Profitable
Sales Management
and Marketing
for Growing Businesses

Profitable Sales Management and Marketing for Growing Businesses

Robert J. Calvin

VNR VAN NOSTRAND REINHOLD COMPANY

Copyright © 1984 by Van Nostrand Reinhold Company Inc.

Library of Congress Catalog Card Number: 83-25888
ISBN: 0-442-21502-9

Manufactured in the United States of America

Published by Van Nostrand Reinhold Company Inc.
135 West 50th Street
New York, New York 10020

Van Nostrand Reinhold Company Limited
Molly Millars Lane
Wokingham, Berkshire RG11 2PY, England

Van Nostrand Reinhold
480 Latrobe Street
Melbourne, Victoria 3000, Australia

Macmillan of Canada
Division of Gage Publishing Limited
164 Commander Boulevard
Agincourt, Ontario MIS 3C7, Canada

15 14 13 12 11 10 9 8 7 6 5 4 3 2 1

Library of Congress Cataloging in Publication Data

Calvin, Robert J.
  Profitable sales management and marketing for
growing businesses.

  Bibliography: p.
  Includes index.
  1. Sales management. 2. Marketing—Management.
3. Small business. I. Title.
HF5438.4.C34 1984   658.8   83-25888
ISBN 0-442-21502-9

To my wife and in-house editor, Jane,
for her support and assistance.

In memory of eight great salesmen:
Abe, Edwin, Jerry, Larry, Maurice, Marvin, Max, and Stanley.

Acknowledgments

I wish to acknowledge with thanks the contributions made to this book by a number of other individuals: Richard J. Thain, Dean, Graduate School of Business, University of Chicago, who helped organize the subject matter; Dick Harmet, Vice President and Executive Editor of World Book and Science Year, who read and critiqued several chapters; Anne Kass, who typed the manuscript; my daughters, Amy and Susan, who displayed great understanding; and my parents, Joseph and Pauline Calvin, whose encouragement never faltered.

I would also like to thank my editor, Gerry Galbo, who gave the book focus, and David Zimmerman and Roger Golde, who shared their experiences as authors.

Contents

Introduction

THE BOOK

This book, written by a small businessman for the small business person, addresses itself to the needs and resources of the smaller enterprise. It focuses on the situation in which one person performs most sales management and marketing tasks. The book emphasizes practical, inexpensive, and proven techniques for improving sales management and marketing results. Because business is a dynamic process, the reader is asked to question company tradition and present industry practice.

The book blends sales management and marketing theory and practice into an action-oriented guide for success. Each chapter contains useful, concrete information and real life-examples that emphasize a small business's most important resource, people. Each also presents a great deal of step-by-step detail on solving problems of particular interest to the smaller business manager. The scope of the subject matter is broad and the explanations comprehensive.

The reader will learn how to capitalize on a smaller business's strengths, such as its greater flexibility; its capacity for faster decisions and reactions to changes; its opportunities for better service, a more personal atmosphere, and more attention to customers' needs; and its ability to operate profitably in smaller specialized markets. The book also reveals how to compensate for a smaller business's weaknesses, such as limited human and financial resources, lack of diversification, and limited career or advancement opportunities. As larger firms continue to consolidate through mergers and acquisitions into even larger capital bases, survival demands that smaller concerns continually evaluate their competitive advantages and weaknesses.

Good sales management and marketing are of particular importance to smaller businesses, because properly applied, they represent the least expensive, most accessible means of successfully competing with larger firms. The small business may not have the equipment and capital of its larger competitors, but it has equal access to the same sales management and marketing techniques. As the book shows, it costs little if anything more to hire, train, compensate, motivate, and evaluate salespeople properly. Effective performance of time and territory management, forecasting, budgeting, and good communication and control need cost no more than performing these same functions poorly. The book shows how proper application of these techniques can maximize sales.

The book also explains how to innovate new products/services, so important to a small business's growth, inexpensively and with minimal risk, and then how to, also inexpensively but effectively, create a demand for new and existing products/services through advertising, publicity, promotion, and packaging. In addition, the book devotes one chapter to explaining how to maximize profits through proper pricing, and another to maximizing sales by choosing the most appropriate channels of distribution.

Although in a small business, good sales management and marketing cannot guarantee success, poor sales management and marketing greatly increase the probability of failure. Larger firms can afford a few mistakes; smaller ones cannot.

SMALL BUSINESS STATISTICS

Small firms account for a large portion of this nation's business and employment; they also act as customers, suppliers, and sales agents for many larger concerns. Figures prepared by the Internal Revenue Service, Dun and Bradstreet, and the Small Business Administration indicate that there are 7.2 million full-time U.S. nonfarm businesses employing less than 500 people and with revenues exceeding $10,000 per annum. These same sources estimate that there are only 13,000 nonfarm U.S. businesses employing more than 500 people. The 7.2-million small firms generate 40 percent of the gross national product, employ 50 percent of the work force, and create 60 percent of all new jobs. Between 1979 and 1981, 2.8 million new jobs were generated.

The financial risks and rewards of smaller businesses both exceed those of larger concerns. One-fourth to one-third of all new ventures fail within the first year, and over 60 percent fail within the first two years. Smaller firms continue to display a higher failure rate than larger concerns through the first 10 years of their life. Over 550,000 new businesses are started each year. For every 15 started, 10 disappear.

On the other hand, successful, well-managed smaller firms show a higher percentage profit return on equity and sales than larger concerns. Helping you achieve such results through proper sales management and marketing is the purpose of this book.

SMALL BUSINESS DEFINITION

The Small Business Administration defines a small business by the number of employees. It usually considers retail establishments with up to 25 employees and manufacturing firms with up to 500 employees as small businesses.

It has been my experience that a small business cannot be defined strictly by the number of its employees or dollars of annual sales. A small business also reflects management's attitude, perception, state of mind, and point of view.

I have worked with family-owned concerns whose annual sales approached $100,000,000 and employed as many as 1,500 people but were perceived and managed by the owners as small businesses. I have also worked with service companies employing only 10 people and doing $300,000 annually that were the largest businesses in their tiny industries. Their management felt and acted as if they were managing a big enterprise. An astute colleague once characterized a small business as any organization in which one person opens all the mail.

Regardless of how you define a small business, this category of firms contains an immense variety of diverse organizations, products, services, markets, and industries—ranging from a tailor shop to a designer blouse manufacturer, from a home cleaning service to a refuse removal firm, from a machine shop to an electronic component manufacturer, from a specialty drug manufacturer to a health food retailer, or from a supplier of chemical additives to a sales representative organization. Whatever their line, however, all small businesses must sell their product or service, which involves some if not all aspects of sales management and marketing.

ROBERT J. CALVIN

Profitable
Sales Management
and Marketing
for Growing Businesses

1
Hiring Salespeople

Hiring effective salespeople represents your most important responsibility as the sales manager for a small but growing business. Proper training, compensation, motivation, and supervision applied to weak salespeople produce mediocre results at best. In a small but growing business your most valuable resources are not machines but people. Since a smaller business employs a smaller sales force, each person's performance has added importance.

In spite of this, most small-business sales managers possess minimal knowledge or aptitude for hiring effective salespeople. Cast the play correctly, and directing it becomes much simpler. There is no actor-proof play; there is no salesperson-proof product/service. This chapter suggests inexpensive techniques for successfully hiring salespeople, regardless of the product or service your company offers. Basically, successful hiring requires writing a job description and a candidate profile, then using appropriate sources for recruiting, and finally skillfully screening candidates.

In 1980 a new venture introduced a long-distance telephone service which potentially could reduce customers' direct-dialing costs by 40%. Basically, the user dialed into Watts, MCI, or SPC leased lines, then dialed a customer charge code, and finally dialed the desired area code and local number. There were no connection costs or minimums. Salespeople sold the service by phone from various U.S. locations.

The company's management became concerned because new salespeople opened only a few new accounts, and half the recruits quit within ninety days. Management had recruited by running newspaper ads in targeted cities, then interviewing and hiring by phone any candidates who responded. This hiring procedure allowed the company to quickly and inexpensively expand the sales force, but without positive sales results. The company had not outlined the type of person desired, nor employed an effective method of finding or screening applicants. They had not even bothered to meet applicants face to face. Later, by using the techniques described in this chapter (and this book), they obtained a productive sales organization, which helped make this small company very prosperous.

TURNOVER

Hiring the wrong salesperson proves expensive because of the cost involved, loss of potential sales, and/or eventual loss and replacement of the person hired. You can spend several thousand dollars' worth of time and out-of-pocket expense finding, screening, hiring, and training a new salesperson. Losing such a person represents a nonrecoverable, nonproductive cost similar to a bad debt. Smaller businesses have limited financial and human resources. They can ill afford expensive mistakes of this nature.

For a small growing business to succeed, each salesperson must produce optimum results. On a small ship, room does not exist for excess baggage. A poorly selected salesperson allows the competition to make inroads, and eventually he or she must be fired. Firing results in loss of continuity for the sales force and further reduces sales. Customers must trust salespeople, and continually replacing them destroys that trust. A company with high salesperson turnover gains a bad reputation with customers, prospects, and potential salespeople which proves difficult to repair.

Annual turnover rates including resignations, discharges, and retirements generally vary from 15% to 20% of a sales force in consumer, industrial, and service industries. The rate goes up to 33% in insurance, and 100% in door-to-door selling. Smaller companies can achieve lower turnover percentages because of the more personal relationship between the sales force and management, and because the sales force generally contains fewer young people.

The basic techniques for reducing turnover are (1) a realistic job description and candidate profile, (2) contacting appropriate sources for attracting candidates, (3) skillfully screening and selecting from those who apply.

JOB DESCRIPTION

Let's say that one of your salespeople has retired, quit, or been fired, or you are expanding the sales force with a new territory. For whatever reason, you as the individual in charge of sales are faced with hiring a new salesperson. Since yours is a smaller company, you cannot expect assistance from others within the organization. Tasks pertaining to sales or marketing are accomplished by you or not at all.

Since every selling job and company are different, you need a written summary of the person's anticipated duties. You can't go shopping until you know what you need. This job description also becomes a tool for sales training and later for evaluating the salesperson's performance. If your company sells milk, beer, soft drinks, bread, fuel oil, a diaper or cleaning service through route delivery people to consumers, selling duties will be different than if your company sells Christmas ornaments, hosiery, window shades, lawn mowers, or office furniture through field salespeople to retail outlets. Similarly, if your company sells a refuse removal service, ethical drugs, or rum through "missionary" salespeople, their duties will differ from selling industrial robots, metal-cutting fluids, gears, or nail-making machines through sales representatives to industrial users. Also, selling books or insurance, fund raising, and advertising to corporations require different duties and skills than selling cosmetics, brushes, and household goods door to door.

Most selling positions can be divided into two major categories: passive order-takers or active order-writers. Passive order-takers sell a pre-sold product, and their main job involves service. This category would include the "inside" customer service person, most retail salespeople, and delivery or route salespeople. Active order-writers must find and influence their customers. This category would include engineers selling a technical product to an industrial user, door-to-door selling of cosmetics, selling of intangibles such as I.R.A. plans, and sales of apparel to retail stores.

Most smaller-company managements do not bother with formulating job descriptions for salespeople, but then complain about poor results in hiring. Let us assume that the smaller company for which you are sales manager sells expensive high-fashion ladies' dresses to specialty stores in major cities. You take a sandwich, pencil, and paper to the park one spring day and start writing a job description. You expect a salesperson to accomplish the following:

Selling.   Make twenty sales calls a week—fifteen calls to service and sell existing accounts, and five calls on prospective new accounts. The salesperson must find new prospects without help from you. Existing customers require servicing for reorders four times a year, and should review the entire line twice a year. The salesperson's objective is to increase unit sales 10% annually. Orders are to be mailed in twice a week.

Servicing.   Where necessary, the salesperson assists the department manager with merchandising and displaying the dresses; reacts promptly to customer complaints; and educates the retail sales clerks on the selling points of your merchandise.

Reporting.   Each Friday the salesperson must submit an informative call report for the previous week and a route sheet for the next week. Twice a year a sales forecast is to be submitted, which includes a list of prospective new accounts along with a list of new items the salesperson plans to sell to existing accounts.

Administrative.   You expect each salesperson to inform you of any significant competitive changes in the territory, and to maintain a comprehensive customer record system. In a small business, your boss, the president, also handles credit and collection. Although the president hardly has time for this important function, present volume does not justify a separate credit manager. Therefore, you expect the salesperson to fill in credit application forms for new customers and to collect past due invoices.

Housekeeping. You expect samples, sales literature, and sales aids to be maintained in mint condition.

Try to keep the job description to a page, but be sure you create one. Review and revise it each year to meet changing market conditions and needs.

CANDIDATE PROFILE

You must now translate the job description into a written candidate profile. The job description lists duties. The candidate profile describes personal characteristics required to perform those duties in your organization.

Continuing with our high-fashion ladies' dress example, you most likely will seek a person who has the following qualifications:

1. Knows the territory, the customers, and the buyers because he or she previously successfully sold a related line in the territory.

2. Owns a car, can occasionally travel overnight, but lives near your major accounts. If Los Angeles represents most of your California business, don't hire a salesperson who resides in San Francisco. It is hard to effectivley sell in Cleveland when you live in Cincinnati.

3. Is over forty with career ambitions only in selling and not in management. Since you are sales manager with no immediate intentions of leaving, since your boss is president and owner of the company, and since there are no regional sales managers, no career ladder or opportunities for advancement exists for the sales force. A salesperson with ambitions to move into management would only be frustrated and quickly leave such a situation. Smaller-company management must be realistic about this limitation. However, many excellent salespeople are strictly interested in selling and earning more money through increased sales.

4. Is a self-starter who will enjoy the freedom, flexibility, self-expression, recognition, personal relationships, and feelings of belonging and usefulness available in a small organization. Although you train, travel with, and supervise your people, not enough hours exist for you to monitor their everyday routines. You need someone who does not have to be continually pushed. If they perform well, you allow them considerable freedom and flexibility.

In a small growing company, suggestions from the sales force can actually create satisfying and valuable changes in policy. The sales force often feel they participate in decision making. In a smaller company, each salesperson has met the president and has had dinner with the sales manager. As the sales manager for such a firm, you must attract candidates whose needs for freedom, flexibility, self-expression, recognition, belonging, usefulness, and personal relationships are greater than their needs for advancement into management.

5. Does not have a college degree. A person with four years of college most likely would not find this job challenging. To sell industrial equipment often requires an engineering degree. To successfully sell ladies' dresses requires intelligence, but not formal college education. Hiring overqualified people creates frustration resulting in high turnover.

6. Does not necessarily know the product. Except in highly technical industries, product knowledge is easily obtained. Knowledge of the product or service represents a plus, but not a necessity. Knowledge of the territory and customers, plus a successful history in selling related products or services, rank much higher on the candidate profile.

7. Displays empathy, enthusiasm, confidence, and drive. A successful salesperson wins customers through empathy, enthusiasm, and confidence, and is motivated by a strong drive to succeed. These four qualities are probably the most significant personal characteristics to look for in a candidate.

Empathy allows the salesperson to discover customer needs and establish trust. Once needs are identified and trust established, the salesperson enthusiastically and with confidence presents product or service benefits to satisfy these needs.

Successful salespeople also possess tremendous drive. They derive satisfaction beyond monetary rewards from closing a sale. Each selling experience represents a new challenge, and new challenges represent a necessary part of their daily diet. They are compelled to sell, which makes them behave like superstars and prima donnas. Some salespeople are terribly insecure, with a strong need to be liked and admired. Selling satisfies that need.

A legendary salesman became a star performer before the age of thirty for a giant men's shoe manufacturer. He invested his money well, married well, and accumulated a fortune. He could live off his investments, but when his employer reduced the size of his territory, he quit and joined a smaller firm. In five years he became their top salesman, and in ten years the highest shoe volume producer in the country. This man, and successful salespeople like him, possess a drive, a need to close the sale, a need to succeed far beyond any monetary rewards.

Confirm the validity of your candidate profile by writing an actual profile of your most successful present salespeople and then comparing the two. Does a similarity exist? Check the validity of your candidate profile by comparing future performance of the people you hire to their merits based on the profile.

In writing your job description and candidate profile, and during the entire recruiting process, keep in mind that the 1964 Civil Rights Act requires that minorities, older people, women, and the handicapped receive a fair and equal opportunity for employment. Each requirement in the job description and candidate profile must be justifiable in terms of job performance.

The most unusual candidate profile I have encountered involved hiring a precious-stone salesperson for Central America. The position required a woman who knew self-defense, could speak Spanish, English, and Lebanese, could identify rare stones at a glance in poor light, was not afraid of carrying large amounts of currency, could handle a firearm, and could travel one month out of two.

SOURCES FOR ATTRACTING CANDIDATES

Many smaller growing companies feel they lack the necessary financial resources for attracting the best candidates. Often they merely do not know how or where to look for them. Qualified applicants for sales positions can be found by:

1. Advertising in the classified sections of trade media and the local press.
2. Informing customers and employees that you are looking.
3. Contacting desirable applicants at competitors.
4. Contacting professional organizations, educational institutions, and armed forces discharge centers.
5. Using employment agencies.

What source or combination of sources you use depends on your job description and candidate profile. Each job search is different, but if in the past one source has produced better results, start with that.

Advertising

Most companies advertise for candidates, but complain of high costs and poor results. A smaller company can ill afford unproductive advertising expense. With financial resources limited, all expenditures must produce results.

Hopefully, a classified ad will produce qualified applicants for you to screen. If a great many unqualified candidates respond, your valuable time is wasted. If no qualified candidates respond, you also lose. Successful advertising for salespeople requires the correct copy and the appropriate media.

Copy.   Blind ads do not produce qualified applicants. Therefore, the copy should include the company name, address, telephone number, and your name as the person to contact. Ask candidates to write or call you specifically if they feel qualified for the position. Your name humanizes the company and the ad, and informs the applicant whom directly to contact.

Your company name may not be well known, but it is necessary in a classified ad for salespeople. Salespeople hesitate to respond to blind ads, because the advertiser may be their present employer. Blind ads also cause suspicion: What sort of employer won't divulge its name in an ad? Replacing a present salesperson requires secrecy, but rather than run an unsuccessful blind ad, I suggest using other sources.

Your ad must contain an honest description of the position. If too much information is given, qualified candidates might find something that discourages them from applying. If you include too little information, unqualified candidates are encouraged to apply. Remember that the ad's objective is not to hire and select the salesperson, but only to produce qualified applicants. You will do the selecting from those who reply.

An honest description of the position states the product or service to be sold, type of selling, territory available, type of customer, what experience is necessary, and amount of overnight travel, if any. I would not include a compensation range, since this generally varies greatly depending on the applicant's ability. I would not mention whether the territory contains established volume or requires pioneering. This information changes quickly, and can best be handled in a personal interview.

The ad should contain words that describe the job's nonmonetary benefits, such as "rewarding," "steady," "interesting," "challenging." Choose the words honestly. For example, a route salesperson's work is steady; a door-to-door salesperson's work is challenging.

An ad for the person described in our job description might read:

CHALLENGING REWARDING OPPORTUNITY
APPAREL SALESPERSON

Salesperson wanted to sell our line of high-fashion women's dresses to better specialty stores in Southern Florida. Prior selling experience in the territory desirable. Occasional overnight travel.

Call or write: Your name _____

Company name _____

Company address _____

Company telephone number _____

Personal interviews will be held in the near future.

Media. Some salespeople read the classified "lines offered" section of trade publications when job searching, but others read the "help wanted" section of their local paper. In certain industries—for example, advertising, apparel, and technical products—trade publications prove especially effective for reaching qualified candidates. Salespeople generally do not read financial publications, so advertising in *The Wall Street Journal* would not prove productive.

There may be one day a week when your trade publication specializes in your market segment or in employment ads. You will obtain better results by advertising on that day. In the local press, for best results advertise on Sundays using newspapers with more than 100,000 circulation. Generally, classified "lines offered" ads in trade publications cost less than "help wanted" ads in local newspapers. Only experience obtained from actual ads can show which media, trade or local, produces the best results for your company.

An effective technique in advertising in the Sunday paper involves asking the reader/applicant to call you that Sunday. This requires you to devote a Sunday to the project, but it produces results. If the ad is run outside your area code, it must specify a toll-free number, or state that collect calls will be accepted.

In addition to the copy suggested above, this Sunday ad should state: "Don't write, but pick up your phone now and call me, (your name), at this number. I am the sales manager of (your company) and will be at my telephone between 9 and 5 today. I will tell you about the job opportunity, and you can tell me about your qualifications. I will not ask your name unless you wish to tell me." The personal aspect of this ad, and the possibility of immediate easy response, produce qualified candidates. Also, it allows people who are presently employed to call without fear that their employer will know about it.

Certain advertising agencies (Nationwide Advertising Service Inc. is one) specialize in employment ads. In exchange for the 15% commission collected from the media, they will advise you on copy and choices of publication.

Informing Customers and Employees

Informing customers and employees represents a very inexpensive source for producing applicants, but cannot be used when privacy is important. Often your customers know of an appropriate salesperson who wishes to change employment. As sales manager, you should call customers who could be helpful, and explain the job's requirements. Choose customers with whom you have a personal relationship and in whom you have confidence. Otherwise someone might be offended by your request, or just recommend unemployed friends. Tell customers that you are asking for their assistance because they will be dealing with your new salesperson.

This approach, asking for help, admits a certain amount of weakness to your customer, but most are flattered. Unless you wish to lose an account, never hire a customer's employee without first asking permission from the employee's supervisor.

Present employees of your own company often know qualified salespeople who might find the available position attractive. Use a bulletin to inform the sales force and other managers of the job's availability and requirements. Your sales force probably know other salespeople, presently employed elsewhere, who might be interested in the position. Salespeople trade stories, successes, problems, and opportunities over coffee and drinks. Similarly, if you know salespeople selling related lines for other companies, ask them for recommendations.

Occasionally, one of your firm's employees in a nonselling capacity may be interested. A small refuse removal company lost a key salesperson and informed their staff of the job requirements. The controller recommended one of his accountants who knew the business, enjoyed people, and had trouble distinguishing debits from credits. The accountant transferred to sales, and all lived happily ever after.

Offering a bonus to the employee who finds a successful candidate acts as an incentive. Again be aware, however, that unqualified friends may be referred.

Seeking Salespeople from Competitors

Although very appealing, this approach contains problems. Make sure you know why the competitor's salesperson wants to leave, or else you may inherit someone else's troubles. He or she may not be performing, or may be having personal difficulties. Also, an individual who leaves a competitor may easily leave your company for yet another opportunity. Sometimes customers lose trust in salespeople who one month extol brand X and the next month brand Y. Salespeople exist who have worked for almost everyone in an industry, leaving just before the present employer realizes their incompetence. In addition, you will have more difficulty changing bad selling habits, because the salesperson recruited from a competitor feels already trained.

On the other hand, a small growing company should not overlook a good candidate who works for a competitor. Often, mature salespeople leave a competitor because their territory faces reduction, or the competitor desires a younger, less expensive person who does not have large vested interests in a pension plan. Corporate mergers, market changes, new compensation plans, and recessions also make competitors' salespeople receptive to offers. The right candidate may bring captive customers, no bad habits, good product knowledge, and little need for training.

Contacting Professional Organizations, Educational Institutions, and Armed Forces Discharge Centers

These are inexpensive, productive sources of salespeople. Most industries have professional associations, occasionally just for salespeople, which publish lists of available positions for their membership. Many groups have a local chapter in each state or major metropolitan area. Such associations range from the Men's Apparel Clubs in each state to the Industrial Robot Division of the Society of Manufacturing Engineers. Be sure to list your job opening with the appropriate industry club or association.

Many smaller businesses do not take advantage of free placement facilities offered by educational institutions. Junior colleges and technical high schools represent fertile ground for recruiting salespeople. Most colleges maintain a service for graduates who later in life wish to change jobs. List your job requirements with the appropriate educational institutions.

Armed forces discharge centers offer placement services which prove effective for some selling jobs. It costs nothing to list your position with the local office.

Employment Agencies

A capable employment agency earns its fee of 10% to 15% of a person's first-year compensation, but good agencies dealing with salespeople are scarce. Most agencies dealing with middle-level salespeople lack professionalism. Their main interest is a match, but not necessarily a good fit.

If you desire to use an agency, ask colleagues and other sales managers in related fields for references, and then check them out. If you engage an agency, choose one you trust, and provide them with all the information available on job and candidate requirements. Ask to meet the person handling your account. Be sure you have a written contract stating how the firm charges: contingency or front-end fee, fixed dollar or percentage. Be sure you establish a realistic time frame for performance: 30, 60, 90 days. When candidates emerge, interview them immediately before they lose interest.

Choose the sources you use for attracting sales applicants according to how they fit the job and the candidate requirements. Then maintain accurate records of results obtained from each source. You will note a pattern developing. Put emphasis on the most productive sources, and in the future your task will be easier.

SCREENING AND SELECTING FROM THOSE WHO APPLY

Choosing the best candidate from a qualified group requires not only intuition and insight but also structure and technique. The probability of success can be enhanced by following certain procedures. Being the sales manager of a small growing company means you must absorb this extra work load on top of the demanding everyday tasks of running a sales force and producing sales. Most likely you receive no assistance from other staff members, since they are also spread thin. Because of these time limitations, the temptation to take shortcuts in the selection process exists; but shortcuts only increase the risk of failure, forcing you to accept a mediocre salesperson or eventually seek a new one. Do it right, or do it again.

By using proper sources for candidates, you have obtained possibly thirty applicants. From some you have received resumes, but for others your notes from telephone conversations represent the only written record. The techniques and structure employed in successfully narrowing the field involve (1) preliminary screening of resumes and notes; (2) requesting personal history application forms; (3) a preliminary personal interview; (4) reference checking and background investigation; (5) testing; (6) a second interview for finalists; (7) a physical exam.

Not every selling position requires all these steps, but as you can see, the process requires considerable time. The more time available to contact sources and screen applicants, the higher your probability of success.

To maximize the available time for recruiting, try to anticipate hiring needs. Don't wait for a salesperson to retire before you start looking. Set up a ninety-day program for the hiring process. If you suspect that one of your salespeople may be planning to leave, start looking now.

Preliminary Screening of Resumes and Notes

You begin the screening process by reviewing the resumes received and the notes written from telephone conversations. Half the thirty applicants probably do not have sufficient experience for the position, or have a record of constant job shifting. You write a cordial letter to these people, expressing appreciation for their interest, but informing them that their fine backgrounds do not meet the position's requirements. The hiring process represents an opportunity for the company to make friends. Job applicants sometimes become customers, suppliers, politicians, managers, or repeat applicants. I know of many situations where an applicant originally rejected for one selling position was hired years later for another. You should write rejection letters with this in mind, and keep a file for future reference of all resumes and notes.

Requesting Personal History Application Forms

You send the remaining fifteen applicants a letter asking them to fill out and submit the enclosed personal history form. Explain that when you receive the form, the applicant will be called for a personal interview.

The personal history form asks the applicant for the following information: name and address; marital status; number of dependents; educational background; employment history (including military) with dates and responsibilities; health restrictions; and outside interests. Keep it simple, and don't ask for unnecessary information. Time represents a valuable resource for you and the applicant.

If you do not have this information for your present sales force, ask each salesperson to complete the personal history form. Then rank your salespeople by performance: strong, average, weak (we all employ them); and analyze each group to find what background characteristics seem most conducive to success and failure. This knowledge proves helpful in evaluating the applicants' backgrounds.

A small firm that sold through telephone solicitation discovered that 70% of their most successful salespeople were divorced high school dropouts. Another business that manufactured transformers found that over 75% of their most successful salespeople were college dropouts whose hobbies involved citizen-band radios. A company that sold sailboats learned that sailors represented their worst sales performers and skiers the best. Many companies discover that their best performers had past experience selling a related product or service in the present territory. By using this technique, you may uncover obvious or obscure clues which will assist you in screening applicants. The information is available at no cost.

Preliminary Personal Interview

Of the fifteen applicants who received your personal history form, let us assume that eight have replied, the other seven have lost interest. Now you begin the art and black magic of interviewing. If applicants live nearby, you can make arrangements for the interview in your office. If the available territory is out of town, interviews should take place at a hotel in that area. Some small companies use telephone interviews to save time and money, and make selections based on these conversations. However appealing this shortcut may appear, you really require a face-to-face interchange to obtain appropirate information and develop intuitions.

Interviews prove more productive if you know exactly what type of candidate you seek and if you prepare a written list of questions based on the candidate's personal history. Again, you may seek people similar to your present best performers.

The most reliable guide to a salesperson's future performance lies with their past record; therefore, obtaining a reliable picture of the past record represents the most important aspect of screening. In your interview, ask the candidate to comment on specific past achievements with each employer. Salary history becomes an extremely important indicator of past performance.

Unfortunately, people seldom change their bad working habits. The mediocre past sales performer continues to perform at mediocre levels. The job hopper continues to hop. The person with financial problems usually finds new ones. The salesperson who works four days a week seldom switches to five, in fact often regresses to three.

Discussing the job description provides an effective means of starting an interview. Ask the candidate why he or she feels capable of performing the job. Find out why the candidate has changed jobs in the past, and why he or she wishes to change jobs now. As the interview progresses, discuss past compensation and future opportunities. If health or personal difficulties appear to be a problem, discuss them at the preliminary interview. Tailor the questions to the candidate.

Under the 1964 Civil Rights Act, you may ask any job-related question unless it expresses willful prejudice based upon religion, race, sex, or age. Often, open-ended questions produce answers which it would be illegal to ask for directly.

The more the applicant talks, the more you will learn. Know what information you seek, and what questions you wish to ask; then listen openly and concentrate on the responses. You can discover a great deal about an applicant's skills and experience by asking how they organize their day, what they think of their present employer, what they liked most and least about past positions, and their own opinions of personal strengths and weaknesses.

Create a nonthreatening atmosphere in which candidates feel free to talk, and they will volunteer all the information you desire. You can best put the candidate at ease by being punctual, not accepting phone calls, not putting a desk between the two of you, and sitting in chairs of equal status. Display sympathy and understanding, but don't talk about yourself even though you may be more interesting. Also don't criticize the candidate, or you will find future responses guarded. When you desire more information on a subject, agree with the applicant. When the conversation veers from the desired subject matter, subtly steer it back in the desired direction. Once you have established rapport, keep the candidate talking about himself or herself, and don't let the conversation drift into the 1983 World Series.

Occasionally a candidate will give fuzzy replies or no replies to such questions as "Why did you leave your last job?" or "What was your compensation?" To elicit a clearer response, drop the question for a while and go on to something else. Then return later to the elusive subject by phrasing the question differently. For example, "What sort of a person was your boss?" If related questions continue to produce fuzzy or weak replies, you have found a problem area, which after the interview requires independent investigation through reference checking.

When possible, immediately after the interview record in writing your impressions and key information. After six interviews, as after six sales calls, information and impressions merge unless you have written notes.

As you record information, I suggest marking each item with a plus, minus, or zero, depending on its bearing on the candidate's desirability. Try to look for information which helps you reject or accept the applicant.

I know of one instance where a sales manager hired the wrong candidate from two finalists because he trusted the information to his memory. When the candidate, now employee, reported for his first day of work, the sales manager realized his mistake, but decided not to admit it. The story has a happy ending, though, because that salesman proved highly successful. When the sales manager retired, he told the story at his farewell dinner, while his successor, the wrongly hired salesman listened.

What to Look for Behind the Answers.   You have prepared questions for the interview based on the candidate's personal history application, and the company job description. Hopefully, the interview will produce answers to these questions, plus useful unsolicited information.

Be cautious of candidates who frequently move from one company to another, or who have gaps in their employment record, such as a salesperson who left a job in June and did not find new employment until November. Be careful of candidates whose records show no improvement, such as a salesperson whose shipments and compensation have remained unchanged for many years, or a salesperson who traded a better line with a top company for an inferior line with a second-rate organization.

Domestic and money problems interfere with a salesperson's job performance. A general open-ended question concerning family, vacations, or inflation sometimes elicits information in these areas.

Salespeople who criticize past employers and bosses signal a problem which requires further investigation. The fault often does lie with the previous employer, but you need more information to know for sure.

The rigors of some sales positions require a great deal of energy, which not all people possess. In such a situation, look for active people who channel their energy into work and don't just talk about working hard. A person who works long hours and Saturdays generally meets this requirement.

During the interview, watch for verbal slips, and for stories or anecdotes that could reveal personal weaknesses. A candidate once told me a "funny" incident about missing an important selling date because he accidentally walked under a sprinkler and got his suit wet. I didn't think it was funny, but considered it revealing. Another candidate told me that every Friday he "got gassed," then corrected himself to say every Friday he "bought gas."

Watch for body language when the candidate answers certain sensitive questions. Does he or she look you in the eye, wet their lips, wring their hands? Most people can't hide anxiety, and anxiety points to problem areas.

Just because you happen to be the interviewer, don't assume that you are more clever than the applicant. Some salespeople have taken more interviews than you have given, and some have even read books on interviewing techniques. Often this person dresses well, speaks well, but cannot close a sale. He or she drifts from job to job, is likable, charming, wonderful at interviews, and sometimes proficient at twisting facts. A clever recruiter spots this person because of constant job changes or lack of increased compensation, and by proper reference checking.

Reference Checking and Background Investigation

You have now finished the eight preliminary personal interviews, and, based on information obtained, eliminated four candidates. During the interviews, you asked for personal references who could be called, and for permission to contact past employers, customers, and competitors. If the applicant presently holds a job, you usually cannot contact the present employer.

Because checking references is time-consuming, burdensome, and awkward, most small-business sales managers neglect it. Next to the personal interviews, reference checking represents the most important screening technique. If you don't have the time or inclination to contact references, then try flipping a coin or throwing darts to choose the best applicant.

A sales manager's aversion to reference checking stems partially from mistrust of references and partially from a misunderstanding of the technique. Sales managers typically complain that "Candidates only give us the names of people who provide good references." I agree, and so you must call references which the candidate has not provided. Many sales managers feel that reference checking challenges their infallible judgment based on personal interviews. As you will see, reference checking helps make preliminary interview information more meaningful, and provides questions for the final interview.

Disregard written references provided by the candidate, since obviously these represent a form of advertising. However, telephone interviews with past employers, customers, and competitors will provide useful information.

In calling past employers, speak with the applicant's supervisor, and then his immediate supervisor's boss. Reaching these people can prove difficult, because sometimes they have changed employers, or company policy prohibits telephone references. Also, since you cannot call the applicant's present employer, all information is somewhat dated. Still, the information gained from past employers can prove invaluable in evaluating candidates.

Introduce yourself and explain the reason for your call. Explain something about your company and the available position. Then try to establish a rapport in order to elicit candid responses. Next verify dates of employment and salary level, and ask exactly why your applicant left this former employer. What were his or her work habits, strengths and weaknesses, responsibilities, and performance record? Find out the referee's title and past relationship to the applicant; I once discovered that the referee was the applicant's ex-brother-in-law.

Last and most important, ask, "Would you rehire the candidate?" Company policy often prohibits rehiring. In this situation ask, "If company policy allowed rehiring, would you rehire this individual?" This is the moment of truth, when previously withheld information comes tumbling forth. I have encountered reactions such as "Never," "Only if his father-in-law made me," and "I would, but my boss would not."

As with the candidate interview, listen carefully to the previous employer's responses and tone of voice. Phrases such as "unfortunate circumstances," or "personality clashes," or "chose to resign" usually indicate problems.

If the previous employer is a competitor, you may receive a false recommendation. The competitor may wish to burden you with one of their previous problems.

Customers who the applicant previously called upon often provide useful information, because they dealt with the applicant in a selling situation. When calling them, ask about the candidate's ability to present ideas, his or her work habits, follow through, enthusiasm, and confidence.

If the candidate sold a product or service noncompetitive to yours, and you know a competitor in that industry, their input can be useful. They can provide information on the applicant's employer, and possibly even the applicant.

Background investigations on the finalists provide a useful precaution. Most credit bureaus offer a service which investigates appropriate court and financial records, and verifies places of residences and past employers if necessary. Through such an investigation, one sales manager discovered that the finalist had just lost his driver's license. The job required extensive use of a car.

Under the Federal Fair Credit Reporting Act of 1971, you must advise candidates that credit reports will be used. Should the report provide information leading to rejection, you must supply the candidate with the source's name and address.

Testing

Intelligence, personality, and interest tests for salespeople can be administered and scored by outside services or by yourself. Such tests provide insight into the subject's learning and reasoning ability, emotional stability, confidence, and occupational interests. The problem is interpreting results. Which test results can accurately predict positive or negative job results? As with the personal history applications, you might have the present sales force take the test, and correlate their individual test results to their sales performance.

A sales manager obtains from testing what he or she puts into it. If you are willing to devote time and energy to this area, you can obtain useful information. If interested, I suggest you contact distributors for some of the following tests: Strong Vocational Interest, Minnesota Vocational Interest, Martin Bruce Test of Sales Aptitude, Thematic Apperception Test, California Personality Test, Guildford-Zimmerman Temperament Survey, John G. Geier Personal Profile System, Otis Quick-Scoring Mental Ability Tests, Wesmon Personnel Classification Test, Adaptability Test, Concept Mastery Test, Wonderlic Personnel Test.

Second Interview for Finalists

You have now completed reference checks, background investigations, and testing on the four remaining candidates. Based on information obtained from these sources, you have narrowed the field and now must choose between two excellent candidates. You make appointments with them for a second and, most likely, final interview.

Based on reference checking, and reexamination of resumes, personal history forms, and notes from the previous interview, you prepare a written list of questions to ask. Different from the first interview, these questions are specific, not general. If one former boss reported different employment dates and a different reason for leaving than the candidate gave you, what explains the inconsistency? Or, although the candidate has a marvelous past record selling established products for large companies, how will he or she adapt to selling a relatively unknown product for a small company?

Use the same interviewing techniques suggested for the preliminary meeting, but occasionally inject some stress to see how the candidate reacts. Imply that some of the former employers were not overly enthusiastic about the applicant's performance record. Does the candidate become hostile, or start divulging previously undisclosed information, or politely call your bluff?

If possible, introduce the finalists to your boss, the company president. The applicant will be impressed, and the president might help in the final choice.

Make sure that you have honestly answered all the finalist's quesitons about the company and the position. Allow the applicant several opportunities to ask. When inviting finalists to a second interview, send them product or service literature and general company information. End the interview by telling the applicant that within a certain time frame, you will call.

Physical Exam

Before hiring your final choice, invest several hundred dollars in a thorough physical exam. This represents a nice opening fringe benefit for the candidate, and one more filtering process for the company. If the exam produces no surprises, the screening is complete. Should the exam raise health questions, you may wish to hire the other finalist.

CONCLUSION

You should be aware that most sales managers prefer salespeople who share their common background, make a nice appearance, and do not threaten them. Most sales managers hire people they enjoy; but this natural selection does not necessarily result in the best sales force. I once attended a company sales meeting where no one was taller than five feet five inches and everyone wore a striped tie.

You should also be aware that most sales managers, being sales types themselves, oversell the job. Overselling the candidate results in unmet unexpectations, disappointment, resentment, and high turnover. If the territory requires a great deal of missionary selling, or sales are declining, admit it.

During the entire hiring process, you should maintain accurate and adequate records, so that you may later compare the person's actual sales performance to their interview responses, personal history, references, and test results. What characteristics did the strong performers have in common during the hiring process? This knowledge makes future hiring easier and produces better results.

Occasionally, when you have completed the steps described in this chapter, only a best candidate emerges, not a good candidate. Don't hire the best of a weak group. This will not solve your problem; it only delays it. A weak salesperson can prove more expensive than no salesperson. It is less expensive to continue looking than to hire, fire, and look again.

As this chapter illustrates, hiring competent salespeople is a process with a beginning—the job description/candidate profile; an end—the medical exam; and steps along the way such as advertising the position, personal interviews, and checking references. If you view recruiting as a process, and consider all appropriate steps even if you decide against using all of them, the probability of success increases.

2
Training Salespeople

In a small growing business the most important resource is people. As sales manager your most important task is hiring competent salespeople; your second most important task is training them. Willie Loman, the 1940s' tragic hero of Arthur Miller's play *Death of a Salesman,* worked for a small family-owned business. In preparation for his selling position, he received only a calling card and a sample case. The rest was up to him. However, Willie represented the end of a romantic era for salesmen. Today you need more than friends, a good shoe shine, and a pleasant smile to obtain orders.

The sales manager for a small growing business feels continual pressure to allocate primary energy and time to closing sales, opening new accounts, and the day-to-day details of operating a sales force. Only so many working hours exist in a week, and the company does not employ anyone else to help in the sales management function. Therefore time gets allocated where results are immediate and predictable. No business can exist without orders and customers.

However, the sales manager's job is to create heroes, not to be one. Six competent sales people can sell many times more goods or services than one sales manager. When a sales manager does not devote the proper energy, time, and skills to hiring and training the sales force, then he or she must continually perform extra sales duties to back up a weak organization. Such a sales manager transforms himself or herself into a line salesperson. Sometimes a smaller-business sales manager actually enjoys competing with the sales organization, because he or she can usually outperform them. Such behavior does not reflect good management, but rather, uncontrolled ego. Small-company sales managers must sell, but at the management level, and not in direct competition with the sales force.

Sales training, like any form of education, should never end. Not only do newly hired salespeople require training, so do those who have been with the company for some time. Even the best salesperson continually needs current input on product knowledge and competition. A well-cast and thoroughly rehearsed play has a higher probability of success, as does a company with a properly hired and well-trained sales organization.

A sales organization is no better than its management. Management begins with hiring and continues with training, compensation, motivation, communication, and appraisal. A good training program makes the sales manager's job easier, not harder. A well-trained sales force not only generates more orders, but also results in less turnover. Invest time in training, and you will have to replace fewer salespeople.

Don't delegate sales training to your best salesperson, even though this option may appear attractive. Even the best salespeople develop bad habits, believe some misinformation, and, most important, possess selling styles peculiar to their personalities. If you delegate training to other salespeople, their habits, misinformation, and styles will be passed along. As sales manager, you alone possess the skills, knowledge, and authority for proper training.

A sweater company discovered that their sales of orlon sweaters were declining each year while natural-fiber sweaters increased. This did not coincide with overall market trends. In questioning the sales force, management discovered that the salesperson who trained new recruits liked natural fibers rather than synthetics, and passed this bias along.

To be effective, any sales training program must accommodate the specific type of salesperson and product/service involved. A training program for route delivery people calling on bakeries will be different from a program for salespeople calling door to door offering educational books; different also from a program for industrial computer salespeople, which in turn will be different from a program for men's neckwear salespeople calling on department stores.

Moreover, a sales training program must accommodate the salesperson's experience level. In dealing with seasoned salespeople you need to recognize their worth, ask their opinions, and spend less time on basics. For newcomers, you should slow the pace and expand the subject matter.

A good training program requires goals and objectives that reflect the job description. Review the job description, and decide what training is necessary to meet these requirements. Base your training program on the needs of those to be trained, not on your particular interests.

Salespeople often resist training for the same reasons that adolescents resist sex education: they really think they know it all, and they are afraid to admit what they don't know. You can overcome this resistance by creating a nonthreatening, participatory training atmosphere, where information is shared rather than taught. Don't present the sales training program as a penalty, or as remedial for weak or potentially weak performers. Present the sales training program as a sharing of proprietary knowledge about the company and the industry. A proper training program makes the salesperson feel wanted and privileged. He or she should understand that learning these skills and obtaining the knowledge will result in increased sales and higher compensation. Inform the salesperson of other people's increased sales after training.

Whenever practical during the training process, outline in advance how time will be spent, what information will be discussed, and the objectives. After each step, summarize the same outline, information, and objectives. Present material in logical order. For example, when discussing selling skills, don't talk about closing the sale before you talk about qualifying leads.

Make sure that the trainees ask questions, and you also should ask questions periodically to establish that they understand the material. Encourage their participation and discussion. Tell the trainees in advance what feedback and participation you expect.

INTRODUCTION

This chapter describes the knowledge and techniques necessary for a successful small-business sales training program. The structure of this program allows it to be inexpensively and efficiently administered by one person, the sales manager. Basically, salespeople require training in: product/service knowledge, competitive advantages, customer knowledge, customer service, nonselling activities, time and territory management, company background and organization, company policy, and selling techniques. Salespeople receive this training by visiting the home office, by the sales manager visiting the field, by group sales meetings, and to a lesser extent through bulletins, telephone calls, tapes, and manuals.

A salesperson requires enough product knowledge to feel confident in presenting the goods or services and to fulfill the customer's information needs for making a buying decision. Salespeople require knowledge not only of their own products/services, but of their competitors'. To sell effectively, a salesperson must know the competitive advantages or disadvantages of each style, model, or service in the marketplace.

You and the salesperson should also review the customer and prospect list. For each customer in the salesperson's territory, review sales by product or service in units and dollars. Is the trend up or down, and why?

A salesperson also requires knowledge and skills in nonselling activities including customer service. Consult the job description and make a list of nonselling activities and customer service functions which your salespeople should handle. Then discuss with them the skills they need to perform these functions.

Time represents another important resource for salespeople; therefore, correctly organizing their time represents an equally important skill. As sales manager, you teach the salespeople how to allocate their time between calling on new prospects and on established customers, between qualifying leads and calling for appointments, between visiting large and small accounts.

A customer not only purchases your product or service, but also in effect your company. Therefore, you should share pertinent company information with each salesperson, such as years in business; growth; ownership; major technical, sales, and manufacturing achievements; key financial data, and market share.

To sell some products or services effectively, a salesperson must understand company and competitor policies on allowable returns, advertising allowances, freight costs, payment terms, available displays, cancellation penalties, and minimum orders. You should consult the job description to determine what policy information a salesperson requires, present the policies on a piece of paper, and review them with the new employee.

Every industry, product, or service involves individual use of certain broad selling techniques. A sales force which understands these individual uses and broad techniques produces superior results. These techniques involve: selling benefits, using empathy, being organized, qualifying prospects, obtaining appointments, and employing proper presentation format.

Customers purchase benefits; as sales manager, you must teach salespeople what competitive benefits most appeal to your customers and prospects. Salespeople close sales when the benefits of their product/service meet a need or solve a problem for the prospect. To define the problem or locate the exact need, salespeople must be empathetic.

As sales manager, you should remind salespeople that they must appear, act, and be organized. Being organized involves a neat personal appearance, planning each sales call, thinking before speaking, and proper use of sales aids.

For revenues to increase, a salesperson must understand how to efficiently find additional prospects who have a greater than average need for the product/service. You must teach new people the proven unique techniques which produce qualified leads for your more successful experienced salespeople, or develop and test new techniques yourself. Prospecting creates growth, but the time required and risks involved are not worth the reward unless leads are qualified.

Salespeople who depend on a constant stream of new customers must be taught proven techniques for selling the first appointment. Remind your salespeople that successfully selling the first appointment by phone does not mean selling the product by phone. In the phone call, the salesperson should stress the value of the proposed visit, and the sizzle of the product/service.

Every product or service has a unique selling presentation format which produces the best results. As sales manager you must teach all your people the proven basic presentation format, including the key words and phrases.

Most of the training outlined above relates primarily to new salespeople, and would be handled by the sales manager through two to five day visits to his or her office. Unless the training continues with field visits by the sales manager, its value is limited. Field visits become an opportunity for continued training at the moment of truth, help to humanize the company, establish personal relationships with customers and rapport with salespeople, and allow you to engage in personal management selling at the appropriate level.

You spend two to five days initially training a new salesperson at your office, and then two to four days a year in continued field training. This leaves long periods between visits in which additional training is done. Between field visits, training take place by means of sales meetings, manuals, bulletins, tapes, and telephone calls.

Some sales managers find it helpful to prepare an agenda when initially training a new salesperson. The agenda outlines the material to be covered and acts as a schedule.

Since sales training is an ongoing process, you require a means of recording each salesperson's progress. Often a one-page form outlining the training program proves helpful.

In order to properly train your salespeople, you the sales manager must obtain a thorough understanding of the material involved. You must also measure the results of your training program, and make changes if the results do not meet expectations.

PRODUCT KNOWLEDGE

A salesperson requires enough product knowledge to feel confident in presenting the goods or services. Confidence represents an important characteristic of successful salespeople. Salespeople feel confident when their product knowledge exceeds that of their customers'. A salesperson should feel capable of answering in depth any reasonable customer question about the products or services offered. Customers respect and trust salespeople who have complete product knowledge. A salesperson should also know where to obtain additional information when required.

Refer to the job description for assistance in determining how much product knowledge is required. If your sales force offers a technically based product such as industrial robots to plant engineers, the salespeople must possess very complete product knowledge. For example, they must know the electrical characteristics of all components, plus the alloys and thickness of all involved metals.

But if your sales force offers a technically based product such as hand-held calculators to department store buyers, the salespeople need only limited product knowledge. They must know how to operate the calculator, its uses, and its performance capabilities. However, component and construction knowledge become unnecessary, because the department store buyer is not an engineer, and his or her concerns pertain to product features and salability.

If your sales force offers a cleaning service to hospital purchasing agents, the salespeople require a knowledge of the people to be employed and the chemicals to be used. They don't need to know what gauge metal is used in the buckets.

If your sales force offers life insurance to individuals, the salespeople need to understand tax benefits, term versus whole life features, cash values, balloon payments, life expectancy tables, inflation rates, interest rates, and double payments under certain conditions. They do not need to know the risk ratings of rare diseases, or which banks accept insurance policies as loan collateral, or the name of the insurance company's founder.

One leasing firm that specialized in financing used computers taught its salespeople a great deal about the equipment, but nothing about figuring monthly payments. Customers and prospects were impressed by their knowledge until the discussion turned to numbers.

Essentially, then, you must teach the sales force whatever product/service knowledge the customer requires in order to make the buying decision. Initially, basic product/service knowledge can best be learned by asking the new recruit, or established salesperson who needs assistance, to spend time at your office. Send pertinent catalogues and manuals to the salesperson for review before your meeting. Make a list of the information you wish to discuss. If possible, have pictures, models, prototypes, charts, graphs, or sampels of your service/product. Spend whatever time may be necessary explaining the pertinent details of the product/service.

Next, where appropriate, accompany the salesperson on a tour of your factory, warehouse, or processing facilities to see the product manufactured or service prepared. Don't delegate the tour, because then you lose control of the situation and the salesperson may receive information not appropriate to the selling process.

If possible, take the salesperson with you to see the product or service "in use." If you sell a hospital cleaning service, visit the hospital and watch the service being performed. If you sell sweaters, visit some stores that offer your merchandise. If you sell industrial robots, visit some factories that employ them. To save time and money, visit customers near your office.

COMPETITIVE ADVANTAGE

Salespeople require knowledge not only of their own products/services, but of their competitors'. To sell effectively, a salesperson must know each style's, model's, or service's competitive advantages or disadvantages in the market place. Do your company's automatic welding robots cost more than competitors', work faster, last longer, move up and down as well as sideways? Do your firm's wool/nylon sweaters require hand washing while your competitor's can be laundered in a machine? Do your sweaters offer a large color range, faster deliveries, more wool content? Does your service clean hospitals two shifts a day while your competitor is available only one? Do you use union help while the competition is non-union? Do you specialize in cleaning operating rooms while the competition specializes in cleaning food facilities? Does your refuse removal company pick up twice a week while the competition picks up once? Is your equipment capable of removing furniture as well as trash? Does your firm's life insurance policy offer dividends or dividend reinvestment while others do not? ... allow borrowing on cash value at 5% while competition charges 10%? ... suspend payments when the insured is disabled, while the competition only reduces the premium?

After you and the salesperson have discussed product information, reviewed company sales literature, looked at models, visited appropriate facilities and a customer or two, you should compare each of your firm's styles, models, or services to what major competitors offer. This can best be accomplished by means of information sheets.

Use one page for each major product, product group, model, major service, or service group. List your company and all your competitors down the left hand side. Across the top put appropriate topic headings of competitive features such as price, reliability, durability, yarn content, delivery, colors, dividend reinvestment, welds per minute, components, double indemnity, gauge, drying time, availability, cost per hour. Fill in each space with the appropriate information, and indicate how it compares with your product or service: "more, less, better, or worse."

Explain and discuss this information with the salesperson and leave him or her copies of the sheets for future reference. This competitive material requires continual updating. Also establish a shelf in your office for competitive literature. You should continually collect, save, and update competitors' calalogues and product/service brochures, and make this material available to any person receiving training. Friendly customers can provide a great deal of competitive literature and information.

You should also discuss with each salesperson the strengths and weaknesses of your company's size versus the competition. For example, being medium-sized for your industry, your firm is more reliable than smaller competitors, but more flexible and personal than larger ones. Your company policy on returns and credits may be more lenient than larger firms'. Possibly your president personally answers any complaints. With less bureaucratic paperwork, possibly your firm's orders can be shipped in 24 hours versus 72 hours for competitors, and decisions on product/service variations to meet customer needs can be made in hours rather than months. In a small or medium-sized firm, each customer receives more attention and is more important.

Be honest in your appraisal of the competition. All companies' products and services have strengths and weaknesses. Accurate knowledge allows the salesperson to call on appropriate customers with the greatest needs for your products/services' strengths. Accurate competitive knowledge allows the salesperson to feel more confident, and to more effectively and forcefully present features and benefits. Knowledge increases the probability of success, ignorance the probability of failure.

CUSTOMER KNOWLEDGE

Your new or experienced salesperson has now obtained additional essential knowledge of the company's products/services and of competition. Next you and the salesperson should review and discuss the customer and prospect list.

For each customer in the salesperson's territory, review sales by product or service in units and dollars. Is the trend up or down, and why? How can sales to each customer be expanded?—by increasing usage of present services/products, or by attempting to sell the customer new ones?

For each customer and major prospect, discuss who does the buying, his or her personality, company buying policies and procedures, highest and lowest ranking person involved in the purchasing decision. What is the buyer's or purchasing agent's attitude toward your company?

Does the customer or prospect have specific problems, such as seasonal business; or specific needs, such as overnight delivery? What competitive products/services are bought?

Supply the new salesperson with addresses and telephone numbers of all customers and major prospects, along with names and titles of all people involved in the buying process.

If your company sells insurance to individuals, educational books door to door, or magazine subscriptions by phone solicitation, new customers generally are more important than repeat sales. For such services/products, knowledge of existing customers becomes less available and less important.

CUSTOMER SERVICE AND NONSELLING ACTIVITIES

A salesperson not only requires product, competitor, and customer knowledge, but also knowledge and skills in nonselling activities, including customer service. A salesperson for a sweater manufacturer must help the retailer display merchandise, and help count his stock for reordering. A life insurance salesman assists in handling claims, and in processing paperwork for cash value loans. An industrial robot salesperson assists in installing and maintaining the equipment.

Consult the job description and make a list of nonselling activities and customer service functions which your salespeople should handle, and the information/skills they need to perform these functions. If possible, review these functions during a customer visit when the salesperson sees the product/service in use, and then again in your office.

Most small growing companies complain that salespeople write orders incorrectly, requiring clerical help at the office to rewrite them, or causing the factory to ship incorrect goods, or causing the computer to incorrectly calculate inventory figures. Most small growing companies don't take the time to instruct their salespeople in proper order writing. So while you have the salesperson's attention, hand him or her an order form and describe the proper procedure for writing and submitting orders. One company eliminated a part-time order clerk, and another reduced delivery time 25% by educating salespeople in proper order writing.

Using the job description, prepare a list of other nonselling activities required of the sales force, and then instruct new employees in their use. If you require route sheets, call reports, or prospect lists, this is the moment to inform your people. Give them a copy of the form, show them how to fill it out, where and when to send it. One small company complained that only half the sales force sent in call reports. I discovered that the other half didn't know how to fill them out and were embarrassed to ask.

Salespeoples' compensation is primarily based on sales, not customer service, proper use of order forms, or prompt submission of call reports. You should use this initial sales training session to explain why these nonselling activities are important to the salesperson. After all, good service creates repeat business, new referrals, and a positive reputation. All this benefits the salesperson. Call reports allow you to help salespeople properly use their time and increase their sales.

TIME AND TERRITORY MANAGEMENT

Hopefully, at this point the salesperson has a good understanding of the product/service, competition, customers, prospects, and nonselling activities. Time represents another important resource for salespeople; therefore, correctly organizing their time represents an equally important skill. Although management decides on a territory's boundaries (we devote a chapter to this later), it is the salesperson who decides each day how to best utilize a finite amount of time within the territory.

Depending on the job description, the salesperson allocates time between calling on new prospects and on established customers, between qualifying leads and calling for appointments, between visiting large accounts and small ones. In addition, a salesperson has to organize his or her travel to minimize time between calls and maximize time spent with customers.

As sales manager you know what time allocation produces the best results for your particular service/product. You know that prime selling time is far too precious to waste. Share this knowledge with your people.

Keep a map of each territory showing the locations of major accounts and prospects. Discuss with the salesperson clusters of accounts which can be called on in one day and good highway systems for moving between accounts.

An office furniture distributor which did a magnificent job of training its sales force in product knowledge and competition experienced high turnover of salespeople. New salespeople with previous strong performance records in other industries expressed frustration over weak sales. Finally, the sales manager spoke to her three best and three weakest established salespeople about how they allocated their time. The best performers spent more time with small accounts than with large ones, more time with established business than in prospecting, more time on the phone than in the car. The worst performers allocated their time in just the opposite manner. The sales manager adjusted this information for differences in the six territories, and a strong pattern evolved. Then as part of the sales training program, she suggested this successful time allocation. Turnover of new salespeople dropped in half, and orders from new salespeople doubled.

COMPANY BACKGROUND AND ORGANIZATION

A customer not only purchases your product or service, but also in effect your company. A person selling home smoke alarm systems door to door in Chicago will find it easier to close a sale after telling the prospect that the company: has been making industrial smoke alarms for fifty years, installed the first home system in California ten years ago, makes the detector for the portable Sears unit, has been owned and managed by the same family since its inception, and has never had a year when sales grew less than 10%.

So share pertinent company information with each salesperson. Such information might include years in business; growth; ownership; major technical, sales, and manufacturing achievements; key financial data; and market share.

Salespeople do not function in a corporate vacuum. For instance, they require information on deliveries and credit, and they must know who in the organization has these responsibilities. They may wish information on the group insurance plan or commission checks, and need to know who to write. Salespeople perform better when they feel part of their company; this involves knowledge and understanding of the organization's structure.

In a smaller firm you have an opportunity to genuinely make salespeople feel part of the company. Share the entire organization chart with each new recruit. Explain who does what, from the president on down. Point out what person to contact for certain information, and who not to bother. If practical, introduce him or her to the appropriate administrative people and company officers. Meeting the president shows that the company cares about its employees. A salesperson remembers this in the field after a disappointing day.

COMPANY POLICY

Not only does a salesperson require product/service knowledge, but also knowledge of company and competitors' policies. To sell some products or services effectively, a salesperson must understand company and competitor policy on allowable returns, advertising allowances, freight costs, payment terms, available displays, cancellation penalties, and minimum orders. Again, consult the job description to determine what policy information a salesperson requires, present the policies on a piece of paper, and review them with the new employee.

Your policies on returns, minimums, and cancellation penalties may represent the competitive advantage which allows a salesperson to close the sale. Similarly, salespeople can't be faulted for misstating payment terms if those terms have never been explained to them. A dog food company established one truckload as their minimum order, but neglected to notify the sales force in writing, and then wondered why most orders were written for smaller quantities.

SELLING TECHNIQUES

Every industry, product, or service involves individual use of certain broad selling techniques. A sales force which understands these individual uses and broad techniques produces superior results. Often, large businesses with large market shares neglect these techniques in favor of "clout." For very little cost, the smaller-business sales manager can gain advantage by teaching and utilizing these skills. The techniques involve: selling benefits, using empathy, being organized, qualifying prospects, obtaining appointments, and employing proper presentation format.

Selling Benefits

Customers purchase benefits; as sales manager, you must teach salespeople what competitive benefits most appeal to your customers and prospects. The automotive manufacturing engineer and procurement agent purchase welding and painting robots because they reduce costs and increase reliability. Families buy educational books from door-to-door salespeople so that their children might do better at school. Auto owners buy undercoatings to increase the life and resale value of their cars. Family heads purchase life insurance for protection and tax relief.

Effective salespeople know why their company's robots are more reliable and cost efficient than the competition's; or why their encyclopedia rather than a competitor's gives youngsters an edge in world history; or why their form of life insurance rather than another creates more after-tax cash. Effective sales managers teach these benefits to their sales force.

The sales presentation must be need-oriented rather than product- or service-oriented. However, a salesperson requires complete product/service knowledge to adequately show how the product/service fills the need. Convert features into customer benefits and teach them to the sales force.

Using Empathy

Salespeople close sales when the benefits of their product/service meet a need or solve a problem for the prospect. To define the problem or locate the exact need, salespeople must be empathetic. Empathy means understanding the customer's situation as if it were your own.

A yarn manufacturer has lost its head dyer who formulated all colors. Your company sells an automated dye machine which uses a minicomputer to formulate, weigh, and dispense dyes. If your salesperson can discover this yarn manufacturer's problem, your product has the benefits to solve it, which might result in a sale.

A retailer must carry high inventories of calculators because deliveries from the present supplier are erratic. You can deliver calculators a week after order receipt. If your salesperson, through empathetic listening, uncovers this problem, a sale is likely.

Empathetic selling involves listening, concentrating, and responding. Teach your salespeople to ask key questions which will lead the prospect or customer to discuss problem-oriented areas. The questions might involve returns, retail markup, inventory levels, down time, manufacturing margins, or plant size. With minimum encouragement, most people tell a great deal more than you need to know. Remind your salespeople that customers respond to personal warmth and a real interest in their situation (empathy). Once the buyer perceives an honest concern—interest, respect, and understanding on the part of your salesperson—a positive sales relationship develops.

Once the customer or prospect starts talking, your salespeople must know what problem areas to listen for. Complaints about high turnover of minimum-wage help in a hospital probably means that a need exists for an outside cleaning service. Complaints concerning unexplained inventory loss from a retailer might indicate a need for security devices.

You should also teach salespeople that all buying behavior is a complex mixture of reason and emotion, which can result in both corporate and personal gain. Purchasing agents, plant managers, design engineers, retail store buyers, or merchandise managers want their company to succeed. They participate by buying goods and services which lower costs, improve efficiency, improve sales, and most important, increase corporate profits. However, these individuals also want to move up the corporate ladder toward management. They fulfill this need by drawing attention to themselves through making successful changes. These individuals also want to make their jobs easier by obtaining as much service as possible from vendors, and avoiding problems and mistakes by dealing with reliable resources. Many buyers and purchasing agents develop strong egos, and most have a need to feel important and be respected. Any salesperson who does not "massage" the buyer's ego loses a certain amount of effectiveness.

Being Organized

Remind your salespeople that they must appear, act, and be organized. A neat personal appearance and appropriate attire convey a sense of organization. A salesperson's appearance represents a kind of personal packaging that reflects on himself or herself as well as on the entire company.

Also, if you sell a consumer product which can be worn, make sure your salespeople wear it. If your company manufactures ties, your salesmen should not wear sport shirts. If your company manufactures dresses, your saleswomen should not wear slacks.

Before each call, a salesperson should organize the presentation. Before speaking during the call, salespeople should organize their thoughts. Salespeople visit the customer or prospect for a specific purpose. Before sitting down with the customer, the salesperson should know what questions to ask and what statements to make. The homework should have been done beforehand.

A card with information on each customer and prospect proves helpful to the salesperson. If the visit pertains to a reorder, the salesperson often needs a stock count. If the visit pertains to expanding a present service, the salesperson should pre-think the benefits. Remind your sales force to organize each call, and to think before speaking.

A small office supply concern employed one saleswoman who made sixteen calls a day but sold only half as much as another who made only eight calls. The first woman would walk into the purchasing agent's office and say, "What do you need today?" The second woman opened with questions about paperwork flow specifically relating to the customer, then mentioned that certain stocks must be low, based on previous orders, then suggested specific fill-ins, and wrote business.

Before each sales call, samples, pictures, and sales aids also require organizing. To a customer, samples and sales aids, even calling cards, represent the product or service being sold. A worn sample, a dirty calling card, or a wrinkled chart invite a negative response. You should train new salespeople to keep samples and sales aids in mint condition.

The sales manager for a small men's tie company questioned a salesperson for not selling its "hottest" style. During a field visit, the sales manager discovered that the sample for this particular style was soiled. After replacing it with a fresh sample, the salesperson's sales of the style rose.

A new salesman for a small company selling clear plastic window shades underperformed his potential. The sales manager discovered many fingerprints and smudges on the salesman's samples. This immediately reminded potential customers of problems, not benefits. With clean samples, the new man's sales rose.

You also need to train new salespeople on how and when to use sales aids to the best advantage. Timing is important and varies in different situations. For example, in selling industrial robots, a most appropriate time exists for pointing out cycles-per-minute in the product brochures. In selling life insurance, the potential customer loses interest when shown a cash value and premium schedule before a need has been established. The door-to-door salesperson must offer the free gift when first greeting the prospect, not after a rejection.

Qualifying Prospects

You and your new salesperson have previously discussed the strengths, weaknesses, and personalities of present customers and certain known prime prospects. For revenues to increase, the new salesperson must understand how to efficiently find additional prospects with a greater than average need for the product/service. You must teach the proven unique techniques which produce qualified leads for your more successful experienced salespeople, or develop and test new techniques yourself. Prospecting creates growth, but the time required and risks involved are not worth the reward unless leads are qualified.

Some businesses, such as smoke alarms, emergency lighting, or hot tubs, rely heavily on new customers, because repeat orders are few. Here the ability to produce qualified leads inexpensively means survival.

The sales manager for a small distributor of ice-making machines initially instructed salespeople to call on all restaurants, taverns, and food processors. One out of every hundred calls led to a sale. Sales-force turnover was high, and those salespeople that stayed were marginal. One day the sales manager realized that following an ice delivery truck, and then calling on establishments that purchased ice, could produce a more select prospect with a greater need.

Each salesperson was informed of this technique, which resulted in one out of every ten calls eventually producing a sale. Turnover decreased and salesperson caliber rose.

The sales manager for a small distributor of solar heat-reflecting window shades had similar problems. Salespeople made cold calls on building managers and interior decorators. One saleswoman began calling directly on offices with large windows and southern exposures. She eventually closed one out of every four calls. The sales manager informed the other three salespeople, and their business prospered.

You should inform salespeople of appropriate lists for prospecting. If you sell a cleaning service to hospitals, you should make use of a publication which lists all private and public hospitals by state and city with telephone numbers and addresses. If you sell men's belts, you should make use of a publication which lists major men's wear retailers by state and city with telephone numbers and addresses. Trade publications, trade associations, and certain specialized business publishers sell such lists. Local Yellow Pages listings can also prove an invaluable help for selling certain products/services.

Supplying salespeople with a list of inactive accounts and previous customers sometimes produces good results. Similarly, salespeople should not neglect qualified prospects presently sold by a competitor. Business is a dynamic process, and buyers, needs, salespeople, quality, service, and prices continually change. You never know when a prospect will become unhappy with your competitor. Caution your people not to attack the competitor's product/service, because then they insult the customer's judgment. Instruct them merely to sell your benefits, and listen to the prospect's comments on the competition.

Remind your salespeople that referrals from satisfied customers represent an excellent introduction to qualified prospects. Suggest that the sales force ask for referrals; there is no charge.

Remind your sales force that noncompetitive salespeople can supply excellent leads. The institutional food purveyor might know which hospitals need a cleaning service. The hosiery salesperson calling on retail outlets might know a buyer who complained about the present sweater resource. Encourage your sales force to exchange market information with noncompetitive salespeople.

Some small growing businesses produce qualified leads for their sales force through advertising, trade shows, and direct mail. One small firm that sold hot tubs produced leads by advertising on UHF television with a number to call, and in TV guides with a return coupon. Another small firm produced leads for a unique industrial cutting fluid by exhibiting in regional machine-tool trade shows. We discuss advertising, trade shows, and direct mail in a later chapter. If your company produces leads for salespeople, explain the process, train them in efficient, quick follow-up, and ask them to evaluate the quality of prospects.

Obtaining an Appointment

Salespeople with delivery routes don't require appointments. Salespeople calling on repeat customers for reorders have little difficulty arranging appointments. However, salespeople who depend on a constant stream of new customers must be taught proven techniques for selling the first appointment. These techniques vary for each company, product, service, and industry.

If your company falls into the latter new-customer category, remind your salespeople that successfully selling the first appointment by phone does not mean selling the product by phone. Trying to sell the product/service by phone generally fails. The objective of the phone call is to obtain an appointment, and a by-product is to further qualify the prospect. In the phone call, the salesperson should stress the value of the proposed visit, and the sizzle of the product/service. The call should stimulate the prospect's curiosity, add a certain element of mystery, and of course, mention any referral. Teach salespeople key phrases and words which produce the desired result, an appointment.

For example, in calling establishments which purchase ice, the ice-machine salesperson would mention that his or her machine could save the prospect money, time, and space. The prospect might ask how much the machine costs. The salesperson should reply that the price depends on the prospect's needs, which they can discuss at their appointment.

Similarly, in calling establishments whose large windows have southern exposures, the solar heat-reflecting shade salesperson would mention that his or her shades could reduce the prospect's room temperature ten degrees in summer, reduce glare, and prevent fabric fading without reducing necessary sunlight. The prospect might ask how the shades affix to the windows. The salesperson should reply that that depends on the particular shade and window, which they can discuss at their appointment.

The telephone appointment request can also result in a "No" or "Call me later." The ice purchaser might say no because his nephew drives the ice truck. The shade prospect might say no because the firm is moving out of state in ninety days. The telephone call requesting an appointment has allowed these salespeople to efficiently determine that these two prospects are not qualified. Should the prospect reply "Call me later," this information is recorded on a file card and referred to in the future for the call back. Encourage your people to maintain file cards on each porspect with all appropriate information.

Presentation Format

Every product or service has a unique selling presentation format which produces the best results. All salespeople will vary it to fit their individual styles and the customer's needs. Some salespeople will not use it at all. However, as sales manager you must teach all your people this proven basic presentation format, including the key words and phrases.

The sales manager of a small men's tie company realized that few retailers purchase an entire line of ties from one manufacturer, but rather buy the best styles from a number of resources. Therefore, the four salespeople currently employed by this tie company were trained to analyze a retailer's present selection, find weak areas, and show only strong styles which filled a need in one of these weak areas. The sales manager then hired a fifth salesperson from a shoe company, whose previous shoe customers had wanted to see and purchase an entire shoe line from one resource. The sales manager neglected to inform him about analyzing needs, and about presenting selected styles, not the entire line. The new salesperson performed poorly until the sales manager made a field visit, realized his mistake, and corrected the problem.

Teach your new salespeople how to understand customer needs, and the ways in which your product specifically satisfies those needs. Suggest certain questions to ask concerning customer problems and opportunities, which will elicit information on needs. Then show them how to completely and clearly explain the major benefits associated with your product/service. Explain which product features concern the buyer and which do not. Explain how to relate the customer needs learned earlier to benefits and product features. Share the type of objections the salesperson is likely to encounter, and how to overcome them.

For example, if your small company sells ice-making machines to concerns presently buying ice, you might suggest the following approach to your sales force. After introductions and a limited amount of small talk, the salesperson should ask the customer what he uses ice for, how many pounds are purchased each week, and how often it is delivered. The customer might respond that deliveries are irregular in the summer, but three times a week in winter. Purchases average a ton a week, which they use in processing certain meat products.

You would advise the salesperson to acknowledge the difficulties and inconvenience of irregular ice deliveries. Then suggest that the salesperson show a picture of a machine capable of producing 350 pounds of ice daily, two of which would satisfy the buyer's needs. Next you would recommend that the salesperson discuss the space needed for the machines, electrical requirements, type of ice made, and reliability. The salesperson should then point out that the machines would solve the delivery problem, because ice would always be on hand; and that after energy costs (showing a chart with the information), money would, in fact, be saved. If the customer asks for exact figures on savings, you teach the salesperson how to calculate them.

The buyer might complain that their last ice-making machine broke down often and was expensive to repair. You should give the salesperson information on frequency of machine failures, and the cost of a maintenance contract. Suggest that the salesperson remind the buyer that breakdowns will be less of a problem with two machines. The buyer might contend that machines break down in summer when repair people and ice delivery firms lag days behind. You suggest countering by explaining that your repair staff will deliver ice made at your facility at no cost until the machine has been repaired.

This buyer might ask the cost of these two machines with installation, and then possibly complain about the funds needed for such a purchase. You suggest that the salesperson mention a lease plan and figure out suitable monthly payments.

Remind your salespeople never to lose their temper or argue with a customer. Keep disagreements polite and friendly. An infamous chain-store buyer gave any salesperson who angrily argued with him two orders: "get out" and "stay out." Whether an order is written or not, salespeople always need to leave a good impression, so that they may return.

Remind your salespeople to obtain buyer agreement at each stage of the presentation by asking questions; for example, "This machine would save you money, wouldn't it?" Remind your salespeople that a presentation where the buyer does not raise objections or ask quesitons indicates that they have lost contact, and this must be reestablished. Salespeople should know that letting the buyer talk, and not interrupting, helps establish good rapport.

Tell your salespeople not to answer questions if they are unsure of their facts. They should admit this to the buyer and promise an answer later by phone.

Next, suggest the key phrases, questions, and unique techniques which close sales for your product/service. Remind your people that if the previous selling process has been handled correctly, closing develops naturally. For ice machines, the salesperson might ask, "Where would you like the machine installed?" The door-to-door hot tub salesperson might ask, "Would you like redwood or oak?" The tie salesperson might suggest, "An order today can be shipped at once, but because of limited inventories, an order taken next week might take longer." The hospital cleaning service salesperson might just say, "What action would you like to take? We are ready if you are."

Finally, remind your salespeople that selling is a process, which starts with prospecting, moves forward with a sale, and ends with service. Using the suggested presentation techniques improves the probability for success, but no more than the salesperson's enthusiasm and confidence. If a salesperson is not enthusiastic about the product/service, why should the buyer be? If a salesperson has no confidence in himself or herself, why should the buyer? Salespeople must establish relationships which create long-term customers, not just short-term sales. Salespeople not only sell a product/service, but themselves.

FIELD TRAINING

Most of the training previously discussed would be handled by the sales manager through two to five day visits in his or her office. Training then continues with field visits by the sales manager. Within thirty days after the home office training sessions, the sales manager should spend a day or two with each new salesperson calling on accounts in the salesperson's territory. Then, at least twice a year, the smaller-company sales manager should visit customers and prospects with each salesperson in his or her territory. Since your sales force probably contains between five and twenty people, this does not represent an unmanageable task.

Field visits have a variety of functions: they become an opportunity for continued training at the moment of truth, help to humanize the company, establish personal relationships with customers and rapport with salespeople, and allow you to engage in personal selling at the appropriate level. Field training and supervision give salespeople confidence in you as a sales manager. Field visits also present a first-hand opportunity for you to learn more about problems and opportunities with customers, with the product/service, and with salespeople. When a customer complains about deliveries to you in person, it has more impact than a salesperson complaining over the phone. Often a salesperson teaches you an important technique, or a customer gives you information which can be successfully employed elsewhere. Field visits to customers and prospects create buyers' confidence in your company. Field visits, including training and supervision, present smaller concerns with an inexpensive opportunity to outperform larger competitors by maintaining superior sales organizations and good customer relations. Many larger-company sales managers don't have the time or inclination to travel with salespeople and call on accounts.

Before the Sales Call

You should call the salesperson at least a week ahead to arrange a mutually convenient day or two. Depending on circumstances, you may wish to spend one day visiting large prospects or customers that you choose, and another calling on smaller accounts which the salesperson chooses. Decide which of you will set up appointments with specific buyers, and then schedule appointments to fill the same full day that you expect your salespeople to work. If your company sells door to door or uses prearranged routes, appointments may not be necessary.

Be sure you arrange field trips with both new and experienced salespeople, and with both weak and strong performers. Field visits represent a unique personal opportunity for building a relationship with your people. Strong perform-ers need the relationship if not the training. Salespeople with whom you don't travel may become insulted or begin developing bad habits. Sometimes strong performers wish to show you off to their customers; sometimes they wish to show off to you. You may learn successful techniques from strong performers, which can be passed on to other salespeople. Also, the time you spend with a strong performer may show more dramatic and immediate sales results than the time you spend with a weak performer.

A small furniture company employed a star salesman who the sales manager chose not to visit because no problems existed. Although the salesman's ship-ments grew each year, he never called on the two major department stores in his territory. When questioned by the sales manager, he claimed that other customers kept him busy. His boss correctly suspected that it was a fear of rejection, because department stores were more difficult to sell. The sales man-ager arranged a visit to the territory, and had the salesman make appointments with the two "majors." Once in the buyer's office, the salesman did a magnif-icent job, and left with an order. Having overcome the fear of rejection and gaining confidence, he went on to open many other department stores.

A small sweater manufacturer employed a woman over sixty-five to repre-sent them in New Jersey. She resented the sales manager, thirty years her junior, and resisted any visits by him to her terriotry. On his initial trip, they called on retail customers in Atlantic City and then checked into a casino hotel on the Boardwalk. When the reservation clerk asked if they were married, everyone had a good laugh. Suddenly they had shared a funny experience, became friends, and thereafter sold together for many years.

During the Sales Call

With new salespeople, the sales manager should make the presentation to the first several customers, and then allow the salesperson the opportunity to do it. The new salesperson will learn from watching you in action, and from your analysis of his or her performance.

With seasoned salespeople, let them make the presentation, unless agreed upon otherwise. Sometimes major customers or prospects wish to be sold by management. Similarly, when you are calling on management rather than on the buyer, purchasing agent, or design engineer, a presentation by sales man-agement may be preferred. Discuss with your salesperson which of you will make the presentation before the call.

Regardless of who makes the presentation, it is necessary before each call to discuss the objectives, the plan of attack, and background information. The objective might be to see if the customer needs another ice machine, to see whether the present robot installation performs as promised, to count stock for a fill-in order on ties, to determine the insurance needs of a doctor who responded to a direct-mail piece, or to sell educational books on a cold call. The plan of attack includes specific questions which determine customer needs, a list of benefits you offer which satisfy known needs, and answers to objections which might be raised. Background information appears on the salesperson's customer or prospect file card, and might include the buyer's name, personality traits, past purchases, present resources, and known needs. This pre-call analysis and review of information allows for proper planning.

When the salesperson makes the presentation, try not to interfere; and if you must interject something, be gentle. You accompany the salesperson on this call primarily for training purposes, not necessarily to write an order. Salespeople learn from failures as well as successes. If you interfere, the buyer becomes confused and the salesperson embarrassed, which strains the relationships. You may gain an order but lose a customer and a salesperson. You travel with a salesperson four days annually, but the other 236 he or she travels alone. When the sales manager sells for the sales force, the sales force stops selling.

When you must interrupt, use a question to make the point indirectly. If the salesperson suggests the wrong model, ask if the customer might also have an interest in the correct model. If the salesperson concentrates on price when another benefit should be emphasized, ask if the customer might wish the other benefit explained.

After the Sales Call

Critique each call immediately afterwards, and before the next one. You can accomplish this on your way to the next customer or over coffee. A good salesperson eventually employs self-analysis after each sales call. To help develop self-analysis, ask the salesperson how he or she felt about the call. What went well? What went poorly?

After this self-analysis, share your thoughts on the strengths and weaknesses of the presentation. If you first tell the salesperson what he or she did right, it will be easier to accept criticism on what he or she did wrong. Your comments should be action-oriented, so that corrective steps can be taken on the next call. You will obtain best results through analysis rather than outright criticism. Use questions to make points. "Do you think you emphasized the lease plan enough?" Salespeople are self-conscious and often not at their best when accompanied by their sales manager. You must factor this into your evaluation.

The curbstone analysis after a solar heat-reflecting window shade sales call might proceed as follows. The sales manager begins, "Well, Joan, how do you feel the call went?" Joan replies, "We found out the problem areas—high air-conditioning costs in summer, high heat loss in winter, ultraviolet damage to furniture, too much sunlight in the morning, not enough in the afternoon; and

I presented the benefits of our solar shades to solve those problems. But I didn't feel their objection to price was handled well." The sales manager agrees. "You did an excellent job of determining their needs, and getting the purchasing agent to talk; but the presentation would have been stronger if you had mentioned that the shades reduce summer air-conditioning costs 25% and winter heating bills 15%. This information also could have been covered when the buyer questioned the price." Joan smiles. "That's right, I forgot, but I'll use that material on our next sales call."

A door-to-door Bible salesman was making household calls with his manager. The company offers attractive editions of the Old and New Testaments along with other religious items. The salesman wanted to close a sale for the Old Testament by showing pictures from the edition. Without thinking, he picked up the New Testament, unintentionally offending the customer, and lost the sale. The two men walked in silence to the next prospect, because a verbal critique was not necessary.

At the end of each day, write notes for yourself on the calls so that on your next field visit with the salesperson you have a basis for compaison. Sometimes check lists prove helpful in evaluating salespeoples' strengths and weaknesses and in determining areas which require further development. A check list might include time and territory management; appearance; organization; product, customer, competitor knowledge; selling skills; paperwork; enthusiasm and confidence. When you return to the home office, write the salesperson a letter, thanking him or her for their time, acknowledging certain strengths, and reminding him or her of certain weaknesses.

Management Selling

As mentioned previously, certain major customers and management-level decision makers prefer to be sold by vendor management, not a salesperson. In a smaller company, this process, known as management selling, becomes part of most sales manager field visits, and therefore part of sales training. Major customers or management represent an appropriate level for the sales manager to sell on. With these accounts you help the salespeople; you do not compete with them. They require your help, and appreciate it. On most field trips, at least one major account requires a visit by the sales manager.

Before the call, you again discuss objectives with the salesperson, along with a plan of attack, background information, and possible objections. You do a complete pre-call analysis. But on these calls, you the sales manager, not the salesperson, makes the presentation. If obtaining an order represents the objective, you use all your skills to obtain it. This call belongs to the sales manager, but the salesperson participates where appropriate. The salesperson might provide information on customer usage and local conditions. Salespeople handle some calls on major accounts themselves, but once or twice a year your presence is required.

After the call, ask your salesperson what they thought: "How did it go?" Their suggestions will help in future customer visits, and will provide further insight into their understanding of the sales process. At one such critique, the salesperson told the sales manager he had forgotten to mention the same product feature that the salesperson had forgotten the previous day. The sales manager asked why she had not corrected him with the customer. She replied that the sales manager had not embarrassed her with the customer yesterday, and she returned the courtesy today.

SALES MEETINGS, MANUALS, BULLETINS, TAPES, AND TELEPHONE CALLS

You spend two to five days initially training a new salesperson at your office, and then two to four days a year in continued field training. Between field visits, training takes place using sales meetings, manuals, bulletins, tapes, and telephone calls. As you can see, sales training is a continual process with a beginning, the office visit, and then a logical progression of events including field visits, sales meetings, manuals, bulletins, phone calls, and tapes.

In a smaller company, you generally hire one or two new salespeople each year, which does not facilitate initial group training. Unfortunately, you must train each person individually, unless by coincidence several are hired at once.

However, at periodic sales meetings, you engage in training a group, or they engage in training each other, which represents a more efficient use of time and requires different techniques from individual training. We devote an entire section to sales meetings in Chap. 6, "Communication and Control." At a sales meeting you must limit the training subject matter to such broad topics as new product knowledge, opening new accounts, and follow-up service. Time is limited, and subject matter must be applicable to the entire group. Group training loses its effectiveness unless all participants share a similar level of proficiency. Training the most experienced salesperson with the least experienced, or training the strong performer with the weak, dilutes the results. For certain training, you may remedy this problem by forming subgroups at the sales meeting.

Chapter 6 also deals with manuals, bulletins, tapes, and telephone calls. The sales manual presents in writing much of the training material you have presented orally, and thus becomes a salesperson's reference book. Bulletins keep salespeople informed on such items as new policies, competitive advantages, product developments, and market changes. Through periodic telephone conversations and/or audio tapes, the sales manager discusses matters relating to each salesperson's individual territory, such as specific orders, customers, or prospects. The material discussed involves a continuation of the training process.

TRAINING AGENDA

Some sales managers find it helpful to prepare an agenda when initially training a new salesperson. For the trainee, the agenda outlines the material to be covered. For the sales manager, the agenda acts as a schedule allocating appropriate time to various subject matter. The following is an example of a training agenda.

Salesperson's Name _____Date _____

Monday, April 27

    9:00–12:00   Review our product line.

    1:00–5:00   Review competitors' product lines.

Tuesday, April 28

    9:00–12:00   Visit Bloomingdale's and Macy's to see how our merchandise and competitors' merchandise is displayed.

    1:00–5:00   Visit our factory to see the goods being made.

Wednesday, April 29

    9:00–12:00   Discuss customers and prospects.

    1:00–3:00   Review customer stock taking, merchandising, order writing, prospect lists, call reports, route sheets, forecasts, and appraisals.

    3:00–5:00   Discuss how to allocate time between customers, and the most efficient way to travel the territory. Review a road map of the territory, and show where customers and prospects are located.

Thursday, April 30

    9:00–10:30   Discuss our company's organization chart and personnel.

    10:30–12:00 Discuss our company history and achievements.

    12:00–1:30   Lunch with the president.

    1:30–3:30   Discuss company and competitor policies on terms, advertising allowances, promotions, box sales, returns, freight, display racks, and minimum order size.

    3:30–5:00   Review the sales manual and bulletins.

Friday, April 31

    9:00–12:00   Present the line to the salesperson as if he or she were a customer. Review selling techniques.

| 1:00–4:00 | Have the salesperson present the line to you as if you were a customer. Critique the presentation. Review selling techniques. |
| 4:00–5:00 | Discuss sales aids, qualifying prospects, and making appointments. |

TRAINING RECORD

Since sales training is an ongoing process, you require a means of recording each salesperson's progress. Often a one-page form outlining the training program proves helpful. Such a form might list the training subject matter down the side and the types of training sessions across the top. The sales manager would fill in dates and remarks where appropriate. The following is an example of such a training record.

Salesperson's Name _____ Date Hired _____

	Home Office	Field Visits	Sales Meetings
Product Knowledge			
Competitive Advantage			
Customer Knowledge			
Customer Service			
Nonselling Activities			
Time and Territory Management			
Company Background and Organization			
Company Policy			
Selling Benefits			
Empathy			
Organization			
Qualifying Prospects			
Obtaining Appointments			
Presentation Format			

SALES MANAGER'S KNOWLEDGE

In order to properly train your salespeople, you the sales manager must obtain a thorough understanding of the material involved including product/service, competitive, and customer knowledge; customer service; time and territory management; company background, organization, and policy; and selling skills. Unless you possess this knowledge, the training program fails. Fit the specific training program to company needs, but do obtain this knowledge. If you are a sales manager with no sales force—not uncommon in a small business—you must still have this knowledge.

MEASURING RESULTS

Measure the results of your training program just as you did with hiring. Between field visits, does the salesperson perform as you desire? If not, change the program. Smaller businesses are flexible—a competitive advantage—and can change quickly. If salespeople fail to present benefits, find out why, and make adjustments in your training. If 20% of your sales force accounts for 50% of your sales, reexamine your training program. If 30% of your new salespeople leave within two years, reexamine your training and hiring programs.

CONCLUSION

Hire the right salespeople, train them well, and the remainder of sales management becomes much easier. As you can see from these first two chapters, hiring and training involve considerable time and energy. However, if they are performed correctly, you obtain a tremendous advantage over your larger competitors. Aside from your time, doing these tasks correctly does not require much more money than doing them incorrectly.

3
Compensation

Many smaller businesses inherit their salesperson compensation plan from pervious management, or follow industry tradition, or they may merely copy plans employed by larger competitors. As sales manager, you should review the compensation plan annually. Business is a dynamic process, and the plan must meet changing human and commercial requirements. Each company and often each salesperson has different and changing needs.

Correct compensation represents an important, although not the sole, ingredient in attracting, retaining, and motivating good salespeople. Other ingredients for motivating salespeople include achievement, recognition, freedom, status, personal relationships, belonging, company policy, and fear of failure. Good salespeople have a strong drive to improve results each year, regardless of compensation. They have an insatiable appetite for writing orders. Salespeople generally have a high need to be recognized and praised for their achievements. A congratulatory letter from the company president will be prized and shared for many years. Salespeople value the personal freedom involved in planning their own time and the status of their positions. They enjoy the personal relationships with customers, management, and other salespeople. However, strong salespeople are also sensitive and insecure, with a need to belong, a distaste for inefficient policies, and a fear of failure. They enjoy feeling part of a successful organization, and have unreasonable fears of not succeeding personally. Chapter 5 deals with motivative in detail.

Few smaller businesses realize that they can offer salespeople more of these motivational ingredients than a larger concern can. In a smaller business, salespeople can more easily receive recognition and status for achievements, enjoy personal freedom and relationships, and feel that they belong. Not enough smaller businesses take advantage of this strength.

On the other hand, career advancement opportunities for a salesperson outside of direct selling are very limited in a smaller business, whereas they are unlimited in larger concerns. You are the sales manager; your boss, the president, runs the company; and no other management positions exist in sales or marketing. As mentioned earlier, this influences your candidate profile, and represents a weakness in attracting, motivating, and retaining salespeople.

Smaller businesses, because of their flexibility, can compensate salespeople as well or better than larger concerns. Compensation must be equitably based on sales performance and must be flexible. For example, a salesperson who unexpectedly opens an account outside of his or her territory should receive extra pay, even if this is not covered in the original compensation plan. The smaller company can easily accommodate such variances, while the larger concern, being more rigid, finds such action difficult.

Proper recruiting and training, discussed in previous chapters, also influences compensation. If you hire the correct people, and train and manage them well, they perform, and can be well compensated. A good compensation plan proves useless for a weak or badly trained sales force.

This chapter deals only with compensation. Later chapters deal with the other ingredients for attracting, retaining, and motivating salespeople. Creating a compensation plan involves: setting objectives, determining compensation mix, creating an expense policy, and determining fringe benefits.

INTRODUCTION

The objectives of a sales compensation plan include: balancing the needs of the company and salespeople, quickly and effectively rewarding positive action, simplicity, fairness, rewarding superior performance, and establishing a minimum level of stability. Basically, the company needs to attract, retain, and motivate salespeople who produce desired levels of sales at a cost which generates profits and allows the necessary percentage returns on sales and invested capital. Good salespeople need a compensation plan which relieves them of basic financial worries, gives them pride in what they earn, reflects their qualifications and experience, and equals or betters competition.

A compensation plan should quickly and effectively reward positive action which is important to company success. As sales manager, you consult the job description and establish specific goals which are measurable, realistic, and achievable through salespeople's efforts.

A universal objective for all sales compensation plans is simplicity. Salespeople do not understand or remember complicated plans, and companies have difficulty administering them.

A good sales compensation plan must also be fair and equitable. For example, nothing dulls a salesperson's enthusiasm more than "house accounts."

A good compensation plan always rewards superior performance. You must build into the compensation plan means for the superior performer to receive superior pay.

A good compensation plan provides a certain level of stability, so that salespeople have some downside protection for their income. Rewards must reflect results, but with assurances of certain minimum levels.

Once you have decided on the objectives for a sales compensation plan, next you determine the proper combination of salary, commission, and bonus to achieve these objectives. Salary provides salespeople with a fixed amount of pay per period regardless of immediate activities or results. Salary deemphasizes the immediate importance of writing orders, but emphasizes the importance of certain nonselling activities and encourages the salesperson to engage in these activities. Since payments are the same each period, salary is easy to administer, and direct selling expenses remain fixed regardless of volume. The major disadvantages of salary plans are their lack of financial incentive, their tendency to reward poor performers at the expense of strong performers, and the lack of proper percentage relationship to sales volume.

Salaried compensation plans generally attract salespeople who are team players, ambitious to climb the executive ladder, steady rather than top performers, more professional than commercial, and who prefer pre-sold products. Because of all these characteristics, salaried compensation plans lend themselves to selling products/services which are pre-sold or cyclical; require considerable prospecting, missionary work, or long negotiating periods; require service not related to reorders; and/or involve team selling.

Commission provides an immediate reward for successful performance. Commission emphasizes the importance of writing orders, and encourages salespeople to engage in activities which culminate in order writing. Commission plans are easy to understand and compute, and sales compensation costs remain a fixed percentage of revenues. Commission provides incentive for the sales force to work hard and earn a great deal of money. The major disadvantages of commission plans are that they lack emphasis on nonselling activities, encourage calling on a few volume accounts at the expense of many smaller ones, can result in high sales force turnover during weak sales periods becuase of decreased income, and can encourage salespeople to oversell unneeded features in addition to overloading customers with inventory.

Commission compensation plans generally attract aggressive career salespeople with no ambition for promotion into management. These salespeople are lone wolves, top producers but erratic, and more interested in the sale than the selling technique.

Because of all these characteristics, commission plans do not lend themselves to selling products/services which require a great deal of non-order-related service, which are cyclical, or which require missionary work or team selling. Commission plans do lend themselves to nontechnical, unsophisticated products/services where reorders create a steady flow of business, and where unit prices are not high.

A bonus provides an extra deferred reward for some form of outstanding performance. Generally, bonuses are paid once a year or once a selling period in addition to salary or commission. Bonus plans can be difficult to administer, but they do allow a great deal of flexibility.

Some combination of salary, commission, and bonus represents the most widely used form of sales compensation. Since the objectives of a compensation system usually involve quickly and effectively rewarding a combination of positive actions, rather than one simple action, combination plans prove most appropriate. However, combination plans lack the simplicity of straight commission or straight salary, which makes them more difficult for the company to administer and the salesperson to understand.

Most companies pay all or some of their salespeople's expenses in addition to salary, commission, and bonus compensation. Expense categories include travel by automobile, airlines, and railroads; lodging; telephone; entertainment; samples, promotion; and office or clerical help. Salespeople should have an economic incentive for controlling their expenses, for using expense money productively and efficiently.

The total direct cost of your sales force includes salary, commission, bonus, and expenses, plus fringe benefits. Most small businesses pay their salespeoples' primary fringe benefits such as social security, unemployment compensation, medical, life, accident, and disability insurance, and vacations. Most small businesses don't pay for their salespeoples' possible secondary fringe benefits such as profit sharing, pension plans, personal use of company car and credit cards, club and association membership, reimbursed educational expenses, dental insurance, and reimbursed moving expenses.

SETTING OBJECTIVES

The objectives of a sales compensation plan include: balancing the needs of the company and salespeople, quickly and effectively rewarding positive action, simplicity, fairness, rewarding superior performance, and establishing a minimum level of stability.

Balancing Company and Salespeople's Needs

Basically, the company needs to attract, retain, and motivate salespeople who produce desired levels of sales at a cost which generates profits and allows necessary percentage returns on sales and invested capital.

One small company manufactured silver-coated reflective plastic film for application to windows, using an adhesive. In the winter, like a silvered coffee pot, the film reduced heat loss through windows. In the summer, the film blocked some of the sun's rays, reducing indoor temperatures and air-conditioning expense. With energy costs skyrocketing, this was a good product for the 1970s.

Management tried to sell the product through window applicators, air-conditioning representatives, and retail shade departments, but none had the interest or knowledge to be effective. Finally the company hired its own full-time field sales representatives, and devised an "ingenious" compensation plan which included base salary plus a commission on sales plus bonuses for achieving quotas. Every year sales doubled, until the company went out of business! The compensation plan had equaled 20% of sales, which did not leave enough cash flow to support increased inventories and accounts receivable.

Good salespeople need a compensation plan that relieves them of basic financial worries, gives them pride in what they earn, reflects their qualifications and experience, and equals or betters competition. Compensating salespeople based on the cost to replace them, or the cost just to keep them from leaving, does not satisfy these needs. Because of these needs, you obtain better results with fewer but more-qualified and higher-paid salespeople than with a larger sales force that includes less-qualified, lower-paid people.

Rewarding Positive Action

To fulfill this objective, return to the job description and establish the specific goals of your compensation program. What positive action do you want the compensation system to quickly and effectively reward? Select specific objectives important to company success which are measurable, realistic, and achieveable through salespeoples' efforts.

If your business sells Bibles door to door, the compensation plan should quickly reward only a sale. The job description calls for no customer service after the sale and no "missionary" work preceding the sale.

On the other hand, if your company sells underwear to retailers, the compensation plan should quickly and effectively reward not only the initial sale, but also fill-in orders, display work with clerks, credit and collection activities, handling complaints and delivery information, sales forecasting, record keeping, and call reports. The job description requires salespeople to engage in all these activities.

If your company sells industrial gears for oil drilling equipment, the compensation plan should not only quickly reward an initial sale, but also replacement orders, the missionary work with customer design engineers that led to getting your gears specified, and the follow-up work with customer production engineers teaching the correct application. Again the job description requires salespeople to engage in all these activities.

A new territory requires a compensation plan that places more emphasis on opening new accounts and less on servicing existing ones. In recessionary times, the compensation plan needs to reflect more emphasis on collections than in prosperous times. These two examples show why compensation plans require annual reviews and flexibility in approach.

Simplicity

A universal objective for all sales compensation plans is simplicity. Salespeople do not understand or remember complicated plans, and companies have difficulty administering them.

A small company which sold abrasive grinding wheels fired the sales manager after two successive years of declining orders. The new sales manager discovered that the compensation plan included a different commission rate for each of twenty major products, a different bonus system for each month, and a salary which was adjusted each quarter to reflect the last quarter's shipments. The program totally confused the sales force and required a full-time administrative person. Each month the salespeople and the administrator would waste a day arguing over the accuracy of paychecks. The new sales manager established a different commission rate for each of five product groups, one bonus system for summer, one for winter, and a level monthly salary. Orders immediately began increasing, and half of the administrator's time became available for other tasks.

Equitable

A good sales compensation plan must also be fair and equitable. For example, orders which customers phoned or mailed directly to the office should be credited to the salesperson's account just as if they had been written in the field. Also, nothing dulls a salesperson's enthusiasm more than "house accounts." Taking lucrative accounts out of a territory for handling by management hurts morale. Unless absolutely necessary, don't do it.

Similarly, paying lower commissions on certain sales which involve the same effort as those on which you pay higher commissions generates negative feelings. Also, not splitting commissions on orders involving joint effort is not equitable. One sales meeting of a food purveyor abruptly ended in a hot-tempered fist fight between two salesmen over commission splitting.

Salespeople who display equal ability and effort but have different type territories require compensation plans that take this into account. It is not equitable, for example, to pay a person in a new territory with no accounts straight commission, just because you pay straight commission to the people in established territories with many accounts. It would not be fair to compensate the New York salesperson who rides the bus between accounts on the same basis as the Colorado salesperson who drives hundreds of miles between customers.

Rewarding Superior Performance

A good sales compensation plan always rewards superior performance. Using the job description, you have decided which positive action the compensation plan is to quickly and effectively reward. Now you must build into the compensation plan means for the superior performer to receive superior pay. Don't place an upper limit on salespeoples' compensation, because this dulls motivation. Earning potential for salespeople should remain open-ended.

If you employ six salespeople in well-developed territories with similar potential, and one salesperson's orders grow much faster than the others, then your compensation plan should pay that person more money. If, from the job description, you decide the compensation plan should reward the opening of new accounts, and if one salesperson opens twenty new accounts in six months versus ten from the other salespeople (assuming equal territory potential), your compensation plan should pay more money to the salesperson with twenty new accounts.

Providing Stability

A good sales compensation plan provides a certain level of stability, so that the salespeople have some downside protection for their income. The income of a salesperson who loses a large account should decline, but not to a level which threatens his or her mortgage payments. Such a salesperson requires time to obtain another major account. The income of a salesperson selling to cyclical industries such as auto, aircraft, steel, and farm equipment should be less in bad times than good, but not so bad as to threaten food on the table. Such a salesperson must survive the bad times in order to write orders when business improves. Rewards must reflect results, but with assurances of certain minimum levels.

Outlining the Objectives

Take a few minutes to outline the objectives of your particular sales compensation plan. If your small business sells custom-printed forms for data processing, your objectives might read:

1. Reward salespeople for opening new accounts and expanding existing ones through developing forms which solve a customer problem. Reward salespeople for diligently seeking reorders.
2. Encourage salespeople to assist in obtaining credit information, collecting overdue balances, occasionally delivering small orders, and handling complaints.
3. Provide a guaranteed minimum monthly paycheck for new salespeople, new territories, and weak sales periods.
4. Require administration by present payroll clerk, monthly payments, and simple reporting to each salesperson.

5. Require commission splitting on regional accounts where two salespeople share the work.
6. Provide 5% more compensation than competition, but do not exceed 10% of company sales.
7. Do not limit top earnings.

COMPENSATION MIX

Once you decide on the objectives for a sales compensation plan, next you determine the proper combination of salary, commission, and bonus to achieve these objectives. Remember, your compensation plan should encourage productive activity which achieves these objectives and satisfies salespeople's needs.

The 1981 Dartnell "Compensation of Salesmen" report* shows that 22% of American companies surveyed employed straight salary, 19% straight commission, and 59% a combination of salary and incentive. The middle group (removing the top and bottom 25%) of straight-salaried experienced salespeople earned from $21,500 to $36,000 with a $28,335 average; straight-commissioned salespeople $24,000 to $38,000 with a $30,897 average; and combination plans $25,000 to $38,000 with a $30,954 average.

For 1982 the American Management Association's Executive Compensation Service reported that 22% of American companies surveyed employed straight salary for salespeople, 6% draw against commission, 28% salary plus commission, 32% salary plus bonus, and 12% salary plus commission plus bonus. For 1982 they also reported average sales trainees' compensation of $22,350, average salesperson's compensation of $29,087, average senior salesperson's compensation of $36,000, and average sales supervisor's compensation of $43,400. These compensation figures include salary, commission, bonus, and other incentives, but do not include expenses or fringe benefits.

The Conference Board's "Compensating Field Sales Representatives Report No. 828" states that for 1982 the average annual salesperson compensation was $30,000, with a high average of $42,400 for textiles and apparel and a low average of $27,200 for consumer chemicals. Compensation includes salary and incentive, but no expenses or fringe benefits.

The same report states that the 1982 medium straight-commission annual compensation for average performers was $45,000, for below-average performers $24,000, and for top performers $89,000. The 1982 medium salary-only annual compensation for average performers was $30,000, for below-average performers $25,000, and for top performers $34,400. For average performers

---

*By permission from *Sales Force Compensation*: Dartnell's 21st Biennial Survey, Dartnell Corp., 1982.

the medium on combination plans ranged from $29,200 to $31,900, for below-average performers $20,800 to $23,500, for top performers $38,500 to $41,500. This data was based on a survey of 319 salesforces.

Sales & Marketing Management magazine's 1983 Survey of Selling Costs* reports the following medium 1982 salesperson compensation figures: account representative $35,350; detailed salesperson $30,250; sales engineer $38,250; industrial products salesperson $40,200; and service salesperson $38,850.

Salary

Salary provides salespeople with a fixed amount of pay per period regardless of immediate activities or results. Nonetheless, when results exceed or fall short of management expectations, salaries can become adjusted accordingly. However, the reward for good performance or penalty for weak results is not immediate or direct.

Advantages. Straight salary provides the salesperson with a steady income and does not emphasize the immediate importance of writing orders. Salary emphasizes the importance of certain nonselling activities and encourages the salesperson to engage in these activities. Often a salesperson must perform services after the sale, which will not necessarily result in a reorder. For example, the salesperson for a small concern selling expensive tropical plants to offices may be required under the sales agreement to check and treat plants monthly for two years.

Since payments are the same each period, salary is easy to administer, and direct selling expenses remain fixed regardless of volume. Before each month begins, you know the exact amount required for salespeoples' compensation.

Salary compensation for salespeople, however, contains certain theoretical advantages which in practice do not exist. In practice, salary does not allow greater control over the sales force, develop a greater sense of company loyalty, or allow greater flexibility in realigning territories. Control, loyalty, and flexibility are not reasons to use a straight salary plan, but excuses because straight salary is so simple.

The correct level of compensation, whether salary, commission, bonus, or some combination, helps maintain proper control over the sales force and builds loyalty. A salesperson receiving $70,000 annually in straight commission will more likely respond to your directions than a salaried person receiving $10,000, and certainly will display more company loyalty. In smaller companies, proper

---

*By permission from S&MM's 1983 Survey of Selling Costs. © 1983, Further reproduction is prohibited.

control and loyalty also result from nonmonetary factors such as personal relationships, recognition of achievement, a feeling of belonging, fear of dismissal, and use of tools such as call reports and route sheets.

Theoretically, salary compensation makes salespeople more flexible about territory and customer realignments. However, regardless of the compensation plan, no salesperson easily accepts a weaker territory or reassignment of a major customer.

Disadvantages. The major disadvantages of salary plans are their lack of financial incentives, tendency to reward poor performers at the expense of strong performers, and lack of proper percentage relationship to sales volume. Salary does not offer that special incentive required for extra effort. It encourages adequate but not superior performance. Generally, salaries overpay the unaggressive salesperson and underpay the "hustler," thus favoring the less productive.

Salaried compensation as a percentage of revenues can vary drastically depending on sales. When sales rise, the percentage falls; but when sales decrease, the percentage painfully increases, which may prove critical to your profits and/or survival.

Type of Person. Salaried compensation plans generally attract salespeople who are team players, ambitious to climb the executive ladder, steady rather than top performers, more professional than commercial, and prefer pre-sold products. Once hired, salaried salespeople often develop rigid but comfortable routines, and often expect considerable sales assistance from management. The type of sales compensation plan you choose acts as a natural filter or selection device in attracting candidates. In this way your job description, candidate profile and compensation plan objectives again become interrelated.

Type of Selling. Because of all these characteristics, salaried compensation plans lend themselves to selling products/services which are pre-sold or cyclical; require considerable prospecting, missionary work, or long negotiating periods; require service not related to reorders; and/or involve team selling. Salary also proves appropriate for trainees, new undeveloped territories, and situations with no adequate measure of performance.

For example, sales of durable goods, such as machine tools, fluctuate dramatically with business cycles; require considerable time working with customer engineers, purchasing agents, and plant managers to make a sale; often require the salesperson to be accompanied by a sales engineer; and involve the salesperson's assistance with installation. Machine tools, like many big-ticket technical products that involve few orders but many dollars, lend themselves to salaried sales compensation.

As another example, items presold through national advertising such as ethical drugs, soap, toothpaste, liquor, and petroleum lend themselves to salaried sales compensation. In these situations the salesperson functions as order-taker, not active seller.

Some new salespeople require salaries during their training period because they could not survive financially based on performance. Salespeople assigned to new territories with no established business require a salary until they can build their volume. People selling to government agencies which require bids represent a situation with no adequate measure of performance. Was the salesperson or the bid responsible for the sale? Here again, salary is appropriate.

Commission

Commission provides an immediate reward for successful performance. If sales increase, your people make more money; if sales decrease they make less. Commission emphasizes the importance of writing orders, and encourages the salesperson to engage in activities which culminate in order writing. Increased sales often require the salesperson to perform many tasks beside writing orders, including prospecting for new accounts, setting up display fixtures, and counting stock.

Advantages. Generally, commission plans are easy to understand and compute. You multiply a fixed percentage times dollars of sales, or a fixed dollar amount times units of sales. Each day your salespeople know their earnings. Each month the payroll department clerk performs simple multiplication to arrive at each person's compensation.

Where commissions have to be split, because the sale involved more than one person's efforts, or when different rates are used for different products, administration proves more difficult. To prevent arguments, details of commission splits must be decided before a sale, not afterwards.

With commission, sales compensation costs remain a fixed percentage of your revenues whether they rise or decline, protecting profit margins and helping cash flow. When sales decline, the company is not saddled with a large fixed expenditure. For smaller companies with limited capital, this feature proves very important. New ventures especially benefit from commission, because initial sales costs are lower, reflecting the low sales volume.

Commission provides incentive for the sales force to work hard and earn a great deal of money. Only time, energy, and territory restraints limit the salesperson's compensation. Since no career ladder exists in the smaller-business sales force, the opportunity to earn large sums on commission takes on added importance. In some small and medium-sized concerns, top salespeople earn more than the sales manager or president. Commission also proves more appropriate for smaller businesses, because often the sales force is smaller but the territories are larger and have unlimited potential. Don't place an upper limit on salesperson compensation, because this dulls motivation. Earning potential for salespeople should remain open-ended.

Disadvantages. The major disadvantages of commission plans are that they lack emphasis on nonselling activities, encourage calling on a few volume accounts at the expense of many smaller ones, can result in high sales force turnover during weak sales periods because of decreased income, can result in excessive income from large nonrecurring sales, and can encourage salespeople to oversell unneeded features in addition to overloading customers with inventory. Commission compensation stresses the benefits (immediate orders) of shorter-term customer relations rather than the longer-term benefits of a growing relationship. However, proper sales training and supervision can overcome many of these disadvantages.

It is certainly more difficult to convince commissioned rather than salaried salespeople to collect past due accounts, unless commissions are penalized for bad debts. It requires more salesmanship on the part of management to obtain weekly call reports from commissioned people than from salaried; the salespeople must believe that call reports help their performance.

Because large accounts generate more sales and commission dollars, a nonsalaried salesperson often concentrates his or her efforts on the majors and neglects small accounts. Through proper training and supervision, management must convince the sales force that smaller accounts also have virtues. For example, smaller accounts often take less time to sell, remain loyal, and require less service.

Large fluctuations in sales cause large fluctuations in dollars of commission income, which can result in high sales force turnover. Few salespeople quit when their commissions rise, but many leave when their income falls.

When unusually large windfall orders create unusually large commissions, problems also may occur. Sometimes the salesperson rises to the next tax bracket, or just becomes complacent, and the following year's results are sure to be a letdown. The additional compensation may also upset fellow employees, who feel entitled to more money. A commission salesman for a small industrial gear company increased his income tenfold on one order from a conveyor concern. He used the six-figure commission check to buy out the family that owned the small gear company.

Some commission salespeople sell customers unneeded features and overload inventory. However, proper sales training can prevent this. Commission people must understand that there will be less commission next year if they mistreat customers this year, simply because their sales will be lower.

If a compensation plan allows commission people to earn a good living, then management can obtain their cooperation in correcting some of the disadvantages. A salesperson earning a good living does not wish to lose his or her job. A commission sales force which trusts and respects management will modify its behavior.

As prices rise for a product or service, so do commission dollars. A salesperson gets paid more dollars for selling the same unit this year than last if the unit price increases. However, a decrease in unit volume becuase of the price increase can offset this gain. Commission rates require annual review to measure the effects of inflation.

Commissions can cause frustration when small territories limit sales volume. In Chap. 4 we discuss factors involved in setting territory boundaries.

Type of Person.   Commission compensation plans generally attract aggressive career salespeople with no ambition for promotion into management. These salespeople are lone wolves, top producers but erratic, and more interested in the sale than the selling technique. Sometimes these characteristics strain customer relations, or result in a salesperson who prefers to highlight a large territory rather than saturate a smaller one.

Type of Selling.   Because of all these characteristics, commission plans do not lend themselves to selling products/services which require a great deal of non-order-related service, which are cyclical, or which require missionary work or team selling. Commission plans do lend themselves to nontechnical, unsophisticated products/services where reorders create a steady flow of business and unit prices are not high.

For example, sales of some soft goods such as men's white underwear to retail stores are a nonfashion, nontechnical, unsophisticated, low-ticket item with frequent orders, little missionary work, and no team selling. Men's underwear, like most apparel, lends itself to commission selling. Door-to-door salespeople and part-time salespeople almost always receive commission.

Rates of Commission.   The rate of commission must allow a salesperson to earn a competitive and living wage from average results, but a superior wage from superior results. Also, the rate of commission must allow your company to maintain necessary profit margins and return on capital. Commission rates vary from 3% on the sale of food products and lumber to 20% on medical supplies and scientific research equipment.

Some concerns vary commission rates on different products or services as an incentive for salespeople to push slow sellers or high-margin items. In practice this does not achieve its goal. A salesperson's job involves finding customer needs/problems and then selling a product/service with benefits that meets the needs and solves the problems. Management's job includes pricing products/ services to create a desired return, developing products/services which meet needs in the marketplace, and eliminating products/services which no longer meet these needs. Commission plans which encourage salespeople to sell something that is not best for the customer generally do not work. Salespeople complain about the lower commission rate, rather than selling the items with a higher rate, customers complain that salespeople push inappropriate items, and administrative people complain about the difficulty of computing monthly pay checks.

However, large quantites of goods sold off-price or large service contracts at below list price sometimes justify a lower commission rate. The company and the salesperson share the cost of such a discount. Many concerns pay only one rate even on large off-price orders. They feel a salesperson should not be penalized for large off-price orders, because if some orders are less profitable, management does not have to accept them.

Some concerns pay lower commissions on the first dollar of sales, progressive rates; others pay lower commissions on the last dollar of sales, regressive rates; others use constant rates. Progressive and regressive rates tend to confuse and discourage salespeople and complicate administration. A salesperson puts the same effort into the first sale of the month or year as the last and deserves equal compensation for both. If you pay more for the first sale than the last, salespeople may lose enthusiasm toward the end of a sales period. If you pay more for the last sale than the first, salespeople may concentrate their orders in one period at the expense of another.

Bonus

A bonus provides an extra deferred reward for some form of outstanding performance. Generally, bonuses are paid once a year or once a selling period, in addition to salary or commission. You decide on a specific activity which most benefits the company, and then set realistic goals or quotas with each salesperson relating to performance of these activities. If goals are approached or exceeded, the salesperson receives a predetermined sum of money. Generally, salespeople who reach 125% of their goal or quota receive a larger bonus than if they reached only 75%.

Base the salesperson's goals on expected performance and territory potential. Setting unreachable goals frustrates salespeople, dulls their motivation, and defeats the purpose of a bonus.

Since bonuses are not paid frequently or immediately after the successful performance of a task, they lose some motivational value. This loss of motivation can be partially offset by informing each salesperson monthly about their performance progress toward their annual goal and resulting bonus. Also, a portion of annual bonuses can be paid quarterly if the previous quarter's performance exceeds a pro-ration of the annual goal.

Bonus plans can be difficult to administer, but they do allow a great deal of flexibility. You can reward different activities at different performance levels with varying sums for different salespeople. Depending on your company needs, you can pay a bonus to the Wisconsin salesperson for new accounts, to the Ohio salesperson for increasing average order size, and to the Florida salesperson for increasing dollar sales. Depending on company needs, bonus arrangements may be changed annually. Make sure each salesperson understands the ground rules.

The flexibility of a smaller business allows it to custom design the bonus for each territory. The lack of management opportunity makes the bonus especially important for smaller-business salespeople. The bonus rewards an outstanding performance in lieu of a promotion. Also, bonus compensation being contingent upon proven performance creates less resentment from nonselling employees over salespeoples' higher income levels.

Combinations

Some combination of salary, commission, and bonus represents the most widely used form of sales compensation. Dartnell Corp.'s 1981 Sales Force Compensation Report* shows that 59% of American companies surveyed employed a combination of salary and incentive. The most frequent combination-plan percentage split reported was 70% base salary/30% incentive, with 60%/40% a close second, and 80%/20% third.

Since the objectives of a compensation system usually involve quickly and effectively rewarding a combination of positive actions, rather than one simple action, combination plans prove most appropriate. Straight salary plans lack enough financial incentive, result in fixed selling expenses, and reward poor performers at the expense of strong performers. Straight commission plans lack emphasis on nonselling activities, encourage calling on volume accounts at the expense of smaller ones, result in high turnover during weak periods because of decreased income, and encourage salespeople to oversell. Combination plans can be tailored to encourage the specific behavior most beneficial to your sales effort, and to eliminate the disadvantages of straight commission or straight salary.

Because smaller concerns are more flexible, and can even use different compensation plans for different salespeople, combination arrangements prove par-

---

*By permission from *Sales Force Compensation*: Dartnell's 21st Biennial Survey, Dartnell Corp., 1982.

ticularly suitable for them. What motivates one salesperson may not motivate another. Combination plans provide security plus incentive for salespeople at a cost that most smaller businesses can afford.

However, combination plans lack the simplicity of straight commission or straight salary, which makes them more difficult for the company to administer and the salespeople to understand. A common mistake of combination plans involves specific compensation for too many activities, rather than emphasizing the most important ones. Because of their complexity, combination plans require more frequent revision than either straight salary or straight commission.

An office furniture company in St. Louis employed five local full-time salespeople, all on straight commission. Two of the salespeople who had ten years with the concern earned a good income, but only sold large customers in their territory. The other three salespeople had less than two years with the company, and replaced a previous parade of representatives who had quit. The president, also sales manager, kept himself busy selling "house" accounts, but worried because total company sales had stopped growing.

After attending a sales management seminar in Hawaii, the president decided to make some changes in his sales compensation program. He set sales goals/quotas 20% higher than previous actual figures for the two older salespeople, and established a bonus which would start when they achieved 90% of quota and would become very substantial if they achieved 110% of quota. He also paid these men a small bonus for every new account they opened.

For the three newer salespeople, he guaranteed a base salary in addition to commission, but lowered the previous commission rate. He added a bonus based on achieving certain percentages of their sales quotas or goals. He also agreed to split commissions on what were previously house accounts. As a result of this new plan, revenues grew and turnover declined.

An emergency lighting company in California employed salaried full-time salespeople in Los Angeles, San Francisco, and Sacramento. They made a good living, but sales had stagnated, and selling expenses as a percentage of revenues had increased, producing lower profit margins. The company enlisted the help of a consultant who recommended more incentive compensation. The sales manager put each salesperson on a draw equal to his or her previous salary. A monthly commission was paid against the draw. The rate and dollars of commission at present sales levels would have left each salesperson 20% overdrawn at year end. The sales manager agreed not to limit higher compensation, but also informed his people that draws would be reduced each year to equal the previous year's actual commission earned. One salesperson quit and had to be replaced, but two years later company revenues started increasing and selling expenses as a percentage of revenues decreased.

A person who leased guard dogs required his salesmen to deliver and pick up the animals. This service activity was as important as opening new accounts. He paid his people a fee for each animal delivered and returned, plus a commission on each sales dollar, plus a bonus on new accounts. His business thrived, but at the expense of several bookkeepers.

EXPENSES

According to Dartnell's 1981 "Compensation of Salesmen" report,* 85% of all companies surveyed paid all or some of their salespeople's expenses in addition to salary, commission, and bonus compensation. For these firms, sales force compensation plus expenses averaged 13% of their annual sales volume. Expense categories include travel by automobile, airlines, and railroads; lodging; telephone; entertainment; samples; promotion; and office or clerical help. Most companies pay between $6,000 and $20,000 of expenses per salesperson, with the average at $12,000; and so this becomes a major selling cost which must be kept under control. Over the past five years, salespeoples' expenses have risen faster than their commissions, salaries, and bonus compensation.

Sales & Marketing Management magazine's 1983 Survey of Selling Costs** reports that in 1982 annual auto, travel, and entertainment expenses averaged $10,450 for account representatives, $12,000 for detail salespeople, $15,450 for sales engineers, $18,550 for industrial products salespeople, and $16,450 for service salespeople. The same survey reports that the average cost of meals, lodging, and auto rental for a salesperson has risen from $50 per day in 1972 to an estimated $137 a day in 1983. The most expensive cities are New York, San Francisco, Chicago, and Washington. The least expensive major cities are Dayton, Canton, Omaha, and Wichita.

A smaller business does not possess the financial resources of a larger concern and so must selectively put its available resources to the best use. A small electronics firm which manufactured components for cable television and microwave transmission hired three new field sales representatives, one to cover the government market in Washington, one to cover the West Coast from Los Angeles, and one to cover Europe from London. Each person received a modest salary, plus a commission based on sales; but each also received an open-ended expense account, since these new territories required a great deal of travel and entertainment. These three salespeople accounted for $200,000 in expenses in two years plus their salaries and commission. Although they wrote $1,000,000 in orders, they almost put their employer out of business.

---

*By permission from *Sales Force Compensation*: Dartnell's 21st Biennial Survey, Dartnell Corp., 1982.
**By permission from S&MM's 1983 Survey of Selling Costs. © 1983, Further reproduction is prohibited.

A company which employs part-time salespeople to sell magazines door to door needs to reimburse a different variety of expenses at a different level than a concern which sells office supplies by phone; or one which uses representatives to sell wallets to chain stores; or one which employs full-time people to sell cleaning services to hospitals; or a concern with one salesperson covering the entire country selling nail-making machines to steel mills. This section discusses the objectives of an expense plan, the various types of plans available to obtain those objectives, and proven means for lowering salespeoples' expenses.

Objectives

Regardless of your product or service, any expense plan should be fair, controllable, fast, simple, easy to understand and administer, and flexible. Salespeople should have an economic incentive for controlling their expenses, for using expense money productively and efficiently. If no economic incentive exists, if expenses are open-ended, salespeople use them as an additional form of compensation. Similarly, management cannot ask the sales force to pay for expenses which lower their total compensation to an unacceptable level.

Salespeople should be paid and expenses reimbursed promptly. Many smaller companies finance themselves by remaining months behind in paying portions of their sales force's compensation or expenses. Such behavior increases turnover of salespeople, and certainly hurts morale and productivity.

Salespeople must thoroughly understand what is included in the expense plan, so they can act appropriately. An industrial gear salesman who lived in Los Angeles covered the entire state of California by auto. His employer reimbursed auto expenses. On one trip he flew to San Francisco and submitted his expense report for the plane ticket, only to find out his employer did not reimburse air travel.

Make your expense plan as simple as possible to facilitate administration and understanding. A small securities brokerage firm paid 100% of its institutional salesperson's air fare, plus 80% of first night's lodgings, 70% of second night's lodgings, and 60% thereafter. In addition, it reimbursed 50% of breakfast expense, 80% of lunch, and 70% of dinner. The expense reports and vouchers looked like physics formulas.

A good expense plan requires a certain amount of flexibility for exceptions. Your Denver salesperson receives a call from a hot prospect to be in his Salt Lake City office at ten o'clock the next morning. The salesperson flies both ways to save time, since he also has appointments in Denver the day following the Salt Lake visit. Your company policy reimburses auto expense but not airfare. You might consider making an exception in this case.

Types of Plans

Salespeople can be asked to pay all of their own expenses out of their basic compensation, the firm and the sales force can split expenses, or the company can reimburse the salespeople for all their expenses. Many variations exist within each of these possibilities. Expense policies, like salesperson compensation plans, require annual review and constant updating to reflect changing conditions.

Salespeople can be asked to pay all their own expenses if the level of compensation takes this into account. Commissioned salespeople in the apparel business, for example, receive a rate of commission high enough to pay all their own expenses. The rate of commission varies according to the level of anticipated expenses. The New York salesperson who travels between customers by subway might receive a lower commission rate than the Iowa/Nebraska salesperson who drives fifty miles between accounts.

If possible, making the salesperson responsible for his or her own expenses proves best for the smaller business. Under such a plan, the salesperson, who has the most to gain or lose and is the best judge, has total responsibility for expenses. Money will not be wasted on unnecessary trips or entertainment. If salespeople feel that money spent for travel or entertainment will result in orders, they will spend it. Certainly this arrangement represents the easiest to administer and understand.

A similar but more complicated arrangement involves the salesperson submitting reports and receipts for certain designated expenses, which the company reimburses until the total reaches a certain percentage of sales volume. Anything over that becomes the salesperson's responsibility. At year's end the salesperson receives a portion of the amount saved, should expenses total less than the agreed percentage. Here again the salesperson has an economic incentive to spend wisely. The percentage rate varies depending on the territory, volume, and expense requirements. The sales volume figure against which you apply the percentage rate to arrive at a dollar expense limit may be last year's actual, this year's forecast, or this year's actual cumulative to date.

Some concerns agree to pay a predetermined percentage of allowable expense items. For example, they may agree to pay 65% of the salesperson's entertainment, travel, and telephone expenses. Salespeople submit invoices, receipts, and reports verifying their expenses, and the company then reimburses only 65%.

Some concerns simply give salespeople a flat monthly expense allowance to use as they feel necessary. Others allow a flat amount for certain expenses; for example, $40 a night for lodging and $25 a day for food. Both arrangements must vary dollar amounts to accommodate different expenses in different territories. A hotel room in Omaha will not cost as much as a hotel room in San Francisco. The flat monthly allowance allows you to accurately forecast this expense item. Both these plans are easy to understand and administrate.

Some capital goods companies allow salespeople unlimited expense accounts on certain items, but such an arrangement can put a smaller concern under tremendous financial pressure. A good expense plan gives the salesperson an incentive to spend wisely and limit expenses.

Some expense plans involve combinations of the above choices. Air fare might be 100% reimbursable, but lodging and meals paid for with a flat allowance.

Expense plans which require vouchers, receipts, invoices, and reports involve a great deal of administrative time on the part of salespeople and the sales manager. The salesperson must submit accurate information, and you must verify its correctness.

Unless salespeople pay their own expenses or you pay a flat monthly allowance, these costs prove difficult to forecast. It is difficult to estimate in November what travel expenses might be incurred during the following year. For a smaller concern this can prove especially problematic.

Reducing Expenses

The following specific suggestions should help your salespeople reduce their expenses. When possible, they should use the telephone rather than a personal visit to qualify prospects, arrange appointments, handle service items, answer specific questions, or write small orders. They should plan the day ahead, so that more customers are seen and less miles traveled. They should only travel economy class by air, and where possible stay at budget-class lodgings. Lastly, they should make fewer but longer trips. Also, management should try to negotiate special corporate hotel, auto rental, and telephone rates for the sales force.

As salespeople and buyers have become more professional, entertainment has become less important as a selling and promotional tool. Personal relationships established over lunch and diner continue to be extremely significant, but golf in the afternoon, gifts, paid vacations, and expensive nightclubs have given way to price, quality, and service. Many concerns frown on any entertainment or gifts for their buyers or purchasing agents outside of a business lunch. As sales manager you can reduce expenses by discouraging salespeople from engaging in excessive entertainment.

Company cars and company credit cards prove difficult for the smaller concern to control and administrate. Reimbursing travel and entertainment expenses is one thing, having primary financial responsibility is another. When the company provides a car and a credit card, it initially pays for the salesperson's personal and business use of both. The salesperson then reimburses the company for personal use. When disputes result, the company must prove the salesperson wrong. When the salesperson owns the car and credit card, personal use is expected; but the company does not pay for it. When disputes result over expenses submitted for reimbursement, the burden of proof lies with the salesperson. As sales manager, you can reduce expenses by not issuing company credit cards to salespeople or allowing them to use company-owned vehicles.

However, a few smaller concerns do allow personal use of certain sales expenses such as a company-owned automobile or credit card as a fringe benefit, because these items often can escape income taxes. If you choose to do this, be sure to consult the company accountant.

FRINGE BENEFITS

The total direct cost of your sales force includes salary, commission, bonus, and expenses, plus fringe benefits. As stated previously, in 1981 the middle compensation range for experienced salespeople whether paid through commission, salary, bonus, or some combination was $23,000 to $35,000 with the average at $30,000. Also, annual reimbursed expenses ranged from $6,000 to $20,000 with an average of $12,000. Smaller companies are generally at the upper end of the commission, salary, bonus scale, but at the lower end of the reimbursed-expense scale.

Now you must add to those figures the cost of primary fringe benefits such as social security, unemployment compensation, medical, life, accident and disability insurance, and vacations; plus possibly the cost of secondary fringe benefits such as profit sharing, pension plans, personal use of company car and credit cards, club and association memberships, reimbursed educational expenses, dental insurance, and reimbursed moving expenses. Fringe benefits vary from 15% of salary, commission and bonus to 40%, and thus represent a significant expense item.

In 1981 the cost of a sales call including compensation, expenses, and fringe benefits averaged $107, up 49% from 1979. The average cost of a sales call varied from $10–$12 in the tobacco and beverage industries to $200–$300 for nonferrous metals and transportation equipment.

Primary Fringe Benefits

Regardless of the compensation mix, most smaller businesses pay their share of a salesperson's social security and unemployment taxes if the salesperson works for them more than half-time. Protection against major illness, accidents, disability, or death through group insurance can be purchased less expensively by the employer than the individual. Some companies offer coverage for dependents, some just for the salesperson. These primary group insurance benefits are necessary to attract competent salespeople in today's business environment, plus they promote good morale and peace of mind. Premium payments are tax deductible to the company, but not taxable to the insured, making these benefits more valuable to both parties.

If your smaller business does not possess the resources to pay the entire premiums for primary group insurance benefits, ask the sales force to share the cost. If the company pays half and the salesperson pays half, he or she still benefits, and gets the necessary protection at group rates. Major medical insurance with a $500 or $1,000 deductible, or health maintenance organizations represent other means of lowering medical insurance costs.

Vacations represent an inexpensive fringe benefit for salespeople. Generally, customers write larger orders to cover themselves before or after a period when your salesperson takes a vacation. During the latter part of December, and the early part of July, many buyers and purchasing agents vacation themselves or close their order book. Encourage your salespeople to take their vacations when business is seasonally slow. Salespeople require a rest from the rigors of their work, and generally return from such a rest with renewed vigor. If you schedule vacations correctly, no business will be lost.

Secondary Fringe Benefits

Because most smaller companies remain privately owned, profit sharing is not practical. For competitive or personal reasons, most smaller-business owners don't care to divulge their profits. Most small-business salespeople want a reward for selling performance, instead of company profits, since they have little control over profitability. Profit sharing in good years causes unmet expectations and disappointment in bad years. For these reasons, profit-sharing plans in smaller businesses cause more disappointments than motivation.

Because pension plans involve complicated legal requirements and excessive administrative work, most smaller businesses do not employ them. A pension plan for the sales force would also have to be available for all other employees on the same basis. You may desire a pension plan for executives and salespeople only, but generally it must be offered to hourly help also. In addition, pension plans require establishing reserves and filing reports on financial condition with various government agencies.

For smaller businesses, selectively paying certain salespeople more, and encouraging them to use I.R.A. plans for retirement, proves more practical than a pension plan. You can assit key salespeople in establishing I.R.A. plans by introducing them to financial institutions that offer these services.

Also, you can purchase group life insurance for a salesperson which converts to an annuity at retirement. These whole life policies carry a cash value which belongs to the salesperson and becomes an incentive for continuing employment. However, the company premium payment on such policies presently becomes taxable income for the insured.

Because pension-plan benefits grow with years of employment, they represent an incentive for good salespeople to continue with their present employer. When a person terminates, he or she loses a significant portion of the pension-plan benefits. Since smaller concerns generally cannot offer pension plans, the incentive to stay must come from other sources, such as current income, achievement, recognition, freedom, status, personal relationships, a feeling of belonging, and generally pleasant working conditions.

In a smaller company, paying for salespeople's educational costs does not produce positive results, because opportunities do not exist for advancement. To reimburse salespeople for attending classes in sales management only causes frustration, and might lead to loss of key personnel.

Dental insurance, reimbursed moving expenses, club and association memberships prove too costly for most smaller businesses. A good medical, life, accident, and disability insurance program satisfies salespeople's major needs for expense protection.

As discussed in the previous section, personal use of company cars and credit cards proves difficult for the smaller business to afford, control, and administrate. Success in today's competitive markets requires careful use of resources. As a result, only a few small businesses employ company cars or company credit cards as fringe benefits for salespeople.

INDIVIDUAL WRITTEN COMPENSATION PLANS

Because small businesses are flexible, you can tailor-make different compensation plans for different salespeople. Each salesperson has different and changing needs, and each territory presents different problems and potential. What motivates and is appropriate for one salesperson may not motivate and be appropriate for another.

In creating a compensation plan, you may wish to consider each salesperson separately. For instance, the New York salesperson may primarily sell major department stores that require considerable stock-taking service, or corporate headquarters which require considerable missionary selling. The Ohio salesperson may be pioneering a new territory, and the New England salesperson may sell many established small accounts. Therefore, you may decide to pay the New York salesperson primarily on salary with a small commission, the Ohio salesperson primarily on salary with a small bonus, and the New England salesperson on straight commission against a small draw. You may reimburse all travel expenses up to $1,000 a month for the Ohio person, pay the New

York salesperson a flat $250-a-month travel allowance, and have the New England salesperson pay his or her own expenses.

Whatever the individual plan, each salesperson should receive a complete written presentation of his or her compensation arrangement. For instance, the New York salesperson would receive the following form.

Name: Bill Locke   Time period: Calendar 1984

Salary: $4,000 a month payable every other week.

Commission: 2% of sales when shipped less uncollectable accounts receivables, returns, and advertising allowances. Payable on the 20th of each month for the preceding month.

Expenses: $250 a month for travel and entertainment, payable on the 15th; expense reports required each week.

Fringe Benefits: Social Security, unemployment, group life, disability, and health insurance.

The Ohio salesman would receive the following form.

Name: George Geroan   Time period: Calendar 1984

Salary: $3,000 a month payable every other week.

Bonus: $2,000 if shipments exceed 90% of quota, $3,000 if shipments exceed 100% of quota, $4,000 if shipments exceed 125% of quota. Maximum total bonus $4,000 payable on January 30, 1985.

Expenses: Up to $1,000 a month cumulative for travel and entertainment payable two weeks after expense reports are received. The difference between 12 months actual expenses and $12,000 to be split 50/50 if actual is under $12,000.

Fringe Benefits: Social Security, unemployment, group life, disability, and health insurance.

The New England salesperson would receive the following form.

Name: Kevin Kelly   Time period: Calendar 1984

Commission: 10% of sales when shipped less uncollectable accounts receivables, returns, and advertising allowances. Payable on the 20th of each month for the preceding month.

Draw: $2,000 a month payable every other week against commission earned.

Expenses: All travel and entertainment expenses are paid for by the salesperson.

Fringe Benefits: Social Security, unemployment, group life, disability, and health insurance.

COMPLACENCY PLATEAU

Whatever their financial rewards, most salespeople eventually reach a complacency plateau or comfort zone. Money does not motivate most salespeople beyond a certain level. When income taxes claim 40% of each additional commission dollar, or when a salesperson has acquired the desired material possessions, or when the children have graduated from college, a salesperson questions the extra effort necessary to increase orders each year. When a salesperson reaches the complacency level, other rewards such as achievement, recognition, and status, which are discussed in later chapters, become important motivators.

ANNUAL REVIEW

Every compensation plan represents a compromise between company objectives and salespeoples' needs, and since these continually change, a good compensation plan requires annual review. When changing your plan, avoid loss of uniformity. For example, raising or lowering commission rates or salaries maintains uniformity, but suddenly changing from 100%-salary plan to a 100%-commission plan destroys it. Your type of compensation plan attracts a partiuclar type of salesperson. Change the direction too quickly, and you most likely will change the sales force also.

TERRITORIAL PROFIT-AND-LOSS STATEMENTS

A smaller business requires reliable information on resource use and people productivity. The "bottom line" for each salesperson is the profitability of his or her territory.

Once a year you should subtract from each salesperson's annual shipment dollars his or her salary, commission, bonus, field sales expenses, and fringe benefit costs. Then you subtract other direct sales expenses identified with customers in that territory such as advertising, rebates, promotion, and freight. Finally, subtract the estimated manufacturing costs (labor, material, factory overhead) for the goods shipped into the territory. This will result in dollars contributed by the territory to cover fixed selling, general, and administrative expenses. Such an analysis allows you to compare each territory's profitability, and if appropriate, adjust the compensation plan. Territorial profit-and-loss statements can also be used as a forecasting and budgeting technique and are discussed in greater detail in Chap. 7, "Forecasts, Budgets, Appraisal, and Evaluation."

4
Sales Force Organization—Time and Territory Management

Have you ever calculated the total expense of a typical representative in your sales organization or the average cost of each sales call and order? The surprisingly high results of such calculations emphasize the importance of proper organization and full utilization of each salesperson and each territory. Only with proper sales force organization and proper time and territory management will salespeople economically make the optimum number of effective calls on the right customers and prospects.

You arrive at the cost of a typical experienced salesperson in your firm by taking the annual compensation—salary plus commission plus bonus, say $30,000; adding to it reimbursed or company-paid selling expenses such as travel, auto, entertainment, telephone, samples, and clerical support, say $6,000; then adding the cost of fringe benefits such as social security, unemployment taxes, company-paid insurance, say $4,500. This $40,500 total then would equal the annual expense of your firm's typical sales representative.

Divide the total, in this example $40,500, by the average number of sales calls your typical salesperson performs in a year. You calculate this figure by multiplying average calls per day, say 5, times average working days in a year, say 240, to arrive at 1,200 calls per year. In this example, the average cost per call would be $40,500 divided by 1,200, or $33.75. If obtaining an order generally requires five sales calls, the average selling cost per order becomes $168.75.

Since you have invested a great deal of personal time in recruiting and training a salesperson, further refinement of this calculation might involve prorating the one-time cost of hiring a salesperson, say $4,000, and his or her training costs, say $3,000, and adding this sum to each year's total salesperson selling cost. Then you divide this higher total by sales calls per annum.

The 1981 Dartnell "Compensation of Salesmen" report,* which surveyed companies in many industries, indicated that the average cost per sales call varied from $10.50/$12.00 for tobacco and beverages to $30.50 for household

---

*By permission from *Sales Force Compensation*: Dartnell's 21st Biennial Survey, Dartnell Corp., 1982.

appliances, $40.00 for cosmetics, $50.00 for printing, $72.27 for computer products, $75.37 for food products, $85.00 for life/casualty insurance, $94.00 for chemicals, $98.93 for electrical equipment and supplies, $113.50 for textile and apparel, $120.90 for electronics, $125.17 for general machinery, $134.58 for fabricated metal products, $200.00 for housewares, and $306.25 for transportation equipment. The average cost of a sales call for all industries surveyed was $106.91.

For 1981 McGraw Hill estimated the average cost per sales call at $178. For 1982 *Sales & Marketing Management* magazine* estimated the average cost per call at $81.25 versus $152.75 for the Cahners survey. The figures vary because of the variety of firms included in the different surveys and different methods for averaging costs and number of calls. In addition, some averages include fringe benefits and others do not.

Sales & Marketing Management using figures from the American Management Association 1982 personnel report estimated 1982 average cost per sales call at $83.40 for account representatives, $41.35 for detail salespeople, $95.15 for sales engineers, $77.85 for industrial products salespeople, and $54.80 for service salespeople. These figures include compensation and expenses, but not fringe benefits. For the purposes of their surveys, account representatives are salespeople who call on a large number of already established customers; detail salespeople do not directly solicit orders but rather concentrate on promotional activities; sales engineers sell products which require technical knowledge; industrial products salespeople sell nontechnical products to industrial or commercial purchasers; and service salespeople sell intangibles such as insurance or advertising.

Another recent survey shows that the average salesperson spends only 40% of his or her time with customers, versus 33% traveling between calls, 24% doing paperwork reports and attending sales meetings, and the remainder on service matters. With costs per call increasing each year, and "eyeball-to-eyeball" selling time limited, using a salesperson's time efficiently represents a potential competitive advantage for smaller businesses.

In a smaller business, human and financial resources are limited, and so you must obtain maximum results from a sales manager's most important asset, the salespeople.

Proper hiring, training, and compensation, discussed in previous chapters, represent an important aid in obtaining maximum results, as do proper motivation, communication, planning, and appraisal to be discussed in future chapters. However, unless you organize the sales force correctly, structure territo-

---

*By permission from S&MM's 1983 Survey of Selling Costs. © 1983, Further reproduction is prohibited.

ries effectively, and help salespeople to manage their time, results will not be maximized.

A sales manager's job is making heroes, not being one, which involves helping his or her people. All this requires time and thought when you have everyday pressures to generate sales, crises requiring immediate attention, and no one to assist you. However, as with correct hiring, training, and compensation, properly organizing the salespeople and their territories eventually decreases everyday pressures and crises.

Remember, business is a dynamic process. Therefore, question past methods of sales force organization to make sure you are not inheriting and perpetrating mistakes, and each year, review customer and territory assignments.

ORGANIZATION

Your sales force can be organized by product, account/customer, geographic territory, function, no restrictions, or some combination. Each method of organization has strengths and weaknesses. The choice depends on your particular products, accounts, markets, sales force, people, and objectives.

If your company offers a wide variety of dissimilar products/services, you should consider a sales force organized by product line.

If your company sells large quantities of products/services to a limited number of major customers, especially customers with many branches, then you should consider a sales force organized by account.

If your company sells closely related products/services to a large number of widely dispersed customers in the same industry, then you should consider a sales force organized by geographic territory.

If you offer a product which requires considerable service after the sale, and which requires different skills for selling than for servicing, consider a two-tier sales organization.

If the methods described above for organizing your sales force do not appear appropriate, consider "no restrictions." Salespeople who sell consumer services often operate without restrictions as to products/services, accounts, or geographic territories.

The most effective use of your sales force may involve combining elements of product, account, geographic territory, function, or no restrictions. Because of varying market structures, you may wish to use a different organization type in different geographic areas, or a different organization type for different product lines.

Product-Line Organization

If your company offers a wide variety of dissimilar or unrelated products/services, especially if they are complex; or if your company's products/services are sold to totally different markets; then you should consider a sales force organized by product line. A product-line sales organization allows each of the various markets and each of the diverse or complex product lines to receive a high degree of specialized attention. It is difficult for the same salesperson to effectively sell drilling equipment to oil companies, shoes to department stores, and a data-processing service to small offices.

A California electronics company with sales under $1,000,000 manufactured power sources for laboratory lasers, professional-quality flash guns for photographers, and emergency lighting for buildings. From a technical standpoint, all these product lines used pulse to power electronics. From a manufacturing standpoint, all these product lines used batteries. However, from a sales and marketing standpoint, these lines had little in common. The lasers were for laboratory use and were sold mainly to universities; the flash guns were for consumer use and were sold to photographic stores; the emergency lighting was for commercial use and was sold to building contractors or managers.

The company employed three salespeople who sold all three product lines— one salesperson in greater Los Angeles, another in the San Francisco Bay area, and a third for Sacramento, the state capital. The company offered excellent products, but could not push annual sales beyond $1,000,000. The sales manager, who also handled customers outside California, decided to reorganize the sales force by product line. The Sacramento person would cover all of California for emergency lighting, the San Francisco person all of California for lasers, and the Los Angeles person all of California for photographic equipment. Travel expenses tripled, but unit sales doubled in five years.

A men's belt company with $5,000,000 of annual sales manufactured a line of better designer merchandise for department and specialty stores, plus a low-end private-label line for chain and discount stores. The company employed fifteen salespeople, organized geographically, who called on both department/specialty stores and chains/discounters. Some salespeople showed unit growth with chains/discounters, but declines with department/specialty stores. Other salespeople showed unit growth with department/specialty stores, but declines with chains/discounters. The same salesperson had a difficult time selling price to chains/discounters and brand name, quality, and service to department/specialty stores. This performance resulted in no growth for the company.

The sales manager reorganized the sales force by product line. The five best chain/discount store salespeople received larger territories, but just carried the private-label lower-end line. The ten best department/specialty store salespeople received larger territories, but just carried the designer-label better line. Territories overlapped, but customers did not; travel expenses doubled, but unit sales of both lines grew at 20% annually.

Organization of the sales force by product/service line does not always have positive results. An institutional cleaning service with annual revenues of under

$1,000,000, but rapid growth, had three salespeople, each calling on restaurants, factories, and hospitals in different parts of Dallas. The sales manager, also owner and president, felt that even more rapid growth would result by having one salesperson specialize in food services, one in commercial services, and one in medical services. He reasoned that each type customer had different needs, and a specialized salesperson could better meet those needs. He also reasoned that since no territory would exceed greater Dallas, only nominal increases would occur in travel expenses.

Under the new arrangement, growth rates slowed; both customers and salespeople expressed unhappiness. All three salespeople were calling on the same hospital purchasing agent—one to clean the halls, one to clean the operating rooms, and one to clean the kitchen. Both the food-services and commercial-cleaning salespeople called on the same factory and office building purchasing agents, in a similar overlap.

Two or three salespeople from one company calling on the same buyer caused confusion and frustration on both ends. Purchasing agents resented spending extra time with multiple salespeople from the same company. Salespeople resented competing against each other for the same sales dollar.

As the three companies illustrate, a sales force organized by product line can increase effectiveness for businesses with diverse or complex products/services, because each product/service receives a higher degree of specialized attention. However, this often results in greater travel expense; and when more than one salesperson from a company calls on the same buyer/purchasing agent, confusion, resentment, and frustration can result. Within a sales force organized by product line, each salesperson is assigned a specific geographic area or customer list to call on.

Account / Customer Organization

If your company sells large quantities of products/services to a limited number of major customers, especially customers with many branches, then you should consider a sales force organized by account. A sales force organized by account allows each each major customer to receive a higher degree of specialized attention.

Eighty percent of a ladies' pantyhose mill's production was sold to Sears, Ward's, Penney's, and K Mart. The central buying offices choose programs twice a year, but reorders were placed by individual stores or regional branches. The pantyhose company assigned one salesperson to handle the central buying office, all regional branches, and all individual stores for each chain. That person had the specialized knowledge, contacts, and experience necessary to produce optimum results.

Ninety percent of all nail-making machines in North America are purchased by various branches of Armco Steel Corp., Atlantic Steel Co., Bethlehem, Bostitch, Continental, Dominion Steel & Coal Corp., Keystone Steel & Wire, Mid-States Steel & Wire, Northwestern, U.S. Steel, C.F. and I. Corp., and Steel Company of Canada. Each machine costs about $30,000, resulting in total annual North American shipments of $3,000,000. Two companies compete in this marktet; both organize their two-person sales force by customer. One salesperson services the headquarters and all the branches of half the steel companies; the second salesperson performs the same task for the other half.

A local refuse-removal company in Eastern Michigan which specializes in automotive waste has three sales/service representatives—one for General Motors plants, one for Ford plants, and one for Chrysler plants. Each representative knows the specific needs of each company.

As these three examples illustrate, a sales force organized by customer proves best for businesses where a few key accounts or national accounts represent a large percentage of sales. However, as with a sales force organized by product, this often results in greater travel expenses than organizing by geographic area. Within a sales force organized by product line, each salesperson might also be assigned specific customers to call on.

Geographic Territory Organization

If your company sells similar or closely related products/services to a large number of widely dispersed customers in the same industry, then you should consider a sales force organized by geographic territory. This means that salespeople sell all your products/services to any appropriate customers within their assigned territories.

The geographic organization of territories allows salespeople to more intensely cultivate local markets by becoming more familiar with local problems, people, and conditions. Also, a person living in the territory often receives a more receptive ear than an outsider. Texans know how to handle Texans, and New Yorkers know how to handle New Yorkers. Similarly, salespeople living in a territory can provide better service at less expense, because generally less travel is required.

A small St. Louis company imports fine Italian, brand-name men's ties with exclusive sales rights for the U.S. market. Potentially, 15,000 department and specialty stores might purchase these ties. The company sells through twenty independent sales representatives, who also carry other nonconflicting lines, and call on all department and men's specialty stores within certain non-overlapping geographic territories.

A small Texas finance company purchased used computers from their present owners and leased them back, allowing the previous owner an option to buy when the lease expired. The company offered this one specialized service to any business owning a computer. Although customer industries varied, the service remained specialized. The company chose to organize its sales force by non-overlapping geographic areas, because of the large number of widely dispersed customers.

Products and services sold door to door such as fire alarms, books, cosmetics, home repairs, magazines, and political and religious solicitations involve assignment of salespeople to non-overlapping specific streets, neighborhoods, or towns. Similarly, route delivery salespeople (beer, bread, industrial fasteners) generally have exclusive geographic territories.

Functional Organization

If you offer a product which requires considerable service after the sale, and which requires different skills for selling than for servicing, consider a two-tier sales organization with different functions. A men's underwear company with a sales force of ten stopped growing when annual sales reached $5,000,000. The sales manager asked each salesperson why his or her sales had stopped increasing. Each salesperson replied that he or she was so busy servicing present accounts that they had no time to open new ones. The sales manager hired part-time salespeople to count stock and fill display fixtures for existing accounts. The full-time salespeople then had time to open new accounts. Eventually this grew into a two-tiered sales force with different functions—one concentrating on new account development, and one concentrating on account maintenance. The new-account salespeople continued to receive a partial commission on customers turned over to the account maintenance sales force.

In a functional sales organization, sometimes customers dislike the change of salespeople, and sometimes the salespeople dislike the change of customers. However, if your salespeople show superior account development skills but a lack of interest in account maintenance, try the two-tier approach. You can test it in one territory at a time.

No Restrictions

If the methods described above for organizing your sales force do not appear appropriate, consider no restrictions. Salespeople who sell consumer services often operate without restrictions as to products/services, accounts, or geographic territories.

A small Minneapolis concern selling real estate and oil tax shelters employs four salesmen who may sell any type shelter to any potential customer regardless of location. Independent insurance agencies allow their agents to write any type of policies without territorial limitations.

Security brokers may sell their services to anyone who cares to buy. Real estate salespeople generally do not have territories or customer limitations.

Combinations

The most effective use of your sales force may invovle combining elements of product, account, geographic territory, function, or no restrictions. Because of varying market structures, you may wish to use a different type organization in different geographic areas, or a different type organization for different product lines. Remember, simple but flexible structures work best. Generally, smaller companies are more flexible than larger ones, allowing them to more readily use combinations. Use this flexibility to your advantage.

A branded running-shoe company with annual sales of $6,000,000 organized salespeople by geographic territory in the Midwest, where it sold small accounts. However, on the East and West Coast, where it primarily sold regional chains, the sales force was organized by key accounts.

A specialty book publisher with revenues of $2,000,000 employed one salaried full-time salesperson to call on the ten major bookstore chains, including B. Dalton, Kroch's and Brentano's, Crown Book, and Waldenbooks. However, it used commissioned sales representatives, who carried other nonconflicting lines, to call on the remainder of the trade, and organized them by geographic territory.

A sweater company with annual sales of $3,000,000 employed two representatives in New York City—one for men's styles and one for women's. In Los Angeles it also employed two representatives—one for selling new accounts and one for servicing existing customers. In Chicago it employed one salesperson for department stores and one for specialty stores. In the rest of the country, the salespeople sold all company products and performed all services to any account within their geographic territory.

Human Resource

In a smaller company your most important resource is the human resource, and decisions concerning sales force organization must recognize this factor. If one of your salespeople has excellent contacts with certain major accounts, you may wish to assign him or her these customers, while organizing the rest of the sales force by geographic territory. If one of your salespeople has a very close relationship with a major customer, you may wish to have him or her sell all your products to that account, while organizing the rest of the sales force by product line. If one of your good salespeople does well with smaller accounts but poorly with large, you may wish to place two salespeople in this territory rather than the usual one. The second person would call on large accounts, allowing the original salesperson to continue concentrating on the smaller ones. If one of your good salespeople cannot travel overnight, but your sales force is organized by widely spread key accounts, you may wish to build a geographic territory of nonkey accounts within a day's drive of this person's home.

The flexibility of a small business allows you to fully utilize the human resource by combining various types of sales force organizations.

TERRITORY AND TIME MANAGEMENT

Once you have decided on the most effective means of organizing your sales force—product, account, geographic territory, function, no restrictions, or some combinations—you now must determine the exact size or limits of each territory. A territory which is too small will not financially support a salesperson. A territory which is too large may be expensive to travel, and will not maximize company sales.

To create territories which most effectively use salespeople's time and maximize company revenues, you should examine each territory's present and potential sales, present and potential customers, each salesperson's call rate and contacts, plus the territory's physical characteristics and highway system.

After reviewing present sales volume by territory, determine what statistics best indicate the market potential for your product/service, and investigate sources of these statistics. Once you obtain the information, use it to assist in establishing territories with proper potential to meet your marketing objectives.

Next you analyze the number and type of actual and potential customers in each territory. Salespeople's results are limited by the number of visits they can make in a day, week, month, or year, and by the number of different type customers they can handle. Maximum number of accounts limits a territory's size.

In a small company, personal relationships play a major role in selling. Your most important resource is the human resource, and decisions concerning territory boundaries must reflect this.

Although market information on buying power, potential sales, and number of possible accounts is generally available by county, zip code, city, state, or region, sales territory boundaries may not lend themselves to city, county, or state lines. Highway systems, subways, and mountains must be considered. Also, major market areas cross state lines.

Once you have determined the exact size or limits of each territory, you must help salespeople organize and schedule their time. Salespeople need to follow logical customer cluster routes or they will spend too much time traveling and too little time with accounts. Effective salespeople have to know how often to call on major accounts vs. smaller ones; how often to call on prospects vs. established business; how much time to devote to one product line versus another; and how much time to devote to service versus selling.

Territories

Often, smaller-business sales managers inherit the territory structure from their predecessors; or just divide their market area into seven territories of equal physical size for seven salespeople; or just assign each salesperson to one of the seven largest cities in the total market area; or divide the market area into seven territories with equal past sales or equal number of active accounts. Such arrangements do not most effectively use salespeople's time or maximize company revenues.

For example, one company created territories which reached 100 miles in any direction from the salesperson's home. Another allowed salespeople to sell any potential customer within their home state. Yet another established territories extending ten miles in either direction from certain parts of major highway systems.

Because business is a dynamic process, you should analyze territories each year. To create territories which most effectively use salespeople's time and maximize company revenues, you should examine each territory's present and potential sales, present and potential customers, the salesperson's call rate and contacts, plus the territory's physical characteristics and highway system.

Present and Potential Sales.   After reviewing present sales volume by territory, determine what statistics best indicate the market potential for your product/service, and investigate sources of these statistics. Once you obtain the information, use it to assist in establishing geographic or product-line territories with proper potential to meet your marketing objectives. This information does not prove terribly helpful for a sales force organized by major account.

As an example, let us say you have recently been hired as sales manager for a men's hosiery company with annual sales of $2,600,000. Presently, the company employs ten salespeople with the following territories and annual shipments: New England, $400,000; greater New York City, $500,000; Eastern Pennsylvania/Maryland/D.C., $300,000; Florida, $200,000; Texas, $200,000; Michigan, $200,000; Ohio, $200,000; Illinois, $200,000; Rocky Mountain states, $100,000; and California, $300,000. The ten salespeople live in Boston, New York City, Philadephia, Miami, Dallas, Detroit, Cleveland, Chicago, Denver, and Los Angeles. Your quality line of branded hose is sold to department and specialty stores.

Present sales by territory indicate great unevenness in market share or market potential. Possibly some territories contain more experienced salespeople or had no sales representation until recently.

You decide to analyze each territory's potential sales by referring to the most recent edition of *The New Yorker Guide to Selective Marketing* and the most recent "Survey of Buying Power" published in *Sales & Marketing Management* magazine. You also have a copy of the *1980 Census Users' Guide* published by the Bureau of the Census, U.S. Government Printing Office, Washington, D.C.

Most better men's hose are purchased in department stores by people with incomes over $15,000. Therefore, you accumulate data by geographic area on population, households, retail sales and buying power per household, families with annual incomes of $15,000 and over, annual dollars of retail sales, annual dollars of department store sales, and annual dollars of men's and boys' clothing (including hosiery) sold in department stores and in all stores.

Based on these figures, you discover that the market potential in greater New York City appears only slightly smaller than Chicago and Los Angeles combined, and so you consider adding a second person to the New York area. You also discover that Northern California including greater San Francisco contains market potential almost equal to either Michigan or Ohio, and so you consider having separate salespeople for Northern California (San Francisco) and Southern California (Los Angeles). These figures also reveal that greater St. Louis, Atlanta, and Minneapolis each contain market potential almost equal to Cleveland, and greater than the Rocky Mountain states. You therefore consider eliminating the Denver-based territory, combining Michigan and Ohio into one, and adding a salesperson for Georgia, Missouri, or Minnesota.

These figures also show that about one-third of U.S. households live in the ten largest metropolitan areas, and that 65% of all U.S. families with annual incomes over $15,000 live in the forty largest metropolitan areas. This information starts you thinking about some longer-range changes in the sales force.

If your company sold home smoke alarms door to door, and you wished information on market potential or buying power in various areas, you would consult census figures on "Families with Incomes over $25,000" and "Owner-Occupied Housing Units Valued at $35,000 and Over." If your company leased ice-making machines to restaurants, and you wished market-potential information for various areas, you would consult The National Restaurant Association for statistics on number of restaurants, their revenues, and number of employees in certain geographic areas. If your company sold a cleaning service to hospitals, and you wished information on market potential, you would consult The American Hospital Association for statistics on number of hospitals, number of beds, number of employees, and dollars of annual revenues in certain geographic areas.

The amount of helpful market-evaluation information available from industry trade associations and trade publications, from national, state, and city governments, and from local Chambers of Commerce will surprise you. You are not the company economist, but general market statistics will help you create equitable territories containing the greatest potential. For every significant economic activity, there is an association that represents it, a government agency that monitors it, and a magazine that covers it. Obtaining statistical data is a matter of identifying the associations, government agencies, and publications in a specific field and getting the information directly from the source. There are a number of reference books which identify these sources: *Encyclopedia of Associations, National Trade and Professional Associations of The United States, Statistical Abstracts of The United States, The United States Government Manual, Guide to Special Issues and Indexes of Periodicals,* and *Standard Periodical Directory.*

Companies with several product lines may require a variety of statistics which indicate greater potential for one line in a territory than the other. Management then must weigh the importance of each line in establishing territories.

For companies with several territories in condensed geographic market areas, such as one city, statistics can be obtained by neighborhood or zip code. Also, in this situation, the Yellow Pages prove helpful. For example, the potential market by area for products/services sold to restaurants or hospitals in Chicago can be partially ascertained by looking under appropriate listings in the Yellow Pages.

In addition to general buying power information, more specific market statistics may be available from government, industry, and civic organizations showing actual unit and dollar sales of your product/service for certain geographic territories. For example, industry sources can provide information on unit purchases of semiconductor devices, reed relays, horn antennas, robots, and many other items by state.

Present and Potential Customers.   Analyzing potential sales or buying power in an area allows you to determine general outlines for each territory, but now you must fine-tune the focus by analyzing the number and type of actual and potential customers. Salespeople's results are limited by the number of visits they can make in a day, week, month, or year, and by the number of different type customers they can handle. Maximum number of accounts limits a territory's size.

This analysis begins by identifying the number of actual and potential accounts in each area, and then classifying accounts as to sales potential and time or call frequency required to service them. Whether your company sells men's hosiery to retail stores, smoke alarms to home owners, or ice machines to restaurants, you can obtain information on present accounts in a territory from company records, and on potential accounts from reference books, trade publications, trade associations, and Yellow Pages.

Next, you determine the number of days each salesperson works in a year, and the number of calls possible each day and each year in that area. By talking or traveling with salespeople, and by reading call reports and order copies, you can obtain information on total calls possible per day, month, or year, and varying time/call frequency necessary for different types and sizes of accounts.

Last, you compare the number of annual calls possible for each salesperson to the number of annual calls and time required to service present and potential accounts in an area. You factor this information with desired market share, and the boundaries of a territory emerge. Territories become defined then by classifying accounts as to importance, sales potential, and necessary call frequency; then comparing present and potential accounts to desired market share, and the physical call limits of a salesperson.

Returning to the men's hosiery company, you obtain an active account list for each present territory by reviewing last year's invoices. The New England territory contains 185 specialty store and five department store accounts; greater New York City contains seven department store accounts with 55 branches; the Pennsylvania/Maryland/D.C. territory contains 70 specialty stores and five department store accounts; the Florida territory contains 90 specialty store accounts; the Texas territory contains 40 specialty stores and 10 department store accounts; the Michigan territory contains one department store and 100 specialty store accounts, the Ohio territory contains 20 specialty store and 10 department store accounts; the Illinois territory contains 110 specialty store and two department store accounts; the Rocky Mountain territory contains 30 specialty store accounts; and the California territory contains 20 specialty store accounts plus three department stores with 40 branches.

After discussions with each salesperson, you realize that the New England representative can average five sales calls a day, because his territory contains few department stores but many specialty stores located close to one another. Department stores require more time, because the salesperson must count stock at each branch and then deliver the counts to a central buyer located at the main store, who writes an order. Specialty stores, although they also require stock counts at their single location, have smaller quantities, and the buyer resides at the store. Also, waiting time to see department store buyers exceeds that of seeing the specialty store buyer.

Moreover, specialty stores require stock-counting every eight weeks, department stores and their branches every four weeks. Therefore, 185 New England specialty stores necessitate 1,100 calls annually, and the five department stores, each with five branches, require 300 calls annually for a total present-customer annual call load of 1,400.

The New England salesperson works 240 days annually, times five average calls a day, resulting in total potential annual calls of 1,200. Obviously, no time exists for the New England salesperson to call on new accounts, and some existing accounts must not be receiving full service. You arrive at average work days per year for a salesperson by deducting time required for vacation, holidays, weekends, sick days, and sales meetings.

Next you examine the total number of potential hosiery accounts in New England by using a trade reference book, *The Salesman's Guide to Men's & Boys' Wear Buyers,* plus Yellow Pages for major market areas under "Men's Wear Retail," plus information on the number of men's wear retailers supplied by the men's wear section of the National Retailers Association. From this information, you estimate that 3,000 potential specialty store customers exist in New England, plus 50 department stores. That means you presently sell 6% of the potential New England specialty stores and 10% of the department stores. On a national basis, the company's dollar market share approximates five percent.

Although company market penetration of New England in terms of number of accounts exceeds national market share in terms of dollar sales, and your salesperson has produced excellent results, he has no time to pursue new accounts and barely time to look after present customers. You consider adding another salesperson in New England for certain areas like Southern Connecticut where present distribution appears weakest.

You repeat this analysis by ranking customers and prospects according to dollars of potential sales, analyzing how large a sales volume one person can efficiently handle, then comparing this to the territory's total estimated sales figure and your desired market share. The New England salesperson presently sells $400,000 worth of men's hose a year. The present 185 specialty store customers produce $300,000 of this volume with a potential of $400,000. The present five department stores produce $100,000 of this volume with a potential of $200,000. Past experience shows that a salesperson has difficulty handling more than $600,000 of annual volume. Trade sources reveal that approximately $12,000,000 of better men's hose are bought by retailers in New England, which means your present dollar market share is 3.3% and your potential dollar market share from present accounts is 5%. Fifty more specialty stores and five more department stores with a potential volume of $350,000 can be identified as prime prospects in New England. This analysis confirms the previous one. Although your New England salesperson has produced excellent results, potential exists to support another person in the territory.

The New York City salesperson, dealing with 55 department store branches and urban auto traffic, averages only three sales calls a day, or 720 annually. The 55 department store branches require 660 calls annually. Obviously, little time exists for the New York City salesperson to call on new accounts. From the same market sources used for New England, you learn that 5,000 potential specialty store customers exist in greater New York City, plus 50 department stores with 500 branches. You decide to add another salesperson to call on specialty stores along with the department stores not presently sold. Statistics on buying power and potential sales mentioned previously reinforce this decision.

This type of customer analysis shows that the potential number of accounts and dollars of sales in Texas may eventually require two people, and that a second person should be added now for Northern California plus Northern Nevada. The number of accounts in the Rocky Mountain states do not justify a salesperson, and travel expenses appear large. Again, earlier statistics on buying power and market potential reinforce the decision concerning Northern California and the Rocky Mountain states.

This type of customer analysis shows that Ohio contains too many potential accounts for one salesperson, and that all the present business clusters in the Northern section. Illinois contains too many potential accounts for one salesperson, and all the present business clusters around Chicago. Michigan does not contain enough potential accounts for a salesperson, and present market penetration is unlikely to grow. You therefore create a new territory composed of South and Central Illinois, Indiana, and Ohio; and you add Milwaukee to the old Illinois territory, Detroit to the old Ohio territory, and Northern Indiana to the new Michigan territory.

Although these examples deal with redefining existing territories, you use the same techniques to define the boundaries of new territories. However, with a new territory, you often have no actual sales volume or existing accounts and must base your analysis entirely on potential and prospects.

Using a customer analysis and salesperson work load to define territories for key account selling proves easier than for geographic territories with no customer restrictions. You can expand or decrease the number of specific key accounts, depending on necessary call frequency and sales potential, more easily than you can change the physical boundaries of a territory.

Many industrial products have limited customer bases, which makes defining territories easier for the companies that sell those products. If your small business sells parabolic antennas to telephone companies, railroads, utilities, and the government for use in microwave systems, salespeople spend some time with all potential users. Generally, you know exactly which customers require how much time.

In contrast, companies offering a wide variety of products/services to many customers in different markets incur a more complex task. Establishing territories based on the potential number of accounts or market potential proves difficult for a distributor of paper products or grinding wheels. Management must assign a relative importance to each product line or customer group.

Using these analytical techniques to establish territory boundaries does not represent an exact science, but a logical approach to improving salespeople's performance. However, the human element, your salespeople, their needs and contacts, also require serious consideration.

Human Element.   In a smaller company, personal relationships play a major role in selling. Again, your most important resource is the human resource, and decisions concerning territory boundaries must reflect this. Flexibility represents a competitive advantage for smaller concerns, allowing you to temper the analytical territory approach with important human considerations.

A small concern offering imported gourmet food to restaurants and hotels in the West employed an excellent salesman in San Francisco. The salesman, an older bachelor, enjoyed skiing at Lake Tahoe once a month in the winter and gambling once a month in the summer at Reno. Over the years he had met socially most major hotel and restaurant managers in these two areas. When he requested that his territory be expanded to include Tahoe and Reno, management wisely agreed. The salesman already had established the contacts, and he made a trip to Nevada once a month anyway.

The Ohio salesman for a Midwest gear company had excellent contacts with the steel company buyers in Pittsburgh because he had covered Pennsylvania for his previous employer. The gear company added Pittsburgh to the Ohio territory.

The St. Louis saleswoman for a Midwest Christmas ornament distributor had a daughter attending college in Kansas City. She visited her daughter once a month, and asked if she could cover the entire state of Missouri. Her employer agreed.

The top salesman for a Midwest office supply company traveled the entire state of Minnesota. When family problems developed at home, his employer agreed to reduce the territory so that overnight stays were unnecessary.

Physical Characteristics and Highways.   Although market information on buying power, potential sales, number of possible accounts is generally available by county, zip code, city, state, or region, sales territory boundaries may not lend themselves to city, county, or state lines. Highway systems, subways, and mountains must be considered. Also, major market areas cross state lines.

For example, the highway system connecting Columbus, Dayton, and Cincinnati to Indianapolis is better and shorter than the highway system connecting Columbus, Dayton, and Cincinnati to Northern Ohio. The greater Cincinnati trading area also includes counties in Kentucky and Indiana. Therefore, many companies create a territory which includes Central and Southern Ohio, Central and Southern Indiana, and Northern Kentucky.

Similarly, highways and distances allow Springfield, Illinois, to be covered more easily from St. Louis than Chicago. However, highways and distances allow Milwaukee, Wisconsin, easy access from Chicago.

When dividing the state of Florida into two territories, many companies establish an East and West Coast rather than a North and South division, because the major cities are connected by highway systems running north and south on either coast. When dividing the island of Manhattan into two territories, experienced companies establish an East and West Side rather than Uptown and Downtown division, because the subway systems basically run up and down the island, not across.

Although Denver and Salt Lake City look close on a map, the Rocky Mountains cause many hours of driving between these two major Western markets. Most companies do not include them in the same territory. Similarly, because of mountains in the Northwest, Seattle and Portland generally form one territory, with Eastern Oregon and Washington covered from Western Idaho.

Time Management

Based on present and potential sales, and present and potential customers; the salesperson's workload limitations, contacts, and needs; plus transportation systems and distances between major market areas, you have established territory boundaries. Now you must help your salespeople plan their time within the territory. Time represents an important resource for salespeople, and they must understand how to best utilize a finite amount of time within their specific geographic area.

Salespeople need to follow logical customer cluster routes or they will spend too much time traveling and too little time with accounts. Effective salespeople have to know how often to call on major accounts vs. smaller ones; how often to call on prospects vs. established business; how much time to devote to one product line versus another; and how much time to devote to service versus selling.

Route Analysis.   Planning efficient travel routes optimizes salespeople's selling time. You help each salesperson organize his or her travel to minimize time between calls and maximize time spent with customers and prospects. The smaller a territory, the easier to meet these objectives, because less time and expense are required for travel.

During the initial home office training sessions or during a field visit, you mark a map of the territory, with locations of each present account and major prospect. You classify accounts and prospects by the frequency in which they must be seen—once a month, twice a year, whatever. Factory or store branches requiring service are also classified and marked.

Next, you and the salesperson review this map and discuss the most efficient schedule and routes for meeting these call requirements. Look for clusters of accounts and prospects which can be seen in a day, with the first and last calls closest to home. To reduce expenses, schedule as few overnight trips as possible. Discuss efficient highway or public transporation systems for moving between accounts.

Experienced salespeople don't enjoy being told how to organize their day. So present your map merely as an aid, and let them tell you how they plan to organize their schedule. Provide suggestions and information where you feel it necessary to accomplish the desired goals.

Some sales managers feel that helping their people schedule calls is not worthy of their time, and represents a skill possessed by every salesperson. If your average sales call costs $30, as calculated previously, and if proper scheduling results in one more call a day, or 220 more calls a year per salesperson, then you might be increasing efficiency or lowering expense by $6,600 per salesperson. Considered in this light, scheduling deserves and needs your time and attention.

Also, sometimes the best salespeople possess poor planning skills, or have developed bad scheduling habits. As an objective voice from outside the territory, you can suggest changes.

One salesman for a small industrial chemical company had a large customer that required a visit each Friday. The visit only took thirty minutes, but the trip required 90 minutes of driving in each direction. The salesman deadheaded 90 minutes each way, because no established customers were located on the route. The sales manager suggested calling on a dozen major prospects located along the way to and from the large customer. Within a year, three of the prospects were customers, and the salesman had income-producing stops to make each Friday on the way to and from his major customer.

A salesman for a small packaging company called exclusively on toy and Christmas ornament manufacturers located in four nearby buildings in New York City. He organized his schedule by floors of each building.

Call Frequency. With each salesperson, share your knowledge of call frequency required by each account and prospect. Remember that large accounts and prospects do not always demand the most frequent calls, and that all accounts have different needs.

An office supply saleswoman felt it necessary to call on her ten largest accounts each week. She felt they all wished to place orders that frequently, and so her weekly call represented a service the customer would appreciate. Her sales manager suggested that she inquire about necessary call frequency with each of these ten majors. They appreciated her asking, and she discovered that five wished to continue weekly orders, three wished to order every other week, and two once a month. Their volume continued to grow, and her time was freed for other sales calls. The saleswoman then selected three small but growing accounts who might benefit from more frequent service. She called on them once every two weeks rather than once a month, and orders increased rapidly.

Prospects vs. Established Business. With each salesperson, share your knowledge of how to allocate time between prospects and established business. You should suggest a different allocation for matured territories with many established accounts than for a newer territory with only a few established customers. Growth occurs not only from opening new accounts, but from correct cultivation of existing ones.

The Cincinnati salesman for an abrasive grinding wheel distributor had two large accounts, each of which required 20% of his time. His salesmanager suggested spending only 10% with one, because the company had 100% of its grinding wheel business, and increasing time spent with the other to 30%, because the company had less than half of its possible business. Outside of these two major customers, the salesman had only a few worthwhile accounts. The sales manager suggested splitting the remaining 60% of the saleman's time equally between present and prospective accounts.

Service vs. Selling. With each salesperson, share your knowledge of service versus selling time required for each customer, type of customer, or territory. What allocation produces the best results?

A small cosmetic company in Detroit manufactured and sold beauty and hair care aids to drug stores. Only one salesperson showed shipment increases under 20% a year. The sales manager discovered that this one salesperson spent 60% of her time filling in stock and setting up displays for customers, and only 40% actually calling on buyers for reorders. He suggested she reverse the ratio, and soon her orders increased at over 20% annually.

One Product Line vs. Another. For companies with more than one product line, the sales manager should share his or her knowledge with each salesperson on how to allocate time between lines. What allocation produces the best results? A small local pet food company manufactured dog and cat food for several Southern states. In Texas, where the dog population surpasses the cat population, the sales manager instructed salespeople to allocate 60% to 70% of their time selling dog food. In Florida, where the cat population exceeds dogs, the sales manager instructed salespeople to allocate 60% to 70% of their time selling cat food.

SUMMARY

This chapter has dealt with alternative ways of organizing your sales force: by product, account, geographic territory, function, no restrictions, or some combination. It also dealt with establishing sales territory boundaries by examining present and potential sales, present and potential customers, plus transportation systems and market clusters. Both analytical processes should be tempered with flexibility, and consideration of the salespeoples' needs and contacts. This chapter also dealt with assisting salespeople in time management through route analysis, call frequency, and time allocation between prospects and established business, service and selling, and various product lines.

The objective of all this information is to get salespeople to economically make the optimum number of effective calls on the right customer and prospects. The emphasis is on helping the salesperson work smarter, thus creating a more productive and efficient sales force.

5
MOTIVATION

You have hired capable sales people, trained them well, created an equitable system of compensation, effectively organized your sales force, and created efficient territories which optimize sales. Now you must motivate each salesperson to fully capitalize on his or her potential.

You cannot offer a promotion for expending that extra effort, because, as previously discussed, the career ladder in a smaller company is limited. Your compensation plan should offer appropriate remuneration for the results generated from extra effort. However, money alone does not represent a universal incentive once the salesperson reaches a desired standard of living, which depends on social status and needs. In Chap. 3 on "Compensation," we called this a complacency plateau or comfort zone.

A small medical instrument company employed twelve salespeople. The New York City salesman had flunked out of college trying to pursue his father's profession as a physician. He had grown up in sumptuous surroundings on Long Island and wanted to maintain that standard of living and social status for himself, his wife, and three children. Earning enough money to achieve this personal goal motivated him to work long, hard, and smart. The more he made, the more he needed.

The Los Angeles salesman had been a history major in college, had no children and a working wife. He and his wife had grown up in a small town in Iowa. He was content to rent an apartment in Pasadena and was not terribly motivated by money.

The Chicago salesman was in his mid-forties with grown children and considerable savings. Ten years ago he had worked long days to support his growing family. Now he was content to work a six-hour day.

The Dallas saleswoman, the single daughter of an oil company executive, worked like a demon and invested most of her money in real estate. She needed little more motivation than her pay check.

As these examples illustrate, salespeople have different aspirations and needs, and so different sparks light their fires. Stated another way, different people react differently to identical stimuli. Your job is to find the particular stimuli that lights each salesperson's fire.

Your success as a sales manager depends on the efforts and therefore the motivation of your salespeople. Although you cannot force a salesperson to be successful, you can learn to recognize people's motivational problems and develop techniques for solving them. The temptation exists to motivate people and solve problems with rank, power, punishments, and threats, but generally, offering positive incentives produces better results.

Because a smaller business is more personal and more flexible than a larger one, the sales manager should find it easier to motivate people individually. Also, a smaller-business sales manager needs to be less concerned with company politics, because the organization is smaller, and so he or she has more energy to devote to the problems and motivations of the sales force.

MOTIVATIONAL PROCESS

To motivate salespeople, you must first understand their individual specific needs or desires, and then the actions or goals which will satisfy these needs. Each salesperson has a particualr package of needs and goals, which are not necessarily rational or random. Most salespeople need varying degrees of recognition, sense of achievement, usefulness, and leadership. In addition, some salespeople may have a strong need to belong, while others may be loners; some may requre job/financial security, others may not.

Needs create tensions, and to relieve the tensions, salespeople engage in goal-directed, motivated action and behavior. When they achieve their goal, the tension is reduced. Other individuals and social groups influence people's needs, and the goals they choose to satisfy these needs. A salesperson might desire certain positive results such as leisure, recognition, security, more money, or better use of time. Achieving these results will create peace of mind and prestige. Not achieving these results will create humiliation, a sense of rejection, and worry.

Motivating a salesperson involves finding an idea, need, emotion, or desire within that individual which with proper goals will incite action leading to greater sales. As sales manager, your job involves finding these needs, and the goals which satisfy them for each salesperson. Then, using the individuals's needs and goals, you motivate the salesperson to optimum performance. You logically and convincingly persuade the salesperson that taking certain positive action will meet his or her goals, and produce his or her desired results. Of course, the results of this action will also increase sales.

Proper motivation can convert complacency into the salesperson's elixir, enthusiasm. Eventually, salespeople obtain enough pleasure from these activities and enough fear of failure to become self-motivated.

Also, once you have some insight into individual needs, and have created an environment which encourages self-motivation, it is much easier to sell your ideas to the sales force, whether this involves correcting a salesperson's bad habits or suggesting some new direction. You can accomplish much of this persuasion on field trips by actually demonstrating the benefits of certain techniques, or pointing out the success of other salespeople who use them.

Generally, a smaller company presents a better opportunity for knowing the sales force than a larger one. During field visits, try to develop a personal relationship with your people, and to find out what they want from life. At dinner after the work day ends, or between calls in the car, involve them in some relaxed soul-searching, self-revealing conversation. Although you are not the company psychologist, in order to create a proper working environment which promotes motivation and job satisfaction, you need insight into those who work for you.

You will find that most salespeople desire success and enjoy working hard at something. Your job involves transferring more of their effort to their selling.

A small Midwest office equipment company employed a Minneapolis salesman who produced great results when he worked, but did not work often or hard enough. On a field visit, the sales manager was invited to the salesman's home for dinner. The sales manager noticed several old cars in the garage. At dinner the salesman spoke about his passion for fixing old cars, but complained about his lack of funds to buy spare parts.

The next day between calls, the sales manager asked how much money the parts required. He then showed the salesman that by selling one more machine a month, he would generate sufficient commission income to pay for the parts.

That year, Minneapolis sales increased by one machine a month. In subsequent years, the sales manager set up a quota/bonus plan for the salesman. The bonus equaled the salesman's cash needs for auto parts, and the quota equaled the sales manager's needs for increased annual sales.

NEEDS, GOALS, AND MOTIVATIONS

Introduction

In a smaller company, salespeople's needs, goals, and motivations can be classified as those related to praise and recognition; a feeling of usefulness; challenge and achievement; authority and freedom; self-realization and fulfillment through personal growth; esteem and status; belonging; interpersonal relationships with management and peers; leadership; company policy and administration; job security and compensation. For a larger company this list would also include advancement.

Salespeople want to be noticed, praised, and appreciated for their performance, and as sales manager, you should reinforce and reward positive results with recognition. Recognition becomes a more effective motivational tool when it is sincere, receives publicity, is recorded, and involves top management.

Salespeople need to feel that their work serves a useful purpose and contributes significantly to the company's success and well-being. A salesperson's motivation can be destroyed overnight by a feeling of worthlessness.

Many salespeople thrive on the challenge and achievement of opening new accounts and increasing the volumes of existing ones. Generally, such salespeople enjoy personal responsibility for problem-solving, will take calculated risks, enjoy participating in management decisions, and need constant feedback on their performance.

Many salespeople prize the authority and freedom available in selling. To satisfy such peeople's needs, you can remove some of the controls, allowing them more freedom and authority. Also, you can allow them to work directly with customers on certain nonselling activities, hold them accountable for performance results, and issue them titles.

Most salespeople require personal growth for self-realization and fulfillment. Are they more effective, more skilled salespeople today than they were two years ago or ten years ago?

Many salespeople desire esteem and status from their fellow salespeople, company employees, management, customers, friends, and family. For some, esteem and status can be achieved from praise, recognition, job titles, and/or money. Others need more direct or more frequent menas of expression, such as elegant calling cards, club memberships, company automobiles, company credit cards, or entertainment allowances.

Many salespeople have a strong need to belong. Within the work organization, any group activities, such as sales meetings, conferences, contests, social events, and training seminars, can satisfy this need to belong.

Pleasant personal relationships with management and peers represent a positive motivational force for salespeople, and also foster a feeling of belonging. Unpleasant relationships represent a negative motivational force, which reduces a salesperson's productivity.

Salespeople require consistent, motivated, and competent leadership in order to maintain their own motivation. A sales force is seldom more motivated or competent than its sales manager.

Company policy and administration which maintain an open, constructive, and relaxed environment and embody trust, faith, and fairness will promote job satisfaction and positive motivation. Equally important, company policy and administration which promote inefficiency, ineffectiveness, and frustration within the organization, and which do not embody the positive attributes in the previous sentence, will cause job dissatisfaction and damage salespeople's motivation.

A salesperson who feels underpaid or on the verge of termination will not put forth that extra effort you are looking for. All the other motivational techniques we have mentioned will prove unsuccessful if a salesperson perceives his or her job as threatened, or feels that remuneration, including fringe benefits, is inadequate.

Recognition

Salespeople want to be noticed, praised, and appreciated for their performance, and as sales manager, you should reinforce and reward positive results with such recognition. Recognition involves everything from a casual thank you over the phone to a formal awards dinner. Salespeople seem to possess an insatiable appetite for recognition.

Salespeople must understand exactly which positive results will be rewarded with recognition: for example, more new accounts, increased sales, or better collections. The required results and the form of recognition—for example, plaque, sales club, or prize—should be different for different salespeople. Moreover, you must create different levels of recognition for varying levels of performance.

Also, lack of recognition can be a powerful tool. Make sure the person you choose not to recognize knows why.

Recognition becomes a more effective motivational tool when it is sincere, receives publicity, is recorded, and involves top management. Insincere praise has a negative effect on the recipient. Say it like you mean it, or don't say it at all.

Where appropriate, such as a sales contest winner, publicize the recognition in a bulletin sent to all salespeople. If the recognition involves an award, consider press releases to local papers.

Where appropriate, record recognition with plaques, sales clubs, or annual awards. For example, if a salesperson goes 50% over annual quota, issue a plaque or certificate with his or her name commemorating the results.

You might establish a special club or honor society for any salespeople whose annual or cumulative volumes exceed a certain amount. Each year you might also give an award for the most new accounts opened or the greatest percentage sales increase.

For really superior performance, a congratulatory letter or phone call from the president proves very effective. Salespeople need to feel that someone at the top knows and cares, and in a smaller concern, that particular someone is the president.

The sales manager for a local St. Louis greeting card company went to a sales seminar in New York City. Company sales had stagnated, and salespeople were underperforming their potential. During the seminar, the sales manager realized that he seldom privately or publicly praised or recognized his salespeople. He did have an excellent combination compensation plan, with bonuses for outstanding performance, but he never said "Thanks for a good job," or established formal awards for high performers. After talking with the company president, he created an entire recognition program with awards, publicity, honor clubs, a contest, and management involvement. Depending on the territory, some salespeople were recognized for new accounts, some for dollar increases in shipments, some for unit increases of a particular line.

Most important, whenever the sales manager wanted to encourage a particular type of behavior, he would praise the salesperson who performed it. "Thank you, Carl, for servicing that major drug store even though you did not receive an order." "Susan, I received your call report and found it very helpful." "I saw that great order you sent in last week, George."

Usefulness

Salespeople need to feel that their work serves a useful purpose and contributes significantly to the company's success and well-being. A salesperson's motivation can be destroyed overnight by a feeling of worthlessness. Salespeople receive a feeling of usefulness from training programs and from management's attitudes, good communications, appreciation of their work, and sensitivity to their problems.

Many salespeople approach their jobs with a feeling of insecurity and inferiority. They live with customer rejection every day. Their skills are intangible, difficult to describe, and nonselling co-workers often don't respect them.

Your investment of time and the company's investment of money in training a salesperson, or in a good sales meeting, creates a feeling of usefulness. During the initial training period, annual field visits, and sales meetings, management should make a clear statement that the company could not exist without its salespeople. Without a sales force, there would be no orders, shipments, or revenues to employ anyone else.

Between trianing periods, field visits, and sales meetings, management should maintain an attitude which acknowledges the salesperson's usefulness. Not only does the sales force sense this positive attitude, but so do other nonselling employees, which further reinforces a feeling of usefulness.

Also, good communications, appreciation of their work, and sensitivity to their problems help make salespeople feel useful. For example, when a salesperson has invested effort in opening a new account or obtaining an order, respond to the situation with the attention it deserves. Don't let orders for new accounts lie on someone's desk for weeks before obtaining credit information. Such lack of action tells the salesperson he or she is useless; it communicates the message that new accounts, and the salesperson's efforts, don't count.

For example, if an order arrives which cannot be shipped on time, discuss it with the salesperson immediately. Don't wait until after the proposed shipping date. Again, such lack of action damages the salesperson's feeling of usefulness, morale, and motivation.

Similarly, as sales manager, you should promptly answer all correspondence and phone calls from your people. Make sure they receive samples, catalogues, bulletins, and sales aids on time. When you wait days or weeks to answer a call or letter from your people, you place their usefulness in question.

Some smaller companies, especially those using commission compensation, do not pay salespeople promptly. Checks may arrive late, or payments may be deferred until next month. The message conveyed by such action says the salesperson's work contributes little, and this quickly destroys motivation.

The Philadelphia salesman for a men's clothing company called on a number of major accounts who preferred to review his line at the New York showroom. The Philadelphia salesman asked his sales manager, who ran the New York showroom, if he could come to New York to work with these major accounts. The sales manager replied that this was not necessary, because he would work with these accounts himself. The sales manager assured his salesman that all commissions on such sales would be credited to the salesman. The sales manager felt the Philadelphia salesman had plenty to do calling on the many smaller retailers in his territory.

These major accounts did purchase clothing through the New York office, and the salesman did receive his commission. The salesman continued to complain that he wanted to participate in the selling, even though he received commission for no effort. Management refused to let him participate, and after two years, the salesman joined a competitor. At his previous job, he had felt useless.

As sales manager, keep in mind that a salesperson must feel useful, must feel a sense of worth in relation to the company. Temper your actions and words with a knowledge of this need, and treat salespeople as mature professionals performing significant work.

Challenge and Achievement

Many salespeople thrive on the challenge of opening new accounts and increasing the volumes of existing ones. They possess a high need to achieve, which exceeds any monetary rewards. Long after they have satisfied their financial needs, these achievers continue expending extra effort to do better. Generally, such salespeople enjoy personal responsibility for problem-solving, will take calculated risks, enjoy participating in management decisions, and need constant feedback on their performance. Since they are your best performers, you must continue to motivate them by providing outlets for their achievement-related needs. Assign such a person difficult customers, possibly expand their territory, and let them participate in decisions.

A small Denver company erected towers for radio, telephone, and television transmission. Its California salesperson had an insatiable appetite for achievement and challenge. When its largest national customer threatened to take his business elsewhere, the sales manager asked the California salesperson to accompany him on a visit to the customer's national headquarters in Washington. Together they won the business back, and the salesman talked about his participation in this success for the next year.

When a Chicago insurance agency received an opportunity to bid on a large group program in Dallas, they sent their high-achieving salesperson to make the presentation. He failed to obtain that business, but he enjoyed the opportunity, appreciated the recognition, and worked even harder upon his return.

Many high achievers enjoy participating in management decisions, and you should develop vehicles for accommodating this need. For instance, invite these people to participate in committees which set agendas for sales meetings, approve new products or services, discuss field problems with management, or develop new sales techniques. Encourage them to make positive suggestions for change. Let them know that you seriously consider their recommendations. From this participation they receive a special sense of achievement and self-worth.

Reducing a high achiever's territory can severely damage his or her motivation. Such people need to perceive unlimited opportunities for challenge and achievement.

A small children's pajama company in Tennessee was acquired by a large conglomerate in Atlanta. The pajama company's New York salesperson also covered Boston and Philadelphia. He worked six days a week, never took a vacation, and produced 25% of company sales. The conglomerate reduced his territory to New York City, so less traveling would be involved and so that Philadelphia and Boston could each have a resident salesperson. His salary remained at the same high level, making him the highest-paid person in the pajama company.

After six months, he quit and went to work for a competitor. Since he had sold every major account in New York, no challenge remained, and he lost interest in the job.

A larger concern can offer the achiever advancement into management, for which he or she may or may not be qualified. A smaller concern cannot offer advancement, but through flexibility, it can offer challenging selling opportunities, and participation in management decisions. In this situation, the smaller-company approach often proves more satisfying for the high achiever; and so, properly handled, these people often prefer a smaller concern.

Authority and Freedom

Many salespeople prize the authority and freedom available in selling. They thrive on planning their own day, not going to an office, representing the company to a customer, and making their own decisions. Many salespeople feel they are in business for themselves, and enjoy managing their own territories.

To satisfy such people's needs, you can remove some of the controls, allowing them more freedom and authority. Also, you can allow them to work directly with customers on certain nonselling activities, hold them accountable for performance results, and issue them titles.

For instance, you might let them make certain decisions on their own which previously had required your approval. As an example, if an account met volume and credit requirements, you might let the salesperson vary prices, terms, freight, and advertising allowances within certain limits. If you normally required weekly route sheets and call reports from most salespeople, you might only require them biweekly from this person. Like the high achiever, you might assign this person more responsibility for forecasting monthly sales in his or her territory, calling on the management of major customers and prospects, or handling national accounts which have headquarters in his or her territory.

Such a person often enjoys working directly with customers on nonselling, service-related projects. Depending on the product/service, this might involve advertising, promotions, plant layout, estate planning, or displays. Allow this person the time and authority to get involved with these sorts of activities.

Salespeople with a high need for authority and freedom like to be held accountable for performance results, and generally enjoy the performance appraisal process discussed in Chap. 7. If they understand profitability, you can share information on each product line's margins and set goals relating to their territories' profits.

Salespeople of this nature also like titles which suggest authority. Instead of being called a sales representative, they prefer titles such as national account manager, territory manager, account executive, marketing representative, sales engineer, technical representative, sales counselor, sales coordinator, sales consultant, sales specialist, account representative, or market specialist. Since advancement opportunity above the sales force is very limited in a smaller company, you can use a series of these titles to create a career path program indicating level, rank, and promotion within the sales force. Your salespeople might start as Account Representatives, and after several years of successful performance, move up to Account Executive, with the ultimate goal of promotion to Territory Manager.

The star salesperson for a small printer in Columbus, Ohio, was a chronic complainer, which annoyed the sales manager and disturbed the general morale. He openly criticized the company and the sales manager. Criticisms often started with "If I were sales manager . . .". At the root of this problem lay his frustration over lack of advancement opportunity into management. Since the printing company depended on this star salesman's results, the sales manager decided to turn the salesman's need for authority into a positive rather than a negative motivational factor.

During lunch at the local country club, the sales manager assigned the star performer responsibility for a national account currently handled by the company president, and assigned him the title of National Accounts Sales Manager. He also granted him authority to quote prices on stock jobs, and to assist customers in designing forms. The salesman's complaining tapered off, and his job satisfaction improved.

In Chap. 4 we discussed the small California company which manufactured emergency lighting, professional photographic flash equipment, and power supplies for lasers. As mentioned, this company assigned one product line to each of three salespeople. The sales force and the company prospered. Eventually the sales manager gave each salesperson the title of sales manager for his or her respective product line, and total responsibility for forecasting sales. The sales force responded by putting forth even more effort.

Self-Realization and Fulfillment Through Personal Growth

Most salespeople require personal growth for self-realization and fulfillment. Are they more effective, more skilled salespeople today than they were two years ago or ten years ago? Most salespeople desire to continue growing. Continual training helps to satisfy this need.

Most salespeople enjoy a certain amount of change and dislike "being in a rut." As sales manager, you should create an environment conducive to productive change and personal growth.

The sales manager of a successful company selling highway safety devices to various government agencies detected growing dissatisfaction among his three best salespeople. These three individuals were well compensated, received adequate recognition, were allowed considerable authority, each had been with the company over fifteen years, and all were over fifty years old. Their dissatisfaction puzzled the sales manager until he realized that these three salespeople had stopped growing personally, and had developed bad self-images.

The sales manager decided to send one salesman to a conference in Washington on highway safety; another to a marketing association three-day seminar on selling municipal customers; and the third to view a new European safety system being installed in Mexico City. The next two years he repeated this type of experience, but rotated each salesperson's activity. The salesmen learned, grew, and a feeling of self-realization and fulfillment replaced that of dissatisfaction.

Esteem and Status

Many salespeople desire esteem and status from their fellow salespeople, company employees, management, customers, friends, and family. For some, esteem and status can be achieved from praise, recognition, job titles, and/or money. Others need more direct or more frequent means of expression.

Little items such as elegant calling cards establish self-esteem and status every day. When an auto parts distributor stopped using embossed calling cards in favor of offset ones to save money, several of its salespeople paid to have their own embossed cards printed.

A successful salesman of small steel products did a great deal of customer entertaining with his wife at company expense. They wined and dined customers twice a week, played golf with many, and even took a few on vacations. When industry sales declined because of a recession, the sales manager cut back on these entertainment expenses. The salesman asked for the expense allowance to be continued even if it meant a decrease in his salary. The life style made available by the expense account was critical to this man's company status and personal self-esteem.

The salesperson with a high need for esteem and status requires special treatment. Consider satisfying this person with a special privilege such as a company credit card, automobile, membership in a private club, entertainment allowance, or fancy calling card. Most important, as sales manager, you should give every salesperson esteem and status through your respect.

Belonging

Many salespeople have a strong need to belong, which they express through club and church memberships, strong family ties, community involvement, and of course, participation in their work organization. Within the work organization, any group activities, such as sales meetings, conferences, contests, social events, and training seminars can satisfy this need to belong. If the sales force resides within a day's drive of your office, frequent group activities are more practical than if they live far away. If the sales force sells out of one central office, the every-day personal social contact creates a focal point for belonging. Satisfying the need to belong for a national field sales force spread from Boston to Los Angeles proves the most difficult.

Sales bulletins, which contain news of other salespeople or other employees, remind the sales force they belong to an organization. Both personal news involving births, new houses, vacations, illness, and retirement; and business news concerning contests, promotions, quotas, and new accounts prove effective.

Once or twice a year, resources permitting, a well-planned sales meeting (discussed in Chap. 6) can provide a productive means of communication, motivation and training. The sales meeting is of particular importance, because it offers a prime opportunity for one-to-one human interaction within the sales force and between management and the sales organization. All this satisfies a salesperson's need to belong.

Also, in a smaller company, the sales manager's and president's expressions of sincere concern for salespeople's well-being create a feeling of belonging. In addition, the sales manager's field visits remind salespeople that they belong to an organization.

The sales manager of a small men's necktie company visited each of sixteen field sales representatives twice a year. The first question salespeople asked concerned news of their colleagues in other territories. The company could only afford one national sales meeting a year, but the sales manager sensed a strong feeling for or need for belonging. He decided to have shorter, less expensive regional sales meetings six months after each national meeting.

He also asked his secretary to write a newsletter for the sales force. Each salesperson submitted information which they felt would be of interest. A nice spirit developed, and the sales force seemed even more willing to put forth that extra effort.

Interpersonal Relationships with Management and Peers

Pleasant personal relationships with management and peers represent a positive motivational force for salespeople, and also foster a feeling of belonging. Unpleasant relationships represent a negative motivational force, which reduces a salesperson's productivity.

The Los Angeles representative of a small West Coast gear company did a satisfactory selling job in his territory, but had a personality clash with the sales manager. The sales manager was an authoritarian, high-powered generalist, and the salesperson a low-key, detail man. The sales manager recognized their difference in styles as a problem, and knew that his salesman would do better if their relationship improved.

Over the next few months, the sales manager showed more flexibility toward, and applied less pressure on the Los Angeles salesman. He also provided this salesman with more detailed information on his territory. The relationship improved, and so did sales in that area.

A Detroit office furniture company employed five excellent salespeople for the greater metropolitan area. One of the people annoyed the other four to the point where sales were being affected. This member of the sales organization always knew the right answers; told his colleagues what to do, and how to do it. His ideas were right; everyone else's wrong.

The sales manager realized that this dissident salesman's problem probably stemmed from lack of self-esteem and self-discipline. One day at lunch, the sales manager expressed his respect for the salesman's judgment, but noted that the salesman must also respect his colleagues' opinions. Thereafter, the two had many discussions concerning this matter, and finally the problem subsided. As a result, the performance of all five people improved.

Leadership

Salespeople require consistent, motivated, and competent leadership in order to maintain their own motivation. A sales force is seldom, more motivated or competent than its sales manager.

Successful sales managers vary greatly in style, from autocratic to democratic, from sales- or task-oriented to employee-oriented, from persuasive to consultive. However, successful sales managers do have two common traits: they realize that their job is getting things done through the cooperation of others, and they believe in what they are doing. This belief creates strong personal motivation, which they communicate to their sales force.

The sales manager for a Christmas ornament company asked his salespeople to call on certain specific retail accounts. If they didn't call on the accounts within ten days, the sales manager would make an appointment to see the retailer. Soon the sales manager was calling on more accounts and the sales force fewer. As a result, company sales declined. This sales manager had failed to realize that his job depended on getting things done through the cooperation of others.

When the Surgeon General issued his initial warning on smoking, an entrepreneur started marketing no-tobacco lettuce-leaf cigarettes. The sales manager for this new product continued smoking the same brand he had for many years, and this contributed to his sales force's lack of motivation. Sales managers must believe in what they are doing.

The sales manager for a regional soft-drink company told the sales force not to call on restaurants, because of credit problems; then the next month he introduced a special-size bottle just for that market. One week this sales manager would use persuasion to implement policy; the next week, threats. During the soft-drink company's busiest month, August, he took a three-week vacation. The sales force responded by losing their motivation. This sales manager was neither competent, consistent, nor motivated.

Company Policy and Administration

Company policy and administration which maintain an open, constructive, and relaxed environment and embody trust, faith, and fairness will promote job satisfaction and positive motivation. Equally important, company policy and administration which promote inefficiency, ineffectiveness, and frustration within the organization, and do not embody the positive attributes mentioned above, will cause job dissatisfaction and damage salespeople's motivation.

For example, a company policy prohibiting salespeople from calling the factory to check on delivery dates or outstanding customer balances can create frustration and job dissatisfaction. A more sensitive, less rigid policy which allows salespeople to call only once a week would satisfy management's need to limit the time and expense involved, while satisfying the salesperson's need for information.

As another example, a company policy prohibiting salespeople from calling the sales manager "collect" can cause frustration and unhappiness; while a company policy which asks salespeople to pay for every other call allows them to share the cost, which is more equitable. The latter policy embodies trust, but prevents salespeople from abusing a privilege.

An administrative policy requiring the company president to review each order can unnecessarily delay order processing, and therefore, shipping by four or five days. Such a policy might cause job dissatisfaction and damage salespeople's motivation. A more moderate policy requiring presidential review of only new-account orders probably would not cause a problem with either salespeople's morale or deliveries.

A credit policy prohibiting additional sales to any account that pays invoices late, no matter what the reason, might cause frustration and unhappiness in the sales force and seriously damage motivation. A credit policy notifying the salesperson of any account which pays late, and prohibiting shipments if payments are over 30 days late twice in a row, probably would be less damaging.

A company policy establishing certain national house accounts on which salespeople receive no income certainly dulls motivation. A policy which splits national accounts among a number of salespeople, who then share the income, would improve motivation.

Job Security and Compensation

A salesperson who feels underpaid or on the verge of termination will not put forth that extra effort you are looking for. All the other motivational techniques we have discussed will prove unsuccessful if a sales person perceives his or her job as threatened, or feels that remuneration, including fringe benefits, is inadequate.

A St. Louis securities firm employed seven brokers to handle its "retail" business with individual investors. When the firm's major partner passed away, the brokers (salespeople) became concerned about their jobs. They became much less aggressive about pursuing business, because of persistent rumors about the firm's imminent liquidation. To offset this concern, the other partners increased the brokers' commissions, called them Account Executives, and held weekly sales meetings; but to no avail. Finally after a year, the brokers realized that their fears had been unfounded, and they once again started producing additional business.

A small company selling housewares door to door employed five excellent salespeople. During the 1981 recession, sales dropped slightly and expenses increased significantly. The sales manager announced that one of the five would have to be terminated. The final decision was to be made in four weeks. During that four weeks, sales dropped dramatically—and they continued to drop after that for the remaining four people. Feeling insecure about their future, none of the salespeople could get very motivated.

In 1981 a specialty shoe importer lowered its salespeople's commission rate from 10% to 6% because inflation had raised the price of their line 40%. The sales manager never fully explained the reason for lowering the commission rate to his people. Even though their dollars of commission income rose slightly, because dollars of sales increased by more than 40%, the sales force failed to produce that extra effort. They felt underpaid.

Summary: A Delicate Balance

A capable sales manager realizes that his or her success depends on properly motivating the sales force, and that each salesperson has a different package of needs. Your job is finding those needs, whether they include recognition, usefulness, achievement, authority, freedom, personal growth, status, or belonging; and establishing goals which satisfy them. Hopefully, these same goals create positive sales performance for your company. Your job also involves eliminating negative factors from the corporate environment such as unpleasant interpersonal relationships, inconsistent leadership, ineffective company policies, unfair compensation, and job insecurity. All this requires a delicate, ever-changing balance.

SALES CONTESTS/INCENTIVE PLANS

Sales contests represent a powerful commonly employed tool for improving sales force motivation and increasing sales. Sales contests provide fast and frequent reinforcement to a salesperson's needs for recognition, achievement, fulfillment, status, belonging, and additional compensation.

Sales contests prove most helpful for meeting specific, short-term objectives, such as smoothing out seasonal sales dips, bringing attention to a good product or service which has been neglected, launching a new product, or increasing the number of active accounts.

Sales contests can also be used to reinstill enthusiasm for meeting longer-term goals, such as improved collections, reduced expenses, increased number of cold calls, increased dollar volume, increased number of orders, increased average order size, new prospects, increased use of displays, and revival of inactive accounts.

In all cases, these contests attempt to elicit extra "beyond the normal" effort from the sales force by generating enthusiasm and excitement. A well-thought-out incentive plan/sales contest will generate a continuing momentum even after it has ended, because salespeople will have experienced the satisfaction of higher sales and earnings. Also, a good incentive program can assist in creating good working habits that will make the sales force more productive on a continuing basis.

However, poorly conceived sales contests can lower morale, reduce sales, and lead to resignations. For example, don't use a sales contest to revive an inferior or obsolete product or service which has seen its day. Don't use a sales contest if you can't deliver the product or service being sold. Don't use a sales contest for a product or service where you already control over 70% of the market. In all three cases, salespeople become frustrated rather than motivated. During contests, salespeople have been known to cheat, overstock customers, and move orders from one period to another. You must realize this, and set up safeguards.

Contests lose their ability to excite and motivate when used too frequently, or when the same contest is repeated. Generally, one to three different contests a year satisfy the sales force's appetite.

Introduction

There are three basic types of incentive plans. The first type—direct competition among salespeople with prizes for one, two, or three winners—does not motivate or involve the entire sales force. The second type—competition between teams of salespeople for a prize shared by the winning group—involves more people than plan one, but dulls the motivation of your star performers. The third type plan—a contest in which salespeople win prizes by meeting or exceeding certain individual goals—produces the best results.

A sales contest without specific short-term objectives, and some more general longer-term goals as well, wastes time and money, and often fails. Using the specific objectives, you assign each activity a time frame and each territory a goal.

Sales contests/incentive programs prove especially suited for smaller concerns with limited financial and human resources, because, if properly structured, they can increase sales and profits from existing personnel with minimum increases in overhead. To achieve this, you must understand the economics of your objectives, and have a budget.

Sales contests which are too long or too frequent lose their effectiveness, because participants lose their enthusiasm and interest. Sales contests which are too short do not allow the sales force sufficient time to become involved, or to translate their enthusiasm into results.

You can best motivate salespeople with luxurious, exotic, fascinating prizes that they normally would not purchase themselves—prizes which capture the imagination. In addition to prizes, you might also consider issuing inexpensive certificates and plaques.

Like the product/service you sell, a successful sales contest requires creativity, merchandising, and promotion. A sales contest must capture the salesperson's imagination by injecting some "pizzazz," drama, and adventure in the everyday corporate routine.

Many contests fail because participants do not understand the rules. Therefore, keep the rules as simple as possible, and ask for individual feedback to make sure that salespeople have a complete understanding.

Types of Incentive Plans/Contests

There are three basic types of incentive plans. First, contests in which salespeople compete directly against one another, resulting in prizes going to a winner and several runners-up. Second, contests in which salespeople are divided into teams by region or product line, and each team competes against the others for prizes. Third, contests in which salespeople win prizes by meeting or exceeding certain individual goals.

Direct Competition.   The first plan—direct competition among salespeople with prizes for one, two, or three winners—does not motivate or involve the entire sales force. At the beginning, half the sales force decide they don't have a chance to win, because the cards are stacked against them, and so they do not get involved in the contest.

For example, if the contest rewards the three salespeople who open the most new accounts in April, many salespeople immediately lose interest because they know their territory does not contain the potential new accounts of another salesperson's territory. Then, halfway through the contest, when it becomes evident which three people will win, all but the winners give up. The losers are left unmotivated, and with a feeling that management does not care about them.

A contest which does not involve the entire sales force will not achieve its motivational or specific performance goals. Active participation by the entire sales organization is vital.

Teams.   The second plan—competition between teams of salespeople for a prize shared by the winning group—involves more people than plan one, but dulls the motivation of your star performers. The stars feel that the group dilutes their individual efforts and results. When the star performer produces, he or she wants the spotlight. Therefore, in group contests, the stars, who may produce most of your sales volume, generally underperform their potential.

Team contests do create good group spirit and positive peer pressure. More experienced salespeople will help and advise less experienced team members in achieving desired goals. Also, no team member wants the responsibility for being the person causing the loss. Therefore, all team members exert some extra effort.

Team contests do not produce resentment against individual winners, because a group wins, but they can produce general resentment unless each team has equal potential to win. When improving group spirit is more important than motivating star performers, consider using a group incentive program.

Individual Goals. The third plan, a contest in which salespeople win prizes by meeting or exceeding certain individual goals, produces the best results. In these contests, salespeople do not compete against each other, but simply against their own individual target. Everyone becomes interested and involved, and participates, because everyone can win prizes.

If the contest's objective was opening new accounts in April, then you as sales manager would set a goal or quota for each salesperson. These individual objectives should reflect the territory's potential. A territory with 100 potential new accounts might carry a quota of ten, while a territory with 50 potential new accounts might have a quota of five. You can obtain information on potential new accounts from the reference material used to design territories and from field trips. Before setting the quota, discuss your reasoning with the involved salesperson to make sure he or she accepts the quota as realistic, obtainable, and fair.

Any salesperson who achieves 80% of his or her goal should receive a prize, but a salesperson achieving 120% of quota should receive a more valuable prize. Prizes for reaching various percentage levels of quota are the same for each salesperson, regardless of territory or quota size.

For example, if the salesperson with a quota of ten new accounts opens eight, he or she receives the same prize as the salesperson with a quota of five new accounts who opens four. Both achieved 80% of quota. Similarly, the salesperson with a quota of ten new accounts who opens twelve receives the same prize as the salesperson with a quota of five new accounts who opens six. Both achieved 120% of quota.

This third, individual-goals, incentive plan bears a striking resemblance to the quota/bonus form of compensation discussed in Chapt. 3. However, the quota/bonus form of compensation rewards superior performance spanning six months or a year with considerable money, while the individual-goals incentive plan/sales contest rewards superior performance spanning one to three months with noncash prizes. The sales contest provides a more immediate reward for superior performance. Also, while bonus plans might reward one salesperson for new accounts and another for dollar sales increases, sales contests reward all salespeople for one type of performance. In addition, winners of sales contests receive publicity, no matter how many reach their objective, while quota/ bonus compensation plans remain private information.

A variation of this individual-goal plan involves a point system. A salesperson receives points for achieving 80% of his or her target in the sales contest, and receives an increasing number of points as the percentage of or over target increases. When the contest ends, the salesperson uses these points to buy prizes.

Another variation involves adding overall winners to the individual-goal plan. For example, the three people who achieve the largest percentage gain over quota receive a prize in addition to their other awards. Everyone continues to have individual goals and individual awards, but you add additional awards for overall winners. This creates some element of direct competition between the salespeople, and added incentive for the star performers.

Setting targets for these individual-goal plans can prove time-consuming, because past sales records require studying and each salesperson requires a meeting. Also, administration of these individual-goal plans can prove time-consuming, because hopefully everyone wins prizes. In a smaller concern, setting targets and administration of the program falls on the sales manager, who is already short of time. However, the results generally will justify the extra time required.

Regardless of which plan you use, direct competition, teams, or individual goals, properly handled sales contests require objectives, budgets, time frames, appropriate prizes, adequate promotion, and simple, clearly explained rules.

Objectives

A sales contest without specific short-term objectives and some more general longer-term goals wastes time and money, which a smaller business can ill afford. Generally, sales contests without specific objectives fail. Company policy stating there should be one sales contest a year does not serve as an objective. You need a reason for this project, and the reason must support your basic marketing plan.

The objectives of a sales contest might include increased sales of a particular product, increased overall unit or dollar sales during a certain period, increased order size, increased number of customers, improved collections, reduced selling expenses, better use of selling aids, or more prospecting. Using the specific objectives, you assign each activity a time frame and each territory a goal. For example, how many additional units of a particular product, how many additional dollars of sales, what percentage increase in sales, do you wish from each salesperson during the contest period? How many additional customers do you want each salesperson to add? If improved collections are a goal, how many days accounts receivable do you want in each territory? If reduced selling expenses are a goal, how many dollars, or what percentage, decrease do you want from each salesperson?

All sales contests should have as long-range goals the reinforcement of salespeople's motivational needs for recognition, achievement, fulfillment, status, belonging, and additional compensation. The contests should also seek to generate continuing momentum by establishing good work habits and exposure to higher income levels.

Budgets

Sales contests and incentive programs prove especially suited for smaller concerns with limited financial and human resources, because, if properly structured, they can increase sales and profits from existing personnel with minimum increases in overhead. To achieve this, you must understand the economics of your objectives, and have a budget. A small concern can ill afford to pay out more in prizes than they reap in additional profits.

Here you will require the assistance of the company president, controller, or accountant. For example, if the contest increases sales by five percent or $100,000, how much additional profits will be generated before contest costs? Look at the profit potential for the best possible, worst possible, and most probable sales results.

Next, decide with the help of your president, controller, or accountant what percentage of the increased profits should pay for the contest costs. If a $100,000 sales increase produces a $10,000 pretax profit, your colleagues might budget 20% or $2,000 for contest expenses. A more successful contest generates greater sales and profits, but if you use an individual quota plan, it also results in greater prize expenses. You must also take into account that a contest not only affects current but also future sales and profits, and that there are motivational benefits which cannot be measured in dollars.

Let us assume that the most probable result of your individual quota contest is a five percent or $100,000 sales increase, resulting in a $10,000 pretax profit increase, and thus creating a $2,000 budget for the program. First, you deduct from the $2,000 $200 for out-of-pocket promotional costs. This covers extra phone calls, mailing expenses, and certain promotional literature, and leaves $1,800 to purchase prizes for your four salespeople.

Now you work backwards, assigning each salesperson a portion of the $100,000 increase appropriate to the contest's objectives and to the potential of his or her territory. This portion, whether $15,000, $20,000, $30,000, or $35,000, becomes related to his or her quota. If they all reach quota, the cost of their prizes would be $1,800 ÷ 4, or $450 each. If one, several, or all exceed quota, you increase the $450, on a prorated basis. If they miss quota, you decrease the $450 on a prorated basis. These numbers then become your budget.

Contests and incentive plans which do not produce immediate sales or profit increases are more difficult to budget. If the contest's objectives involve more prospecting or improving collections, it is difficult to measure the immediate impact on sales or profits. In such instances you use the same techniques, but must place a value on the longer-range benefits.

Time Frame

Sales contests which are too long or too frequent lose their effectiveness, because participants lose their enthusiasm and interest. Contests are temporary schemes to elicit extra effort in a particular area. Sales contests which drag on or come to be expected lose their excitement and will no longer light your sales-people's fire.

Sales contests lasting from one to two months usually prove most effective. Generally, one to three contests a year will provide enough extra motivation for a sales force.

Contests lasting less than a month do not allow salespeople sufficient time to become involved, or to translate their enthusiasm into results. The minimum time span for a contest would be that required to perform the necessary tasks. For example, if a contest involves increasing dollar sales to achieve certain goals, you must allow enough time for the salespeople to contact all their important customers. If a contest involves opening new accounts, you must allow enough time for proper prospecting, appointment setting, and call backs.

To maintain interest and enthusiasm, longer contests require more substantial prizes than shorter contests. You may obtain good results by offering a free French dinner for two to any salesperson who reduces his or her territory's overdue accounts receivable by 10% in the next 30 days. Such a prize would not generate sufficient enthusiasm for a contest lasting 90 days which involved opening a substantial number of new accounts. By comparison, enthusiasm for the 90-day contest might require a free weekend on the town at a local hotel.

Prizes

You can best motivate salespeople with luxurious, exotic, fascinating prizes that they normally would not purchase for themselves—prizes which capture the imagination. Cash, therefore, is not the best contest award, and it also interferes with your regular compensation plan.

If your budget is $100, dinner for two at a fine restaurant along with theater tickets might provide an appropriate prize. If your budget is $500, a weekend for two on the town might prove an appropriate prize. If your budget is $1,000, a video tape recorder; home computer; weekend in New York, San Francisco, or New Orleans for two; quadrophonic sound system; or fine camera might provide an appropriate prize.

Always offer a choice, because one type of prize seldom is acceptable to all the participants, yet you want all participants to be motivated to try for a prize. For example, some salespeople do enough traveling during the week and would prefer a prize for the house rather than another trip.

Prizes that benefit both the participant and spouse work well. This produces a little extra pressure at home to perform well, and a little extra prestige for winning. Also, prizes such as home computers, auto accessories, telephone answering machines which a salesperson can use on the job prove very appropriate.

The Internal Revenue Service considers the cash value or cost of most prizes as taxable income to the recipient. However, some prizes valued under $400 might not be taxable to the employee if considered a gift. You should consult the proper company financial officer for details, and inform your sales force.

In addition to prizes, you might also consider issuing inexpensive certificates and plaques. These represent a lasting form of recognition, and, as we have discussed, recognition represents an important motivational force.

Promotion

Like the product/service you sell, a successful sales contest requires creativity, merchandising, salesmanship, and promotion. A sales contest must capture the salesperson's imagination by injecting some pizzazz, drama, and adventure into the everyday corporate routine.

If possible, announce the contest at a sales meeting, where you can personally sell it to the group and answer questions. Prepare an innovative promotional piece, clearly explaining the rules and describing or picturing the prizes. If a sales meeting is not practical, mail the promotional piece to each salesperson with a covering letter, and follow up with a telephone call. Sales contests require personal enthusiastic selling by the sales manager to excite the participants.

Create an appropriate name and theme for your sales contest, which relates to the prizes. If most prizes are home entertainment devices, you might call it "Electronic Whirl." If most prizes are trips to Florida, you might call it "Sunny Skies."

Even properly organized individual-goal sales contests which start out well can begin losing salespeople's interest at midpoint. To maintain this interest, issue weekly bulletins on results, write personal congratulatory letters to the leaders, and remind all salespeople of the prizes involved.

If possible, end the contest with a dinner announcing the results. If this is not possible, issue a bulletin with the results. You and the president should write congratulatory letters to all prize recipients. Remember that a sales contest not only achieves certain specific company objectives, and awards prizes to participants, but also reinforces salespeople's needs for recognition, achievement, fulfillment, status, and belonging. A good sales contest boosts personal morale and pride in the company.

Rules

Many contests fail because participants do not understand the rules. Therefore, keep the rules as simple as possible, and ask for individual feedback to assure that salespeople have complete understanding. Make certain that everyone knows the opening and closing dates; what achievements are sought by the company; by what date products/services have to be sold or shipped; what products/services, customers, expenses, or accounts receivable are included; how sales, expenses, or new accounts are reported and validated; the basis for awards; how and when prizes will be awarded; and what assistance the company will provide salespeople in the contest.

Summary

Sales contests and incentive plans represent a powerful commonly employed tool for improving sales force motivation and increasing sales. They provide fast and frequent reinforcement to a salesperson's needs for recognition, achievement, fulfillment, status, belonging, and additional compensation. Sales contests elicit extra "beyond the normal" effort from the sales force, and prove most helpful in smoothing out seasonal sales dips, bringing attention to a good product or service which has been neglected, launching a new product, or increasing the number of active accounts.

Sales contests generally involve one of the following types of plans: Salespeople competing directly against each other, teams of salespeople competing against each other, or salespeople trying to achieve individual goals. The latter plan produces the best results, because it encourages more people to participate.

Sales contests require specific performance objectives, budgets, and time frames. In addition, prizes must be unusual, the promotion creative, and the rules clear.

6
Communication and Control

In order to hire, train, compensate, organize, motivate, and evaluate a sales force, you must be able to communicate with your salespeople. Often a sales manager communicates well with customers and with bosses, but not with the sales force. Many sales managers lack the understanding, sensitivity, and skills required for good communication with their subordinates. Significant differences exist between selling, and managing those who do the selling. A saleswoman once told me that her sales manager talked well, but communicated poorly.

Managing salespeople involves influencing their thoughts and causing actions. Therefore, communication not only means explaining, but also persuading and changing.

Often companies with a small number of employees have greater communication problems than concerns with more employees. Good communication does not depend on the number of people involved, but upon the skills, techniques, concern, and sensitivity of those people. In many smaller companies the attitude prevails that "everyone will find out sooner or later, so why waste time telling them." Moreover, in a small organization a person may become more essential if he or she holds on to information rather than passing it along. Good communication involves open doors and open minds.

Effective communication is essential not only within the sales organization of a smaller business, but also among all levels of sales, production, and accounting. At a small paper products company in Cincinnati, the plant continued manufacturing an item that had been discontinued six months previously, because sales and manufacturing did not talk. In another instance, accounting continued to send pay checks to a salesperson who had quit months before, because the sales manager had failed to notify the payroll department. As these examples illustrate, a breakdown in communication can prove more expensive than a breakdown in machinery.

Managing a successful small business, in particular an effective sales program, is very difficult *with* good communication; without good communication, it is impossible. When management, beginning with the chief executive officer, communicates well, other employees find good communication easier. Good communication is contagious.

To communicate effectively, a sales manager must understand the skills, techniques, sensitivities, and human dynamics involved, such as feedback; perception; initiation of action through commands and persuasion; organization and clarity of expression; simplicity; recognition of personal prejudices, and informal or unconscious communication; listening; and measuring results. To communicate effectively, a sales manager must also establish tangible channels/vehicles for interplay with the sales force, such as route sheets, call reports, customer analysis, product analysis, commission statements, expense reports, orders, sales forecasts, expense budgets, performance appraisals, phone calls, bulletins, letters, audio tapes, manuals, catalogues, sales meetings, individual meetings, staff meetings, training sessions, and bulletin boards.

COMMUNICATION SKILLS AND TECHNIQUES

Introduction

All communication involves a sender and a receiver trying to achieve a commonness of meaning. Therefore, all successful communication involves four basic factors: a sender, a message, a receiver, and feedback. Commonness of meaning is not achieved until the sender receives feedback that his or her message was received by the recipient in its intended form.

When you communicate with salespeople, they may receive a message different from your intended one, or you may receive a message different from their intended one, because their experience, desires, and expectations differ from yours. You should convey messages in terms of the recipient's perceptions, and you should receive messages with a sensitivity for the sender's perceptions.

Much of what you communicate is intended to initiate action or change on the part of the recipient. Initiating action or change requires issuing demands rather than reports and involves persuasion and selling.

Many failures in communication stem from not organizing our thoughts before we speak. Whatever you wish to communicate, think it through first, keep it simple, and use visual aids wherever appropriate.

As a sales manager, you must recognize that you have negative personal feelings about certain salespeople which influence your ability to effectively communicate with them, and that you may express these negative feelings in certain nonverbal, unconscious communication. As sales manager, you don't have to like all your salespeople, but you do have to communicate with all of them.

Good communication has two sides, talking and listening. Proper listening involves concentrating and thinking about the sender's intended message, perceptions, and expectations; and then feedback to the sender confirming the intended meaning. Good listening involves not interrupting the sender.

Feedback

All communication involves a sender and a receiver trying to achieve a commonness of meaning. This is not achieved until the sender receives feedback that his or her message was received by the recipient in its intended form. When communicating with a salesperson, do you ask for feedback to assure that he or she understands the meaning of your message? Do you give feedback to assure that you have understood the meaning of his or her message?

For example, the sales manager of a ladies' dress company told his five salespeople "not to call on discounters any more." After three months, one salesperson continued selling to discounters, because she thought the sales manager meant not to open any new discount store accounts. Another salesperson stopped selling both chain and discount stores, because he considered chain stores as discounters. Another salesperson thought she could continue selling discount stores through the current season.

The sales manager should have asked each salesperson for specific feedback to assure proper understanding of the message. For example, "What discount stores are you presently selling?" "When will you see them next to inform them of this policy change?"

Perception

When you communicate with salespeople, they may receive a message different from your intended one, or you may receive a message different from their intended one, because their experience, desires, and expectations differ from yours. You should convey messages in terms of the recipient's perceptions, and you should receive messages with a sensitivity for the sender's perceptions. This necessitates using terms, expressions, and analogies which the person can readily understand. When communicating with salespeople, use language that is part of their daily experience—language they themselves would use.

Remember that words have different meanings to different people, and that an expression common to you may not be common to your sales force. This holds especially true for technical terms, clichés, abbreviations, initials, and "businessese." Many sales managers build a mystique around their trade using buzz words and jargon, resulting in poor communication. Also, certain words have hidden emotional meanings which can produce friendly or hostile feelings. For example, the words "house accounts," "paperwork," and "expense account" produce negative feelings in many salespeople. A female salesperson might react badly if you referred to her as a salesman. A good communicator knows and is sensitive to the audience and chooses words carefully. A good communicator also listens with a sensitivity for the sender's perception of words.

One sales manager told a trainee that all shipments were "F.O.B. factory, 2% 10 days E.O.M. net 60." The trainee had previously been employed as a sales clerk in a retail store. When the sales manager questioned the trainee's orders calling for his employer to pay freight, the trainee explained that his understanding of "F.O.B. factory" was that the vendor/shipper paid freight to the customer's factory, not the opposite. When the trainee's customers started paying invoices late, the sales manager discovered that his new salesman thought "2% 10 days E.O.M. net 60" meant 60 days after the 10 days E.O.M. (end of month), not 60 days from invoice date.

This sales manager spoke accounting and shipping language to an inexperienced salesperson. The sales manager should have said, "On all shipments, customers pay all freight charges from our factory to theirs, which we call 'F.O.B. factory.' Invoices must be paid 60 days after the goods are shipped, but a 2% discount can be taken on invoices paid within 10 days after the month in which goods are shipped. We call these payment terms 2% 10 days E.O.M. net 60." Then the sales manager might have asked for feedback by saying, "If an order is shipped on April 15, when must it be paid to take the discount, and when must it be paid before it becomes delinquent.?"

People hear what they expect and desire to hear, which is not necessarily the sender's intended meaning. Therefore, to communicate effectively, you must understand what the recipient expects and desires to hear as well as his or her experience and perceptions. This enables you to express your message accordingly to achieve your desired meaning. Similarly, as a listener you must understand the sender's expectations, desires, experience, and perceptions to accurately interpret the desired meaning of the message.

In July, a sales manager told a salesman whose sales had declined, "I will have to reduce your salary 10% unless sales improve." The salesperson, expecting orders to increase in the fourth quarter, a major shipping period, thought he had until year-end to show improvement. The sales manager, expecting the salesperson's orders to decline in the third quarter, and wanting to reduce expenses, had decided that he would make the decision in October. The salesperson's orders did decline in the third quarter, which resulted in a salary cut. The salesperson quit, because he had expected and perceived a longer time period to improve results. The sales manager lost a valuable employee simply because he did not realize that the two had different expectations and perceptions of the time period involved.

In July, the sales manager should have said, "I will have to reduce your salary 10% unless sales increase above $10,000 a week by October 1. Do you think that is fair?" A discussion would have followed, which might have led to a compromise date; but certainly the salesperson would have completely understood the sales manager's message.

The sales manager for a sweater company told the sales force that "all off-price orders for promotions must be limited to 20% of a customer's purchases." The sales manager's goal involved reducing off-price volume, thus improving profits. He wished to restrict any off-price promotional orders to 20% of *that item's regular-price* unit volume the *previous* twelve months. The sales force's goal involved maximizing orders, thus improving their commission income. They interpreted the sales manager's message to mean that off-price promotional orders could not exceed 20% of the account's *total expected* dollar volume for the next twelve months. This misunderstanding resulted in the sales manager continually reducing, scaling back, off-price promotional orders written by the sales force, which upset customers. The sales force and the sales manager had different expectations and perceptions of "off-price orders for promotions" and of "20% of a customer's purchases." These different expectations and perceptions led to a misunderstanding which caused embarrassment, waste, and bad feelings.

The sales manager should have said, "Off-price orders for promotions must be limited to 20% of a customer's regular-price unit purchases of that item for the past twelve months. Now, please look at the shipments for your largest accounts, and let's discuss their allowable quantities for their next promotion." Asking for this feedback establishes whether the salesperson received the correct message.

Initiating Action

Much of what you communicate is intended to initiate action or change on the part of the recipient. Initiating action or change involves persuasion and selling. You sell a particular action by giving a reason for it, and the reason must promise a desirable result for the listener.

Initiating action or change also necessitates direct commands. Many sales managers assume that their salespeople know what is expected of them. If the sales manager "thinks" the desired action, he or she believes the sales force can read minds and somehow perceives it. You must verbally communicate demands to initiate change or action, not just think them.

Sales managers often try to initiate action by giving a *report* when they intend to issue a *demand*. Then they complain that no one listens or follows instructions. If you want route sheets on your desk by noon each Friday, do not tell the sales force, "I review route sheets each Friday afternoon so I can discuss them with each salesperson Monday morning." You are reporting or describing an event and will be lucky to receive route sheets from half the sales force. Instead, issue a direct command/demand by saying, "You must have your route sheet on my desk by Friday noon, or I will call you Saturday." "What day will you mail it?" (Feedback.)

If you want to meet with a salesperson Monday morning, don't say, "We better have a meeting Monday," and then wonder why he or she does not show up. You are giving a report, not issuing a command/demand. Instead say, "I want to discuss several of your accounts. Please be in my office Monday morning at 8:30 for a meeting. Is an 8:30 meeting convenient?" (Feedback.)

To initiate action, you must make demands which produce desirable results for the listener, demands which persuade by appealing to his or her motivation. If you make demands which go against the listener's motivations, aspirations, self-image, or values, they will be resisted. The fewer demands you make in each communication, the more likely you will achieve the desired action. Messages with too many demands weaken the communication's effectiveness.

You can persuade the Ohio salesperson, who lives in Cleveland, to make more trips to Cincinnati and Columbus by reminding him that more trips should result in more orders, which in turn will result in more commission income. You do not tell him to make more trips to Toledo and Pittsburgh while discussing Cincinnati and Columbus. Make one demand for action at a time, and point out the personal benefits.

You could persuade the Illinois salesperson to call on more prospects by noting that such action might help him win the new-account sales contest. You would have difficulty persuading him to take a booth at the Chicago trade show, because he will not get credit for orders from customers outside Illinois.

You convince the New York salesman to lead a discussion at the sales meeting by appealing to his need for recognition and achievement. You convince the same person to call on the Navy Exchange buying office in Brooklyn by arranging a lunch date with the company president to discuss the meeting.

Your Michigan salesman is sixty-eight and plans to retire in two years. He only works three days a week, but has the good health to work five. You remind him that working five days a week will increase his income; but money no longer motivates him. You cannot threaten early retirement, because his wife is the president's sister. As a last resort, you write a special bulletin to the entire sales force praising the Michigan salesman's record and years with the company. You note that his sales have risen in each year with the company. Suddenly he starts working five days a week to maintain his record of unbroken sales gains.

Organization and Clarity of Expression

Whatever you wish to communicate, think it through first, keep it simple, and use visual aids wherever appropriate. Many failures in communication stem from not knowing exactly what idea, information, demand, or instruction you wish to express. Many failures in communication stem from not organizing our thoughts before we speak.

The sales manager of a specialty steel distributor in Atlanta discovered that his star salesman wanted his job and was "bad mouthing" the sales manager to the other salespeople. This sales manager had a dilemma, since he did not plan to vacate his job and could not afford to lose his star performer. Initially, the sales manager responded by getting angry and verbally attacking the salesman rather than analyzing the problem.

Eventually, the sales manager discussed the problem with his boss, the company president. They decided that the sales manager should communicate the following message to his star salesman: (1) The salesman was a valuable, appreciated member of the company organization. (2) The sales manager's job was not available. (3) The salesman's responsibilities would be enlarged to include handling certain national accounts, plus helping to plan sales meetings, new products, advertising, and contests. (4) The salesman would be promoted to national accounts sales manager, but would still report to his present boss, the general sales manager.

The sales manager arranged a meeting with the star performer to discuss points one through four. The sales manager clearly and calmly presented the program, stressing the benefits for the listener. He spoke to the problem rather than attacking the person. This time the sales manager had thought out and organized exactly what he intended to communicate.

When customers of a small Omaha industrial fastener company started complaining to the sales manager about late deliveries, he called the warehouse manager. The warehouse manager complained that three salespeople were writing orders incorrectly, which necessitated time-consuming rewriting at the warehouse, thus delaying shipments. The sales manager immediately called the first salesman and expressed anger at his stupidity, because correct order writing had been explained many times. The sales manager attacked the person, not the problem.

When the sales manager called the second salesman, his anger had subsided. He said, "Customers have complained about poor deliveries, and the warehouse manager says this results from your incorrectly writing orders." The salesman replied, "Be specific; what have I done wrong?" The sales manager replied, "Your handwriting is sloppy, customers' addresses are incorrect, you wrote quantities in the wrong column, data-processing codes do not have all the digits, quantities by page are not totaled, and product descriptions carry incorrect abbreviations. Refer to the sales manual and straighten this out." The sales manager had answered the question, but he still had not thought through and organized exactly what he wanted to express.

By the time the sales manager called the third salesman, he had thought through the problem and organized his message. He said, "Your customers are complaining about poor deliveries, which may cost you some business unless you take the following corrective action in order writing: (1) Ask each customer for their correct billing and shipping address. (2) Only place quantities in column six, and total them for each item and page. (3) All data-processing codes must use seven digits including zeros. (4) Abbreviate product descriptions by using the first two letters of each word. (5) Print or typewrite each order." The sales manager continued, "I am returning several incorrectly written orders. Please correctly rewrite them and mail them back to me by Monday." (Feedback.) The first and second salesmen continued to write faulty orders; the third salesman did not. Eventually, the sales manager wrote a bulletin on order writing, and discussed it at the next sales meeting.

Attempt to organize your written and verbal communications in a simple, concise, uncomplicated way. More words do not necessarily make communication clearer.

The sales manager for a small specialty chemical company sent out the following bulletin to all salespeople:

Many of you have requested that the company have a sales meeting this spring. Although the cost of the meeting will be high, we feel the benefits will be greater.

In searching for a central theme or focal point, we considered "opening new accounts," "handling objections," "organizing time," and "new product development." After much thought, we decided on the latter.

You may drive, take a train or bus to the meeting. The opening night dinner begins at 7:00 p.m.

We debated whether to have the meeting at a resort or in a city, and whether to have it in the Midwest, East or West Coast. We finally decided to have it at Stouffer's on Fountain Square in Cincinnati, because of the factory location and good transportation.

We finally decided to have a three-day meeting rather than two or four. The meeting begins on April 3rd and ends on April 5th.

After receiving this bulletin, every salesperson called the sales manager with questions, confusion, and comments. A clearer message could have been sent by simply saying:

There will be a spring sales meeting at the Fountain Square Stouffer's in Cincinnati, beginning with an opening dinner at 7:00 p.m. on Friday April 3, and ending at 5:00 p.m. on Sunday April 5. Arrange your own transportation, but inform me of the details by March 15. (Feedback.) The meeting will concentrate on new product information.

Often charts, diagrams, and photographs communicate messages better than words. Always consider using visual aids. The sales manager for a small San Francisco specialty food purveyor condensed a three-page written explanation of a sales contest into a one-page memo with pictures of prizes and graphs explaining the performance necessary to win prizes.

Personal Prejudices and Informal Communication

Our personal prejudices are very precious to us and we relinquish them reluctantly if at all. As sales manager, you don't have to like all your salespeople, but you do have to communicate with all of them. Recognize that you have negative personal feelings about certain people which influence your ability to effectively communicate with them. Also, recognize that you may express these negative feelings in certain nonverbal, unconscious communication.

The sales manager for a local truck-leasing company inherited a salesperson who continually complained about business, his family, his customers, and his employer. However, the salesman had excellent contacts with the purchasing agents of major customers, and wrote substantial business. The sales manager couldn't stand talking with this salesman. He communicated only by mail, and only when absolutely essential. As a result, the salesman always underperformed his potential, and the complaining grew worse.

Sales managers may dislike individual salespeople for many reasons: the way they dress, the money they earn, their complaining, their lack of performance, their bragging, or their lack of maturity. You should be aware that these prejudices are not abnormal, but that you must deal with them in order to communicate with all your salespeople.

Also recognize that you not only express negative personal feelings in words, but also in certain nonverbal, unconscious communication, the "silent language." Your eye contact, physical touch, tone of voice, body posture, facial expression, and silence can all convey strong messages to subordinates. You probably have experienced the "silent treatment" from a cold and uncommunicative boss. On the other hand, eye contact can communicate concern, warmth, and understanding to the recipient.

The sales manager for a small insurance agency employed a salesperson who resisted any sort of change. The sales manager dealt with this by personally explaining and selling all desired changes. During their meetings, the sales manager never looked the salesperson in the eye and always sat with his arms folded. He used long pauses with deep breaths in answering questions. The message of dislike, though expressed indirectly, came across strongly to the salesperson. The sales manager might have better achieved his goal of selling change if he had recognized and better controlled the nonverbal communication.

Listening

Good communication has two sides, talking and listening. No matter what your position—salesperson, sales manager, president, purchasing agent, or foreman—good listening skills are essential to communication. Proper listening involves concentrating on and thinking about the sender's intended message, perceptions, and expectations, and then issuing feedback to the sender to confirm the intended meaning. Good listening involves not interrupting the sender. When a sales manager listens properly and sensitively to a salesperson, it communicates a sense of recognition and worth.

The sales manager for a St. Louis commercial laundry asked his salespeople to increase their calls on hospitals and uniform rental companies, which they did. The salespeople reported back to the sales manager that hospitals required one-day service rather than the three-day service currently offered to other customers. Also, uniform rental firms required a specific type of folding not currently offered by the laundry. The sales manager heard this, but did not really listen.

Had he listened, two alternatives would have emerged: either offer one-day services to hospitals, and/or special folding for rental concerns, or don't have the sales force waste any more time calling on these types of prospects. Instead, no changes were offered in the service, but he insisted that the salespeople continue wasting time on these type accounts.

The sales manager for a door-to-door cosmetic company asked her best salesperson why she was not selling the newest natural shampoo. She replied that customers objected to the ingredients. The sales manager pointed out that the ingredients were finer than those of the competitors. Had the sales manager been listening, concentrating, thinking, and aware of the salesperson's perceptions, she would have realized that the salesperson's problem involved selling the product's chemistry rather than its benefits, more beautiful hair. The problem was not the product, but the presentation; and the sales manager should have noted this to the saleswoman.

The sales manager for a paper-recycling company received an urgent call from his best salesman: unless the company increased his salary by 25%, he would resign. The sales manager asked why. The salesman replied he had received an offer from a competitor at the higher salary level. The sales manager asked what other advantages the competitor offered, and then listened very carefully to the reply. It became obvious that the salesman was flattered by the offer, and that the higher salary was contingent on performance. The salesman wanted recognition and the chance for more money.

The sales manager responded by changing the salesman's compensation from straight salary to salary plus commission, which created an opportunity for greater earnings, and by changing the salesman's title from "Sales Representative" to "District Sales Manager." The salesman stayed with his current employer, and both benefited.

Measuring the Result

Communication is a never-ending process, and you should continually try to improve your skills. On the way home once a week, or after an important conversation, analyze and rate your performance. Did you ask for feedback to confirm a common understanding of your meaning? Did you take into account the listener's perceptions, expectations, and experience? Did you speak the listener's language? Did you sell action by giving a reason which produced a desired result for the listener? Did you ask for action with clear demands rather than vague descriptions? Did you calmly organize your thoughts before speaking, keep the communication simple, and use visual aids if appropriate? Were you aware of your indirect or unconscious communication and possible personal prejudices? Did you concentrate while listening, think about the message, and establish feedback with the sender? Did your communication achieve its intended objective? If not, why not?

COMMUNICATION CHANNELS, REPORTS, VEHICLES, AND DEVICES

Introduction

As sales manager you must not only understand the previously described skills and techniques for effective communication, but also the means and methods for using these techniques. The major channels of communication include route sheets, call reports, customer analysis, commission statements, expense reports, orders, product analysis, sales forecasts, expense budgets, performance appraisals, phone calls, bulletins, letters, tapes, manuals, catalogues, sales meetings, individual meetings, staff meetings, training sessions, and bulletin boards. Through these channels, information, instructions, and demands are communicated.

The route sheet lists who the salesperson *plans* to visit in the *coming* week, and what he or she *plans* to accomplish. The call report lists who he or she *actually* visited in the *past* week, and what actually was accomplished. These two reports help the salesperson plan time and measure results, while also communicating this information to management.

The customer analysis shows shipments and/or orders, in units and dollars, for the period and year to date, by product/service, for each customer, organized by territory and compared to the previous year. The customer analysis allows each salesperson and also the sales manager to compare this year's results to last year's, and then to use this information to prepare sales forecasts and evaluate performance.

If you compensate salespeople with any form of commission, you must provide them with monthly information on invoices and how you calculated the commission earned. Such statements can also compare commission earned and dollar product line sales for this month and year-to-date to last year.

If your company reimburses salespeople for certain travel, telephone, entertainment, and clerical expenses, their expense reports will provide you with valuable information about their activities. In a smaller firm, the sales manager should receive and review copies of all orders, because they provide the most immediate hard information on a sales force, its markets, and its results.

The product analysis presents total company cumulative orders, sales, or shipments in units and dollars totaled by product, style, model, or service compared to the previous year. Sales forecasts, expense budgets, and performance appraisals require the sales manager and each salesperson to agree on future goals and a plan of action for reaching these objectives; periodically the sales manager meets with each salesperson to compare actual performance to these plans/goals, agreeing on corrective action where necessary.

Regular weekly or biweekly fifteen-minute telephone calls from the sales manager to the field people create a personal, inexpensive, effective means of communication. However, for efficiently communicating certain information applicable to the entire sales force, the sales manager needs to write bulletins. Information which does not require immediate response or feedback lends itself to communication using tapes, manuals, and catalogues.

Route Sheets and Call Reports

Typically, sales managers ask the sales force to submit weekly route sheets and call reports. The route sheet lists who the salesperson *plans* to visit in the *coming* week, and what he or she *plans* to accomplish. The call report lists who he or she *actually* visited in the *past* week, and what actually was accomplished. These reports provide you with useful information from the marketplace, but must be kept simple and submitted promptly. Management must devote time to reading these reports, and must realize that they may not be equally helpful to all salespeople.

These two reports help most salespeople plan time and measure results, while also communicating this information to management. Without a call plan, your salespeople can waste time and money by not using the most efficient travel routes and correct call frequency discussed in Chap. 4.

Effectiveness. The effectiveness of both reports depends on simplicity, timeliness, and responsiveness. Neither the salesperson nor the manager can afford to waste time on nonproductive paperwork. Some route sheets and call reports require unnecessary and burdensome detailed information. A manager needs to know simply which customers his or her salespeople plan to see each day; whether they were seen; a short phrase on the visit's objectives and accomplishments; and a report on any special information. Special information includes significant changes in the customer's buying habits, financial condition, staff, or attitude, plus any significant changes in competitors' activities or in your product/services' performance.

As an example, a day on the route sheet might read, "March 12, Cabot Machinery, Montpelier, Vt. Obtain fill-in order for 50 gallons of cleaning fluid. Van Horne Engine Co., Burlington, Vt. Hope to open this new account with our metal cutting fluid." The same day on a call report might read, "March 12, Cabot Machinery, Montpelier, Vt. Wrote a $1,750 order for cleaning fluid. Purchasing agent being transferred to a new position. Met the new buyer, Dick Lang. Van Horne Engine Co., Burlington, Vt. Saw purchasing agent, Alex Gregoris. Likes our product, but sees no reason to change from present supplier, Henkle Chemical, who just lowered its prices."

Route sheets and call reports keep you informed, so that you may help salespeople economically make the optimum number of effective calls on the right customers and prospects. Call reports also provide you with useful information from the marketplace on competition, customers, and your products'/services' performance, which you in turn can pass on to other salespeople. To be most helpful, route sheets and call reports should be submitted each weekend. The information which they contain proves most useful when fresh.

Salespeople should not only send the call reports to their sales manager, but maintain a copy for themselves. The call reports become their diary, the ship's log. They refer to it in the future for customer information, frequency of visits, and order writing results.

Often in smaller businesses, route sheets and call reports are an exercise for salespeople but not read by management. The salespeople speak to management through these reports. Responsive management must listen and reply, using these reports as a significant means of communication and control. The sales force's attitude toward writing route sheets and call reports generally reflects management's attitude toward reading them. If you respond to significant information provided in call reports, most salespeople will faithfully submit them.

Human Element. However, you must build your reporting and communication function around a small business's most important resource, people. You must show flexibility by not necessarily requiring certain salespeople to submit weekly route sheets and/or call reports. Not every salesperson in your organization benefits equally from submitting these reports. For example, the individual who sells and services only one major account has little reason to submit this information. The major men's shirt supplier for Broadway Department Stores in Los Angeles has a salesman who spends all his time servicing their 28 branches. His activity and performance can best be monitored and evaluated by reviewing orders.

Also, some salespeople produce outstanding volumes of business but cannot tolerate any paperwork beyond writing orders. In such an instance, do not argue with success; be flexible, and monitor performance and field intelligence with weekly phone calls, or compromise on biweekly call reports.

A legendary ladies' sportswear salesman wrote his route sheets on the back of match covers while relaxing on Friday evening. Each night at dinner he wrote a daily call report on a paper table napkin. As long as he remained the top salesman in the industry, management never complained about his reports. Detailed reporting is no substitute for success.

Also, sometimes superorganized salespeople obtain little benefit from submitting a formal route sheet. They have their own system.

However, average organizers and nonsuperstar salespeople, who comprise 80% of most sales organizations, do benefit from route sheets and call reports; and even if they object, you must insist on prompt weekly reporting to improve results. Some salespeople with strong needs for freedom and independence consider written reports as symbols of repression which restrict their freedom and independence. They may also view these reports as an invasion of their privacy, an attempt to find out if they are working, to find out where they are every day, to check up, to spy.

To overcome their objections and start receiving these reports regularly, you must persuade such salespeople that the reports will help them improve results. During a field visit, review the reports to make certain they understand their simplicity. During field visits and phone conversations, make helpful suggestions based on information contained in the reports. This assures salespeople that you read and use the information.

Occasionally, salespeople do not submit reports regularly because of embarrassment over penmanship or poor spelling. Assure them that you do not grade the reports. Again, show them how they can improve results by using information in the reports. Compliment them based on performance noted in the reports.

Some salespeople don't submit route sheets and call reports when they contain negative information—for example, a week with few calls or few orders. Let them know that you both need records of disappointing as well as successful periods to help them improve future results.

Sales and Expense Reports

The customer analysis allows each salesperson and also the sales manager to compare this year's results to last year's, and then to use this information to prepare sales forecasts and evaluate performance. The customer analysis provides a basis for productive discussion between sales manager and sales force.

If you compensate salespeople with any form of commission, you must provide them with monthly information on invoices, and how you calculated the commission earned. Such statements can also compare commission earned and dollar product line sales for this month and year-to-date to previous year.

If your company reimburses salespeople for certain travel, telephone, entertainment, and clerical expenses, their expense reports will provide you with valuable information about their activities. In addition, you should receive and review all order copies, because in a small firm they provide the most immediate hard information on a sales force, its markets, and its results. Lastly, the product analysis presents total company cumulative orders, sales, or shipments in units and dollars totaled by product, style, model, or service compared to the previous year.

Customer Analysis. Route sheets and call reports ask the sales force to maintain and submit certain helpful information to management. For effective communication, management must also collect and submit to the sales force certain helpful information, such as sales reports. Many smaller businesses neglect to do this because of the cost and effort involved. It is easier to ask the sales force for reports if you are providing them with data in return.

Every month, or every three months, six months, or year, depending on the selling cycle, your accounting department should produce a customer analysis. The customer analysis shows shipments and/or orders, in units and dollars, for the period and year to date, by product/service, for each customer, organized by territory, and compared to the previous year. For example, if your company sold men's hosiery, and issued a quarterly customer analysis, the columns across the top would read:

MINNESOTA TERRITORY

CURRENT YEAR		PREVIOUS YEAR	
SHIPMENTS THIS QUARTER	SHIPMENTS YEAR TO DATE	SHIPMENTS THIS QUARTER	SHIPMENTS YEAR TO DATE
DOZENS DOLLARS	DOZENS DOLLARS	DOZENS DOLLARS	DOZENS DOLLARS

The columns down the side would read:

Nathan's Clothing Store
Style 112—Orlon Crew Sock
Style 845—Nylon Dress Hi Rise
Style 1050—Wool Anklet
   Total Store

Jack's Department Store
Style 1240—White Athletic Hose
Style 66—Cotton Dress Anklet
Style 99—Argyle Mid-Length
   Total Store

Every account in each salesperson's territory would be listed with total dozen and dollar sales accumulated for the entire territory.

For example, if your company sold printing, the customer analysis format might read:

NORTHWEST SIDE TERRITORY

	CURRENT YEAR		PREVIOUS YEAR	
	ORDERS THIS MONTH	ORDERS YEAR TO DATE	ORDERS THIS MONTH	ORDERS YEAR TO DATE
	UNITS DOLLARS	UNITS DOLLARS	UNITS DOLLARS	UNITS DOLLARS
Omaha Symphony Orchestra				
Programs				
Fund-Raising Brochures				
Annual Report				
Total Account				
Union Pacific Railroad				
Office Forms				
Employee Magazine				
Menus				
Total Account				

Each salesperson only receives the customer analysis for his or her territory. The sales manager receives the customer analysis for all territories. If possible, sales by model, style, product, or product group should also be totaled and compared for the entire territory.

The customer analysis allows each salesperson and also the sales manager to compare this year's results to last year's, and then to use this information to prepare sales forecasts and evaluate performance. The customer analysis provides a basis for productive discussion between sales manager and sales force. The sales manager might remark to the Ohio salesperson, "I see your sales are up in Northern Ohio but down elsewhere. How often do you travel to Cincinnati, Dayton, and Columbus?" The salesperson might reply, "I still travel there once a month, but unemployment continues high in Southern Ohio and business is weak."

When the salesperson calls on Nathan's Clothing Store, he or she can point out to the proprietor that their sales of crew socks this year are up, but nylon dress hose are down. When Jack's Department Store wants an off-price promotion on argyles, the salesperson can refer to the customer analysis for information on total unit purchases the previous year.

Capable salespeople thrive on this type of information. They want details of their performance, so they can set future goals to improve it. Similarly, capable sales management needs the information, so they can evaluate salespeople's performance and help them improve.

The customer analysis is as important to good sales management as the profit-and-loss statement is to good financial management. If you employ a data-processing service bureau to keep track of invoices and inventory, they can use the same information to print a customer analysis. If you use a billing machine or a small computer for processing invoices, it can be programmed to produce the customer analysis. In both cases, the additional cost is nominal compared to the valuable information created.

Commission Statements.   If you compensate salespeople with any form of commission, you must provide them with monthly information on invoices, and on how you calculated the commission earned. The commission statement should list invoice numbers and amounts, and applicable commission rates, arriving at the total commission earned.

Commission statements can also contain other useful information. They can compare commission earned and total dollar sales for this month and year-to-date to last year's figures. If easy to calculate, they can compare total dollar sales by product line for this month and year-to-date to last year's. All this information can be quickly accumulated through data-processing from the same invoices used to calculate commission earned.

For example, the mens' hosiery commission statement might include information on monthly and year-to-date dollar sales compared to the previous year for branded versus unbranded business; or for crew socks, athletic hose, and dress hose; or for department stores versus specialty stores. (See p. 130)

Page two of the commission statement would list all current-month invoices by number and date, showing the customer and dollar total, applicable commission rate, and resulting commission dollars due. (see p. 130)

Total dollars of sales and commissions on the second page must be reconciled with these same figures on the first page of each salesperson's commission statement.

MINNESOTA TERRITORY

	SHIPMENTS			COMMISSIONS		
	CURRENT MONTH	PREVIOUS TOTAL	YEAR TO DATE	CURRENT MONTH	PREVIOUS TOTAL	YEAR TO DATE
Branded:						
Department Stores						
Dress Hose						
Athletic						
Casual Hose						
Total Department Stores						
Branded:						
Specialty Stores						
Dress Hose						
Athletic Hose						
Casual Hose						
Total Specialty Stores						
Total Branded						
Unbranded						
Chain Stores						
Discount Stores						
Total Unbranded						
Grand Total Territory						

	PREVIOUS YEAR					
	SHIPMENTS			COMMISSIONS		
	CURRENT MONTH	PREVIOUS TOTAL	YEAR TO DATE	CURRENT MONTH	PREVIOUS TOTAL	YEAR TO DATE
Branded:						
Department Stores						
Dress Hose						
Athletic						
Casual Hose						
Total Department Stores						
Branded:						
Specialty Stores						
Dress Hose						
Athletic Hose						
Casual Hose						
Total Specialty Stores						
Total Branded						
Unbranded						
Chain Stores						
Discount Stores						
Total Unbranded						
Grand Total Territory						

| INVOICE # | DATE | CUSTOMER | DOLLAR AMOUNT | COMMISSION DUE | |
				RATE	DOLLAR
50026	11/4/84	Nathan's Clothing	$1,250	10%	$125.
55534	11/5/84	Jack's Dept. Store	$2,712	9%	$244.
55689	11/7/84	Peoples Discount	$4,509	8%	$360.
and so on.					

As another example, the printing company commission statement might include information on monthly and year-to-date dollar sales and commissions compared to the previous year for magazines, office forms, books, and annual reports.

NORTHWEST SIDE TERRITORY

| | SHIPMENTS | | | COMMISSIONS | | |
	CURRENT MONTH	PREVIOUS TOTAL	YEAR TO DATE	CURRENT MONTH	PREVIOUS TOTAL	YEAR TO DATE
Magazines						
Office Forms						
Books						
Annual Reports						
Other						
Total Territory						

PREVIOUS YEAR

| | SHIPMENTS | | | COMMISSIONS | | |
	CURRENT MONTH	PREVIOUS TOTAL	YEAR TO DATE	CURRENT MONTH	PREVIOUS TOTAL	YEAR TO DATE
Magazines						
Office Forms						
Books						
Annual Reports						
Other						
Total Territory						

PAGE 2.

| INVOICE # | DATE | CUSTOMER | DOLLARS | COMMISSION DUE | |
				RATE	DOLLARS
2260	10/6/84	Union Pacific	$8,460	5%	$423.
2316	10/10/84	Omaha Symphony	$4,612	5%	$230.
2409	10/15/84	Mutual Savings	$6,644	5%	$332.

Again, good salespeople thrive on comparative information, because they enjoy measuring themselves and planning for improvement. Good sales management thrives on comparative information as a means of measuring sales force performance, and as a basis for discussion with the sales force.

Expense Reports.   If your company reimburses salespeople for certain travel, telephone, entertainment, and clerical expenses, their expense reports will provide you with valuable information about their activities. Under such a plan, each week salespeople submit invoices or receipts for motel rooms, telephone calls, auto mileage, tolls, meals, airline tickets, and/or secretarial expenses. They record and total these items day by day on an expense report, along with the names of each city visited and each person entertained. Standard expense report forms are available at most office supply stores. The expense reports and receipts supplement information on the call reports, besides verifying expenditures and acting as a basis for cost control and reimbursement. In a smaller company, the sales manager should review all expense reports.

For example, by reviewing monthly long-distance telephone invoices, a sales manager knows what customers were called and how often. The telephone represents an important sales tool, and monthly bills reveal how effectively this sales tool is being utilized. Monthly telephone bills also reveal how often a salesperson called the factory, warehouse, or home office. An excess of such calls indicates a possible problem which may require your investigation.

Expense reports also quickly tell you how much time a salesperson devotes to each part of the territory. By reviewing a salesperson's expense reports for a six-month period, you can tabulate how many days he or she spent in each city.

Similarly, you can review which customers or prospects were entertained. Did the salesperson entertain the same purchasing agent, possibly a close personal friend, on each visit; or were different customers and prospects entertained?

Orders.   In a smaller company, the sales manager should receive and review copies of all orders; this is the moment of truth. Route sheets tell you what a salesperson intends to accomplish, call reports tell you about accomplishments, the customer analysis and commission statements summarize and compare results, and expense reports contain related cost information. However, orders provide the most immediate hard information on a sales force, its market, and its results.

By reviewing orders, a sales manager keeps his or her hand on the pulse of the business. For example, last week's call report from the Georgia salesperson promised a large order from a major customer in Macon, but it hasn't arrived yet. Such inconsistencies deserve an inquiry. Why does a large order from a small customer contain last year's prices? A large order from California calls for containers which may be in short supply, requiring a memo to the plant manager.

Orders indicate that one new product is selling more than all the other new products combined. This information should prompt a call to production control. This information should also cause the sales manager to question whether the sales force understands the other new products.

Customers in one territory submit orders directly to the company rather than through the salesperson. Is the salesperson actually calling on these customers? Are customers circumventing the salesperson because they don't care to deal with him or her?

Product Analysis.   As sales manager, you require certain sales information not necessarily produced by and/or shared directly with the sales force. On a weekly or monthly basis you need to know for the entire company cumulative orders, sales, or shipments in units and dollars totaled by product, style, model, or service compared to the previous year.

For example, the hosiery company product analysis might read:

	CURRENT YEAR SHIPMENTS				PREVIOUS YEAR SHIPMENTS			
	THIS MONTH		YEAR TO DATE		THIS MONTH		YEAR TO DATE	
	DOZENS	DOLLARS	DOZENS	DOLLARS	DOZENS	DOLLARS	DOZENS	DOLLARS
Style 112 Orlon Crew Sock								
Style 115 Cotton Athletic Sock								
Style 845 Nylon Dress Anklet								
Style 945 Nylon Dress Hi Rise								
Style 1050 Wool Dress Anklet								
Style 1150 Wool Dress High Rise								
Style 99 Argyle								
Style 250 Cotton Dress Anklet								
Style 350 Cotton Dress Hi Rise								
Total Company								

For example, the printing company product analysis might read:

	CURRENT YEAR ORDERS				PREVIOUS YEAR ORDERS			
	THIS MONTH		YEAR TO DATE		THIS MONTH		YEAR TO DATE	
	PIECES	DOLLARS	PIECES	DOLLARS	PIECES	DOLLARS	PIECES	DOLLARS
Programs								
Brochures								
Annual Reports								
Office Forms								
Magazines								
Menus								
Books								
Posters								
Letterheads								
Total Company								

Whether you require this information on orders, shipments, or both depends on your particular industry. Such comparative information on orders or shipments by product or service allows you to measure total company performance, spot trends, and forecast future sales. Why are total company orlon crew sock unit sales 10% less than last year, while wool anklets are 15% ahead? Why are dollar orders for annual reports down 20% this year, while orders for magazines have risen 14%? Did you change the commission rate on certain products? Did the company open a major new account or lose a major existing customer? Did you realign territory boundaries? Have you lost or gained any salespeople? What corrective action should you communicate to the sales force?

Sales Forecasts, Expense Budgets, Performance Appraisals

The next chapter deals in detail with sales forecasts, expense budgets, and performance appraisals. These three activities require the sales manager and each salesperson to (1) agree on future goals and a plan of action for reaching these objectives; and (2) compare actual performance to these plans/goals, suggesting corrective action when necessary. At least once a year, you meet with each salesperson to discuss future anticipated sales, plus the specific activities and costs necessary to generate these sales. At least once a year, you meet with each salesperson to discuss how actual sales, costs, and activities compared to the anticipated levels discussed at previous meetings. As you will observe in the next chapter, the sales forecast, expense budget, and performance appraisal process represents a critical means for communication between sales manager and sales force.

Phone Calls

Regular weekly or biweekly fifteen-minute telphone calls from the sales manager to the field people create a personal, inexpensive, effective means of communication. If the sales organization resides locally, a fifteen-minute personal meeting can replace the phone call. The time, day of the week, and length of conversation, whether in person or by phone, should be decided previously and adhered to.

Before the meeting or call, the sales manager should carefully prepare a list of items for discussion, including suggested action to improve results. Route sheets, call reports, customer analysis, commission statements, expense reports, orders, product analysis, sales forecasts, expense budgets, and performance appraisals all provide information that can become the basis for discussion. The sales manager might remark, "Gene, according to your call and expense reports, you visit Premier Hardware once a week, and take the buyer to lunch. Do you feel their volume or potential justifies that much attention?" Gene might reply, "Probably not." The sales manager would then respond, "I agree, so please concentrate more on Central Supply, which, according to your route sheets, is unhappy with their present vendor. I suggest you call on both Premier and Central twice a month. What is the buyer's name at Central?"

Or the sales manager might remark, "Alex, I see that Atlas Chemical did not order any dyes last week. Is there a problem?" Alex might reply, "Yes, the purchasing agent has been promoted and replaced by a trainee." The sales manager could respond, "That sounds like a potential problem, Alex. Please set up a date for you and me to visit the plant manager."

Or the sales manager might remark, "Amy, your commission statement shows a 20% improvement in shipments so far this year, and I see from the customer analysis that you have both opened new accounts and expanded existing ones. Keep up the great job."

Also, during the weekly discussions, the sales manager should listen to his or her people's needs and respond to them. If a salesperson reports that "deliveries arrive late," you should offer an explanation, or promise to follow up at the factory. If a salesperson requests your help in opening a "fat" prospect, make arrangements for an appointment with the buyer. If a salesperson has suddenly run out of catalogues, price lists, or order forms, immediately mail out the required material.

Bulletins and Letters

In communicating with the sales force, the telephone with its personal touch and human interaction generally proves more effective than an impersonal bulletin or letter. However, for efficiently communicating certain information applicable to the entire sales force, the sales manager needs to write bulletins. Such matters as price, policy, procedures, sales meetings, sales contests, product changes, and copies of advertisements, press releases or publicity can best be transmitted in a bulletin, so that all parties have a permanent copy.

Also, letters prove effective when you want to communicate certain types of information to one salesperson but still desire a permanent copy. For example, after a field visit, you may wish to summarize for future reference what action was agreed to—customers to be seen, programs to be offered, closing techniques to be used, and so on. Certainly when hiring a new salesperson, territory boundaries and compensation require a letter for future reference. Any disciplinary action also requires a letter.

Tapes, Manuals, and Catalogues

Information which does not require immediate response or feedback lends itself to communication using tapes, manuals, and catalogues. For example, detailed information on new products or selling techniques can be effectively communicated by tape. The sales manual permanently presents basic training material and thus becomes a salesperson's reference book. Catalogues keep salespeople informed on changing items such as price, colors, and construction.

Some companies send a half-hour tape to each salesperson once a month with suggestions for improving sales. The tapes carry the same initial message for everyone, but then present individual suggestions in the last ten minutes.

Generally, a new salesperson receives the field manual after his or her initial training. A manual might include subjects such as correct order-writing procedure, advertising and freight policy, company history and organization, and reporting requirements. You can add and delete information from the manual by sending the sales force new pages and asking them to destroy obsolete ones.

Generally, you issue a new catalogue when a selling season changes. Catalogues benefit both customers and salespeople. Often a catalogue shows a salesperson pictures of new products. A catalogue gives detailed product/service information on components, characteristics, variations, price, terms, availability, and benefits.

Controlling Paperwork and Communication

Reports can become so institutionalized, complex, and inflexible that they take on a life of their own. Instead of being a means of communication, the report becomes an end in itself. One report often generates another. The activity of writing and submitting a report can become more important than the proposed result of communication. Information and communication are not synonymous.

The format of route sheets, call reports, customer and product analysis, commission statements, expense reports, and bulletins should be reviewed once a year. Sometimes these reports can be made simpler, sometimes two reports can be combined into one.

Also once a year, the sales manager should examine all the reports which he or she receives and submits, and all the reports the sales force receives and submits. Who reads the report? How is the information used? Is the reason for creating the report still valid? Does the report help the salesperson and/or sales manager do a better job? Can the report be simplified or incorporated into another report? Based on the answers to these questions, you may wish to take action.

One notorious sales manager collected all these reports once a year and weighed them. If they weighed over three pounds, he began eliminating.

Regardless of the form—telephone calls, meetings, or reports—communication involves time and money. In some sales organizations, time and money are wasted on excessive, unnecessary communication. As sales manager you don't have to know everything a salesperson does, and they don't need to know all the information available to you. Routine matters do not require notification, but exceptions do.

For example, when a customer who normally orders monthly fails to do so, you need to ask the salesperson for an explanation. When a customer who normally orders monthly continues to do so, no communication on this matter is required.

SALES MEETINGS

Once or twice a year, resources permitting, a well-planned sales meeting can provide a productive format for communication, motivation and training. The basic purposes of a sales meeting are (1) continual training of sales personnel; (2) sharing of problems and successes by salespeople and management; (3) salespeople feeling part of something larger (belonging), and receiving recognition for achievements; (4) salespeople personally meeting management; (5) management disseminating policy to the sales force; (6) an opportunity for management to visit salespeople with minimum travel.

Contrary to popular belief, being a field salesperson is lonely and full of disappointments and rejections. The sales meeting helps to assure a salesperson that someone cares. He or she arrives dusty and tired from the commercial battlefield, and leaves refreshed, enthusiastic, vibrant, and ready for new challenges.

To justify the cost, time, and energy involved, the specific objectives of your sales meeting must be well thought out. Holding a meeting because you had one last year does not count as a justifiable objective. You need a more concrete reason. Decide in advance what you specifically hope to achieve, and then carefully plan toward those goals. The objectives might include introduction of a new product or service; alleviation of tensions between the sales force and management; explaining a sales contest, appraisal form, or new compensation plan; convincing the sales force you can stay in business; or analyzing competition.

Sometimes even with proper objectives, these functions become stale, tiresome, and monotonous. At that point everyone needs a rest. If you feel the meetings no longer achieve their goals, change the format, or stop convening them for a while.

Many sales managers have a strong dislike for sales meetings because the salespeople outnumber them, causing lack of control. Also, they must listen to salespeople's complaints and accept criticism in front of the entire group. A good sales manager, however, will be sensitive to complaints and criticisms, because they generally contain important messages. A properly managed sales meeting minimizes these problems, and should be not only productive but enjoyable for all those involved.

Introduction

The cost of a sales meeting can strain the budget of a growing business, so you should consider regional rather than national gatherings, not inviting all salespeople to each meeting, and choosing a location which offers reasonably priced accomodations. The frequency and length of sales meetings depends on how far apart your salespeople live.

Sales meetings consist of formal group meetings, formal individual meetings, informal social gatherings, and official social functions. Participants should receive an agenda before they arrive, so that everyone knows where to be, when to be there, and what material is going to be covered.

Sales meetings fail when administrative matters receive more time than selling matters, when one or several salespeople dominate the meeting, when trivial matters encroach on more important subjects, and when participants do not share a similar level of proficiency. Sales meetings can be made more interesting by having salespeople present certain subjects themselves, having competitors' products available for inspection, inviting a friendly customer to address the meeting, or by including a factory visit, skits, role-playing, films, video tapes, and brainstorming. Also, you should devote 30 minutes each day to a presentation and discussion of company functions outside of selling, and allow 30 minutes for any complaints or criticisms which involve company-wide issues.

At formal individual meetings you may share concerns which do not affect the entire group. Salespeople probably learn more from casual conversations with each other than in formal gatherings, and so you should allow opportunities for socializing. Official social gatherings include a dinner each evening which might involve a speech or award presentation.

Costs

The cost of ten or twenty people gathering together for two or three days has risen astronomically and can strain the sales budget of a growing business. You can reduce the travel expense of such a group through a series of regional meetings rather than one central gathering. Management can also lower costs by not inviting all salespeople to each meeting. For example, you can have two meetings annually, each with half the sales force, and each time a different mix of people. You might include more-experienced salespeople in one group and less-experienced in another.

The choice of city and meeting place also affects costs. It is less expensive for a Midwestern sales force to meet in a central location, such as Chicago, which is serviced by a reduced-fare airline such as Midway, than in Florida or California. It is less expensive to stay and dine at a suburban motel in Chicago than at a downtown hotel. Often, weekend hotel rates and Sunday return air fares can save the company money.

According to *Sales & Marketing Management** magazine's 1983 Survey of Selling Costs, the average per-person, per-diem cost of lodging, meals, and meeting rooms at a sales meeting is $111. This does not include transportation, guest speakers, or audio-visual aids. The cost varies from a high of $167 in New York City to a low of $82 in Milwaukee.

If the entire sales force resides within a few hours' drive of your office, the sales meetings can be held there, and attendees can return home the same evening. Lunch can be ordered in, and dinner arranged for at a local restaurant. Such a meeting would involve minimal costs.

Frequency

When the entire sales force resides locally and overnight accommodations are not necessary, meetings can be held more frequently, but for shorter periods of time. For example, meetings could be held on the first Saturday of every other month.

When the sales force resides plane trips apart, economics necessitate less frequent but longer meetings. In such instances, two- to three-day gatherings once or twice a year generally provide the best use of time and money.

---

*By permission from S&MM's 1983 Survey of Selling Costs. © 1983, Further reproduction is prohibited.

Annual or semiannual sales meetings which require several days should be scheduled during slack periods and/or at the start of a selling cycle. You don't want to remove a salesperson from his or her territory during a peak selling period. For example, many menswear manufacturers and book publishers schedule sales meetings in early December, because at this time retailers are too busy to see salespeople, and January begins a new wholesale selling season.

Format and Agenda

Regardless of cost, location, frequency, and length, sales meetings consist of formal group meetings, formal individual meetings, informal social gatherings, and official social functions. Participants should receive an agenda before they arrive, so that everyone knows where to be, when to be there, and what material is going to be covered. The agenda should state that once a formal group meeting begins, you will lock the doors until break time. This eliminates a tendency for people to straggle in later and interrupt the gathering. Actually, once you initiate the locked-door policy, no one arrives late.

A typical sales meeting agenda might read:

Friday December 3

    6:00   Cocktail hour in Suite 201.

    7:00   Dinner in private dining room B.

    8:30   Welcoming address by president.

Saturday December 4.   Suite 201*

    9:00–10:00   Discussion of new products, their prospective customers, and sales presentation. Sales manager.

    10:00–10:30   Credit information needed for new accounts. Credit manager.

    10:30–11:00   Break.

    11:00–12:00   Techniques for opening new accounts and overcoming objections. Salesperson. Presenting benefits. Salesperson.

    12:00–12:30   Discussion of complaints and criticisms.

    12:30–2:00   Lunch in main dining room.

    2:00–5:00   Individual meetings in Room 150. Schedule to be announced.

    6:00–7:00   Cocktail hour in Suite 201.

    7:00   Dinner in private dining room C.

    8:30   State-of-the-company address by president.

    9:00   Award presentations.

Sunday December 5.   Suite 201*

9:00–10:00	Competitive advantages of machines #72, #84, #96 presented by Forman, Rosenblatt, and Turner (salespeople).
10:00–10:30	Quality control. V.P. manufacturing.
10:30–11:00	Break.
11:00–12:00	Explanation of new sales contest. Sales manager.
12:00–12:30	Discussion of complaints and criticisms.
12:30–2:00	Lunch in main dining room.
2:00–5:00	Individual meetings in Room 150.
5:30	Bus to airport.

---

*The doors to Suite 201 will be locked from 9:00–10:30 and from 11:00–12:30, so be punctual.

Formal Group Meetings

Whether you conduct three-day sales meetings twice a year or one-day sales meetings six times a year, you should plan a session each morning from 9:00 to 10:30, with a 30-minute break, and then from 11:00 to 12:30 for all formal group matters. The company president should attend some of these formal group meetings.

In these sessions, management introduces and everyone discusses subjects such as new or problematic products, services, programs, company policies and organization, selling techniques, promotions, advertising, competition, sales contests, compensation plans, evaluation, forecast, and budget procedures. The subject matter must be applicable to the entire group, and capable of being meaningfully presented in the allotted time. For example, discussion of individual customers does not involve the entire group and would therefore not prove an appropriate subject. Likewise, selling in general represents too broad a topic, but selling benefits, or opening new accounts, or qualifying leads could be handled in 90 minutes.

Problem Areas.   Sales meetings fail when administrative matters receive more time than selling matters, when one or several salespeople dominate the meeting, when trivial matters encroach on more important subjects, and when participants do not share a similar level of proficiency. Do not devote more than 25% of a meeting to administrative matters such as proper order-writing, credit and collection, sales reports, expense reports, or putting enough postage on order envelopes.

Do not allow any salesperson, whether it be the superstar or a laggard, to turn your meeting into a personal speaking platform. Remind these people that you have scheduled individual meetings in the afternoon to discuss individual problems. Also, involve people who have not participated by asking them questions. You must run the meeting, and not let the meeting run you.

Do not let the discussion digress into unimportant aspects of important matters. When a salesperson notes that the welding seam in your new ultrasonic cleaning tank raises one-half inch rather than one-quarter, remind this person that the new tank degreases customer components at half the cost in half the time of any competitive product.

Group meetings can also lose their effectiveness unless all participants share a similar level of proficiency. Mixing the most experienced salepeople with the least experienced, training the strong performer with the weak, can dilute the results. For certain subjects, you may remedy this problem by forming subgroups at the sales meeting.

Making It Interesting. Sales meetings can be made more interesting by having salespeople present certain subjects themselves, by having competitor's products available for inspection, by inviting a friendly customer to address the meeting, or by including a factory visit, skits, role-playing, films, video tapes, and brainstorming. Also, you should devote 30 minutes each day to a presentation and discussion of company functions outside of selling, and allow 30 minutes for any complaints or criticisms which involve company-wide issues.

Since most salespeople are not classroom types, the best way to involve them and hold their attention is through individual participation. Therefore, certain portions of the program should include presentations by the salespeople themselves. The person who opened the most new accounts could have fifteen minutes on the agenda to share his or her techniques. Another salesperson might lead a discussion on phone solicitation. Product presentations can be organized so that different salespeople present different features and benefits. Be sure to review appropriate material with the salesperson before his or her presentation. Remember, salespeople learn best through provocative group discussion, through sharing problems and information, not through lecture-type presentations by management.

Having a competitor's product, product line, or service brochure at the meeting generates a lively and informative discussion. You might assign each salesperson one competitive product to analyze for the group. In such a discussion, be sure that the sales force understands both your competitive strengths and weaknesses. Just concentrating on strengths does not prepare a salesperson for the realities of the marketplace.

Inviting a friendly customer to address the meeting for 30 minutes on how he or she views your company, its products/services, and sales force can prove enlightening. You might then allow your salespeople to ask the customer questions. This approach allows salespeople to receive the customer's point of view.

Films, video tapes, and guest speakers discussing appropriate topics such as selling techniques, or good listening, or time management can spice up your meeting. Both Dartnell Publishing and Xerox Learning Systems offer films and video tapes. Most local telephone companies offer free guest speakers for sales meetings.

If you hold the sales meeting near your manufacturing facility, take the sales force on a plant tour and introduce them to key administrative people. A sales force finds selling a product easier if they understand something about manufacturing. Also, the order and billing people or customer-service people find it easier to deal with a sales force they have met.

Skits and role-playing which enact an "eyeball-to-eyeball" customer-salesperson interchange can prove a powerful learning technique at sales meetings. One salesperson takes the role of a customer, the other plays him or herself. Pick two people who will take the task seriously; and if they wish, allow them to rehearse. Use a tape recorder, and occasionally stop the action. Then during the playback ask for analysis and comments from the group.

With a group of senior salespeople, brainstorming can produce productive results. You see an unfilled need in the market place for a small nondestructive animal trap which can catch squirrels and other pests without injury but will not attract pets such as cats. You ask the sales force if they perceive the same need. If so, how would they design such a product, sell it, price it, and name it? Hopefully, out of the group discussion and interaction will emerge not only some creative ideas, but also a feeling of usefulness for the participants.

At each group meeting, devote 30 minutes to a presentation and discussion of company functions outside of selling. For example, allow the credit manager and/or vice president of manufacturing an opportunity to exchange information and problems with the people who sell the product. The credit manager might discuss information needed from the sales force to evaluate the financial status of a new account. Possibly the sales force might complain about its lack of information about existing accounts that pay late. Similarly, the vice president of manufacturing might talk about improved quality control, while the sales force might confront him about poor deliveries.

At the end of each formal group meeting, allow 30 minutes for any complaints or criticisms which involve company-wide issues such as late paychecks, poor deliveries, price increases, poor quality, lack of communication, return policy, or freight and advertising allowances. Complaints and criticisms which involve individual issues should be discussed later at the individual meetings. Individual issues would include such items as customer credit problems, territory boundaries, or handling of a particular account. Salespeople require a forum to express their frustrations, and if they know their "day in court" will arrive, the rest of the meeting proves more productive.

Listen to their complaints and criticisms. Answer them, disagree where appropriate, promise remedial action where appropriate. Salespeople represent your link to customers and the marketplace. They should understand why certain things can't be done, such as overnight shipments; and you should understand why certain things must be done, such as eliminating back orders.

Formal Individual Meetings

After the formal group meetings from 9:00 to 12:30 in the morning, followed by a brief lunch, salespeople and management should meet individually for an hour in the afternoon. Here you may share concerns which do not affect the entire group.

You may meet with the salesperson alone in your room or office, or also ask the president to attend. Have a list of items you wish to discuss, and don't let the meeting digress into trivia or small talk. These meetings represent an important opportunity for one-to-one interchange.

At such an individual meeting you may wish to discuss the change in personnel at a customer, or a prospect who requires a visit. You may have brought for discussion expense reports, call reports, or a customer analysis containing puzzling information. The salesperson may wish to discuss fears that competition has added more service people in the territory.

Do not use these individual conferences at sales meetings for formal compensation reviews or formal performance evaluations. Such procedures require more than an hour and considerable preparation, and they conflict with the learning/social atmosphere of a sales meeting. Compensation reviews and performance evaluations, discussed in a later chapter, deserve separate handling away from the sales meeting.

Informal Social Gatherings

Salespeople probably learn more from casual conversations with each other than in formal gatherings, and so afternoons (between formal individual meetings) and evenings should allow opportunites for socializing. When a group of salespeople get together, they do not discuss sports or politics; they discuss their jobs. "Who did you sell what, and how?" Although order sizes inflate by a third, the participants share valuable information. Maintaining a casual atmosphere even with tight scheduling promotes socializing.

Even in its most social moments, the gathering revolves around shoptalk, and for this reason, plus the additional costs involved, sales meetings work best without spouses. Also, some spouses resent and feel uncomfortable in the commercial atmosphere of a sales meeting.

Official Social Gatherings

Generally, at a multiday meeting, the participants arrive in time for an opening dinner at which acquaintances are renewed, management delivers a welcoming address, and everyone unwinds. During dinner on the second evening, the president presents a state-of-the-company address, and this becomes another opportunity for management and sales force to socialize. The state-of-the-company address allows some insight into the "big picture," enlightening the sales force about overall corporate performance and plans for the future.

A sales force which knows management on a personal basis becomes more involved. "I had dinner with the president of my company. He is a pleasant fellow, and certainly has his hands full." A management which knows the sales organization on a personal basis has more empathy. The company president might comment, "After spending several evenings with the sales force, I more fully appreciate their problems in reopening accounts we have lost because of late shipments. The sales force is a noisy bunch, but they work hard at a difficult job."

After dinner on the second evening, the company president presents awards for outstanding performance and prizes for sales contests. Outstanding performers should be officially recognized by management in front of their peers. If possible, have an employee take photographs of these events, and mail copies to the participants.

Summary

A successful sales meeting requires specific objectives, and attention to costs, location, frequency, and length. Sales meetings consist of formal group meetings, formal individual meetings, informal social gatherings, and official social functions. Sales meetings fail when administrative matters receive more time than selling matters, when one or several salespeople dominate the meeting, when trivial matters encroach on more important subjects, and when participants do not share a similar level of proficiency. Sales meetings can be made more interesting by having salespeople present certain subjects themselves, having competitors' products available for inspection, inviting friendly customers to address the meeting, or by including a factory visit, skits, role-playing, films, video tapes, and brainstorming. Salespeople probably learn more from casual conversations with each other than in formal gatherings, and so time should be allocated for socializing.

Hopefully, everyone returns home from the sales meeting with renewed vigor and pleasant feelings. The sales force has learned, participated, and enjoyed. The company has said "Thank you for doing a fine job" by attending to their needs and showing them a good time. A successful sales meeting strongly influences the salespeople's image of their company, which they pass on to your customers.

Even though larger competitors may offer superior advancement opportunities, greater compensation, and more comprehensive benefits, a smaller business can attract and retain effective salespeople through compassion and good communication. Many salespeople even prefer the flexibility and personal interaction of a smaller organization. The sales meeting is of particular importance, because it offers a prime, but often overlooked, opportunity for one-to-one human interaction between the sales organization and management.

7
Forecasts, Budgets, Appraisal, and Evaluation

Now that you have hired and trained capable salespeople, established equitable compensation, efficiently organized the sales force and territories, created proper motivation and communication, you are ready to engage in planning for and appraisal of your sales organization. A salesperson not only needs to plan each week with route sheets, and measure results with call reports and orders, but also, with management help, he or she needs to set sales objectives and expense goals for an entire season or year. Then, at the end of each season or year, management compares actual results to objectives/goals, and successful performers receive appropriate rewards.

The sum of these individual sales objectives, after certain adjustments by management, becomes the company sales forecast. The sum of these individual expense goals, after certain adjustments and additions, becomes the company sales expense budget, the selling cost necessary to generate the sales forecast.

Sales forecasts, expense budgets, and employee appraisals allow smaller firms to better utilize their limited human and financial resources, and to better compete with larger firms. An effective sales/marketing program starts with a financial plan and concludes with appraisal/evaluation of individual performance. Good management requires planning, and then comparisons of planned to actual results. Good salespeople expect to be given objectives and periodic appraisals.

A business of any size requires a sales forecast in order to schedule purchases, employment, and production; establish inventory levels; estimate cash receipts for paying bills; borrow money; set quotas; and evaluate individual performance. A business of any size requires a selling-expense budget in order to analyze the cost of obtaining sales; estimate cash disbursements for meeting payroll and payable obligations; borrow money; set individual cost goals; and evaluate individual performance.

A sales manager can best control a sales organization that embodies wide geographic dispersion with individual objectives and goals, because in such an organization each salesperson has different skill levels and faces unique problems and opportunities in territories which contain different sets of customers. However, such objectives and goals prove useless unless you periodically compare them to actual performance, and employ rewards or corrective action where necessary.

Forecasting, budgeting, objective-setting, appraising, and evaluating take place only once or twice a year. Therefore, these worthwhile processes do not require a great deal of your time.

Many smaller businesses prepare no sales forecast or expense budgets, and engage in no employee appraisal process. These companies are flying blind in a blizzard without aid of any navigational instruments. Many small-business sales managers dislike sales forecasts, expense budgets, and appraisals because they do not understand or mistrust the mechanics, and also they fear the results. When a sales manager's forecast or budget proves incorrect, it reflects on his or her ability and performance. When you evaluate the performance of one of your salespeople, you also evaluate your own; a salesperson's performance reflects your ability as a manager. A sales force is no better than its management. Many sales managers feel more comfortable avoiding these risks by not forecasting, budgeting, or appraising. Also, managers may feel uncomfortable criticizing a subordinate and handling the inevitable argument that follows.

SALES FORECASTS

Introduction

The sales forecast process involves asking each salesperson, agent, or distributor who sells your product or service to forecast sales in his or her territory. At the same time, you prepare a total company preliminary sales forecast. You and the sales force forecast orders by month or quarter for each customer or industry, and for each product/service/style, or product/service/style group. You may forecast by dollars or units or both.

Once your preliminary total company forecast is finished, you compare it to the sum of the preliminary individual territory forecasts prepared by each salesperson. You then discuss each individual territory forecast with the appropriate salesperson, suggesting and agreeing on certain changes. Finally, you combine the adjusted individual territorial and total company forecasts into a completed version. Next, you review the completed version with other members of management such as the company president, manufacturing manager, and controller/accountant.

In preparing your preliminary company-wide forecast, and in reviewing each salesperson's preliminary territorial forecast, you must take into account total company and each territory's past and present sales trends, along with sales trends by product or product line, customer or customer group, and geographic area. You may arrive at sales trends through moving or weighted averages, rate of change, or average change.

In preparing your preliminary company-wide forecast, and in reviewing each salesperson's preliminary territorial forecast, you also must evaluate the effect upon forecasted sales of anticipated changes in the company marketing plan, such as the addition or loss of a salesperson, changes in sales force remuneration, new products/services introduced, present products/services discontinued, price changes, advertising and packaging changes. Then you evaluate the effect on future forecasted sales of possible changes outside the company in the marketplace, such as loss of existing customers, addition of new customers, changes in customer purchasing personnel or policy or credit standing, and customer expansion or retrenchment plans. Also you evaluate the effect on future forecasted sales of possible competitor's price changes, new products, deletion of existing products, changes in sales personnel and policy.

You may also wish to analyze the total markets in which you sell. Is demand for your product/service increasing, decreasing, or remaining constant? What forces are at work changing the needs and wants that affect your markets and the way your product/service is bought?

Next, you evaluate the effect on future forecasted sales of appropriate changes in the general business environment as indicated by gross national product, housing starts, industrial output, plant utilization, unemployment, personal income, steel output, and/or retail sales. Last, you evaluate the effect on forecasted sales of special factors such as weather or legislation.

From all this input, you prepare a "worst and best case" forecast, stating the assumptions (What Ifs?) that influence results. No one best technique exists for forecasting sales, only the most appropriate for your company's circumstances. Once you have arrived at an annual sales forecast figure, you use these same techniques to distribute sales by month or quarter.

Obtaining the closest estimate of future sales from present knowledge represents the ultimate objective of your sales forecast. Each year, you compare actual results to forecast sales, evaluate how well you met that objective, and take corrective action where necessary. Each quarter, you review the sales forecast for future periods, and based on any new information make appropriate adjustments. Each month, you compare cumulative actual sales for each territory to forecast, analyze the reason for variances, and take corrective operational action.

Format

Thirty to sixty days before the start of your company's accounting year, send each salesperson, agent, or distributor who sells your product or service a forecast form for his or her territory. On this form you ask the sales force to forecast orders by month or quarter for each customer or industry, and/or for each product/service/style, or product/service/style group. You may ask for this information by dollars or units or both. Request information which the sales force finds easiest to work with and which proves most helpful in meeting the forecast's objectives. If the sales force thinks in terms of dollar sales per customer, and if the objective of your sales forecast is cash flow projections, not inventory control, then ask each salesperson to forecast dollar sales per appropriate period by customer, don't ask for unit sales by product/service.

If your firm takes orders for future rather than immediate delivery, then the salesperson must identify what months orders are to be shipped in. If 90% of all orders are shipped within 45 days, you can use a standard factor to translate orders into shipments. Similarly, you can translate any unit forecasts into dollars using standards or averages.

For example, the sales manager of a small ice cream manufacturer in Boston employs the following form:

DOLLAR SALES FORECAST BY QUARTER

	FIRST	SECOND	THIRD	FOURTH	TOTAL
Grocerty Stores					
Restaurants					
Drug Stores					
Vending Services					
Municipal					
Ball Parks					
Other					
Total					

On the other hand, the publisher of a monthly trade magazine asks sales representatives to submit the following unit product line information.

SPACE SALES FORECAST BY ISSUE, IN COLUMN INCHES

	JAN.	FEB.	MAR.	APR.	MAY	JUNE	JULY	AUG.	SEP.	OCT.	NOV.	DEC.	TOTAL
Classified													
Covers													
Page 1-20													
Page 21-40													
Page 41-60													
Total													

If your industry has selling seasons, as the apparel industry does, you may ask for a forecast by season rather than month or quarter. You may also ask salespeople to update their forecast each month or quarter, reflecting the changing dynamics of the marketplace.

In order to prepare these forecasts, the sales force needs the various reports on past actual performance discussed in Chap. 6 on "Communication and Control." If you wish monthly order forecasts in dollars and units by customer and product, then you must supply each salesperson with a customer analysis containing the actual information for previous years.

Process

At the same time as you ask the sales force to forecast orders by territory, you prepare a preliminary total company forecast using a similar format, whether it be units, dollars, customers, product lines, months, quarters, or seasons. Once your preliminary forecast is finished, you compare it to the sum of the preliminary individual territory forecasts prepared by each salesperson. You then discuss individual territory forecasts with the appropriate salesperson, suggesting and agreeing on certain changes. Finally, you combine the adjusted individual territorial and total company forecasts into a completed version.

In preparing your preliminary company-wide forecast, and in reviewing each salesperson's preliminary territorial forecast, you must take into account: past/present sales and trends; changes within the company such as a new product/service, increased prices, or the retirement of a salesperson; and changes outside the company such as the loss of a major customer, a new competitor, demand changes, or a recession.

Past/Present Sales and Trends.   Start your company-wide preliminary sales forecast by reviewing past and present actual sales and trends. To forecast accurately, you require access to appropriate historical information. If you are going to forecast orders by product or product line, or major service or major customer, in units or dollars, by month or quarter, you must begin by reviewing these same actual figures for this and past years. Do you expect orders to increase, decrease, or stay the same, and why? You may wish to analyze trends for total company sales, for product lines, or for customer groups. You may wish to use weighted or moving averages.

In preparing the preliminary 1983 company sales forecast for the Boston ice cream manufacturer, the sales manager relied on the historical information given in the table on p. 152.

First, the sales manager looked at average trends in the total annual sales figures. From 1979 to 1982 (three years) total company sales increased $550,000 (78%) from $700,000 to $1,250,000, an average of $183,333 or 26% annually. As note (1) indicates, higher prices per gallon accounted for 25% of this dollar increase. Therefore, average unit growth per year was about 18%. Assuming a 3% price increase per gallon in 1983, and projecting a continuation

ACTUAL DOLLAR SALES BY YEAR (IN THOUSANDS)[1]

	1982*	1981	1980	1979
Grocery Stores	$610	$580	$530	$480
Restaurants	161	168	160	75
Drug Stores	142	135	123	110
Vending Services	74	35	10	—
Municipal	112	112	38	—
Ball Parks	106	52	—	—
Other	45	43	39	35
Total	$1,250	$1,125	$900	$700

[1]Average selling price per gallon rose 10% in 1980 and 1981 and 5% in 1982.
*An estimate based on actual sales January–October 1982.

of the 1979–1982 18% unit growth rate, the sales manager forecasts a possible 21% dollar increase in 1983 sales from $1,250,000 to $1,512,000.

In forecasting 1984 sales, the sales manager might use a trend projection including 1979–1983 actual results, or he might delete 1979 and only continue with figures for the past four years. Averages computed by removing the oldest period and adding the newest are called moving averages.

Next, the sales manager examined the dollar and percentage increase in each year since 1979. In 1980, total dollar company sales increased $200,000 or 29%; in 1981, $225,000 or 25%; in 1982, $125,000 or 11%. Adjusted for inflation, the increase in average selling price, total unit sales rose 19% in 1980, 15% in 1981, and 6% in 1982. So although the unit growth rate after inflation has averaged 18% since 1979, year-to-year sales are growing at a rapidly decreasing rate. Assuming a 3% price increase per gallon in 1983, and projecting a continuation of the decreasing rate of unit growth, the sales manager forecasted a possible 1983 sales figure of $1,250,000, just equal to 1982. In such a forecast, the sales manager assigned more importance to the current 1982 results than to 1981 or 1980.

Finally, the sales manager examined the trends for each customer group. Since 1979, grocery store sales, which represented about half of 1982 total company volume, have shown virtually no unit growth, and dollar growth only equal to price increases. Restaurant sales, which represent 13% of 1982 total company volume, doubled in 1980, but have actually declined in units since then. Since 1979, drug store sales, which represented 11% of 1982 total company volume, have shown virtually no unit growth, and dollar growth only equal to price increases. Sales to vending machine operators started in 1980, tripled in 1981, doubled in 1982, and now represent 6% of total company dollar volume. Sales to municipalities started in 1980, almost tripled in 1981, but leveled off in 1982, and now represent 9% of total company dollar volume.

Sales to collegiate and professional baseball and football parks began in 1981, doubled in 1982, and now represent 8% of total company dollar volume. "Other" sales, which represented 4% of 1982 total company volume, have shown dollar growth only equal to price increases since 1979. Based on these customer group trends and a 3% price increase, the sales manager forecasts the following 1983 dollar sales: grocery, $620,000; restaurants, $160,000; drug, $150,000; vending, $110,000; municipal, $115,000; ball parks, $125,000; other, $45,000, for a total of $1,325,000.

Based on total company and customer group past and present sales trends, the sales manager has projected three different 1983 dollar sales forecasts: $1,512,000, $1,250,000, and $1,325,000. To determine which sales forecast, which trend projection, contains the highest probability of being achieved, the sales manager now must look at changes within the company and changes outside the company that will affect 1983 sales. These trend projections, whether weighted or moving averages, have established some probable limits for the sales forecast.

Changes Within the Company. Sales for any future period are not only affected by past and present trends, but by anticipated changes in your marketing plan. The ice cream company sales manager employs the following check list for noting anticipated marketing plan changes that might affect his sales forecast: addition or loss of a salesperson, changes in sales force remuneration, new products introduced, present products dropped, price changes, packaging changes, dollars of cooperative advertising.

In 1983 the sales manager anticipates hiring a new salesperson to specialize in vending services, using a distributor to service "other" accounts, replacing a weak salesperson, lowering draws but increasing commission rates, introducing several new dietary flavors and deleting several older nondietary ones, increasing prices 3%, adding a special dixie cup for vending services and a ten-gallon container for restaurants, and increasing cooperative advertising expenditures with drug and grocery stores from $25,000 to $30,000. Now the sales manager must evaluate the effect these anticipated changes can have on 1983 sales.

A new salesperson specializing in vending services should reinforce the past growth trend for that customer group and support the $110,000 forecast. Using a distributor to service "other" accounts should reduce selling expenses but have no effect on sales volume. Hopefully, replacing the weak salesperson will produce greater sales. Hopefully, higher commission rates will act as a stimulant for higher sales. The introduction of several new dietary flavors and the deletion of several older nondietary ones may increase sales in 1984 but should only offset each other in 1983. The effect of a 3% price increase should be nominal and not result in lower unit volume. The new dixie cup for vending companies should produce immediate increased volume for that customer group. The new ten-gallon container for restaurants will immediately sell well, but will primarily replace smaller-container sales. The $5,000 increase in cooperative advertising expenditures should allow the company to maintain its grocery and drug store market share in 1983, and possibly increase its market share in 1984. In evaluating the possible effects of these marketing plan changes, the sales manager feels most comfortable with a forecast between $1,325,000 and $1,512,000.

Changes Outside the Company. Sales for any future period are not only affected by past and present sales trends, and by your anticipated marketing plan changes, but also by changes outside the company in the marketplace, over which you have little control. Again, the ice cream company sales manager uses a check list for noting anticipated changes in the marketplace. The check list contains four main headings: customers, competitors, demand trends, and business environment. Subheadings under customers include loss of existing customers, addition of new customers, changes in purchasing personnel, policy changes, growth customers, and declining customers. Subheadings under competitors include price changes, addition of new products, deletion of existing products, changes in sales personnel, and changes in policy. Subheadings under demand trends include only total national ice cream consumption. Subheadings under business environment include changes in gross national product, local unemployment, local total employment, personal income, retail sales, and the weather.

In 1983 the sales manager anticipates that three restaurant customers will go out of business or become such poor credit risks that sales will have to cease. However, the addition of three new branches to an existing grocery store chain customer should more than offset this loss. The city purchasing agent at a major municipal customer will retire in 1983, and her replacement might ask for competitive bids on ice cream. Two of the vending service customers have just obtained major contracts for industrial lunchrooms which could generate more ice cream business.

In 1983 the sales manager anticipates that his two major competitors will raise prices 5%, making their products slightly more expensive than his. One competitor has licensed a celebrity name for a new higher-priced product line, which could have a negative impact on available shelf space and sales in grocery stores. The senior salesperson of another competitor plans to retire in 1983, which should open some doors for the sales manager's products. Another competitor has changed its terms from 2% 60 days to 2% 30 days, which might make some of its present customers receptive to a new vendor.

In 1983 the sales manager anticipates no unit increase in the total market for ice cream. According to trade association sources, national annual unit consumption of ice cream has remained virtually unchanged for the past three years.

In 1983 the sales manager anticipates a small increase in real gross national product, personal income, retail sales, and local employment, along with a slight decrease in local unemployment. This would reverse present negative trends in these indicators. The sales manager bases these opinions on material published by the Boston Chamber of Commerce, New England Business Association, Merchants National Bank, New England Electric, and articles in *The Wall Street Journal.* His boss, the company president, subscribes to an economic forecasting letter, avidly reads *Business Week,* and concurs with the sales manager's economic forecast.

A correlation exists between ice cream sales and summer temperatures. Generally, 40% of a year's sales occur in June, July, and August. During these months, hot weather can produce ten percent greater sales than cool weather. The National Weather Service's long-range forecast calls for a hot summer in New England.

Worst and Best Case. After considering past and present trends, anticipated changes inside the company, and possible changes in the marketplace, the sales manager decides to prepare a "What If?" or "worst and best case" forecast. If summer 1983 weather proves unusually hot, and the major competitor's senior salesperson retires, and the competition raises prices 5%, and a capable salesperson can be hired for vending services, and a strong salesperson can be hired to replace a present weak salesperson, then annual 1983 sales will be $1,512,000. If none of the above occurs, the sales manager forecasts 1983 sales at $1,325,000. If some of the above occurs, sales will fall between these two numbers. The sales manager decides to use the medium point of $1,420,000 as his preliminary sales forecast. As the year progresses and more of the "What Ifs?" become reality, the sales manager can make revisions to produce a more precise forecast. One small-company president humorously rated his sales manager high on producing accurate annual sales forecasts once the forecasted year's final quarter began.

Combining Sales Force and Management Preliminary Forecasts into One Final Forecast. You now compare your preliminary total company forecast to the sum of the sales force's, agents', or distributors' territorial forecasts. Are the two forecasts close? If not, why not? What assumptions have you made that the sales force has not? What information do they have available that you do not?

These questions are partially answered by comparing past and present sales trends in each territory and in the company to each territorial forecast. If sales for a territory have remained unchanged for two years, why does the salesperson forecast a 28% increase next year?

You should also review how anticipated changes in your marketing plan, and probable changes in the marketplace, will affect each specific territory. Do territorial forecasts reflect your plans to raise prices next year? Has your Omaha agent adjusted her forecast to reflect credit problems in that territory, and the possible loss of a major customer? Does the Minnesota forecast reflect the anticipated retirement of a competitive salesperson? Does the Washington State forecast reflect the depressed condition of the lumber and aerospace industry.? You should apply the same analytical techniques to each territory that you did to the total company forecast. Based on these techniques, you make adjustments, and once again compare your total company forecast to the sum of individual territory forecasts. Are the two forecasts close, or do they require further adjustment?

You then discuss each territorial forecast and your suggested changes with the responsible salesperson, agent, or distributor. You exchange information on how each of you has arrived at the figures, and then agree on a final forecast. These final individual territorial forecasts become the salesperson's objective or quota, which you use to measure, evaluate, and reward actual performance. To accept the sales forecast as a commitment, each salesperson must consider his or her forecast as a realistic, fair, and obtainable objective, which reflects the territorial potential. The sum of these final individual territorial forecasts should equal or exceed your final total company forecast.

Management Review

Because of the final forecast's corporate importance, you should quickly share this information with other management members. Arrange a meeting with the company president, controller, and manufacturing manager to discuss the numbers.

The manufacturing manager might feel he cannot hire enough skilled hourly people to produce the goods required by the sales forecast. He may suggest subcontracting certain work. On the other hand, the forecast might indicate an underutilization of manufacturing, in which case he may wish to solicit subcontract work from another firm.

Based on your forecast, the controller may immediately sense a need to decrease inventories or increase available bank credit. With your sales forecast, the controller can begin a cash flow projection and profit forecast for the next year.

The president may not accept the forecast as realistic, or as meeting long-range goals, or short-term profit requirements, in which case further adjustments may be necessary. He or she may also ask you to verify certain information by calling key customers.

Evaluation of Sales Forecast

Obtaining the best estimate of future sales from present knowledge represents the ultimate objective of your sales forecast. Each year, you must compare actual results to forecast sales and evaluate how well you met that objective. Was your forecast correct in units, but wrong in dollars? Correct in the direction of sales, but wrong in magnitude of that direction? Accurate for one product line or customer group, but inaccurate for another? Analyze the reasons for these variances, and take appropriate corrective action on your next forecast. Possibly you should put less emphasis on general economic indicators and sales trends, and more emphasis on changes in industry demand, pricing, new accounts, and competitors' new products.

In addition, each month, you compare cumulative actual sales for each territory to forecast, analyze the reasons for variances, and take corrective operational action. If the Ohio salesperson forecast $100,000 of sales in the first quarter but only booked $75,000, you would call to discuss the matter. Possibly you need to visit a major customer in Cleveland, which has given more business to competition, or the salesperson needs to travel more, or a major account is having credit problems. If the Minnesota salesperson forecast $225,000 of sales in the first nine months but only produced $150,000, possibly his draw should be lowered or he should be replaced.

Each quarter, you review the sales forecast for future periods, and based on any new information "What Ifs?" make appropriate adjustments. For example, if a large customer unexpectedly goes out of business in the second quarter, the third- and fourth-quarter forecasts require adjustment.

Summary

The sales forecast process involves asking each salesperson, agent, or distributor who sells your product or service to forecast sales in his or her territory. At the same time, you prepare a total company preliminary sales forecast. In preparing your preliminary company-wide forecast and in reviewing each salesperson's preliminary territorial forecast, you must consider past and present sales trends, anticipated changes in your company's marketing plan, and possible changes outside the company in the marketplace.

From all this input, you prepare a "worst and best case" forecast and present it to the company president, controller, and manufacturing manager. Obtaining the closest estimate of future sales from present knowledge represents the ultimate objective of your sales forecast.

SALES EXPENSE BUDGETS

Introduction

At the same time as you forecast sales, you must budget the cost of obtaining those sales. For a company to be profitable, selling expenses must be maintained at a certain percentage of total sales.

Selling expenses can be grouped into fixed costs which do not vary directly with sales volume and cannot easily be changed; variable costs, which do vary directly with sales volume; and discretionary costs, which management has the ability to change on a short-term basis. Fixed expenses include such items as salaries, payroll taxes, group insurance, rent, and utilities. Variable expenses include such items as commissions, bonuses, and royalties. Discretionary expenses include such items as travel, entertainment, telephone, and advertising. Although it is easier to budget fixed costs than variable or discretionary ones, all expense budgeting requires assumptions, judgment, and planning.

The budget process requires accumulating as much detail as possible on anticipated monthly expenses from the sources of those expenses, whether they be the sales manager, the sales force, or the sales forecast. Each category in the expense budget requires testing against the previous year's actuals, and as a percentage of forecasted sales.

The total sales-expense budget requires review and approval by the controller/accountant and company president. The president decides whether your expense budget realistically satisfies the requirements of the company cash flow projection and profit forecast.

Obtaining the most realistic estimate of future selling expenses necessary to profitably generate forecasted sales represents an important budget objective. At year end, that year's budget should be compared to actual expenses; variances noted, accuracy evaluated, and corrective action taken on the next budget. In addition, each month, you compare cumulative actual selling expenses to budget, analyze the reason for variances, and when necessary, take corrective action. Each quarter, you review the budget for future periods, and based on any new information, make appropriate adjustments.

Sales forecasts and expense budgets by territory allow you to prepare territorial profit-and-loss and break-even analyses. You can then compare dollar pretax profits or margins, and their percentage relationships to sales among the various territories. Territorial profit-and-loss and break-even-point analyses allow you to calculate the estimated effect on dollar margins of certain corrective action.

Preparing sales forecasts and expense budgets forces the sales manager and the salespeople to plan the action which influences sales and expenses. These plans become objectives against which actual performance can be measured and controlled.

Format

At the same time as you forecast sales, you must budget the cost of obtaining those sales. For a company to operate profitably, dollars of selling expenses must be maintained at a certain percentage of total sales. In the 1970s, a citizen band radio manufacturer doubled its sales each year until management declared voluntary bankruptcy. Each year, the cost of selling the product unexpectedly increased as a percentage of total sales. Each year, the company lost money, and to remedy this, management promised to lower selling expense as a percentage of sales. However, they never prepared an expense budget to use as a plan for lowering those costs.

Had management prepared an expense budget, it might have looked like this:

CITIZEN BAND RADIO MONTHLY SELLING EXPENSE BUDGET ($000)

	JAN.	FEB.	MAR.	APR.	MAY	JUNE	JULY	AUG.	SEP.	OCT.	NOV.	DEC.	TOTAL
Sales Management Salaries													
Office Salaries													
Salespeople:													
Salaries													
Commissions													
Bonuses													
Total Compensation													
Payroll Taxes													
Group Insurance													
Royalties													
West Coast Warehouse													
Coop Advertising													
National Advertising													
Store Displays													
Telephone													
Travel													
Entertainment													
Rent & Utilities													
Postage													
Other													
Total													

Budgeting fixed costs such as salaries, group insurance, and rent proves much easier than budgeting variable expenses that depend on sales volume, such as commissions, bonuses and royalties; or discretionary expenses, such as advertising, telephone, travel, and entertainment, which offer a wide variety of choices. However, all expense budgeting requires certain assumptions, judgment, and planning.

Sales Force Discretionary Expense

Thirty to sixty days before the start of your company's accounting year, ask each salesperson, agent, or distributor to prepare a monthly budget for whatever discretionary reimbursable expenses he or she will incur. If you use straight commission to compensate the sales force and do not reimburse expenses, you do not need this information. However, a company which does reimburse expenses should ask the sales force for a monthly telephone, travel, and entertainment budget, including detailed information on lodging, food, transportation, and planned itineraries.

Once received, you compare each of these territorial budgets to the previous year's and this year's actual territorial expenses/sales, and also next year's territorial sales forecast. Why does the Denver salesperson budget a 50% increase in expenses but no increase in forecasted sales? Why does the Minneapolis agent budget expenses at 3% of next year's forecasted sales, when the actual for last year's expenses totaled only 2% of sales? Why does the New York City distributor budget lower expenses but forecast higher sales for next year? You should discuss this type of question with the sales force, reaching agreement and making adjustments where necessary.

Each salesperson must accept his or her final expense budget as a realistic, fair, and obtainable objective and commitment. You use these territorial expense budgets to help plan, control, measure, evaluate, and reward actual performance. As mentioned in the chapter on Compensation, some firms pay bonuses to salespeople whose expenses do not exceed budget. The sum of these adjusted territorial expense budgets becomes part of the total company budget.

Fixed Expenses

Next, start accumulating monthly figures for budgeted fixed costs, such as salaries, group insurance, payroll taxes, and rent. Prepare a worksheet listing yourself and all salaried personnel who report to you. By each name and under the appropriate month, place a figure equal to the budgeted monthly gross salary, taking into account any anticipated raises, retirements, replacements, or additions. Various sums of these figures then become monthly totals for the company expense budget. Compare these totals to the previous year's actual expenses and next year's forecasted sales. Have they risen in dollars and as a percentage of sales? Are the increases justified?

Next, ask the controller or accountant to provide you with budget figures for group insurance and payroll taxes. He or she will ask for a schedule of your personnel and their anticipated compensation. Again, compare total budgeted group insurance and payroll tax figures to the previous year's actuals, and calculate what percentage of total compensation and sales they represent. Be sure you understand the reasons for variances.

If you rent space for sales offices, review the leases and add to the budget appropriate monthly figures for next year's rental and utility expenses. If you share rented or owned space with other company functions, such as manufacturing or administration or research, ask the controller or accountant to allocate a portion of anticipated, appropriate monthly expenses to selling. Compare total budgeted rental/utility expenses to the previous year's actuals and calculate what percentage they represent of total sales. Ask questions, and where appropriate, make changes.

Variable Expenses

Next, calculate monthly figures for variable expenses which are a function of sales. Based on the final monthly sales forecast by territory, calculate each salesperson's commission and/or bonus due (if any). Then place the total figure in the company budget. Based on the final monthly total company sales forecast, calculate your bonus and any royalty due, and place this figure in the company budget. Again, compare these figures to the previous year's actuals and calculate their percentage relationship to sales. Have budgeted commissions and bonuses risen as a percent of forecasted sales, because of a change in the compensation plan, because of an anticipated change in product mix, or because changes in territory boundaries have caused a redistribution of sales among salespeople?

Management Discretionary Expenses

Finally, you should accumulate monthly figures for remaining discretionary expenses such as travel, entertainment, telephone, and advertising. Prepare a monthly travel and entertainment expense budget for yourself using the same format previously suggested for the sales force. To arrive at a company total for this category, add your figures plus all other management sales-related travel and entertainment expense to the numbers, if any, submitted by the sales force.

Using last year's actual figures, plus adjustments for rate increases and possible changes in anticipated activity, budget the sales office and your business-related personal telephone expenses. Add this figure to the total of sales force reimbursed telephone expenses, if any, and arrive at a monthly total company budget for this category.

Prepare a monthly worksheet listing the various categories of sales-related advertising activity engaged in by your company. This might include trade, consumer, cooperative, classified, employment, institutional, newspaper, or magazine advertising; plus displays, press releases, premiums, and samples; or none of the above. Next to each category of advertising, budget the anticipated monthly expense. Then justify these figures with a more detailed plan. In what newspaper or magazine do you plan to run how many column inches of cooperative, consumer, trade, or classified advertising? What product, service, or employment will the ad feature? Which customers require how much cooperative advertising? What will each ad cost? In what months do you plan to purchase which displays, send out press releases, or give away samples; and how much will this cost?

The total of these figures becomes your monthly and annual advertising budget, which you then compare to the previous year's actual, and also calculate its percentage relationship to sales. Are you planning to spend more on advertising next year than last? Is it a higher percentage of sales? Do increased advertising expenditures result in increased sales? The budget becomes your advertising plan, and creates questions which you must answer.

Totals

Finally, you total all the sales-expense categories by month and for the year, then compare these totals to the previous year's actuals. You also calculate the percentage relationship of these budgeted expense totals to forecasted total company sales, and compare this percentage to actual past percentage figures. Negative variances require questions and answers.

Management Review

Because the selling-expense budget totals many dollars and represents a significant percentage of sales, you should share this information with the company president and accountant or controller. The controller/accountant needs these figures for next year's cash flow projection and profit forecast. The president may not accept your budget as realistic or as meeting profit requirements, in which case further adjustments could be necessary. The president may feel that continued growth requires more travel and advertising, or that the entertainment budget does not seem realistic, or that total budgeted selling expenses are too high a percentage of forecasted sales.

Both the sales forecast and selling-expense budget become part of a larger plan, the cash flow projection and profit forecast. The president decides whether your figures realistically satisfy the requirements of that larger plan.

Evaluation of the Sales Budget

Obtaining the most realistic estimate of future selling expenses necessary to profitably generate forecasted sales represents an important objective of the budget. At the end of each accounting year, you compare actual expenses to budget, and evaluate how well you have met that objective. Were actual selling expenses above or below budget because actual sales were above or below forecast? Did advertising expenses exceed budget because a new customer unexpectedly demanded a cooperative ad? Did higher than budgeted travel expense result from an unexpected trip to hire a new salesperson? Analyze the reasons for the variances and take appropriate corrective action in your next budget.

Each month, you should compare cumulative actual selling expenses to budget, analyze the reasons for variances, and take corrective action. If the Ohio salesperson budgeted $500 monthly for reimbursed travel expenses, but after five months has submitted receipts for $4,000, a telephone call is required to find out why. You may have him reduce traveling for two months unless his sales are ahead of forecast, justifying the budget overrun. After six months, telephone expenses may be several thousand dollars over budget because of either personal use or more business activity. You need to find out which.

Each quarter, you should review the budget for future periods and, based on any new information, make appropriate adjustments. For example, if a salesperson unexpectedly resigns in the second quarter, and you decide not to immediately seek a replacement, the third and fourth-quarter budgets require adjustment.

TERRITORIAL PROFIT-AND-LOSS PROJECTION

Sales forecasts and selective expense budgets by territory produce information allowing you to prepare a territorial profit-and-loss projection. You have already reached an agreement with each salesperson on his or her sales forecast and, if appropriate, his or her reimbursed-expense budget. By deducting from the territorial sales forecast all selling expenses directly applicable to that particular territory, the projected costs of manufacturing the goods, and an allocation for general, selling, interest, and administrative expenses, you arrive at various margin figures, which you may relate to the territory's sales as a percentage, and then compare both the dollar and percentage margins between territories.

Starting with the sales forecast, you deduct all selling expenses directly applicable to that particular territory, such as a salesperson's compensation, payroll taxes, fringe benefits, travel, entertainment, phone, and rent costs; plus bad debt, freight, terms, discounts, and advertising (such as cooperative) directly related to customers in that territory. This calculation produces a margin figure which you may relate to the territory's sales as a percentage, and then compare both the dollar and percentage margins of various territories. For example, if the sales forecast for a territory is $400,000, and the direct selling expense budget (as outlined above) totals $45,000, the resulting margin would be $355,000, and the resulting margin percentage would be $355,000/$400,000, or 88.75%.

You then deduct the projected cost of manufacturing the goods or producing the services being sold. Here you must rely on average costs or percentages for the entire company or product/service groups, a figure available from the accountant/controller. You also deduct any royalties due.

For example, if the projected manufacturing costs average 65% of each sales dollar, you would multiply 65% times $400,000 of forecast sales and get a result of $260,000. Subtracting the $260,000 from the previous margin of $355,000 produces a contribution of $95,000 toward the remaining selling, administrative, general, and interest expenses which cannot be identified with a specific territory, and profit. This contribution can be compared in dollars, and/or as a percentage of sales between territories. The $95,000 in our example, which represents 23.75% of sales, could be compared to another territory with $460,000 of sales and a $120,000, or 26% contribution; or one with $300,000 of sales and a $75,000, or 25%, contribution. You might set 18% as the minimum acceptable percentage contribution from a territory. Any territory with less than an 18% contribution would indicate a need for corrective action, such as different salesperson compensation, a change in territory boundaries, less advertising, or fewer discounts.

A further refinement of the territory profit-and-loss projection involves allocating the remaining selling, general, interest, and administrative expenses between territories on a percentage-of-sales basis. For example, if company sales total $2,000,000, and the remaining selling, general, interest, and administrative expenses total $300,000, or 15% of sales, you would allocate 15% of each territory's sales to its selling, general, interest, and administrative expenses. A territory with $400,000 in sales and a $95,000 contribution to selling, general, and administrative expense would receive an allocation of 15% times $400,000, or $60,000, leaving a projected pretax profit margin of $35,000 or 8.75% of sales. You then compare projected pretax profit dollars and margins for various territories, and take corrective action where goals are not met. At year end, actual territorial contributions to selling, general, and administrative expenses or actual territorial pretax profit margins should be compared to the projection and to other territories, and corrective action taken where necessary.

Territorial Break-even-Point Analysis

Using the territorial profit-and-loss projection might reveal unprofitable territories. By using these same techniques, you can forecast what level of sales and direct selling expenses will produce a break-even point, or restore an acceptable level of pretax margin, or acceptable level of contribution to selling, general, and administrative expenses.

For example, a territory with $200,000 of sales, $45,000 of direct selling expenses, a 15% general, selling, and administrative allocation, and a 65% cost of producing the product or service would show a $5,000 pretax loss. By using these territorial profit-and-loss projection techniques, you can calculate the performance necessary to break even: increase annual sales $30,000, or 15%; or reduce annual direct selling expenses $5,000, or 11%. More specifically, you might calculate a necessary monthly sales increase of $2,500, or a certain number of additional units; or a weekly increase of $577, or a certain number of additional units. You might decide to lower the salesperson's salary and travel expense $1,500 each, and cooperative advertising $2,000. You also might decide on a combination of lower expenses and higher sales to reach the break-even point.

You perform this same type of exercise to arrive at the action necessary to earn a certain pretax territorial profit, for example 10% of sales or $20,000. In this case, the salesperson must lower expenses by $25,000, increase sales by $150,000, or some combination of the two. Again, specific action can be planned to produce these dollar changes.

Summary

At the same time as you forecast sales, you must budget the cost of obtaining those sales. Selling expenses can be grouped into fixed expenses such as salaries, payroll taxes, group insurance, rent, and utilities; variable expenses such as commissions, bonuses, and royalties; and discretionary expenses such as travel, entertainment, telephone, and advertising. The budget process requires accumulating as much detail as possible on anticipated monthly expenses from the sources of those expenses. Each category in the expense budget requires testing against previous year's actuals, and as a percentage of forecasted sales. The total budget requires review and approval by the company president and controller/accountant. Obtaining the most realistic estimate of future selling expenses necessary to profitably generate forecasted sales represents an important budget objective. Sales forecasts and expense budgets by territory allow you to prepare territorial profit-and-loss and break-even analyses.

PERFORMANCE APPRAISAL AND EVALUATION

Periodic performance appraisals and evaluations represent an important vehicle for communication with and motivation of the sales force. They inform the salesperson what performance standards you expect; whether these standards are being met; and if not, what corrective action is necessary. The salespeople have a need and a right to know what you think of their work. Performance appraisals help the sales manager and salesperson develop an effective working relationship. Recognition of positive performance motivates a salesperson to do even better, and anticipation of such recognition stimulates self-motivation. The evaluation process involves (1) deciding what you wish to appraise; (2) developing individual performance objectives and measurements for each salesperson; (3) observing, rating, and evaluating actual performance; and (4) sharing the evaluation with the appropriate salesperson. Most important, using the appraisal form, ratings and discussion, you agree on future objectives, and obtain a commitment from the salesperson to a plan and time frame for achieving these goals.

Introduction

You decide what you wish to appraise by reviewing the salesperson's job description and training program, and then determining what characteristics, knowledge, skills, and results are critical to the successful performance of a salesperson in your particular company. The appraisal list would contain ten major categories: sales results, sales quality, selling skills, job knowledge, self-organization, paperwork, expense control, customer relations, company relations, and personal characteristics.

The territorial forecast and budget become the salesperson's sales-results and expense-control objectives or quotas. Many firms include a bonus in their compensation plan for attaining certain objectives such as certain percentages of forecasted sales and budgeted expenses. Now you review the remaining activities on your evaluation check list, and select those which represent the most critical areas for each salesperson. In order to define expected results, and set objectives, you need to define valid methods for counting, measuring, or describing them.

Once you have decided what to appraise and have developed some individual performance objectives and measurements, you must establish a meaningful rating system. Some firms use numbers, some letters, some grades, and some arrows. You should select a rating system most appropriate to your particular sales organization—a rating system which accomplishes your desired results in the simplest, easiest, fairest manner. Overly complicated rating systems prove hard to administer and understand.

The ultimate effectiveness of the appraisal process depends on how you prepare for, organize, and conduct the appraisal interview. You should conduct performance reviews and evaluations once or twice a year. Several months before the interviews, explain the entire evaluation process in a comprehensive memo or at a sales meeting. At the interview, review each section of the appraisal form, asking for the salesperson's assessment and giving yours. Explain your ratings, justify them; but don't argue, complain, threaten, or lose your temper. Using the appraisal form, ratings, and discussion, agree on future objectives; and obtain a commitment from the salesperson to a plan and time frame for achieving these goals.

Often sales managers would rather complain about a salesperson than analyze the underlying problems and attempt to solve them through a formal evaluation process. The salesperson who started out well but has gone downhill and has to be dismissed often might have been rehabilitated along the way through performance evaluations. You have spent a great deal of time, energy, and money hiring, training, compensating, organizing, and motivating the sales force. It only makes sense to finish the process and ensure success with periodic performance evaluations. You can't afford to waste your most important resource, people.

What to Appraise

The evaluation process starts by deciding what you wish to appraise. Prepare a list of activities, characteristics, knowledge, skills, and results critical to the successful performance of a salesperson in your particular company. Start by reviewing the job description used to hire each salesperson; the job description lists a salesperson's anticipated duties. Next, review the format of your training program, which lists the skills and knowledge necessary for success. Then add any other items not mentioned in the job description or training format, but important for effective performance.

Divide the appraisal list into ten major categories: sales results, sales quality, selling skills, job knowledge, self-organization, paperwork, expense control, customer relations, company relations, and personal characteristics. Whether your sales force sells soft goods or durables, products or services, to consumer or industrial or government users, these ten categories should prove helpful in deciding what to evaluate.

Sales results would include such items as total dollar and unit sales volume; sales volume as a percentage of quota or forecast; number of new accounts opened; number of existing customers lost; total number of active accounts;

average number of calls per week on present customers and prospects. Did total sales, total number of customers, total calls grow or decline, and how does this compare to the forecast?

Sales quality would include such items as dollar and unit sales by product or service group, area coverage, credit losses, and territorial gross margin. Did the salesperson sell the entire range of products/services or just a few? Did he or she concentrate on selling the least expensive and/or the least profitable? Did the Ohio salesperson saturate the Cleveland market but neglect Dayton, Columbus, and Cincinnati? How many new and existing accounts pay slowly?

Selling skills would include such items as finding prospects, creating empathy, presenting benefits, answering objections, closing, and using sales aids. You base these evaluations on observations made during field sales visits. Hopefully, you spend at least several days a year with each salesperson, and part of that time is spent observing the salesperson relating to customers and prospects.

Job knowledge would include a knowledge of your company, competition, competitive advantage, product/service features and applications, market and industry information. You base these evaluations on observations made during field visits, plus information exchanged in call reports, phone calls, and meetings. During a customer visit, could the salesperson answer questions on product performance, competitive pricing, industry sales trends, or new applications? Did the salesperson know the buyer's name at all customers and major prospects?

Self-organization would include efficient use of time in traveling the territory, keeping accurate records on customers, setting up appointments, planning each day and week, planning each presentation, keeping samples and sales literature neat. Does the salesperson call on clusters of customers, or spend many hours driving between calls? On Monday morning does he or she call ahead for Friday appointments? Does the salesperson have an objective for each sales call, and know what happened on the last visit? Again, you base these evaluations on observations made during field visits plus information obtained from route sheets, call reports, phone calls, and meetings.

Paperwork refers to promptly submitting accurate route sheets, call reports, expense accounts, customer credit information, requests for advertising material, requests for return permission, and any other required written material. A salesperson who submits call reports once a month when you require them once a week, or submits requests for advertising material after the customer has run an unauthorized ad would not rate well in this category.

Expense control refers to a salesperson maintaining reimbursable travel/ entertainment costs, plus customer terms, discounts, promotions, frieight and advertising allowances at an agreed-upon budgeted level. If a salesperson's reimbursed annual travel expense is budgeted at $10,000 but actually amounts to $15,000, or if annual territorial cooperative advertising and freight allowances are budgeted at $7,000 but actually amount to $10,000, the salesperson probably would receive a negative evaluation in this category.

You may wish to carry the sales quality and expense control evaluation one step further by evaluating territorial profits. Using the territorial profit-and-loss analysis discussed previously, you can rate each salespersons's profitability in total dollars and as a percentage of sales.

Customer relations include such items as solving customer problems, providing technical knowledge, merchandising skills, stock counting, and delivery follow-up. Does the salesperson call on customers frequently, provide necessary service and assistance, and develop positive relationships with customer personnel? A salesperson who only visits customers when he or she can write an order would rank poorly here.

Company relations involve abiding by company policies and procedures and cooperating with other company personnel. If company policy requests salespeople not to call the sales manager more than once a week collect, yet one salesperson calls every other day, this would affect his or her rating. The salesperson who annoys fellow workers as a "know-it-all," or yells at your secretary about late deliveries would not rate well in company relations.

Personal characteristics would include such items as enthusiasm, self-confidence, aggressiveness, drive, flexibility, persistence, judgment, stability, dependability, imagination, initiative, and appearance. The salesperson who fights any change in products, services, prices, procedures, or personnel would not be considered flexible. The salesperson you must remind for six months to call on a specific prospect would rank poorly in initiative.

Developing Performance Objectives and Measurements

Let us assume that you have decided to appraise the following activities for your salespeople's performance evaluation:

Sales Results
    Dollar sales volume
    Unit sales volume
    Percent of quota
    New accounts opened
    Existing customers lost
    Total active accounts
    Average number of calls per week on present customers/prospects

Sales Quality
    Dollar sales by product line

Unit sales by product line
Area coverage
Credit losses
Gross margin

Selling Skills
Prospecting
Empathy
Presenting benefits
Handling objections
Use of sales aids
Closing

Knowledge Of
Product features
Applications
Customers
Prospects
Market
Industry
Competition
Competitive advantage

Self-Organization
Traveling
Records
Planning
Samples and sales literature

Paperwork
Route sheets
Call reports
Expense reports
Credit reports
Return requests
Advertising requests

Expenses
Travel and entertainment
Freight and advertising allowances
Terms and discounts
Promotions

Customer Relations
   Frequency of visits
   Service and assistance
   Personal relationships

Company Relations
   Policies
   Personal relationships

Personal Characteristics
   Enthusiasm
   Self-confidence
   Aggressiveness
   Drive
   Flexibility
   Persistence
   Judgment
   Stability
   Dependability
   Imagination
   Initiative
   Appearance

Now you select specific objectives to fit the needs of each individual salesperson and territory. You have already reached an agreement with each salesperson on his or her forecasted total dollar, unit, and product line sales and on his or her budgeted expenses. The territorial forecast and budget become the salesperson's sales and expense objectives or quotas.

Bonus and Quotas.   Objectives can become quotas which then serve as a basis for both compensation and evaluation. Many companies include a bonus in their compensation plan as an incentive to attain objectives such as certain percentages of forecasted sales and budgeted expenses. For example, the bonus starts when actual sales reach 80% of forecast, but is greater if sales attain 120% of forecast. The bonus may also be greater if the sales mix includes more high-profit items. Bonuses may also be paid for achieving objectives on number of new accounts, credit collections, calls per week, territorial profits, gross margin, or absenteeism.

    A bonus can also be paid if actual expenses do not exceed budget, with the bonus increasing as actual expenses decrease. As previously stated, quotas must be mutually agreed upon by sales manager and salesperson, and obtainable through reasonable effort. Unobtainable quotas do not motivate the sales force to expend extra effort.

Counting, Measuring, Describing. Now you review the remaining activities on your evaluation check list and select those which represent the most critical areas for each individual salesperson. In order to define expected results and set objectives, you need to define valid methods for counting, measuring, or describing them. Territory by territory, salesperson by salesperson, you establish standards for measuring desired skills, activities, knowledge, personal characteristics, and results.

For example, one of your people spends too much time, over 50%, with a few customers. You want that reduced to 35%, with 65% allocated to other customers and prospects. Another salesperson opens many new accounts but loses them the following year. You want that person to concentrate on maintaining accounts, and thus increase total active customers by 5% a year. Another salesperson averages only two calls a day and only on existing accounts. You want that person to average three calls a day including one prospect. Yet another salesperson has only large accounts and needs to open a dozen smaller ones next year. Still another salesperson has only small accounts and needs to open two large ones next year.

One salesperson emphasizes product features rather than benefits; another does not carry catalogues. You want both deficiencies corrected. One salesperson does not write down the buyers' names; another does not stay current with competition. Some salespeople do not submit call reports each week. Others phone orders to the factory rather than mailing the purchase order. These deficiencies also need correcting. Two salespeople show little concern for personal appearance. You will ask them to wear suits when calling on customers.

Rating System

Once you have decided what to appraise and have developed some individual performance objectives and measurements, you must establish a meaningful rating system. Some companies use numbers 1 through 5 or 1 through 10; some use "poor, fair, expected, very good, excellent"; some use "poor, consistently below average, average, consistently above average, excellent"; some use grades A, B, C, D, E with pluses and minuses; some use "strong, fair, need to improve"; some use arrows to show improvement or deterioration; some assign different activities different weights or importance; some use just weakness or strength as ratings.

For example, one sales manager rates each salesperson's skills, knowledge, activities, characteristics, and results on the following basis:

Rating 1—Poor. Accomplishment is significantly below acceptable levels.

Rating 2—Fair. Performance is close to, but not yet at an acceptable level. Some improvement has been made.

Rating 3—Expected. Performance is at an acceptable level, accomplishment is very satisfactory.

Rating 4—Very good. Performance is above acceptable level, accomplishment is very satisfactory.

Rating 5—Excellent. Performance and accomplishments are superior and outstanding.

Each rating is accompanied by an arrow indicating whether there has been improvement or deterioration since the last evaluation. Each item on the evaluation sheet carries a weight indicating importance: sales results carry a weight of 32, sales quality 16, selling skills 9, knowledge 9, self-organization 5, paperwork 2, expenses 9, customer relations 7, company relations 2, and personal characteristics 9. These weightings total 100. Each item's weight is multiplied by the individual ratings, 1 to 5, and the numbers are added to arrive at a total evaluation. This evaluation form also contains room for written comments, and a plan for improving performance.

In contrast, another sales manager rates each salesperson's performance for each activity only as a strength or weakness, with a note explaining any necessary corrective action. Both sales managers consider their evaluations and performance reviews a successful and valuable tool.

Where possible, eliminate the middle ground from your ratings. For example, remove the word "average." If you use numbers 1 through 5, remove 3. If you use numbers 1 through 10, remove 5 and 6. This eliminates the comfortable tendency to overuse middle ratings and forces you to make a judgment.

Select a rating system most appropriate to your particular sales organization—a rating system which accomplishes your desired results in the simplest, easiest, fairest manner. Overly complicated rating systems prove hard to administer and understand.

Appraisal Interview

Once you have decided what to evaluate, developed performance standards and objectives for each salesperson, and established a meaningful rating system, you are ready to begin the appraisal interviews. The effectiveness of the appraisal process depends on how you prepare for, organize, and conduct these interviews. Before the interview, send each salesperson a copy of the appraisal form and fully explain the process. At the interview, using the appraisal form, ratings, and discussion, agree on future objectives, and obtain a commitment from the salesperson to a plan and a time frame for achieving these goals.

Preparation.   Several months before the interviews, explain the entire evaluation process in a comprehensive memo or at a sales meeting. Include information on the goals, rating system, and interview, plus a copy of the evaluation form. Encourage questions, so that the sales force knows what to expect and surprises are minimized. Remember that most salespeople have apprehensions concerning appraisals. Explain that your job involves helping the sales force to improve performance, and that the appraisal form and interview assist in that task.

You should conduct performance reviews and evaluations once or twice a year. If the sales force resides locally, hold these meetings at your office. If the sales force resides an airplane ride away, conduct the appraisal interview in your hotel room at the end of a field visit.

Do not hold appraisal interviews at sales meetings or at compensation reviews. During a sales meeting you cannot devote the proper time to a performance review, and it detracts from the learning/social atmosphere necessary for a successful sales meeting. Combining them confuses and enervates participants.

Although appraisals certainly influence compensation decisions, the appraisal interview becomes too emotional if held as part of the compensation review. Salespeople may feel the performance review is being used to justify lower compensation, and that attitude would make the appraisal much less effective.

Several weeks before the interview, send the salesperson a second copy of the appraisal form and ask him or her to use it as the basis for a self-evaluation. Several weeks before the interview, you start rating the salesperson for each item on the appraisal form. Also make written comments and note any corrective action which you feel is necessary.

Procedure.   At the appraisal meeting, whether in your office or a hotel room, create a relaxed atmosphere. Don't accept phone calls, do offer coffee, and sit away from your desk in comfortable chairs. Give your total attention to the salesperson and the evaluation, adding an element of importance and recognition to both.

After some small talk to set the salesperson at ease, review the reasons for the appraisal process, and what you hope to achieve. Stress the goal of mutually agreeing on guidelines, objectives, and action to improve future performance. Remind the salesperson that you are not here to complain about any substandard performance, and that another appraisal will be held in a year or six months.

Next and most important, review each section of the appraisal form, asking for his or her assessment and giving yours. You will be surprised how often salespeople rate themselves lower than you do, admitting the need for improvement and help. The appraisal form thus becomes a basis or agenda for discussion; it provides a starting point for talking about the job.

Explain your rating, justify it, but don't argue, complain, threaten, or lose your temper. Where appropriate, commend strong performance, good points, or improvement. Most important, using the appraisal form, ratings, and discussion, agree on future objectives, and obtain a commitment from the salesperson to a plan and a time frame for achieving these goals. The goals should correct weaknesses and build on strengths. The time frame should be long enough to achieve the desired goal, but short enough to maintain motivation.

For you the evaluation process creates a vehicle for communicating with salespeople, plus controlling and motivating their behavior. In addition, you should use information from appraisals to improve training and update job descriptions. If you find that most salespeople are not selling benefits, or are not calling on clusters of customers, or are not aware of competitive pricing, possibly your training program requires a change. If you find that most salespeople no longer service customers by counting stock, or working with design engineers, possibly your job description requires a change.

Example.   A Denver company employed three salespeople to sell oil and real estate tax shelter investments. Once a year, the president, who also acted as sales manager, held appraisal interviews. Although he had daily contact with each salesperson, continually commented on their performance, and suggested means of improving results, the annual appraisal process provided a more formal comprehensive opportunity to review performance and set goals. One year he asked me to sit in on the sessions.

After offering coffee and once again explaining the evaluation process and its goals, he asked the salesperson how she evaluated her dollar and unit sales volume. Susan replied, "I gave myself an excellent, a number five, because last year my sales were 22% over quota, and so far this year 9% above quota." "I agree," replied Hal. "You have done a great job in surpassing your total dollar quota, and I also rated you excellent, number five." "Good," said Susan. "How about an increase in my bonus and commission rate?" "We will discuss that at your compensation review in ninety days," replied Hal. "At this meeting I want to discuss objectives for next year. What sort of sales do you expect next year, Susan?" "At least a 10% increase," she replied. "Good," said Hal. "We will discuss your sales quota and forecast in detail next month."

"How did you rate sales quality, Susan?" "I gave myself another excellent, number five, for the same reasons we just discussed," she replied. "How did you rate me?" "I rated you number two, fair, because 80% of your sales are shallow gas projects and only 15% are real estate and 5% deep oil. Susan, do you present deep oil and real estate ventures to prospects?" Susan answered,

"I always present shallow gas first, because the cash return is faster. Usually the prospect won't sit still long enough to listen to another presentation on deep oil or real estate." Hal responded, "What if the prospect is more interested in a larger tax write-off, which real estate makes possible, and less interested in a fast cash return from shallow gas? Assuming you only have the prospect's attention for one presentation, then presenting shallow oil first may lose a sale. Why not ask the prospect some questions to determine their tax shelter objectives, and then choose the appropriate program to present first?" "I see your point," said Susan, "I'll try it." "Okay," replied Hal, "let's say that next year's objectives include a 30% increase in deep oil and real estate sales." "Fine," said Susan, "I'll start working on it today."

"How did you rate product knowledge, Susan?" "I gave myself an average, number three." Hal responds, "You know there is no number three, average, on the evaluation form." "I forgot, Hal. In that case, I rate myself number two, fair, because I am not confident in my knowledge of real estate and deep oil benefits. Maybe that's why I don't sell them." "Actually, Susan, I rated you four, very good, in product knowledge, but if you don't feel confident, I will give you some more training literature today, and let's make some sales calls together this month." Susan replied, "That's fine, I will set up some appointments next week."

"How did you rate self-organization, Susan?" "I gave myself four, very good, because I keep great records." Hal responded, "In this area, I rated you fair, number two, because your call reports indicate a great deal of time spent traveling between prospects. Can you organize your week so that each day's appointments are closer together?" Susan angrily replied, "I see prospects when they can see me. If I travel a great deal between calls, that's not my fault. I deserve a very good, number four, on this rating." Hal calmly responds, "I would rate you a four on your next evaluation if you try to set appointments each day for one area of town. You suggest the appointment day to a prospect, and then see if he or she will accept. Wouldn't that save you time and money?" Susan answers, "I guess it would. I'll try it this month and see if it works."

The evaluation interview lasted 90 minutes, and using the appraisal form, all areas were discussed. Hal simply repeated the techniques illustrated above. As you can see, evaluation is a participatory process. Without the personal interchange of a meeting, the process loses its usefulness.

Management By Objective

Closely related to the evaluation process, but differing in emphasis, is management by objective (M.B.O.). The M.B.O. concept calls on managers and their subordinates to jointly determine personal performance goals in terms of expected results. It requires that managers emphasize results rather than activity, or doing things right. Although the evaluation process places heavy emphasis on results, such as annual sales, it places equally strong emphasis on the activities, characteristics, or skills (self-organization, product knowledge, enthusiasm, call reports, customer service) necessary to obtain those results.

Summary

Periodic performance appraisals represent an important management tool for controlling, evaluating, motivating, and communicating with the sales force. The appraisal process involves (1) deciding what you wish to appraise, (2) developing individual performance objectives and measurements for each salesperson, (3) developing a rating system, and (4) discussing the evaluation with each salesperson. Most important, using the appraisal form, ratings, and discussion, you agree on future objectives and obtain a commitment from the salesperson to a plan and time frame for achieving these goals.

8
The Development and Introduction of New Products

Small-company managers often feel that their firms do not possess the resources to successfully introduce new products. They consider the potential risk and expense of failure not worth the potential gain of success. Eighty percent of all new products/services never recover their initial investment.

The small-business manager reasons that he or she does not have the capital resources available to successfully generate a new product, whether a major technical breakthrough or simply a fashion change; nor the advertising dollars to promote it; nor the distribution channels to fully take advantage of it. He or she may further reason that if their firm does develop a new successful product or service, competition in the form of larger concerns will copy it; and with the larger concern's greater human and financial resources and marketing ability, it will quickly capture a major portion of the sales. Moreover, he or she knows that if their small business develops a new unsuccessful product/service, the firm will not recapture development expense, often must liquidate inventory below cost, and often must terminate recently hired personel. Heads you lose, tails you don't win.

In the early 1970s, a relatively small firm, Bowmar Instrument Corporation, introduced one of the first hand-held electronic calculators. The Bomar Brain popularized this new product category, and suddenly a several-hundred-million-dollar annual market materialized. Within a year, corporate giants flooded the market with similar products, forcing Bowmar to abandon the business.

Such experiences lead smaller businesspeople to feel that "being first may be good, but being big often is better." As a result of such thinking, many smaller firms succeed in the photographic, copier, computer, and apparel fields by cleverly adapting new products or styles developed by the seminal forces in their particular industry, such as Kodak, Xerox, I.B.M., or Calvin Klein.

However, new products/services still represent the fastest means for a small business to expand sales and market share. The successful introduction of new products/services also enhances the company image and improves employee morale. Customers and employees enjoy association with a leader.

Small businesses offering a service can often introduce new ideas less expensively than firms offering a product. A small Miami company, for example, made and delivered ice to restaurants and industrial users. Annual revenues never exceeded $100,000. Assets consisted of refrigerated trucks and an ice-making facility. The firm employed three drivers and a secretary. The owner did all the selling. Competition was keen and profits marginal.

The owner looked for a means of escaping from this commodity-oriented business to something related but proprietary, where competition was not so intense. She decided to lease ice-making machines to her customers, with maintenance service included; and she guaranteed the machines' rated ice-making production 24 hours a day by delivering ice when machines required repair. She leased the ice-making machines from the manufacturer and re-leased them to her customers. Within five years the business produced annual revenues of several million dollars and a handsome pretax profit. Within ten years she had developed branches and franchises in other cities.

Only a handful of small companies are involved in high-technology industries such as gene splicing or fiber optics, where new products require large continual investments in research and capital equipment. Most small businesses offer a nontechnical product, or one involving less-expensive applied rather than more-expensive developmental technology. A larger concern may manufacture the laser, but a smaller one supplies the industrial power source that fires the laser.

In the consumer products field, many small businesspeople feel that the introduction of new products/services requires large advertising expenditures. Most small businesses possess neither the resources nor the need for a national consumer campaign. Later in this chapter, we discuss how to inexpensively but effectively create a demand for new products/services through press releases/publicity; trade shows; mailings; radio and television giveaways; premiums; statement stuffers; catalogues; mail order ads; plus vendor and customer participation in trade and cooperative advertising.

This chapter then deals with techniques for reducing the risks of introducing new products allowing small businesses to participate in this worthwhile endeavor. The risks associated with new products or services can be limited by (1) finding market needs and competitive weaknesses, (2) seeking small markets which would be unprofitable for larger firms, (3) innovating rather than inventing, (4) determining return on investment, (5) using market research, (6) test marketing, and (7) inexpensively creating a demand.

INTRODUCTION

New products or services fail most often because they do not reflect a need in the marketplace or a competitive weakness, but rather the ego of the originator. Even a great idea succeeds commercially only if a need exists; that is, if it satisfies a customer want.

Because of larger overhead, greater start-up expenses, and the economies resulting from higher unit volume, larger businesses often cannot operate as profitably in smaller markets as in larger markets. Therefore, when developing a new product/service, find a need and competitive weakness in a market segment where your size business can operate profitably but a larger one cannot. In this way, you reduce the risk of a competitor with greater resources and better distribution capitalizing on your idea.

A small company generally does not have the human and financial resources for inventing a totally new product, but it does possess the resources to alter an existing product, so that it meets an unfilled need in a specialized market. You can achieve these innovations through (1) different packing and packaging, (2) color identification, (3) unusual sizing, (4) unusual guarantees, (5) adding or subtracting features from an existing product, (6) use of private labels and licensing, (7) adopting from a related market, (8) adopting from an overseas market, and (9) reviving an old idea.

Before you commit dollars to developing and selling a new product/service, estimate the investment involved and the profit potential. By using this type of financial analysis, you eliminate those great ideas in which the probable return does not justify the risk, or where development costs exceed any probable return, or where unacceptable profit margins exist. By using this type of analysis, you can compare return on investment, profit margins, and pay-back periods between several potential new products/services.

Just because you have a great idea which meets a need in the marketplace and produces an excellent return on investment does not guarantee that it will sell. Market research can help you determine a consumer or business-to-business product's/service's salability, and also can produce important suggestions for improving it. Market research involves (1) deciding what additional information you require concerning the new product/service, (2) reading related studies which have already been undertaken, (3) deciding on whether to use mail, phone, or personal interviews and what group you wish to interview, (4) correctly designing a questionnaire, (5) selecting a representative sample of potential customers for interviews and interpreting the data.

Test marketing, like market research, can reduce the risks involved in introducing new products/services, since actual experience can best indicate both acceptance of the new item and possible problems. Test marketing involves picking limited representative markets to test customer responses, asking potential customers to try the new product/service, and then, based on their response, altering the features and marketing strategy. If the response is considerably negative, you abandon the project. If the response is positive, you incrementally increase distribution. Test marketing techniques are different for industrial/commercial products and consumer products.

While it is always helpful if a customer or prospective customer has heard of an existing product or service and knows its selling points, for a new product/service to be successful, it is absolutely essential to pre-sell it. A small business can inexpensively pre-sell a new product/service through press releases and publicity, trade shows, mailings, radio and television giveaways, premiums, statement stuffers, catalogues, mail order advertising, plus sharing the cost of trade and cooperative advertising with suppliers and retailers.

FINDING MARKET NEEDS AND COMPETITIVE WEAKNESSES

New products or services fail most often because they do not reflect a need in the marketplace or a competitive weakness, but rather the ego of the originator. Even a great idea succeeds commercially only if a need exists; that is, if it satisfies a customer want.

Approach your customers and salespeople for new product ideas, because they are most aware of needs in the marketplace and of competitive weaknesses. During field trips, ask major customers for their ideas. They will be flattered, and more receptive to doing business together. This type of closeness to customers represents a competitive advantage of smaller businesses over larger firms. Devote some time at sales meetings and during field visits to discussing new products/services with the sales force. Offer a bonus for successful ideas. Also look for new product/service ideas and information in trade papers and magazines.

The English-manufactured Wilkinson double-edged stainless steel razor blade succeeded in America because the cost per shave was less than any blade offered by a domestic company, it lasted longer, and it produced a closer shave. At the time, American razor manufacturers were unwilling to offer a double-edged stainless steel blade because of their investment in conventional blades, and this created a competitive weakness.

The artificial Christmas tree, first introduced by a company with annual revenue under $100,000, satisfied a commercial and consumer need for a no-fuss, no-mess, reusable fixture that simulated the real thing. At that time, companies in the Christmas decoration industry were unwilling to tamper with the live-tree tradition, and this too created a competitive weakness.

Nontobacco, lettuce-leaf cigarettes failed as a new product not because of unfair practices by major tobacco companies, but because smokers, although concerned with health, were unwilling to compromise the tobacco taste. They might limit the health risk with low-tar filter cigarettes, but not with tobacco substitutes. The nontobacco cigarette certainly represented a competitive weakness, but unfortunately did not satisfy a consumer need.

SEEKING SMALL MARKETS, UNPROFITABLE FOR LARGER COMPANIES

A smaller business, like a larger one, should use size to its advantage. Because of larger overhead, greater start-up expenses, and the economies resulting from higher unit volume, larger businesses often cannot operate as profitably in smaller markets as in larger markets.

Today's markets are very complex and segmented. When developing a new product/service, find a need and competitive weakness in a market segment where your size business can operate profitably but a larger one cannot. In this way, you reduce the risk of a competitor with greater resources and better distribution capitalizing on your idea. Smaller businesses succeed by specializing, not by being all things to all people.

In 1981 the hosiery industry had annual sales at wholesale of three billion dollars, a market large enough to interest any corporate giant. However, specialized equipment and distribution divided this huge market into hundreds of smaller submarkets appropriate for and populated by smaller businesses. For example, panty hose accounted for half of the market, ladies' casuals 20%, and infants' hose 10%. This meant the total wholesale market for men's hose approximated $600,000,000 which could be futher divided into 80% unbranded merchandise for mass merchants and 20% branded goods for specialty and department stores. The $120,000,000 branded men's hosiery business consisted of 20% designer labels and 80% national brands; 30% casual hose, 30% athletic hose, 30% dress hose, and 10% patterns. The casual, athletic, dress, and patterned goods could be further divided between synthetics and natural fibers. These specialized submarkets amounted to total annual sales of only $20,000,000. A smaller company which excels in short run unit production could make money in these submarkets whereas a larger concern could not.

You can obtain this type of statistical market data from trade associations, trade publications, Chambers of Commerce, and government agencies. For every significant economic activity, there is an association that represents it, a government agency that monitors it, and a magazine that covers it.

A larger company prefers to use its resources in markets with larger dollar returns. It is not efficient for a large business to be involved in many small markets. To lower the risk of introducing new products, seek out these specialized submarkets where your company's size creates a competitive advantage.

INNOVATING RATHER THAN INVENTING

The risks associated with introducing new products/services can be further limited by innovating rather than inventing. A small company does not possess the resources for inventing an engine capable of running on alternative fuel. A small company does have the human and financial resources to alter an existing product so that it meets an unfilled need in a specialized market. You can achieve these innovations through (1) different packing and packaging, (2) color identification, (3) unusual sizing, (4) unusual guarantees, (5) adding or subtracting features from an existing product, (6) use of private labels and licensing, (7) adopting from a related market, (8) adopting from an overseas market, and (9) reviving an old idea.

Remember the importance of timing in introducing new products/services. An idea which failed three years ago might succeed today, and an idea which succeeded three years ago might fail today. Business is a dynamic process with markets, needs, and competition continually changing. The first American-made compact cars introduced in the late 1960s and early 1970s failed. Recycling paper failed until inflation made it a necessity; deflation may make it unnecessary. In 1988 smokers might be ready for the lettuce-leaf cigarette.

Innovative Packing and Packaging

Innovative packing and packaging can alter existing products to satisfy unfilled needs in the marketplace. Consider the size of your package, amount supplied, information and instructions which can be printed on it, plus gift and reusable packages.

A small chemical company in whose industry the product was traditionally offered in 100-pound drums increased its market share by also offering the product in 50- and 200-pound drums. A small underwear company whose products were traditionally offered three-to-a-package increased its sales by developing a single-pack and a six-pack. The single-pack used an acetate tube instead of the traditional see-through envelope.

A small financial service company specializing in tax shelters significantly increased its business by lowering the minimum investment from $10,000 to $5,000. Its larger competitors were unable to profitably handle the paperwork involved in such small transactions.

Each year, review your present packaging to determine whether altering it could increase sales. As the chemical and underwear companies did, examine the size of your packaging and the amount of product supplied. If a consumer package contains more than a person can use, the purchaser may feel wasteful. If the package does not hold enough, he or she may feel cheated. If the industrial container holds too much product, overstocking and spoilage can occur. If the industrial container does not hold enough, it causes inefficiency in storage, shipping, and use. However, both consumers and purchasing agents think that packages containing larger quantities represent better buys.

Examine the information, if any, written on your package and containers. Can the directions be made clearer with pictures or larger type? Does the container clearly state its contents? An electrical cable concern increased its industrial sales by printing in bold red letters on all six sides of each container the type and quantity of cable it contained. This allowed workmen to quickly find the exact cable they needed.

A ladies' glove manufacturer increased sales by placing the style number inside each glove. This allowed store personnel to more easily count stock for reorders. An artificial Christmas tree concern increased its sales by printing directions for assembly on the package rather than inside. The directions alleviated consumer fears about the difficulty of assembling the tree.

For consumer products, consider offering a gift package at holiday time. If your product lends itself to gift giving, develop an attractive package specifically for that purpose. A men's hosiery company significantly increased its sales by placing six pairs of socks in a modified beer six-pack and promoting the item as a gift. A handkerchief concern pulled ahead of competitors by developing a three-unit gift pack that resembled a piggie bank.

Whether you sell an industrial or consumer product, consider developing a competitive edge through reusable packages. An industrial cleaning compound company increased market share by shipping goods in metal containers which the purchaser then used as trash cans. A ladies' fragrance company gained market share by packaging soap in a reusable jewlry box. Examine your packing and packaging to determine what changes might prove beneficial to your customers. Seek suggestions from customers and salespeople.

Color Identification

Color identification represents another inexpensive means of innovating to satisfy unfilled needs in the marketplace or to create brand identification. A small industrial gear company significantly increased its market share by placing a red circle on each side of its 2″ pitch diameter gear, and a yellow circle on its 5″ diameter gear. When a gear needed replacing or reordering, an unskilled worker could identify the specific size.

A small men's hosiery company knit a narrow tan stripe into the top of each pair of brown socks, a red stripe into each pair of black, and a light blue stripe into each pair of navy. This allowed the consumer to easily match pairs after washing, and to easily find the desired color each morning in a dark drawer. This simple idea sold millions of pairs of hose.

The most successful company in the branded men's hosiery business went from one million dollars of annual sales to over thirty million by knitting a gold toe into every sock. The company created a brand, "Gold Toe," which could be identified by the consumer after the sock had been worn and washed.

Examine your products to determine if color identification could benefit the users in some way or could establish brand identification. The cost of adding color is usually nominal.

Unusual Sizing

Unusual sizing that meets a need represents another inexpensive means of innovation. In the 1960s many fledgling electrical component manufacturers greatly expanded when they introduced miniature relays and connectors for microcircuitry and oversized versions for heavy industrial equipment. They used the same technology for both, but varied the size. In the 1970s several knitting mills survived the general panty hose business demise by introducing specialty items such as "Queen Size" for larger women, and "Petite" for small. At the same time that Sharp was developing miniature calculators to fit in your pocket, it developed a model for older people with extra-large keys and displays. Certain group health insurance companies were able to profitably enter the individual major medical field by significantly increasing deductibles and offering unlimited maximums. A Midwest firm recently introduced attention-getting five-feet-high, seven-feet-wide telegrams. A Virginia firm successfully developed extra-large stretch denim jeans for truck drivers.

Examine your products/services to determine if larger or smaller versions would satisfy unfilled needs in the marketplace. This strategy will lead you into submarkets, which may prove profitable for a smaller concern but unattractive for a larger competitor.

Unusual Guarantees

Offering unusual guarantees with a product or service represents yet another inexpensive innovation. The mail order business, which is populated by many small firms, owes some of its recent success to "satisfaction guaranteed or return of purchase price"; also to one-, three-, and five-year guarantees or replacement of the product. The long-term corporate and municipal bond markets collapsed in 1980 because of inflation and high interest rates. In 1981 several companies successfully offered 20-year bonds with guarantees to buy them back at par in five year. At the same time, municipalities offered long-term bonds with interest and principal guaranteed by groups of insurance companies. These guaranteed bonds sold out. Similarly, Federal Express created a successful business in a competitive industry by guaranteeing overnight parcel deliveries.

Car undercoatings such as Ziebart traditionally were guaranteed for five years. In 1978 "Rusty Jones" offered a more expensive guarantee for the life of a car with annual free inspections and continual maintenance. If a treated area of the car rusts, "Rusty Jones" repairs the rust or returns your initial fee. The service is very successful.

A men's hosiery company, in conjunction with a mail order concern, offered a lifetime-guaranteed sock. When the sock wore out, the customer returned it to the manufacturer, who replaced it with a free pair. The sock, knit with heavy nylon, generally wore out after 100 wearings, but at that point few people remembered the guarantee. This innovation built two successful businesses.

Examine your product/service to determine if an unusual guarantee would satisfy an unfilled need in the marketplace. Guarantees may relate to time, quality, standards, or customer satisfaction. Be sure to estimate the probable expense, if any, of your guarantee, and reflect that in the product or service cost.

Adding or Subtracting from an Existing Product/Service

Taking something out of or adding something to an existing product/service can often inexpensively create a totally new product/service which will satisfy an unfilled need in the marketplace. Ethyl gasoline, calculator watches, antistatic undergarments, word-processing equipment, phone-a-visions, and clock radios with telephones all represent new products created by adding something to an existing product. Unleaded gasoline, low-alcohol beer and wine, decaffeinated coffee, light beer, and diet soft drinks represent new products with an ingredient removed.

A small knitting mill created a new product by putting anti-static and sanitized chemicals in the dye bath, which prevented trousers from clinging to hose and reduced foot odor. Another company knit socks without heels, producing the tube socks that athletes wear. An electronics mail order concern developed a telephone without a cord, thus making it portable. A running shoe firm added a zippered pocket for keys to one of its models. The dinner-theater concept developed from adding something to an existing service. Coca-Cola has placed a small-screen video game in one of its new lines of vending machines. Cash management accounts introduced by stockbrokers in 1980 are a combination of money market funds, checking, custodial, and margin accounts. Universal life and variable life insurance policies, introduced by several small insurance firms in the late 1970s, are a combination of life insurance, savings accounts, money market funds, and mutual funds. These are all simple ideas which used existing technology to inexpensively alter existing products/services, resulting in increased sales and market share.

Examine your product/service to determine whether adding something to it or taking something away from it would satisfy an unfilled need in the marketplace. To facilitate this, review the parts, ingredients, and components of your present product/service.

Private Labels and Licenses

Offering branded merchandise under private label, and unbranded merchandise using licensed brand names, represents yet another inexpensive product innovation which can satisfy a need and expand sales. Many of the nationally advertised brand name apparel manufacturers found lucrative markets in selling Neiman-Marcus, Bloomingdale's, and Saks Fifth Avenue using the store label. Many of the brand name nationally advertised appliance manufacturers found lucrative markets in selling Sears, Ward's, and Penney's using the store label. Previously this market had belonged to lower-end manufacturers involved only in unbranded merchandise. These retailers had a need for better store label merchandise that only branded manufacturers could provide.

Similarly, major manufacturers of unbranded merchandise have inexpensively developed proprietary branded lines by licensing recognized names from Izod, Polo, Calvin Klein, Yves Saint Laurent, Pierre Cardin, Jordache, Jockey, Levi, Spaulding, Hershey, Winnebago, Barnum, Crayola, E.T., Star Wars, Snoopy, Walt Disney, Joe Namath, the New York Yankees, Pittsburgh Steelers, and the Chicago Symphony Orchestra. In 1981 retail sales of licensed goods grew to $14 billion, with manufacturers paying about $750 million in royalties. Royalty rates range from 5% to 15% of the wholesale price. Think about recognized designers, brands, personalities, athletic teams, movies, and institutions whose names would appeal to your customers. See if they are available for licensing.

In addition to licensing names, you can license entire products. Often an individual, firm, university, or government agency has developed a worthwhile product which they do not have the resources or inclination to produce or sell. Sometimes larger firms have developed proprietary products with markets too small or inappropriate for their organization. Sometimes overseas firms wish to license an American business to manufacture and sell their proprietary product in the U.S. market. To learn of these opportunities, contact Clark Boardman Company Ltd. in New York City, your local office of the U.S. Commerce Department, or the U.S. Chamber of Commerce in Washington. Clark Boardman publishes licensing, trademark, and patent periodicals, and the other two organizations maintain some lists of available product licenses.

Many products in the telecommunications, machine tool, computer, chemical, copying machine, photographic, textile, and fragrance fields are made and sold under licenses from other firms. For example, in 1982 the English firm Sinclair Research licensed Timex Corp. to manufacture and sell its inexpensive home computer in the U.S.

On the other hand, should your firm develop a proprietary product not appropriate for your markets or resources, you might consider offering it for license. The heat-reflecting window shade company mentioned in previous chapters might have fared better by licensing its product, rather than manufacturing and selling it.

Adopting from a Related Market

Often, inexpensive new product/service ideas can be obtained from related markets. Women's tailored clothing came from the men's market. Men's fashion underwear came from the women's market. Frozen dinners were originally developed for Air Force pilots, and digital wristwatches for the space program. Home computers grew out of commercial computers, hospital cleaning services grew out of home cleaning services. Some innovations for fabric-dying equipment came from commercial laundry machines. Guaranteed overnight document delivery grew out of guaranteed overnight freight service. Liquor by wire was adopted from flowers by wire. Portable kerosene heaters have been used to heat boats for many years. When oil prices rose in 1975, a firm named Kerosun, Inc. reintroduced these devices for home use.

See if markets related to yours offer products/services which with appropriate changes could satisfy an unfilled need in your market. Start by identifying previous new products/services which have been successfully adopted from other related markets.

Adopting from an Overseas Market

Often, new product/service ideas can be inexpensively obtained from overseas markets. An American golf enthusiast noticed that English golfers wore shoes with rubber rather than metal spikes. The rubber spiked shoes were lighter weight than the metal, more comfortable, and did not make holes in the turf. The American golf enthusiast contracted to have a similar shoe produced in the U.S., and then successfully sold this product to golf shops.

American manufacturers entered the industrial robot business once the Japanese had proven its commercial feasability. An entire segment of the U.S. ladies' apparel industry survives on products first introduced in Paris. In France there is a fast-food chain based on McDonalds which offers quiche and croissants rather than hamburgers and fries. For many years Europeans have used Telex sending and receiving services rather than owning their own machines. A smart entrepreneur now offers that service in the United States and Central America.

Keep abreast of overseas markets through trade journals and trips abroad. Look for new products/services offered overseas, which could satisfy unfilled needs in your domestic markets.

Reviving an Old Idea

Often, products/services no longer in use provide the basis for a successful contemporary revival. In the 1950s and again in the 1980s miniskirts were revived from the twenties. In Chicago, a small concern called Western Onion successfully revived Western Union's singing telegram. The popular copy-righted card game Uno is a revival of a similar game from Elizabethan England. Rising fuel costs have resulted in the reintroduction of wood stoves. The computer game Dungeons and Dragons revived and updated war and military games played on boards and graph paper. Many computer adventure games revived and updated the plots of children's adventure books. Mousetraps which utilize glue rather than spring-loaded devices originated in 1900, met their demise in 1920, and were revived in 1980. A whole class of highly successful movie theaters now specialize in rotating one-day revivals of old movies. The lettuce-leaf cigarette originated with the American Indians. Consider which products/services no longer in use might provide appropriate new ideas for an item that could meet a need in today's market.

Summary

The risks associated with introducing new products/services can be lessened by using available resources to innovate rather than invent. A small company can achieve these innovations through (1) different packing and packaging, (2) color identification, (3) unusual sizing, (4) unusual guarantees, (5) adding or subtracting features from an existing product, (6) use of private labels and licensing, (7) adopting from a related market, (8) adopting from an overseas market, and (9) reviving an old idea.

DETERMINING RETURN ON INVESTMENT

You can limit the risks associated with the introduction of new products/services by estimating return on investment. Before you commit dollars to developing and selling a new product/service, estimate the investment involved and profit potential. Since your company president, accountant, and manufacturing manager have access to much of the necessary information, involve them in this evaluation.

The investment will include labor, material, and services involved in development; purchases of additional equipment for development and manufacturing; additional advertising, promotional, and selling expenses; plus increased inventories and accounts receivable. The total of these costs represents your total investment.

Profit margin for your new product/service is calculated by estimating the direct labor, material, and overhead costs required to produce each unit, plus allocations for selling, administration, and general expenses. You subtract the total of these unit costs from the unit selling price to arrive at a profit margin. Be sure you have included all appropriate costs, but have not double-counted by including them in both the investment and unit calculation. Chapter 9 on Pricing contains more detailed information on calculating costs and profit margins.

Once you have estimated the required dollar investment and resulting unit profit dollars and margins, you forecast unit sales for the next five years. These projected unit sales will produce certain dollars of profit margin which can be measured as a percentage return on investment, and which can show the time period required to recoup your original investment. You can compare this return and pay-back to other alternatives, and evaluate it against the new idea's probability of success.

By using this type of financial analysis, you eliminate those great ideas in which the probable return does not justify the risk, or where development costs exceed any probable return, or where unacceptable profit margins exist. By using this type of analysis, you can compare return on investment, profit margins, and pay-back periods between several potential new products/services.

For example, a small metal-fabricating company manufactures stainless steel sonic cleaning tanks, which it sells to the government for degreasing everything from rifle bolts to aircraft engines. The tanks are large and expensive, and must meet exacting quality standards. The company sales manager sees an unfilled need for smaller, less complicated, less expensive cleaning tanks for use in the electronics industry. Such a tank must have built-in space for drying parts with forced air, and must meet critical sanitary standards. He discusses the idea with the company president, controller, design engineer, and manufacturing manager. They estimate that it will cost $5,000 to design and build a prototype, but that no additional equipment will be necessary for manufacturing the tank. To launch this product, the company must spend another $5,000 on trade advertising, press releases, and trade shows. The controller estimates it would require another $10,000, between inventory and accounts receivable, to support sales of the new tank. These investment costs total $20,000.

Considering the cost savings this tank could produce for a user, the sales manager feels he could sell each one for $600. The manufacturing manager estimates labor, material, and factory overhead at $300 per unit, and the controller adds another $200 for selling, general, and administrative expenses. Unit costs total $500, leaving a $100, or 20%, pretax profit margin.

The sales manager estimates he can sell 100 machines the first year, 200 machines the second year, 300 machines each in the third, fourth, and fifth years; but after that, a more sophisticated device may be necessary, because of competition, and changes in user requirements. This sales projection produces $10,000 of pretax profit margin in year one, a 50% annual return on investment; $20,000 of profit margin in year two, a 100% annual return on investment; and $30,000 of profit margin in years three, four, and five, a 150% annual return on investment. About six months into year two, the $20,000 investment will be recouped, resulting in an 18-month pay-back period. Over the course of five years, the new product will have produced pretax earnings of $120,000 on an original investment of $20,000, a 600% return or 120% a year.

The sales manager and the company president compare this possible new product's percentage unit profit margin, return on investment, and pay-back period to estimates for several other potential new products; the profit margin and return on present product lines; and the return from investing the same amount in a money market fund. The sales manager also considers the probability of this new product not succeeding as projected, but calculates that only 200 machines must be sold to recoup development and promotion costs, which minimizes the risks involved. As this example illustrates, by calculating the investment necessary to develop and support a new product, and the potential sales and profit margin, you can determine the new item's pay-back period and return on investment. This analysis helps you to measure whether the rewards are worth the risk.

MARKET RESEARCH

You can reduce the risks associated with introducing new products/services by using simple, inexpensive market research. Just because you have a great idea which meets a need in the marketplace and produces an excellent return on investment does not guarantee that it will sell. Human behavior is difficult to predict. Market research can help you determine a consumer or business-to-business product's/service's salability, and also can produce important suggestions for improving it.

First, determine your objectives. What additional information do you require concerning salability of the new product/service, and what questions do you want answered to obtain that information? Before you actually begin gathering data, you should read related studies which have already been undertaken. They provide an excellent source of free material and can save you hours of work.

Next, decide whether mail, phone, or personal interviews are most appropriate for your market research project, and whom specifically you wish to interview: buyer, merchandise manager, purchasing agent, controller, plant manager, quality engineer; men or women under 40, husbands or wives over 45, or high school children. Now you must correctly design a questionnaire to obtain the reliable information that you desire. Finally, you select a representative sample group of potential customers for interviews, and collect and interpret the data.

Objectives

Market research objectives include finding out who specifically are the potential customers; what product/service features do they want most; would they consider buying your new product; who are the most serious competitors; what price will potential customers pay; what media do they read or listen to; from what retail outlet or through what channels of distribution would they purchase the product/service? Such market research questions allow you to pinpoint the most effective distribution and advertising for reaching specific customers; to identify problem areas which need correcting; and to determine what price the buyer will pay. Through market research, the sonic cleaning tank company could determine which specific electronic companies have the greatest need for their product; what features and benefits are most important; whether the purchasing agents read *Electronic News, Electronic Business, Electronic Industry,* or *Electronic Buyers News;* whether they buy this type of equipment from agents or distributors; what specific size and capacity tank would be most appealing; what specific companies offer competive products; whether $600 is too low or too high a price; and how potential customers feel the sonic cleaning tank could be improved.

So start your market research by deciding what additional information you require to determine and maximize the new product's/service's salability. Decide what questions you need answered.

Related Studies

Before you actually begin gathering market research data, read related studies which have already been undertaken. They provide an excellent source of free material and can save you hours of work. Contact the appropriate trade publications and trade associations to see what market research they have published on this subject, and what statistics they have gathered on the market. Review brokerage house, government, and Chamber of Commerce reports on these markets, along with competitors' annual reports and prospectuses. For every significant economic activity, there is an association that represents it, a government agency that monitors it, and a magazine that covers it. Obtaining market research data is a matter of identifying the associations, government agencies, and publications in a specific field and getting the information directly from the source. There are a number of reference books which identify these sources: *Encyclopedia of Associations, National Trade and Professional Associations of The United States, Statistical Abstracts of The United States, The United States Government Manual, Guide To Special Issues and Indexes of Periodicals,* and *Standard Periodical Directory.* College or graduate students majoring in marketing can inexpensively search this literature and bring appropriate information to your attention.

Types of Interviews

Market research data on consumer and business-to-business products and services can be collected through mail interviews, telephone interviews, and face-to-face personal interviews. Each technique has its place, depending on your needs.

Mail interviews prove least inexpensive, since the only costs involve developing, printing, and mailing a questionnaire. However, since a 10% to 15% return is considered excellent, large mailings are usually required to obtain the proper number of responses. If necessary, mail interviews can contain moderately complex questions, and can require up to twenty minutes for completion. However, the shorter and simpler, the better. Include a postage-paid return-address envelope, and a premium to encourage people to complete and mail back their responses. Several concerns have increased the rate of response by including pens or the promise of cash for completing and returning the questionnaires.

Telephone interviews are more expensive than mail interviews, but they produce a 70% response rate. Telephone respondents become aggravated if the interview exceeds ten minutes or contains complicated questions. Again, consider training college students as interviewers. Be sure the interviewer understands the questions, and the purpose of the project.

Personal interviews prove the most expensive, but are necessary when complicated, probing questions must be answered. Personal interviews can last up to thirty minutes. Often, gifts are offered as an inducement for being interviewed. Generally, personal interviews require the services of a professional market researcher.

The sonic cleaning tank company might mail a questionnaire to the quality control managers of 1,000 electronic companies to determine what trade media they read, what devices they presently use for cleaning, and what quality specifications they consider most important. The company might use telephone interviews with the appropriate purchasing agents of 100 select electronic companies to determine price ranges for competitive equipment, freight policies, terms, delivery requirements, and type of distribution used. The company might choose to use personal interviews with twenty plant managers to determine service requirements and any problems with present cleaning equipment.

As this example shows, industrial/commercial purchasing decisions are influenced by several people, and obtaining market research information from each becomes important. To decide on the proper type of interview, you must know whom you wish to interview: buyer, merchandise manager, purchasing agent, controller, plant manager, or quality engineer.

Before deciding on the proper type of interview for a consumer product, you also must decide whom you wish to interview: single men, women, wives, husbands, or children. You must decide who makes the purchasing decision. For example, 70% of all men's hose, ties, and belts are purchased by women, so interviewing only men would not obtain correct information on these markets.

For consumer goods you may wish to interview both consumers and retail store buyers/merchandise managers. You must sell the retail store before the store can sell the consumer.

If the lettuce-leaf cigarette company had used market research to interview smokers, they might have altered or even discontinued this product. At least they would have been more aware of specific consumer objections.

Each type of interview—mail, phone, or personal—has its place, depending on the nature of your market research. Long interviews with complicated questions produce better results in person than by phone. Mail interviews can be used when you have a large, appropriate mailing list and need a large number of replies.

Designing a Questionnaire

Once you have decided what information you desire, whom to interview, and whether to use mail, telephone, or personal interviews, you must correctly design a questionnaire to obtain reliable information and achieve your desired results. Instructions and questions should be clear, simple, easy to read, and easy to understand. Each question should contain only one idea, and questions should follow a logical order. Questions must produce easy to understand and easy to interpret answers. Don't crowd the questionnaire; leave extra room for answers.

A questionnaire should include the name of the interviewer, date of the interview, name, address, and phone number of the respondent. It should begin with a statement concerning the questionnaire's purpose, and then completely describe the product or service. The first question should ascertain in a yes or no fashion the initial negative or positive reaction to the new product/service you have just described. The second question should ask for an open-ended explanation of or reason for the negative or positive reaction. Next you ask whether the respondent would buy the product, and if not, why not.

Then ask why the product/service appeals to the respondent, and what are its advantages. Or if appropriate, why it does not appeal, and what are the disadvantages. This question determines the user benefits, and influences your initial sales presentation, or generates ideas for altering the product.

Next, ask what the respondent thinks such a product would cost, where he or she would expect it to be advertised, and where he or she would expect it to be bought. Ask for suggestions on improving the new product/service.

Last, you obtain information classifying the respondent. In a consumer interview, this might include age, income, sex, and marital status. In a buyer, plant manager, or purchasing agent interview, this might include information on the size of the firm, types of products/services offered, and types of customers.

If this questionnaire is used for a face-to-face or telephone interview, the interviewer reads the material to the respondent, explains instructions, records answers, and answers any questions the respondent might ask. If the questionnaire is used for a mail interview, the interviewer's name is unnecessary, wording requires slight changes, plus it must contain instructions on how to fill out the questionnaire, and on how to return it.

The following illustrates a typical questionnaire.

Name of Interviewer _____

Name of Respondent _____

Address _____

Phone _____ Date _____

Good morning (afternoon or evening), my name is _____,
and I am conducting a market study for a new product/service called _____.

Your name was suggested as someone whose opinion would be important in determining whether or not to introduce this new product/service, and what features it should have. This is not a sales presentation, and you will not be asked to purchase anything. May I have a few minutes of your time to answer some questions?

The name of the product/service is _____.

It is a _____, and its functions/purposes are _____
_____.

The benefits of this product/service are _____.

1. What is your immediate reaction to this idea?

   Positive   *Negative*

   Terrific _____   So-so _____

   Good _____   Don't especially like it _____

   Like it somewhat _____   Don't like it all _____

   Why? Explain: _____
   _____

2. If it were available, would you purchase this product/service?

   Positive   *Negative*

   Yes, positively _____   No, positively _____

   Yes, probably _____   No, probably _____

   Why? Explain: _____
   _____

3. What three features of this product/service appeal to you most or least? What do you consider its three most important advantages or disadvantages?

   Appeals   *Advantages*

   1. _____   1. _____

   2. _____   2. _____

   3. _____   3. _____

4. How much do you feel such a product/service should cost? _____

5. From what type store/distributor/jobber/broker/salesperson/company would you expect to purchase such a product/service? _____

6. How would you expect to hear about such a product/service?

   _____

   Where would you expect it to be advertised? _____

   _____

7. How do you feel this product/service could be improved?

   _____

(For consumer questionnaires:)

8. How old are you?

   Under 15 _____   50–59 _____

   16–21 _____   60–69 _____

   22–29 _____   70–79 _____

   30–39 _____   over 80 _____

   40–49 _____

9. Check one:

   Female: single _____

            married _____

   Male: single _____

            married _____

10. Is your family's annual income above or below?

    $10,000 _____ $20,000 _____ $30,000 _____
    $50,000 _____

(For questionnaires concerning business-to-business industrial/commercial type products/services:)

8. How many people does your firm employ?

Under 50 _____   50 to 99 _____   100 to 199_____
200 to 499 _____   500 to 1,999 _____   2,000 to 5,000_____
Over 5,000 _____

9. What products/services does your company offer? _____

_____

10. What industries use your company's products/services? _____

_____

Once you have developed a questionnaire to obtain the desired information, test it on a group of fifteen potential customers. Their responses will point out any ambiguities, confusion, misunderstandings, biases, poorly worded questions, unnecessary questions, or necessary additional questions. You can then make the required changes for a final version.

Selecting a Sample Group for Interviews

Once you have decided what information you need; read related studies; decided on whether to use mail, phone, or personal interviews; decided who makes the buying decision; and developed and tested a questionnaire, you now must select a sample group of potential customers for interviewing. If, for example, your new product/service is concrete railroad ties, or a data-processing program which allows airlines to forecast empty seats, you can interview all potential customers. If your new product/service is an oven or car cleaner, a data-processing program for banks, or a microwave antenna, you must select a representative group of potential customers to interview. You select this representative group by defining the prime characteristics of potential customers, obtaining a list of firms or consumers with these characteristics, narrowing the sample, and then randomly selecting names for interviewing until the results show agreement.

You start by defining the prime characteristics of potential customers. The prime characteristics, or universe, of potential customers for the car cleaner would be men under 50 who own a car less than five years old. The prime characteristics, or universe, of potential customers for the oven cleaner would be married women with gas stoves over five years old. The prime characteristics, or universe, of potential customers for the microwave antennas would be television networks, telecommunications companies, railroads, utilities, Department of Defense, local, state, and national government agencies.

If you plan to sell your new product to consumers through retail stores, you need to interview both consumers and retail store buyers. You must sell the retail store before the store can sell the consumer, and you must decide what type retail store can best reach your potential customer. The decision concerning type of retail outlet, drug, chain, discount, department, hardware, specialty store, or supermarket, is discussed in Chap. 10 on "Distribution."

In order to interview a representative sample of the entire group, or universe, you need to start with a large enough group of potential customers possessing these prime characteristics. Mailing list companies can provide you with a list of consumers having virtually any set of characteristics you desire. Trade magazines and trade associations can provide a list of companies with virtually any set of characteristics you desire. Now from these large lists, you begin narrowing the sample. You might do this by selecting certain geographic areas for a consumer survey, or certain industries for a commercial survey, or if appropriate, by using your present customer list.

Next you select from the reduced sample those specific potential customers to be interviewed. One approach to selecting a random sample involves use of random number tables, which list numbers involving combinations of the digits 0 through 9 in a purely random way. Each number has an equal chance of selection at any draw. You assign a number to each name in the reduced sample; then choose a number from the random table; and the potential customer assigned that number becomes part of the sample group for interviewing. Another approach to selecting a random sample involves choosing every tenth, or fiftieth, or hundredth potential customer on your list. Still another approach involves selecting a sample at random until you obtain certain quoatas, such as three television networks, five telecommunications companies, two railroads, ten utilities, and twenty government agencies.

The number of potential customers necessary to interview for an accurate sample of the market depends upon the responses. If 50 responses produce strong agreement, then that is enough. For example, if 80% of the responses strongly like or dislike the new product/service, you have a representative group. If only 60% agree, you must interview more people to see if the distribution changes. If after another 50 interviews, only 60% still agree, you have a representative sample. Continue sampling until you feel that further interviewing will not change the results.

Although you must design the questionnaire and select a sample group for interviewing, a college student can competently handle the remaining tasks. Also, a firm specializing in market research can undertake the project for you. Your company will remain anonymous if an outside firm performs the research.

Market research should not be limited to new products. You can use it to determine how your customers and potential customers feel about present products/services. Such information can help you improve the product/service features, pinpoint weaknesses, more effectively sell benefits, better utilize advertising, and set prices which maximize profits.

TEST MARKETING

Test marketing, like market research, can reduce the risks involved in introducing new products/services, since actual experience can best indicate both acceptance of the new item and possible problems. Once you have developed a new product/service which meets a need in the marketplace and which meets your internal standards for return on investment, pick limited representative markets to test customer response. Pick particular regions, states, cities, neighborhoods, industries, or customer groups for the tests. Your test markets should be free from unique or atypical conditions, such as a nonrepresentative climate, unusual income distribution, low freight charges, or domination by one company. If appropriate, include present customers in the test, since you already have a relationship with them.

If possible, the sales manager should accompany the salesperson when presenting a new product/service for test marketing. This emphasizes the new idea's importance to the customer, allows you to participate in the selling process, and observe the reaction firsthand.

Resources and time permitting, it pays to perform both market research and market testing. Market research tells you what customers think about your new product/service; market testing tells you what they do about it. Potential customers' responses to market research can help you refine the product and strategy for market testing. If you must choose between market research and market testing, the latter is generally more critical.

Test marketing involves asking potential customers to try the new product/service; then, based on their response, altering features and/or marketing strategy. If the response is consistently negative, you abandon the project. If the response is positive, you incrementally increase distribution. Test marketing techniques are different for industrial/commercial products and consumer products.

Industrial/Commercial Markets

For test marketing industrial/commercial new products/services you prepare a prototype or audiovisual presentation to show key accounts. Your prospects may have ideas for improvement, they may reject the idea, or they may give you an order. If they reject the idea, move on to another test market. If this second test market also rejects the idea, consider changes which might make it acceptable, but also consider abandoning the project. You may also wish to test different prices or product/service features to see which produce the best response.

If the new product/service is accepted, and you start writing orders, move on to several other test markets and repeat the process. If the response continues positive, offer it to the entire market. Keep inventories at cautious levels until demand becomes more established, and even then build inventories carefully. The cost of late deliveries is considerably less than the cost of unsold inventories. Initially, maintaining minimum inventories further reduces the risks of new product development. For a new service, utilize existing personnel until a positive sales trend develops, and then carefully add to your staff.

Several months after introducing the new product/service, call customers who have purchased it. If possible, question the person who actually bought the product, the purchasing agent; and those who actually use the product, the quality engineer, manufacturing manager, secretary, concerning its actual performance. Were they satisfied? Did it live up to expectations? Could they suggest any improvements? In this way you can further refine the new item's benefits and quickly correct problems. Such follow-up after test marketing represents a continuation of the market research process.

For example, if the microwave antenna company management decided to test market a new increased channel capacity design, they would build a prototype and prepare extensive test data on its superior performance. Management might decide to test market the product on five common carrier telecommunication companies, three of which were present customers. With test data, a video tape, and a model of the product, the sales manager and appropriate salesperson would visit all five telephone companies in a week. Two prospects might suggest improvements, one might ask for more test data, and the other two might place orders. Two weeks later the sales manager and appropriate salesperson might obtain similar results calling on five utilities, and a month later, similar results calling on five government agencies. Based on this response, the company would incorporate certain suggested improvements, and offer the antenna through its sales force to all prospects.

Consumer Products/Services

For consumer products, you generally test market through stores or direct mail. With samples, audiovisual presentations, and market research results, you and the appropriate salesperson visit key stores in the test markets. Try to select stores with sales personnel, display space, and advertising funds capable of emphasizing a new product. Call on stores who presently buy other products from your firm, and those who do not. The stores may have ideas for improving the product, they may reject it, or they may agree to participate in the test and give you an order. A store may ask for return privileges if the new product does not sell, and you may have to accept this condition. If all the stores you approach in the test market reject the idea, move on to another test market. If all the stores you approach in this new test market reject the idea, consider changes which might make the product acceptable, but also consider abandoning the project.

Let us assume that several stores agree to buy and test market the new product. You ship them the new product; advertise, promote, and merchandise it; and analyze the sell-through. What percentage, and how many units, of the new product were sold? If the consumer response is weak, you consider changes in product features, packaging, and price which might increase the sell-through. You test market the product in different stores in different regions to see if the sell-through results remain consistent. You might try different prices, packaging, promotion, merchandising, advertising, and product features in different regions, and compare sell-through results. If test marketing in different stores and in different regions with variations in price, packaging, promotion, merchandising, advertising, and product features consistently results in weak sell-throughs, drop the new product.

If test marketing results in a favorable sell-through, then analyze which combination of price, packaging, promotion, merchandising, advertising, and product features produced the best results. Take that combination and offer it to all the appropriate stores in one region. If the other stores in that region have a favorable sell-through, then offer the new product in another region, and so on.

This approach allows you to better control the risk of high inventories, and to measure sell-through on reorders. Remember, keep inventories at cautious levels until demand becomes more established, and then build inventories carefully. Sometimes consumers will try a new product but not reorder it. Sometimes consumers will buy any potential gift item in December, but not repurchase it the rest of the year. Sometimes nonrecurring factors over which you have no control, such as a snowstorm or a strike, will influence initial sell-through.

If possible, pack a postage-paid return-addressed card with the new product. Ask the purchaser to return it in exchange for something of value, such as a small rebate. On the card, request information concerning the purchaser's name, address, age, sex, occupation, media exposure, store of purchase, reason for purchase, advertising response, product satisfaction, use, and suggestions for improvement. Such information proves helpful in further refining the new product, advertising, distribution, and marketing strategy. This technique represents a blending of market research with test marketing.

For example, the oven cleaner company starts test marketing by producing samples of its new odorless product, along with graphics for its package. The sales manager and appropriate salesperson show the new product, packaging, and market research results to three multi-unit grocery store chains in Houston, Hartford, Milwaukee, Denver, and San Francisco. At least two stores in each city agree to test it in some of their branches. The sell-through is good in all stores, but better in those which use a higher price, larger package, point-of-purchase display, and engage in some newspaper advertising. The company incorporates this information into its marketing plan, and offers the odorless oven cleaner to all grocery stores in the five cities. Sell-through continues strong on reorders, and so the company offers the odorless oven cleaner to grocery stores in Dallas, Atlanta, Miami, Los Angeles, Portland, Chicago, and New York. Once these cities prove successful, the new product is offered in Boston, Detroit, Minneapolis, Seattle, and Miami; and so on. The company also considers offering it through other types of retail outlets such as chain and discount stores.

Test marketing should not be limited to new products/services. By testing a different price, package, display, or advertising program in several regions for an existing product, you can measure the effectiveness before introducing the change nationally. Again, test marketing limits the risks of these proposed changes.

Some consumer products can be inexpensively test marketed through direct-response advertising. For example, you might place an ad for the odorless oven cleaner in *Ladies Home Journal* with a return coupon and telephone number for ordering. You can measure the salability by the number of orders or replies. A month after the product has been shipped, you can interview the purchaser concerning satisfaction, price, product features, appeal, problems, reorders, advertising media, and type retail stores. Such an approach represents a hybrid between test marketing and market research.

Since consumer services generally are not sold through retail stores, you must find other means for test marketing them. Sometimes a new service can be test marketed through existing customers who use a related service. Sometimes a direct-mail piece to a list of potential users in one region proves effective; mail order houses sell such lists. Sometimes newspaper or magazine ads with return coupons and telephone numbers for obtaining more information prove effective.

Beyond this, the procedures and goals of test marketing for consumer services remain the same as those for consumer products. If possible, for a new consumer service, utilize existing personnel, equipment, and materials until a positive sales trend develops, and then carefully add to your staff. If additional personnel, material, and equipment are required for the test market, make minimum commitments.

Test marketing cannot be used in situations where competitors are likely to quickly duplicate your new product/service. In these situations, timing proves critical and test marketing would forewarn competitors, allowing them an opportunity to enter the market. By developing new products/services for small markets, you reduce this risk, because smaller markets have less appeal for larger competitors.

The Procter & Gamble Company test markets many new products at a small downtown Cincinnati grocery store near their headquarters building. The store, known as Fred's place, is a regular stop for P & G competitors. Once a month a competitor's district sales manager checks to see what new products P & G is test marketing, and how well they are selling.

INEXPENSIVELY CREATING A DEMAND/PRE-SELLING

While it is always helpful if a customer or prospective customer has heard of an existing product or service and knows its selling points, for a new product/service to be successful, it is absolutely essential to pre-sell it. The very essence of a new product/service means it is relatively unknown (unsought), and dictates the necessity for creating a demand. Many worthwhile new products which meet specific needs in the marketplace, which offer good return on investment possibilities, and which test market well, still fail for lack of pre-selling. The small-business person who wishes to reduce the cost/risk of introducing a new product because of limited resources has a special set of problems. However, by selectively using and expanding on the techniques discussed here, and later in Chap. 11 (Advertising, Packaging, Promotion, and Publicity), a small company with limited resources can inexpensively create substantial demand for new products/services. You can inexpensively pre-sell a new product/service through press releases and publicity, trade shows, mailings, radio and television giveaways, premiums, statement stuffers, catalogues, mail order advertising, plus sharing the cost of trade and cooperative advertising with suppliers and retailers.

Press Releases and Publicity

Publicity created by press releases represents the least expensive, most effective means of pre-selling a new product or service. A new product/service which receives publicity in a periodical acquires exposure, status, authenticity, and notoriety.

Write a newsworthy story about your new product/service, have photographs made, and submit the package to selected publications. If the new product/service has an industrial end use, submit the material to appropriate trade publications. For consumer products, you must pre-sell both the retailer and the retailer's customer; therefore, submit the material to both retail trade and consumer publications. Select publications read by your potential customer or ultimate user.

Magazines and newspapers always have space to fill. Interesting new product/service press releases represent an easy, inexpensive means for an editor to obtain good material. Eye-catching photographs with captions produce good results. Be sure the press release contains information on how and where to purchase the product or service. Resources permitting, you might initially consult a professional public relations firm. You will quickly learn the techniques, and be able to perform this function admirably yourself.

You can obtain free exposure for new consumer products/services in newspapers and some consumer magazines by using the following techniques. First, decide which section of the publication should receive your press release. If the new product is an oven cleaner or squirrel trap, you would submit material to the home and garden editor. If the new product is apparel, you would submit material to the fashion editor. If the new service guarantees tire repairs for two years, you would submit material to the auto editor.

Next, buy copies of reference books which list publications and their specific editors. For newspapers the reference book is *Editor and Publisher International Year Book,* "The Encyclopedia of the Newspaper Industry," 575 Lexington Avenue, New York, NY 10022. For newspapers and magazines the reference book is *The IMS Ayer Directory of Publications,* 426 Pennsylvania Avenue, Fort Washington, PA 19034. Select cities of interest, publications of interest, and submit the press release package to the appropriate editor by name. The results of such a program will amaze you.

In the early 1970s a small knitting mill introduced men's long underwear with feet. The item was a male, heavier-weight version of panty hose, offering users warmth without weight. Management test marketed the item in two New York City department stores just prior to Christmas. A press release with pictures was sent to the major New York dailies. One of the papers printed the story and pictures on the fashion page. By chance, a wire service picked it up, and several days later the story was in hundreds of newspapers across the country, from Portland, Maine, to Los Angeles, California. Thousands of people started asking retailers for this new product. The little company was besieged with telephone calls and orders from retail outlets. Of course, since it was test marketing, inventories were minimal, creating much frustration.

You would follow a similar procedure for publicizing a new industrial/commercial product or service in trade journals, and a new consumer item in retail trade publications. Select those trade publications read by the decision makers in the appropriate market, prepare an interesting press release with photos, and mail it to the correct editor. Listings of trade publications can be found through *Standard Rate and Data* and the *Standard Periodical Directory.*

An article in a steel trade publication concerning a new inexpensive pollution control device created enough unsolicited orders for two years' production. An article in a hospital management trade publication concerning a new guaranteed 24-hour cleaning service produced inquiries from all over the country.

Although publicity through press releases is most effective in promoting new products/services, don't neglect it as a communication tool for your existing line. A regular program of press releases on older products/services can also produce worthwhile sales results.

Make reprints of worthwhile published articles and photos which appear as a result of your press releases. Combine these reprints with sales bulletins and direct mail pieces, and send them to salespeople, customers, and prospects. Recipients consider reprints important and will take the time to read them.

Trade Shows

In most industries, trade shows represent an effective means of pre-selling or introducing new products/services. To accomplish this, you must choose the trade show attended by the appropriate decision makers, notify important appropriate customers and prospects that you have an exhibit, design an attractive display, and teach salespeople how to make a two-minute presentation.

Since the cost can be considerable—space alone averaged $46 a square foot in 1981—be sure to pick the trade show attended by the appropriate audience, by the appropriate decision makers. Does the person responsible for your new products/services' purchasing decision attend a specific trade show? The 1982 annual *Directory of Trade and Industrial Shows* published by Successful Meetings lists over 10,000 trade shows.

For commercial business-to-business products you can attend an industrial trade show such as the Computerized Office Equipment Exposition, American Hospital Association Convention, or the Communications Network Conference. For consumer products you can attend the appropriate retailer trade show, such as those for shoes, sportswear, consumer electronics, books, furniture, housewares, or gourmet food. In addition, there are a number of trade shows which present specialized consumer products directly to the consumer such as ski equipment and apparel, sail and power boats, automobiles, and camping equipment.

For example, if you have developed a new iridescent scented dripless candle, the Houseware Show might prove effective. If you have developed a new device for accurately pouring cocktails, or an ice machine leasing service, the Restaurant Show might prove effective. If you have a new cutting fluid, the Machine Tool Show might prove effective.

In addition to these large, well-known, and rather expensive shows, there are thousands of less expensive regional trade shows, and some very specialized sub-industry trade shows. For example, the Men's and Boys' Apparel Club of Nebraska holds two trade shows a year in Omaha. The New England

Machinery Equipment Dealers hold a trade show in Boxbourough, Massachusetts, each December. Separate trade shows are held solely for robotics, yarn, knitting equipment, video games, fertilizer, bicycles, fiberglass, ceramics, carpet cleaners, off-shore oil drilling, food-packaging equipment, community antennas, energy-saving devices, model railroads, hospital equipment and services, bread and pastry machines, welding equipment, hospital business machines, and poultry feed. Often, these less costly smaller shows produce excellent results because of limited competition. For a smaller business, the cost of a trade show can be further reduced by sharing your booth with another compatible firm.

The average cost of making a customer contact at a trade show was $68 in 1981, compared to over $100 for an average sales call in the field. The key to a successful trade show lies in effectively contacting a maximum number of qualified prospects. Before a trade show opens, notify important appropriate customers and prospects that you will be exhibiting new products. This can be accomplished through trade publication advertising, or a mailing piece which might include reprints of articles or product literature on your new product/ service. Also, mention in your press releases that the new product/service can be seen at the trade show.

The exhibit itself should be eye-catching and quickly tell your story. A new product or service requires an unusual display showing use, benefits, and competitive advantage. If appropriate, you may wish to demonstrate the new item. At your booth, distribute reprints of published articles on the new product/ service. Offer cards so that interested prospects may leave their names and addresses. The appropriate field salesperson should then receive these cards, and follow up with a sales call and product literature.

Selling at a trade show involves some special skills. For example, customers become turned off by salespeople who smoke, drink coffee, or eat food at the booth. Customers also become turned off by salespeople who pace nervously, talk endlessly with fellow workers, or stand with arms folded across their chests. Salespeople at trade shows need to engage in a series of two-to-five-minute pitches to a stream of strangers. You must teach these salespeople how to give an effective two-to-five-minute presentation, and how to properly greet prospects. Questions such as "May I help you?" only receive a "No thanks" answer. On the other hand questions which demand a response, such as "Does your store sell candles?" or "What type cutting fluid do you presently use?" not only starts the visitors talking, but helps to qualify them as prospects. Ten qualified prospects might walk by while the salesperson is talking to a browser or even an unidentified competitor. Salespeople should not prejudge visitors based on looks.

Remember your objectives at a trade show are (1) to maximize exposure of your new offering to the appropriate decision makers, (2) to produce the names of interested qualified prospects for field salespeople to call on, and (3) to make enough actual sales to at least pay for your participation in the show.

You should investigate the possibility of using a trade show to see if the cost/benefit relationship favors your participation. Trade shows prove very effective for introducing new products/services, but in certain industries and regions, they can also be used effectively on a continuing basis for existing products/services. Many small firms with no sales force rely on trade shows for customer contacts. Solar-heated swimming pools, reed relays, high-speed dental drills, the Attaché portable computer, and many computer software programs were first introduced at trade shows by small companies.

Mailings

A program of mailings to buyers, corporate purchasing agents, and other company decision makers such as merchandise managers, engineers, and production managers also helps to inexpensively pre-sell new products. A mailing can take the form of an interesting newsletter, copies of press releases, reprints of published articles, or just product literature. The piece must be addressed with the recipient's name and title, not just sent to: "Purchasing Agent, Maintenance Supplies, Cabot Machinery." Have each salesperson submit names and addresses of customers and prospects for the mailing. You can selectively supplement these names with lists bought from direct mail houses, and from names obtained at trade shows.

You may wish to draw special attention to your new product mailing by using Western Union Mailgrams or the U.S. Postal Service's E-Com (electronic computer originated mail). Both claim the advantage of strong impact, with over 90% of Mailgrams and E-Coms being read by the recipient. Both services involve your message being read to a computer which then prints the letters at various locations. The mail is guaranteed to be delivered in one or two days in a distinctive, attention-getting envelope. The cost is surprisingly reasonable.

Mailings represent an inexpensive way for smaller businesses to keep their names in front of customers and prospects between a salesperson's visits. Although they are most effective for new products/services, also consider using mailings for existing items. Nonleather synthetic shoes, string ties, miniature transformers, and flexible memory disks were first introduced to the trade through mailings.

Radio and Television Giveaways

Offering new consumer products or services to radio and television shows as giveaways results in excellent, inexpensive exposure. Both radio disc jockeys and television game shows have an insatiable need for unusual items to use as prizes. Before giving the item away, they generally describe it and tell where it can be purchased. Your main cost usually is the donation of the merchandise, although some shows with large audiences also charge a fee.

Certain advertising agencies specialize in performing this service, for which they will ask a small fee. These agencies know which programs in which markets require which items. They handle all arrangements and provide you with information on listenership.

Choosing the appropriate program in the right city can be very important, especially if test marketing is involved. You would receive little value from giving away portable home whirlpools on an AM rock station or thermal motorcycle gloves on an FM better-music station. Choose the program that best reaches your potential customer or target market. A small manufacturer of fishing equipment first introduced the telescopic rod by using radio and television giveaways. Many small cosmetic concerns introduce ethnic products through media giveaways.

Premiums

Many firms successfully launch new products or services as premium items. For example, automobile dealers often offer unusual auto cleaning or repair items free for simply visiting their showroom. Automobile undercoatings were first introduced as a free item for customers who purchased new cars. The auto dealers buy these items from manufacturers and advertise them heavily at no expense to the supplier, in an effort to attract car customers. Through such advertising, consumers hear about the item and may purchase it at their local store.

For example, real estate companies often offer new and unusual home or garden products/services to prospects who visit an available house or apartment. In Minneapolis a new home cleaning service and a tropical plant rental service were successfully launched as free premiums for customers who bought houses or condominiums. The real estate agency heavily advertised the offer, which created wonderful free exposure for the new services. People who had no interest in buying a house or condominium heard of the services and started using them. The real estate agency absorbed the cost of one year's cleaning and one year's plant rental into the cost of the house or condominium.

Parachute-weight purses were first introduced as free premiums for buying a certain package of cosmetics. The cosmetic manufacturer bought the purses and gave them away. Many new toys and games have been launched as premium items for opening or adding to a bank account. Folding sunglasses were introduced as premiums for car rentals. All these premium offers included a great deal of advertising. *U.S. News* offered a pen with a digital clock as a premium for buying a 22-week subscription. They sent out a national mailing with this offer and included a picture of the pen. Possibly the odorless oven cleaner could be introduced as a premium with the purchase of a home appliance.

Consider whether your new product/service could be used and advertised as a premium. If so, contact the appropriate party.

You might also consider whether existing products/services lend themselves to sales as premium items. However, premium buyers generally desire something new or out of the ordinary to attract their customers, and they only offer it for short time periods. Moreover, selling an established product/service as a premium can upset present customers, who may feel it cheapens the item. Also, present retail customers and consumers might object to giving something away for which they had to pay.

Direct Response Marketing

A smaller company with limited resources can inexpensively create substantial demand for new products/services by using direct-response marketing techniques. These include statement stuffers, catalogues, and mail order ads.

Statement Stuffers.   For new consumer products/services, credit card and retail store statement stuffers allow you to create a national demand at minimum cost. Diners Club, American Express, Mobil, Visa, Mastercharge, etc. search out new products/services which might be appropriate items for one of their monthly stuffers. Via a statement stuffer, your message reaches millions of affluent people, and is paid for by the orders received from credit card holders. The same stuffer is seldom sent to all card holders, but rather to select groups who have previously purchased a similar item, live in a certain region of the country, or charge over a certain amount annually. Although only a small percentage of those receiving the stuffer respond by buying the new product/service from the credit card company, the other 98% become aware of the item. Some of these 98% will purchase your product/service at a later date through conventional retail outlets.

Most national credit card concerns will refer you to a subcontractor who handles all their mail order business. The subcontractor chooses the items, designs the stuffer, sets retail prices, buys the merchandise, and ships the orders. Direct-response consulting firms can also help you in this specialized type of marketing. The statement stuffer's pictures and text do the selling. Collapsible umbrellas, carry-on luggage, and certain types of travel insurance were first offered through such an effort. Approach some major credit card concerns to see if your new product/service would be an appropriate item for one of their monthly stuffers.

Retail stores also continually look for new items to promote with statement enclosures, and so, for consumer products sold through retail outlets, their statement stuffers offer the small business another inexpensive means of pre-selling the ultimate user. The benefits are similar to those of a national credit card stuffer, except you generally reach a smaller regional market. Those receiving the stuffer may order your product/service by mail, telephone, or a store visit. Although only a small percentage of those receiving the stuffer respond with an immediate purchase, the remainder become aware of the item and may buy it later at any of your retail outlets.

Contact the advertising departments of your retail customers or prospects to explore this possibility. Generally, you pay the cost of printing the stuffer, and the retailer pays the cost of mailing it with their monthly charge card billing. Generally, orders received from the mailing will cover your costs. Many new cosmetic products have been successfully introduced with retail statement stuffers.

Although new products/services lend themselves best to statement stuffers, existing items can also be sold and advertised by this means. Review your line to see if other items might lend themselves to this sales approach.

Catalogues.   Specialty and retail catalogues represent another inexpensive direct-response means for introducing both consumer and industrial products. You might approach such consumer specialty catalogues as L.L. Bean, Eddie Bauer, Abercrombie & Fitch, or Land's End with a novel outdoor item; Kimballs or Vermont Country Store with a household device; Horchow or Trifles with a new fashion style; and The Fine Tool Shops, Leichtung, or Lynchburg Hardware & General Store with a new do-it-yourself product. Even Harley-Davidson has a very successful catalogue for motorcycle accessories and clothing.

In addition, many industrial/commercial items are sold through specialized business-to-business direct mail catalogues including material-handling, communications, safety, and scientific equipment; maintenance, office, laboratory, printing, and computer supplies; business forms, electronic typewriters, small computers, chemicals, ballot jacks, shelving, temperature control and solar devices, fiber optics, containers, grinding wheels, payroll time recorders, and roofing. Major publishers of business-to-business catalogues include Revere Chemical Products, Xerox, I.B.M., Moore Business Forms, Pitney Bowes, NCR, C & H Distributors (maintenance/material handling), Expandor (data communications equipment), Dozier Equipment (maintenance, material handling, safety equipment), Omega Engineering (temperature controls), McMaster-Carr Supply (110,000 items), Freund Can (containers), and Global Equipment (material handling).

Computer-aided telemarketing has greatly expanded catalogue sales. More than half the customers respond by toll-free phone rather than mail. The operator does not merely take an order, but engages in selling to increase the order size. With desk-top computers and video screens, the operator has immediate access to information on past purchases. He or she might ask if the caller would like to reorder other specific items which might be on sale.

Through such catalogues your message can reach millions of affluent consumers and thousands of corporate purchasing agents. Although only a small percentage of those receiving the catalogue respond by immediately purchasing the new product/service, the rest become aware of the item. Some of these people will purchase your product/service at a later date through conventional retail outlets or other forms of distribution. Immediate sales from the catalogue should pay for your advertising costs, and so the additional market exposure costs nothing.

Contact the specialty catalogues which best reach the specific customers for your new product/service. These catalogues depend on new ideas for their success. Down sleeping bags, organic shampoos, calendar watches, fiber glass roofing, high-strength epoxy, answering machines, and shatterproof safety glass were first offered through such an effort.

Major retail stores print numerous specialty catalogues of items which can be purchased by mail, by phone, or in the store. For consumer products sold through retail outlets, store catalogues offer the small business an inexpensive means of pre-selling the ultimate user. The benefits are similar to those of a national specialty catalogue, except you generally reach smaller, more heterogenous regional markets. Although only a small percentage of those receiving the catalogues respond with an immediate purchase, the remainder become aware of the item, and may buy it later at any of your retail outlets. Contact the advertising departments of your retail customers and prospects to explore this possibility. Retailers generally charge for catalogue space, but write an initial purchase order which covers your costs. New products ranging from men's fashion underwear to energy-saving heating devices first came to market through retail catalogues.

Although new products/services lend themselves best to catalogues, existing items can also be sold and advertised by this means. Review your line to see if older items might lend themselves to this sales approach.

Mail Order Ads.   Direct-response advertising in select periodicals allows you to advertise new consumer products nationally at little or no cost. National periodicals such as *The Wall Street Journal, Smithsonian, Rotarian, Parade* (the Sunday magazine insert), *Runner's World, Hot Rod, World Tennis, Popular Mechanics, Popular Electronics, Better Homes and Gardens,* and *Town and Country* have good readership and carry a great many mail order ads.

Choose an appropriate publication that reaches your specific target market or prospective customer. Buy advertising space for your new product/service, and include a direct mail return coupon and/or telephone number for those who wish to purchase it. By reading the ad, many people become familiar with the product/service, and may purchase it at a retail store or other outlet. Readers who respond by ordering the new product from you by phone or with the direct mail coupon pay for the ad. Home sanding and stripping devices which can be attached to electric drills, and large-size stretch jeans for truck drivers were successfully launched by small companies using this form of advertising.

Trade and Cooperative Advertising

You can inexpensively create a demand for your new product/service through sharing the cost of advertising in trade publications with suppliers and sharing the cost of advertising in newspapers with retailers. Advertising in trade publications allows you to inexpensively reach a very specific market and therefore proves appropriate for pre-selling a new product/service. Trade publications not only reach industrial/commercial markets, but also retail store buyers, merchandise managers, and management. Therefore, retail store trade publications can be used to pre-sell consumer products. Although many choices exist, there is always a most popular or appropriate trade publication. *Standard Rate and Data* lists over 4,000 trade publications including *Airport Service Management, American Laundry Digest, Apartment Construction News, Automotive Engineering, Broadcast Daily, Chemical Age, Chemical Equipment, Coal Industry News, Computer Data, Convenience Store Merchandiser, Cost Engineering, Design News, Forest Products Journal, Gas Digest, Golf Digest, Hardware Merchandising, Hospital Financial Management, Frozen Food Age, Laboratory Management, Light Metal Age, Meat Plant Magazine, Mens Wear, Musical Products News, Nuclear Instruments, Paper Trade Journal, Pollution Engineering, Pulp and Paper, Rubber World, Sporting Goods Business, Telephone Engineering and Management, Textile Industries, Womens Wear Daily,* and *Yard and Garden Product News.* What trade publication reaches the decision maker for your new product/service? Ask your major customers and prospects. Consult responses to your market research survey. You probably read the same publication. Select the trade publication local, national, daily, weekly, or monthly which allows you the best customer exposure.

Ask your suppliers for an advertising allowance to help fund new product advertising in trade publications. If you knit sweaters, approach your yarn suppliers for an advertising allowance. If you make industrial cleaning compounds, approach the chemical companies who sell you the raw material. The quantity you buy from these suppliers depends on the quantity you sell. A larger advertising budget should help sell more goods and services. Most small businesses buy materials and supplies from larger companies with substantial advertising budgets. Often, the small company neglects to take advantage of the advertising dollars available from larger firms. The clever small business should not fail to explore this opportunity.

If your new product can be sold through retail outlets, cooperative advertising produces excellent results for minimal cost. Contact key retail accounts and prospects in important market areas. Offer to share half the cost of a local newspaper or radio ad if they will stock your new product. The retailer's initial order should pay for your share of the ad. Tens of thousands will see or hear the ad and will become aware of your new product. Some will purchase the product immediately at the retail outlet which coops the ad. Many will purchase it later at another retailer as a result of the ad. Such a cooperative program places goods in key accounts, results in some direct sales, and inexpensively creates a much broader demand for your product. Be sure that cooperative newspaper ads contain a coupon for mail orders, and that radio and newspaper ads give a local number for telephone orders.

Since trade and cooperative advertising are an important part of pre-selling existing as well as new products/services, Chap. 11 (Advertising, Packaging, Promotion, and Publicity), deals with them in greater detail.

NAMING A NEW PRODUCT / SERVICE

A good name will not save a product/service which does not meet a need in the marketplace, but the right name can obtain attention for a new item, increasing initial sales and market share. Also, a good name makes it more difficult for firms with greater resources to copy your new item. A good name establishes your new item as proprietary. Equally important, poor names have severely hurt some new products. A name should attempt to neatly describe the product's use, benefits, and qualities taking into account the words' emotional meanings.

Start by determining what you want the name to accomplish. Make a list of qualities you want the product/service to convey, such as durability, knowledge, excitement, reliability, value, sensuality, status, freshness, masculinity, warmth. A manufacturer of wool plaid shirts and coats chose Woolrich; a manufacturer of computers, Sage I; a manufacturer of portable computers, Attaché; a manufacturer of computers which assist in design, Computervision; a manufacturer of small forklift trucks, Little Might; a home cleaning service, Maid-To-Order; and a giant telegram service, Colossal Gram.

Unusual names, or names that quickly tell what a product does, seem to more easily obtain the user's attention, invite interest, and stay in their memory. *Parting Company* was chosen as the title for a book on coping with being fired. Piggy Back was chosen for a service that transported truck trailers cross-country on railroad flatcars. Code-A-Phone, Record-A-Call, Phone-Mate, and Ansafone were chosen as names for automatic telephone-answering equipment. Long Haul was chosen as the name for large-size stretch jeans for truck drivers.

In choosing names, use a word's emotional meaning to arouse needs. Men associate names such as Mustang and Colt with the excitement of being a cowboy, which explains their choice as model names for sporty cars. Such names reinforce the user's self-image. The Thread-O-Life name for ladies' panty hose has strong positive emotional connotations for women, as the Die-Hard battery name does for men. Using the name Kanga Roos to describe athletic shoes with zippered pockets has different emotional connotations for women than for men, and different emotional connotations for adults than for teenagers. Using the name Bio Guard to describe sanitized products produces positive emotional responses, as does the name Weekender to describe casual products.

The men's long underwear with feet described earlier in this chapter was eventually offered by a multitude of firms with names ranging from Mani-hose, Manly-Legs, and Warm Johns to Heatards. The name Warm Johns best described the item's purpose and use with a positive emotional meaning. The name Mani-hose was unusual, funny, and had a good sound to it, but made a direct reference to the item's female counterpart, panty hose; it gave a feminine connotation to a male product. Heatards and Manly-Legs alluded to its derivation from ladies' wear, but unsuccessfully attempted to create a male image.

The heat-reflecting window shades described earlier were eventually offered by a multitude of firms with names such as Solar-X, Solar-Control, Solar-Flex, Clear-View, Kool-Lite, Temtrol, and Cool-Vue. All these names attempt to neatly describe the product's use and benefits.

Once you have selected a name that conveys the new product/service's qualities, test it on potential users through market research and test marketing. If it does not produce the desired reaction from customers and prospects, consider changing or altering the name. Lastly, have an attorney conduct a trademark search to make sure you can use the name without infringing on another firm's registration.

PRODUCT/SERVICE LIFE

You should keep in mind that products/services, like living things, pass through stages: introduction, growth, maturity, saturation, and decline. Each stage requires a different marketing strategy, and preparation for its successor.

Usually only one firm offers a new product/service in the introductory stage. Sales volume rises slowly, distribution is limited, production costs and prices are high.

In the growth stage, competition begins to enter the market. Sales increase rapidly, distribution expands, production costs and prices decline.

During the maturity stage, many competitors enter the market. Sales continue to increase, but not as rapidly as in the growth stage. Spare parts and service requirements become more critical. Due to increased competition, prices decline dramatically and distribution expands further.

By the saturation stage, the most efficient producers have eliminated some of the competition. This now becomes a replacement business.

In the decline stage, total sales drop, because other substitute products/services have been developed. Prices and the number of firms decline further, and only the most efficient remain. Survivors tend to specialize in basic areas where prices have stabilized, and as a result, distribution contracts.

SUMMARY

This chapter has dealt with techniques for reducing the risk and cost of introducing new products, allowing smaller businesses to participate in this worthwhile endeavor. The risks associated with new products or services can be limited by (1) finding market needs and competitive weaknesses, (2) seeking small markets which would be unprofitable for larger firms, (3) innovating rather than inventory, (4) determining return on investment, (5) using market research, (6) test marketing, and (7) inexpensively creating a demand.

You can inexpensively innovate new products/services through (1) different packing and packaging, (2) color identification, (3) unusual sizing, (4) unusual guarantees, (5) adding or subtracting features from an existing product, (6) use of private labels and licensing, (7) adopting from a related market, (8) adopting from an overseas market, and (9) reviving an old idea.

Market research involves (1) deciding what additional information you require concerning the new product/service, (2) reading related studies which have already been undertaken, (3) deciding on whether to use mail, phone, or personal interviews and what group you wish to interview, (4) correctly designing a questionnaire, (5) selecting a representative sample of potential customers for interviews and interpreting the data.

While it is always helpful if a customer or prospective customer has heard of an existing product or service and knows its selling points, for a new unsought product/service to be successful, it is absolutely essential to pre-sell it. A small business can inexpensively pre-sell a new product/service through press releases and publicity, trade shows, mailings, radio and television giveaways, premiums, statement stuffers, catalogues, mail order advertising, plus sharing the cost of trade and cooperative advertising with suppliers and retailers.

9
Pricing

Your product/service should be priced to maximize profit dollars, taking into account both its value and image to the user, plus competition. If you overprice, profit margins as a percentage of sales rise, but because unit sales will decline, you may not attain maximum profit dollars. If you underprice, unit sales may increase, but profit margins as a percentage of sales will decrease, and again you may not maximize profit dollars. This chapter discusses the process for reaching this middle ground which optimizes profits.

Many small businesses set prices on a cost-plus or "follow the leader" basis. Cost plus involves calculating the cost of manufacturing, or doing business—for example, labor, material, and factory overhead—and then arriving at the price by adding a set percentage for selling, general, and administrative expenses, and profit. Cost plus represents the minimum acceptable price, but does not maximize profits, because it does not consider what the market will bear, what the user will pay. At the ancient Maya Indian ruins in Mexico, tickets for the evening light-and-sound show cost natives 50 cents and foreigners $1.00. They are charging what the market will bear.

"Follow the leader" merely involves copying your competitors' prices, which assumes that *their* pricing will maximize *your* profits. Since their cost structures, products/services, and market positions differ from yours, and since they probably did not price correctly to maximize even their own profits, your following their example will hardly meet your objectives. In the lobby of a large office building in Atlanta, Dentyne gum sells for 32 cents at one tobacco store and for 37 cents at another. They both sell the same number of packages.

You should remember that while price indicates what the user must pay, which has negative connotations, it also communicates a great deal about quality, status, and expected satisfaction. Therefore, price becomes an important part of the product/service image. For instance, most people believe that a direct relationship exists between price and quality. Within the confines of Herald Square in New York City, you can obtain a shoeshine for 50 cents, $1.00, and $2.00. People wait in line for the $2.00 shine, while the 50-cent one is seldom busy. If you visited a store and found five marketing books priced at $5.00, $10.00, $15.00, $20.00, and $25.00 all covering approximately the same material, which one would you purchase? Would you trust a business book that only cost $5.00 or $10.00?

Most small-business people are timid about pricing and therefore charge less than they should. Few businesses meet their demise by overpricing, but many struggle along with marginal profits or liquidate because of underpricing.

INTRODUCTION

The pricing process involves determining what the market will bear by looking at your competitive advantage or place in the market, the type of goods or services you offer, and the type of customer you serve. You analyze your product/service features, image, and benefits to determine whether they are better, worse, or the same as competition. You determine whether the type of goods or services you offer are staple, impulse, specialty, emergency, homogeneous, or heterogeneous. You determine whether the type of customer you serve is a leader, early adapter, early majority, late majority, or laggard.

Once you have determined approximately what the user is willing to pay for your product or service and the approximate relationship between price and unit volume, you then determine what specific effect present, higher, or lower prices would have on your profits and what specific effect present, higher, or lower unit sales would have on your costs.

In order to determine what profit you can earn on a particular product or service at a particular price, you must compute its cost. You do this by obtaining from the company controller the direct labor, material, and factory overhead necessary to produce each product/service in the line, and then adding a factor for general, selling, and administrative expenses. The difference between this total and the selling price is that item's pretax profit.

Now you must evaluate whether the pretax profit of each item meets the firm's profit goals, and regardless of this, determine what effect higher or lower prices would have in maximizing profits. If an item's pretax profit does not meet the firm's goals, you have five alternatives: (1) lower costs either by taking something out of the item, becoming more labor efficient, seeking less expensive materials, or subcontracting the work; (2) raise prices to increase margins; (3) lower prices to increase unit volume and possibly raise profit dollars; (4) make no changes, but continue the present situation; (5) discontinue the item. You can use these same techniques to evaluate the effect on overall corporate profits of major changes in pricing strategy and/or cost cutting.

If your firm engages in off-price selling using rebates, premiums, coupons, terms, discounts, promotions, or advertising and freight allowances, these expenses must be added to your net price or reflected in the costs used to arrive at list prices. Management, not the sales force, should set and approve any variations from list prices.

Consumers have developed attitudes and beliefs about odd ($2.99) and even ($4.00) pricing, multiple prices (3 for $9.00), and oddball prices ($11.11).

Depending on your desired product/service image, you can use these to your advantage. Skim pricing, higher-than-normal prices, and penetration pricing with lower-than-normal prices also can be used depending on the competitive situation.

In maximizing dollar profits through pricing, you must recognize certain legal restrictions. The Sherman Act of 1890 and the Clayton Act of 1914 prohibit concerted action by competitors, or any unfair action by a single firm which has the result of limiting competition. The Robinson-Patman Act of 1936 prohibits discrimination in price among different purchasers of the same quality goods if such price discrimination injures a competitor.

DETERMINING WHAT THE MARKET WILL BEAR

Introduction

To optimize profits, you must determine what the user is willing to pay for your product or service. How important is price to your unit volume? If you raised prices 5%, 10%, 15%, or 20%, would your unit sales drop by a corresponding amount? If you lowered prices 5%, 10%, 15%, or 20%, would your unit sales increase by a corresponding amount? To answer these questions, you must understand your competitive advantage and place in the market; type of goods or services offered; and type of customer served.

Each product/service or product/service group in your line must be analyzed separately. Are its features, image, and benefits better, worse, or the same as competition? A product/service can command a higher price and maintain volume if it is new, unique, difficult to imitate, uses difficult-to-obtain material, employs an exclusive name, projects a status image, or contains superior benefits and features.

For example, if you sell designer-name apparel, it should retail for more than private-label and national-brand apparel, regardless of the product's cost. If you sell to exclusive stores, your goods should sell at higher prices than comparable goods in less exclusive stores, regardless of the cost. If your car undercoating is guaranteed for the life of the car, it should sell for more than an undercoating guaranteed for five years, regardless of cost. If you offer overnight delivery of cleaning chemicals and your competitor does not, your product should be higher priced. If you offer 24-hour maintenance service and your competitor does not, you can again command a higher price.

The type of product/service you offer—staple, impulse, emergency, specialty, homogeneous, or heterogeneous—also influences what you can charge. Staple items such as industrial nuts and bolts, dye stuffs, office supplies, printing, groceries, and gasoline are purchased often and priced competitively. Impulse items, such as candy or street food, which are purchased for emotional appeal without preconceived intent can be priced less competitively. Emergency items such as overnight parts or document delivery, nighttime maintenance service, or 24-hour pharmacies command less competitive, higher prices. Homogeneous type goods, which users perceive as being very similar regardless of the manufacturer or provider, such as refuse removal, airplane travel, home appliances, lumber, or typewriters, must be priced more competitively than heterogeneous goods such as apparel, furniture, and machine tools, where users perceive differences in quality, uniqueness, and suitability. Some products/services such as Polo and La Coste apparel, or law firms and doctors with strong reputations in certain specialties, have developed specialty type status and loyal followings, which allow the provider to charge higher prices.

Your type of customer also influences what you can charge. Commercial/industrial firms and consumers can be classified as leaders, early adapters, early majority, late majority, and laggards.

Leaders are large successful companies and wealthy people whose self-images predispose them to try new products/services and buy the best of existing ones. When a new piece of equipment is developed for their industry, these firms want it first, regardless of price. When a new home stereo or video system is developed, these consumers want it first, whatever the price. Early adapters consist of wealthy and successful companies and people who follow the leaders and aspire to eventually becoming leaders. After the leaders purchase equipment or video systems, then the early adapters also purchase them, again with little regard for price.

Early majority customers consist of medium-sized businesses and white-collar workers who look up to early adapters and would like to follow their buying patterns, but at lower prices. Late majority customers consist of small businesses and skilled blue-collar workers who are more concerned about security and price than status.

Laggards consist of marginal businesses and unskilled laborers who buy out of necessity with great concern for price. They are not concerned with following the actions of others.

Because markets, customers, competition, and products/services continually change, you must formally review prices once or twice a year. You probably informally review prices continually.

For a consumer products sold through retail outlets, you not only consider what price the ultimate user will pay, but also what price to charge the store. You must offer the retailer an appropriate and attractive markup margin. Full-service stores offering better merchandise to better customers generally require higher markups than stores offering goods of lesser quality to customers of lesser means. Department and specialty stores work on 50% to 65% markups versus 40% to 50% markups in discount and chain stores.

Competitive Advantage/Place in the Market

To price a product/service correctly, you must understand its competitive advantage and place in the market, its expected pricing zone, and its relationship to other products in your line. At some point, higher prices will decrease demand and unit volume enough to totally offset any profit gains. Likewise, at some point a lesser price will not increase demand and unit volume enough to compensate for lower profit margins. Market research and test marketing can help you determine these points.

You must first determine from the marketplace whether your product/service's competitive advantage is quality, service, price, uniqueness, cost saving, color, durability, lack of maintenance, fidelity, accuracy, fast delivery, image, status, control of critical resources, or possibly the difficulty of imitating. I suggest listing each of your products/services or product/service groups on a separate piece of paper. Then list on each sheet comparative information on competition. How do the benefits or features of your offering realistically compare to those of the others? You acquire this information by talking with customers, prospects, salespeople; reading competitive sales brochures; and conducting market research. You have already accumulated some of this information for training salespeople.

If you offer something better, different, unique, exclusive, hard to compare, or with a status image, you should consider charging more than competition. If possible, do some market research or test marketing to determine how much more. At some point, higher prices will decrease demand and unit volume enough to toally offset any profit gain. Market research and test marketing will help you find this point. For instance, unit purchases of a sales management book might increase until the retail price reaches $15.00, then decrease 10% at $20.00, then decrease another 25% at $30.00, and another 50% at $40.00. In such a pricing decision, you weigh the increased profitability caused by higher prices against the risk and magnitude of lower unit volume. As you will see from the discussion which follows, your type of product/service and type of customers greatly influence this risk.

If you offer a product or service which is easy to compare, and is not especially different, unique, better, or exclusive, or does not contain a status image, you should probably charge the same as or only a little more than competition. If you offer an easy-to-compare product or service with features, image, and benefits inferior to competition, you cannot charge more than competition; you may charge the same, but probably should charge less. Again, market research and market testing can help determine how much less. At some point, a lesser price will not increase demand and unit volume enough to compensate for the lower profit margin.

Consumers, purchasing agents, and buyers all seek and enjoy a bargain. However, lower prices may give the impression that something is wrong, or that no one wants to buy the product/service. As will be discussed later, your type of product/service and type of customer also influence these decisions.

Consumers, purchasing agents, and retail store buyers all develop expected price zones based on past experience with a particular item. Prices that fall below or above those zones have negative connotations of inferiority or extravagance. Try to determine these zones for your products/services and keep their prices within them. A book on sales management retailing for $5.00 might be considered inferior, while one at $30.00 might be considered extravagant. A long-distance telephone service priced at half the Bell System's rates might be viewed as unreliable, while one priced at 20% below Bell might connote reliable value. A small-business computer system at $10,000 might appear inferior, while one at $100,000 might appear extravagant.

In pricing a product/service, you must not only take into account its competitive position in the marketplace, but its relationship to other items in your line as well. You should not price the anklet version of an argyle sock at more than the over-the-calf. You should not price a three-color polyester striped tie at more than your three-color silk striped tie. It would be foolish to price a new nail-making machine which produces 50,000 units in eight hours at less than your present model which produces only 36,000 units, even though the new unit costs less to manufacture.

The American tie licensee for a famous French designer offered a fine line, mostly silks, with retails ranging from $7.00 to $25.00. The licensee's president decided to drop the $7.00 styles, since they appeared unprofitable. The sales manager suggested continuing these styles but raising the retail price to $10.00. They test marketed the idea in several cities and sold more units at $10.00 than they had at $7.00. Customers had considered $7.00 designer ties as inferior, but $10.00 ones as a good value.

A leading manufacturer of hand-held calculators developed a reliable unit to retail at $5.00. It did very poorly until the price was raised to $12.00, at which point sales increased sharply. At $5.00, consumers thought something must be wrong and that no one wanted the device. Both the tie and calculator manufacturers originally had made mistakes concerning the consumer's perception of their product price and their competitive advantage in the marketplace.

An industrial refuse removal firm had old equipment which often broke down, causing unreliable service. Its pickup prices were the same as more reliable competitors with newer equipment, which caused its business to decline. The owner determined that he could reduce prices 15%, and if pickups increased by 25%, the company would be more profitable. Customers were willing to accept the inconvenience of irregular service for a price reduction; thus his strategy proved correct.

When microcircuitry was first introduced, it offered electronic systems manufacturers many benefits in size and reliability, but initial prices were too far above competitive devices. The microcircuitry manufacturers lowered prices until they were more competitive, causing some short-term profit declines, but eventually unit volume and profits grew dramatically.

In pricing a product/service you must take into account its competitive advantage and place in the market, its expected pricing zone, and its relationship to other products in your line. If you offer something better, different, unique, exclusive, hard to compare, or with a status image, you should consider charging more than competition. If you offer a product or service which is easy to compare, and not especially different, unique, better, exclusive, or containing a status image, you should probably charge the same as or only a little more than competition. If you offer an easy-to-compare product or service with features, image, and benefits inferior to competition, you cannot charge more than competition; you may charge the same, but probably should charge less.

Type of Goods and Services Offered

To price a product/service correctly you must understand its user classification (how the user perceives it): staple, impulse, emergency, homogeneous, heterogeneous, or specialty. Staple and homogeneous products/services require more-competitive pricing than heterogeneous, impulse, emergency, or specialty items.

Staples. Staple items such as rivets, business forms, office supplies, electrical wiring, nylon yarn, refuse removal, groceries, and gasoline are purchased frequently by businesses or consumers, and priced competitively. Staples represent basic repeat items, low in unit price relative to other purchases. Although there are some exceptions, firms find it difficult to develop brand loyalty or charge prices above competition for staple items. Users consider reliable delivery, availability, and competitive prices essential. In Chap. 10 on "Distribution" we will refer to staple items as convenience goods, which customers will not spend much time shopping for. If a sweater manufacturer cannot obtain nylon yarn quickly from one supplier, or obtain a competitive price, it will use another. If you need charcoal for the Sunday cookout and the local grocery store is sold out or has raised prices, you merely buy it at the local gas station.

Analyze how the user views your product/service. If it is viewed as a staple, you must offer prices not greater than competition, and must put emphasis on reliable delivery and availability. It is difficult to price staples according to a superior competitive advantage or better place in the market. Unit volume

drops dramatically when you raise prices above competition. A small manufacturer of dry dog food developed a superior product with greater protein content. When priced the same as lower-protein dog food, it sold well. When priced
above the lower-protein dog food, sales declined dramatically. A small quarry
in Northwestern Indiana sold sand and gravel to steel mills, railroads, and construction firms. The owner unsuccessfully attempted to raise prices above competition by offering lower minimum quantities, faster deliveries, and various
stone sizes.

Homogeneous.   Users perceive homogeneous items, such as commercial airplane travel, long-distance phone service, some home appliances, most lumber,
typewriters, copying machines, and material handling equipment, as being very
similar in quality and features regardless of the provider, thus making product
differentiation difficult and competitive pricing essential. Consumers, retail
store buyers, and purchasing agents will shop for the best price. Homogeneous
items are not as basic, or purchased as frequently as staple items, and carry
higher relative unit prices.

If the user perceives your product/service as homogeneous, you must offer
prices not greater than competition and consider the results of prices below
competition. It is difficult to price homogeneous items according to a superior
competitive advantage or better place in the market. Unit volume drops dramatically when you raise prices above competition. Small regional airlines exist
because they underprice the majors. Even the Xerox name has not allowed that
company to rise above the 1980s' price war in office copiers.

Heterogeneous.   Users perceive heterogeneous items such as apparel, furniture, machine tools, consultants, catering services, and hotels as different in
quality, uniqueness, and suitability, thus making product and price differentiation easier for the provider. Consumers, retail store buyers, and purchasing
agents, although concerned with price, will generally base their choice among
alternatives on features, benefits, and image. Heterogeneous products/services,
like homogeneous, are not as basic, or purchased as frequently as staple items,
and carry higher relative unit prices. In Chap. 10 on "Distribution" we will
refer to both homogeneous and heterogeneous items as shopping goods, which
customers want to examine and compare before purchasing.

If the user perceives your product/service as heterogeneous, you can price
according to competitive advantage or place in the market. At some point,
higher prices will decrease demand and unit volume enough to totally offset
any profit gain; and at some point, lower prices will not increase demand and
unit volume enough to compensate for the lower profit margin. Again, market
research and market testing can help determine these levels.

Lifetime-guaranteed hosiery is certainly worth more money to the user than a similarly constructed nonguaranteed pair. The ice-machine rental firm which provides maintenance and free ice delivery when needed can charge a higher monthly fee than other firms which do not offer these benefits. A high channel capacity microwave antenna should sell for more money than antennas with less capacity. These are all examples of heterogeneous products/services.

Specialty. Users develop strong brand loyalties for specialty products and services such as Countess Mara ties, Crabtree and Evelyn beauty aids, Godiva chocolates, Tanqueray gin, Top Sider Shoes, Club Med Vacations, Michelin Tires, *Fortune* magazine, *The Wall Street Journal,* certain investment advisory services, Dun and Bradstreet, the Joffrey Ballet, Harvard Business School, and the Sunday *New York Times.* Specialty products and services have prestige images and status, which can command premium prices. Often you can license designer and brand names, thus putting your product/service in a specialty category. Specialty items are generally but not always heterogeneous products/ services which have been advertised heavily through media, word of mouth, logos, embroideries, point-of-purchase displays, and packaging. The customer will spend considerable time and effort searching out specialty goods. Once purchased, specialty items have high visibility for the user, and generally contain easy identification for the user's associates. The user obtains status through purchasing the specialty item, and through association with others who have also purchased the item.

Analyze whether your product/service lends itself to specialty status. Does it or could it connote an exclusive image? If appropriate, try to develop or maintain specialty status, becuase it allows you a great deal of pricing flexibility.

If your product/service has specialty status, you can price it above competition because the user perceives it as unique and better. Pricing it above competition helps to maintain its image as an exclusive item. Unit volume will not be terribly sensitive to price. Doctors and lawyers with strong reputations in certain specialties can charge twice the rates of others without those reputations. Although Cadillacs and Chevrolets for certain model years may have looked alike, one had an original price which was twice the other. In 1983 *The Wall Street Journal* cost 40 cents a copy, while most city dailies were 25 cents. In 1983 the Sunday *New York Times* sold for at least $2.00 outside New York City, while local Sunday editions cost $1.00. These are all examples of specialty product/service pricing.

Impulse. Users purchase impulse items such as shoe shines, arcade games, and street food without any preconceived intent, because of emotional appeal and accessibility. You purchase popcorn, ice cream, pretzels, roasted chestnuts, cookies, and croissants for immediate consumption from street vendors or franchises because the food looks or smells good and is easily accessible. Your desire for the product is immediate, and no appropriate substitutes seem readily available, so you do not compare prices.

You leave home one December morning without any intention of giving money to the Salvation Army, but when you hear the bell ringing and see Santa Claus, you put a dollar in the kettle. You have just purchased a dollar's worth of satisfaction. On the way home you buy pretty flowers from a street vendor. At the airport, you buy a key chain with your daughter's initials. At an art fair, you have your photo taken or portrait drawn. These are all examples of impulse items.

If users perceive and react to your product/service as an impulse item, price it at the high end of the acceptable pricing zone, but be careful not to make it exorbitant or unit volume will decline dramatically. Price it above comparable non-impulse items. A freshly toasted pretzel bought from a street vendor should sell for more than a packaged pretzel bought in a grocery store. In 1983 Good Humor, Baskin-Robbins, Bresler, Dairy Queen, Tastee Freeze, and Haagen-Dazs sold their basic ice cream cones from 50 cents to $1.00.

Emergency. Emergency products and services such as express mail, overnight freight/document delivery, 24-hour pharmacies, towing services, strike mediation services, boiler repairs, and ambulances command less competitive, higher prices. The user needs them in a hurry, so convenience and availability become more important than price. If you need a part or a document the next day, you will not bother comparing prices of competitive services. Unit volume of emergency products/services is not terribly sensitive to price.

If users purchase your product or service to solve an emergency, price it at the high end of the acceptable pricing zone, and price it above comparable non-emergency items. Guaranteed overnight freight delivery between Boston and New York should command a higher price than the ordinary two-day freight delivery. If the emergency creates an ongoing expense until resolved, such as a strike or an oil spill, consider pricing your problem-solving service based on alleviating that expense.

Combination. Most products/services are not perceived by the user as purely staples, specialty, impulse, heterogeneous or homogeneous in nature. Most represent a combination of these classifications. For example, Haagen-Dazs ice cream is a specialty impulse item, which further reinforces a high-end price. Razor blades are a heterogeneous staple, which allows certain brands to sell for more than others. In analyzing your product/service type to help determine a pricing policy, weigh the relative importance of each element in the combination.

Also, users perceive variations of a product differently. Consumers might consider men's white underwear briefs as a homogeneous staple, but patterned, colored fashion bikinis as a heterogeneous impulse item, and designer underwear as a specialty product. If you manufactured underwear, you might therefore adopt a different pricing strategy for each of these product groups.

Also, different users may perceive the same product/service under a different classification. What might be a homogeneous item to one customer group might be a heterogeneous item to another. You must then weigh the relative importance of each customer group.

Business being a dynamic process, user perceptions and product/service classifications change. Digital watches might start as a heterogeneous item but after a few years become a homogeneous item. For this reason you must review classifications annually.

Summary.   To price a product/service correctly, you must understand its user classification. Staple items are purchased frequently and priced competitively. Users perceive homogeneous items as being very similar in quality and features, thus making product differentiation difficult, and competitive pricing essential. Users perceive heterogeneous items as different in quality, uniqueness, and suitability, and so the provider can price according to competitive advantage in the marketplace. Users develop strong brand loyalties for specialty products and services, and so these command premium prices. Users purchase impulse items without any preconceived intent, because of emotional appeal and accessibility, so you may price them at the high end of their pricing zone. Since the user needs emergency products/services in a hurry, they command less competitive, higher prices.

Type of Customer

To price a product/service correctly, you must not only understand its competitive position in the marketplace, and its user classification, but also its type of customer. For consumer products, type of customer often determines the type of store in which the item is offered. Commercial/industrial firms and consumers can be classified as the following types of customers: leaders, early adopters, early majority, late majority and laggards. Product/services sold primarily to leaders and early adopters require less-competitive pricing than those sold to early majority, late majority, and laggards.

Leaders.   Leaders are wealthy successful people and large successful companies whose self-images predispose them to try new products/services and to buy the best of existing ones. These firms want the best and the newest equipment. These individuals want the best and the newest fashions, autos, stereos, vacations, and restaurants. They are more concerned with status, image, benefits, and features (in that order) than price. When making a purchase, leaders demand a great deal of personal attention from the seller.

If your firm developed a robot to deliver office mail, or if your firm knit cashmere sweaters for Gucci, leaders would be your customer group. The consumer portion of this customer group purchases products at exclusive specialty stores. If the customer group for your product/service consists primarily of leaders and/or is sold through exclusive specialty shops, price your item at the upper end of the expected pricing zone. You can take full advantage of your superior competitive position in the marketplace. Unit volume will not be terribly sensitive to price. A higher price appeals to this customer group and enhances the product image in their view.

A Midwestern citizen band radio company developed an improved navigational device for private company aircraft. Since the device grew out of an existing product, costs were minimal. The sales manager priced the new unit at twice any comparable device on the market. He sold more than the firm could make.

In the 1970s many cashmere sweater manufacturers found that cost increases periodically forced them to raise suggested retail prices from $35 to over $100. Every time they raised prices, unit sales increased.

Early Adopters.   Early adopters consist of wealthy successful people and companies (not necessarily large) who aspire to eventually become leaders, and so follow their behavior. After the leaders purchase the robot, the company jet, and the cashmere sweater, the early adopters follow. However, the early adopters would not purchase these items unless the leaders purchased them first. Also, the early adopter would buy the cashmere sweater at a better department store where he or she shops, not an exclusive specialty store. If the customer group for your product/service consists of early adopters, and/or is sold through better department stores, price your item at the upper end of the expected pricing zone, and take advantage of your superior competitive advantage in the marketplace. Unit volume will not be terribly sensitive to price, but early adopters do require a great deal of attention and service when making a purchase.

Early Majority.   Early majority consists of not terribly prosperous or successful medium-sized businesses and white-collar workers who look up to early adopters and would like to follow their buying patterns, but generally do not have the resources. They would only buy the robots, company jet, and cashmere sweaters "at a price," and, on the consumer level, they shop at chain stores. Early majority customers must get the most for their money, and will shop around until they find the best relationship between price and value. If the customer group for your product/service consists of the early majority, or is sold through chain stores, price your item competitively, regardless of competitive advantages or place in the market. Unit volume will be quite price-sensitive.

Late Majority.   Late majority consists of small businesses and skilled blue-collar workers who are more concerned about security and price than status or image. They have no interest in following the actions of others through buying the robot, company jet, or cashmere sweater; and on the consumer level, they shop at discount stores. When machinery wears out, they replace it with used equipment. When traveling on business, they fly economy and stay at cut-rate lodgings. When buying apparel, they seek synthetic fibers rather than natural. Late majority customers will shop around for the lowest price. If the customer group for your product/service consists of the late majority, or is sold through discount stores, a low price becomes an important competitive advantage. Unit volume will be very price-sensitive.

Used-equipment dealers find these customers very price-sensitive. A seven-year-old piece of machinery that cost $10,000 new might be turned down by a late majority customer because the $2,000 used price is $100 too high. An auto accessory manufacturer increased his business on one item 40% at a discount store by lowering the suggested retail price from $3.25 to $2.95.

Laggards.   Laggards consist of marginal businesses and unskilled laborers who are not concerned with status, image, or following the action of others, and who only buy out of necessity, with great concern for price. As equipment wears out, it often is not replaced. If a sweater is needed, they would visit a resale shop. Laggards regard a purchase as strictly functional. If the customer group for your product/service consists of laggards, price becomes the most important consideration. Volume is very price-sensitive.

A nonprofit resale shop received a used fur coat as a donation. The coat cost $1,000 new, and the resale shop offered it for $100. It finally sold for $25 because this customer group didn't care whether the coat was cloth or fur, only that it was inexpensive.

Combinations.   Most customers exhibit combinations of these types, and few could be accurately described as purely one or the other. Customers may also exhibit different buying behavior toward different types of goods. Also keep in mind that your product/service may appeal to several customer types, each having different buying habits. Therefore, you must weigh the relative importance of each type for your product/service.

Summary.   To price a product/service correctly, you must understand its type of customer. If the customer group for your product/service consists primarily of leaders or early adopters, price your item at the upper end of the expected pricing zone. If the customer group consists primarily of early majority, price your item competitively; if primarily late majority, a low price becomes an important competitive advantage; and if primarily laggards, price becomes the most important consideration.

Interrelationship in Pricing of Competitive Advantage, Type of Product/ Service, and Type of Customer

To optimize profits, you must determine what the user is willing to pay for your product or service, which involves understanding your firm's competitive advantage in the marketplace, type of goods/services offered, and type of customer served. These three factors are very much interrelated and to some extent overlapping.

A product/service which can command a higher price than competition because of superior benefits or features, a status image, newness, uniqueness, or exclusivity probably is a heterogeneous item, possibly even a specialty item, bought by leaders, early adopters, or early majority. This item certainly is not a homogeneous or staple product/service bought by late majority or laggards.

A product/service which must be priced at the lower end of its pricing zone because it is not unique, better, exclusive, or different, but easy to compare, probably is a homogeneous item, possibly even a staple. If it's a staple, customers might include all user classifications. If it's a nonstaple homogeneous item, customers probably would not include leaders or early adopters.

Impulse and emergency items generally are not compared on a competitive advantage or price basis by the user, and they involve all customer types. At some time, most businessess require overnight delivery of a part or document, and at some time most consumers buy food from a street vendor.

DETERMINING THE RELATIONSHIP TO PROFIT OF PRICE AND UNIT SALES

You have determined approximately what the user is willing to pay for your product or service and the approximate relationship between price and unit volume. Now, with the controller's help, you must determine what specific effect present, higher, or lower prices have on your profits, and what specific effect present, higher, or lower unit sales have on your costs.

Your product/service should be priced to maximize profits. If you overprice, profit margins as a percentage of sales rise, but because unit sales decline, you may not attain maximum profit dollars. If you underprice, unit sales increase, but profit margins as a percentage of sales decrease, and again you may not maximize profit dollars. To understand these relationships, you must determine the costs of your products/services by obtaining the direct labor, material, and factory overhead necessary to produce each product/service in the line, and then adding a factor for general, selling, and administrative expenses. The difference between this total and the selling price is that particular item's pretax profit.

Now you must evaluate whether the pretax profit of each item meets the firm's profit goals, and in addition to this, determine what effect higher or lower prices would have on maximizing profits. If an item's pretax profit does not meet the firm's goals, you have five alternatives: (1) lower costs by taking something out of the item, becoming more labor efficient, seeking less expensive materials, or subcontracting the work; (2) raise prices to increase margins; (3) lower prices to increase unit volume and possibly raise margins; (4) make no changes, continue the present situation; (5) discontinue the item. You can use these same techniques to evaluate the effect on overall corporate profits of major changes in pricing strategy and/or cost cutting.

Cost

In order to determine what profit you can earn on a particular product or service at a particular price, you must compute its cost. You do this by obtaining from the company controller or accountant the direct labor, material, and factory overhead necessary to produce each product/service in the line, and then adding a factor for general, selling, and administrative expenses. The difference between this total and the selling price is that particular item's pretax profit. If your firm does not employ a controller or accountant, either the president, the sales manager, or the manufacturing manager must perform these tasks. Regardless of who prepares the numbers, the sales manager must understand the method of their preparation.

Many smaller businesses do not accumulate accurate data on the cost of each item. A California firm with sales below $1,000,000 assembled industrial batteries for use as power sources on laboratory lasers. The more power sources the firm sold, the more money it lost. When the owner finally computed the cost of this item, he discovered that the manufacturing cost alone exceeded the selling price.

The power sources were a specialty research product which represented a small cost item in an expensive system, and at the time, this firm was the only manufacturer. The customers, mainly research laboratories, would have paid "any" price.

Direct Labor. The controller obtains the direct labor costs of producing an item by first listing the labor operations involved in making it. In manufacturing a sweater, for example, you have labor involved in knitting the material, dying it, sewing it into a garment, pressing, packing, and shipping it. In the case of a sonic cleaning tank, you have labor involved in cutting the sheet metal, welding the pieces into a tank, assembling the tank to its legs and sonic vibrator, and crating and shipping it. In the case of a hospital cleaning service, you have labor involved in assembling the necessary supplies and equipment, driving people to the hospital, actually cleaning the hospital, driving people back from the hospital, and cleaning the equipment.

Your firm should keep records of how long each of these operations require per unit. It takes 45 minutes to knit the material for a sweater, 55 minutes to dye a lot of 55 pieces, 35 minutes for sewing each garment, and 14 minutes for pressing, packing, and shipping each unit. It takes 19 minutes to cut the sheet metal for a cleaning tank, 55 minutes to weld the pieces together, 80 minutes to assemble the tank, legs and vibrator, and 90 minutes to crate and ship it. It takes 125 minutes to assemble equipment and supplies for cleaning a particular hospital, 62 minutes to drive the necessary manpower to and from the site, and 83 man hours to clean it.

Next, the controller multiplies the hourly rates involved by the times required for each operation, and adds them all up for a total direct labor cost. If the person who runs the knitting machine receives $9.00 an hour, then the labor cost of knitting a sweater is $45/60 \times \$9.00$ or $6.75. If the person who assembles the sonic tank receives $6.00 an hour, then the labor cost of assembly is $80/60 \times \$6.00$ or $8.00. If the people who clean the hospital receive $4.50 an hour, then the labor cost of cleaning is $373.50.

Some firms pay workers by piece work, paying an agreed-upon rate for each operation, no matter how long it takes. For instance, the knitter receives $6.50 per sweater, the assembler $7.00 per tank, and the cleaning person $1.00 per room. Whether labor is paid by the hour or by the piece/unit, you add up the labor costs per function to obtain a total for your product or service.

Materials. The controller obtains the materials cost of producing an item by listing and then totaling the amount and price of all materials necessary to make or offer it. In the case of a sweater, material would include 12 ounces of orlon yarn at $3.45 a pound, two ounces of dyes and chemical at $5.58 a pound, two ounces of sewing thread at $2.00 a pound, labels, tissues, cellophane envelopes, boxes, and cartons, all at their respective unit costs. The controller multiplies the amount used per unit, in this case per sweater, by the appropriate price for the material, and adds up all these for a total materials cost.

In the case of a sonic cleaning tank, materials would include 28 pounds of stainless steel sheet metal at $1.07 a pound, 22 pounds of structural angle legs and framing at $.22 a pound, two pounds of welding rod at $5.75 a pound, the sonic vibrator bought complete from another supplier, eight feet of wiring, three switches, and wood for crating, all at their respective unit costs. In the case of a hospital cleaning service, material would include the gallons of chemicals required, wax, finishes, and cloth. Again, the controller multiples the amount used per unit by the appropriate price for the material, and adds all these up to arrive at a total materials cost per unit.

Also included in materials costs are services, subassemblies, and components purchased from other firms which become part of the product/service. For example, the controller would include as material the cost of having a designer logo embroidered on the sweater by another firm, or the cost of buying complete sleeves from another knitter. If your firm purchased preassembled legs and frames from a job shop for the sonic tank, you would include these in materials costs. If your firm used a private transportation service to deliver and pick up cleaning people at hospitals, you would include the cost under materials.

Factory Overhead. Factory overhead consists of costs related to the production of a product/service which cannot be easily identified with an individual unit, and so they must be allocated by a formula. Factory overhead includes such items as production employee health insurance, paid holidays, make-up pay, overtime premiums, payroll taxes, supervisory salaries, vacation pay, maintenance labor, depreciation, equipment rental, factory supplies, casualty and business interruption insurance, light and power, freight in, machine parts and repairs, and factory rent.

These actual or budgeted factory overhead expenses are totaled for each year, and then allocated back to the product/service provided by hours or dollars of labor, hours of machine time, units of output, or some combination. For example, the sweater company controller might calculate that the annual cost of all production employee benefits, $140,000, represents 17.5% of total direct labor cost, which is $800,000. Therefore 17.5% of the direct labor cost of each sweater would be added to that unit's cost for employee benefits. The annual cost of depreciation, power, equipment rental, parts, and repairs might total $60,000, which, divided by total annual knitting machine hours, 180,000, equals 33 cents per machine hour. The controller could allocate these factory overhead costs back to each unit of production by adding to the unit cost 33 cents per knitting hour necessary to produce the sweater. The annual cost of insurance, rent, and lights might total $60,000, which, divided by the 240,000 sweaters produced annually, equals 25 cents per sweater. The controller could allocate these factory overhead costs back to each unit of production by adding 25 cents to the cost of each sweater.

Whatever method your firm chooses for allocating factory overhead costs to each unit, make sure that total dollars allocated equal total dollars of actual costs. If annual factory overhead costs total $300,000, be sure you have allocated all $300,000 (no more, no less) back to your product's/service's unit costs. You may have allocated $100,000 using machine hours, $100,000 using direct labor hours, and $100,000 using units produced. As a method of double-checking, multiply the factory overhead assigned to each unit by annual units produced, and compare the dollars to total annual factory overhead expense.

General, Selling, and Administrative Expenses.   General, selling, and administrative (G.S.&A.) expenses consist of all other costs you have not accumulated under direct labor, materials, and factory overhead, except federal and state income taxes. G.S.&A. includes such items as salespeople's commissions, salaries, bonuses, payroll taxes, and fringe benefits; plus salaries, bonuses, payroll taxes, and fringe benefits for the sales manager, president, controller, office manager, accountant, and secretarial and clerical personnel; plus advertising, royalties, prepaid freight, office rental, promotion, entertainment, travel, automobile, samples, and showroom expenses; plus data processing, telephone, interest, credit, collection, and bad debt expenses; plus lawyers, auditors, consultants, and office supplies.

You or the controller total the past year's G.S.&A. expenses and calculate their percentage relationship to last year's net sales. You or the controller total this year's or next year's budgeted G.S.&A. expenses and calculate their percentage relationship to this year's or next year's forecasted sales. You multiply this percentage by each product's selling price and add the resulting G.S.&A. allocation to materials, labor, and factory overhead, arriving at a total cost for the product/service.

For example, the sonic cleaning tank company had total actual G.S.&A. expenses last year of $300,000, or 20% of last year's actual sales, $1,500,000. This year the president estimates G.S.&A. at $330,000, or 21% of the $1,575,000 annual net sales estimated by the sales manager. Next year the president has budgeted G.S.&A. at $350,000, or 19% of the $1,837,000 annual net sales forecasted by the sales manager. In costing out a particular model, the sales manager feels safe using a 20% factor for G.S.&A.

The particular model involved sells for $1,100 and requires $750 to manufacture, $400 of material, $200 of direct labor, and $150 of allocated factory overhead. The sales manager multiples the 20% S.G.&A. factor by the model's selling price of $1,100 with a result of $220. This $220 represents the S.G.&A. allocation for this model and, when added to the $750 of manufacturing expense, results in a total cost for the model of $970. By subtracting the $970 from the $1,100 net selling price, the sales manager arrives at a pretax profit of $130 for this model.

Cost Cards. You or the controller should accumulate all this cost information on a separate card for each model, style, or job, and update it at least twice annually. Business is a dynamic process, and costs continually change.

The cost card for the sweater company might appear as follows:

Date _____

Style Number _____ Description _____

Manufacturing Specifications _____

Yarns	Type	Lbs. per Dozen	$ per Lbs.	$ per Dozen
		Total _____	$_____	$_____

Operation	Labor Cost	Item	Material Cost
Knitting	$_____	Total Yarn	$_____
Seaming	_____	Dyes & Chemicals	_____
Inspecting	_____	Labels	_____
Mending	_____	Tissues	_____
Pressing	_____	Boxes & Cartons	_____
Dyeing	_____	Embroidery	_____
Finishing	_____	Buttons	_____
Stockroom	_____	Sleeves	_____
Shipping	_____	Waist Bands	_____
Total Labor	$_____	Total Material	$_____

Factory Overhead Allocation	Number	Rate	Dollars
Machine Hours	_____	_____	$_____
Labor Hours	_____	_____	_____
Unit	_____	_____	_____
		Total Dollars	$_____

Summary	
Labor Costs	$_____
Material Costs	$_____
Factory Overhead Allocation	$_____
Total Manufacturing Costs	$_____
Selling, General, Administrative Allocation	$_____
Total Cost	$_____
Net Selling Price	$_____
Pretax Profit	$_____

Maximizing Dollars of Profits

You have previously determined approximately what the user will pay for your product or service, and what approximate effect increases or decreases in price will have on unit volume. With the help of the president and controller, you have also calculated the cost of each model, style, or job in your line, and at present prices, its pretax profit. Now you must evaluate whether the pretax profit of each item meets the firm's profit goals, and in addition to this determine what effect higher or lower prices would have on maximizing profits.

Profit goals for each item may involve the dollars of profit or profit as a percentage of selling price. For example, an industrial instrument manufacturer wants a 20% (of sales) pretax profit on all devices selling for under $10,000, which represents the bulk of its business; but on devices selling for over $10,000, the firm accepts any pretax profit exceeding $2,000 per unit.

If the pretax profit does not meet your firm's profit goals, you have five alternatives: (1) lower costs by taking something out of the item, becoming more labor efficient, seeking less expensive materials, or subcontracting the work; (2) raise prices to increase margins; (3) lower prices to increase unit volume and possibly raise margins; (4) make no change, continue the present situation; (5) discontinue the item.

Even if an item's present profit meets your goals, you should still evaluate whether raising or lowering its price would increase dollars of profit. Each product/service should be priced to maximize its dollars of profits.

Lowering Costs.   If a model, style, or job does not meet unit profit goals, you should evaluate whether lowering costs by seeking less expensive materials, taking something out of the item, becoming more labor efficient, or subcontracting the work would best correct the problem. For example, if the sweater manufacturer wanted a 10% (of sales) pretax profit on all wool blend styles, but found that the cable knit yielded only a 5% margin, it could lower costs by using a less expensive yarn, reducing the number of cables in the design, knitting the garment on a faster machine, or subcontracting the dying to a more efficient firm. If the sonic cleaning tank manufacturer wanted a $500 pretax profit on all models, but found that the rifle degreasing tank only yielded a $250 profit, it could lower costs by using less-expensive, thinner-gauge sheet metal, reducing the tank's size/capacity, using more automated equipment to cut and weld the tank, or subcontracting the assembly process to a firm with lower labor rates. If the hospital cleaning service wanted a 7% (of sales) pretax margin, but found that cleaning smaller hospitals only produced a 4% margin, it could lower costs by hiring less-expensive, less-experienced labor and using less-expensive, less-powerful chemicals for these jobs; it could also not clean closets and storage areas, see if fewer people could do the job with faster equipment, or subcontract these jobs to a firm with lower labor rates.

Raising Prices to Maximize Profits. If a model, style, or job does not meet unit profit goals, you should evaluate whether raising prices would correct the problem. Even if a model, style, or job does meet unit profit goals, you should evaluate whether raising its price would increase total dollars of profit from its total unit sales.

For example, the sweater manufacturer presently sells 17,000 cotton crew neck sweaters a year at $13, which the stores in turn retail at $26. The sweater manufacturer's profit on this item is $1.30 per garment times 17,000 units, or $22,100 a year. Based on the product's competitive position in the market, the pricing zone of cotton sweaters, type of product, type of customer, and type of retail store, the sales manager estimates that if wholesale prices were increased 5% from $13.00 to $13.65 (which would result in an increase at retail from $26.00 to $27.30), annual unit sales would fall 5% from 17,000 to 16,150, and profits would increase to $1.30 + $.65 cents times 16,150 units or $31,492. This represents an annual profit increase of $9,392 or 42.5%.

The sales manager assumes that the entire 5% price increase will go to profit, since the price increase causes no cost increases, except possibly a slightly greater unit allocation of factory overhead and G.S.&A. because unit sales have declined 5%. As you can see, a small 5% price increase results in a much larger percentage increase in profits. Theoretically, annual unit sales would have to decline 33% from 17,000 to 11,333 for total dollar profits at the higher price ($13.65) to equal profits at the lower price ($13.00). However, as unit sales decrease significantly, unit costs do rise, because of greater allocation of fixed expenses to each unit. For this style, the risk of lower volume from higher prices appears worth the potential gain of greater profits.

The sweater manufacturer also sells 60,000 orlon V-neck sweaters a year at $9.00, which the stores in turn retail at $18.00. The sweater manufacturer's annual profit on this item is $1.80 per garment times 60,000 units, or $108,000. The sales manager estimates that if wholesale prices were raised 5% from $9.00 to $9.45 in this very competitive chain store market, unit sales would fall 20% from 60,000 to 48,000 sweaters, and profits would theoretically remain unchanged at $1.80 + .45 times 48,000 or $108,000. However, a 12,000-unit decrease in volume would increase fixed-cost factory overhead and S.G.&A. allocations per unit, causing a decrease in actual profits. In this case, the potential dollar profit gain from higher prices would be totally offset by lower unit volume.

To maximize profits through correct pricing, you must do this exercise for each model, style, job, product, or service group in your line. The sonic cleaning firm would perform this exercise for each size and variety of tank. The hospital cleaning firm would perform this exercise for each type of service offered and possibly for each type of account.

Lowering Prices to Maximize Profits.   In addition to evaluating the effect of raising prices on unit sales and dollar profits, you should consider whether lowering prices could increase unit volume enough to generate greater dollar profits. Again, to maximize profits you should perform this exercise on all products/services offered even if they presently meet profit objectives.

An importer of digital watches sells its product through chains, catalogue houses, and discounters. The firm presently sells 8,000 units of one model at $10.50, which the stores in turn retail for $21.00. The importer's annual profit on this item is $1.50 per watch times 8,000 units, or $12,000. Based on the product's competitive place in the market, the pricing zone of this type digital watch, the type of customer, and the type of retail store, the sales manager estimates that the additional profits from any price increase would be more than offset by a decrease in unit volume. He now decides to evaluate the effect on dollar profits and unit sales of lowering the price to $9.50 to retail at $19.00. At this lower price, the sales manager feels he can open several major new accounts, and that sales to existing stores would increase 30%, resulting in a total annual volume of 16,000 units. By increasing volume to 16,000 units from 8,000, the cost per unit of importing the watches decreases by 50 cents. Profits per unit now are $1.50, the previous amount, less $1.00, the price decrease, plus 50 cents, the cost decrease, or $1.00 per watch. At the lower price, annual dollar profits for this item would increase 33% from $12,000 ($1.50 × 8,000 units) to $16,000 ($1.00 × 16,000 units). The sales manager considers the risks minimal of not being able to produce the additional volume at the lower price, and so with management's approval, he announces a price decrease.

A materials-handling forklift truck manufacturer was losing sales to imports from the Orient. By reducing the base price of its least expensive model from $21,000 to $19,500, its unit volume increased enough to offset the lower unit profit, and actually generated more profit dollars. The increased volume also lowered factory overhead and G.S.&A. expense per unit.

Many firms in the electronics and chemical business have found that they can generate larger dollar profits from the volume increases resulting from lower prices. Also, airlines offer discount fares, and theaters discount tickets, because empty seats do not maximize profits. These discounts are a way of reducing prices to increase unit volume.

You may also wish to analyze the effect of lower prices combined with lower costs. If lower prices can significantly increase volume, why not see what steps can be taken to lower costs and further expand margins.

Status Quo.   You may find that lowering or raising prices cannot improve an item's profit dollars, and therefore, your present price maximizes profits. If these profits do not meet your firm's dollar or percentage objectives, and if costs cannot be reduced, you can discontinue the product/service, or accept the less than desired profit and continue the item.

An item may not meet your profit objective, but its loss might create a worse situation. For example, a semiconductor manufacturer made a 1% profit on a basic item, which represented half of its sales. The firm made a 15% profit on the dozens of specialty items that comprised the other half of its business. Lower costs and different prices were not feasible for the basic item. Management could not discontinue the basic item, because it absorbed half of the firm's factory overhead and G.S.&A. It also helped to sell the more profitable specialty items. Had it discontinued the basic item, the firm would have become unprofitable.

An item may not meet your profit objective, but its loss might upset your business with a major customer. For example, a designer tie company found that its least expensive polyester tie generated only a 5% profit margin, versus over 10% for the remaining styles. The sales manager felt that price increases or decreases could not correct the problem, and that costs could not be decreased. The item represented less than 5% of total company volume, and its loss would hardly have been noticed on a financial statement. However, the tie firm's largest customer, which accounted for 17% of its total business, bought 80% of the polyester ties. The firm continued the polyester style because it did not want a competitor to have this business at its largest customer.

Both these examples illustrate situations where you would continue offering an item which did not meet your profit objectives. Many such situations exist in any business.

Discontinue the Product/Service.   Your last alternative is to discontinue a product/service which does not meet profit goals or lend itself to productive cost cutting or positive price changes. Too many small firms continue items which do not meet profit standards and therefore unproductively tie up limited human and financial resources which could be better used elsewhere. Often, these items are unimportant to customers and contribute only a few dollars to fixed expenses. These items continue because of management's chronic inertia. The ability to be flexible and to act quickly should not only help a small firm successfully introduce new products/services, but also discontinue unproductive ones. Review your line at least once a year to consider dropping products/ services which do not meet profit objectives.

A kennel leased guard dogs to retail stores, security agencies, plants, and auto dealers. The kennel had excellent profits, but the guard dog revenues did not cover the costs of delivery and pickup, training, food, insurance, and sales commissions. The owner varied costs, prices, and benefits, but to no avail. Finally he discontinued this service and employed the funds in starting a dog-grooming operation.

Corporate Strategy.   Many small companies do not generate sufficient profits to provide proper working capital or cash flow. To remedy this, management may apply the profit-maximizing technique used for pricing each product/service to a basic corporate strategy. That is, you can use these same techniques to evaluate the effect on overall corporate profits of major changes in pricing strategy and/or cost cutting.

Let us say your firm earns a pretax profit of $65,000 on sales of $1,750,000. The $65,000 is not sufficient to buy new equipment and pay off your term loan. You require a pretax profit of $165,000 to accomplish these objectives. You can increase profits $100,000 by increasing unit sales, increasing prices, lowering costs, or some combination of the three.

The firm's present gross margin after labor, materials, and factory overhead expense is $612,500, or 35% of sales; and S.G.&A. expense is $547,500, or 31% of sales, leaving a pretax profit of $65,000, or 4% of sales. By applying the pricing techniques to this situation, you determine that unit sales would have to increase approximately $300,000, or 17%, to generate another $100,00 of profit; $300,000 times the gross margin percentage of 35% equals $105,000, minus $5,000 for increased S.G.&A., equals $100,000. On the other hand, assuming no decrease in unit volume, prices would only have to be raised $100,000, or 6%, or costs lowered by $100,000 to increase profits to $165,000. Lower costs could be obtained by using less material, by using labor more efficiently, by subcontracting certain work, by lowering factory overhead, or by reducing S.G.&A. expense.

After considerable study, you decide that profits can best be increased $100,000 by combining a 6% price increase with a $35,000 cost decrease. You estimate that the 6% price increase will cause a 6% decrease in unit sales volume, but will still result in an additional $65,000 of profit. The remaining $35,000 of profit can be generated by reducing travel and entertainment expenses $10,000, advertising $10,000, eliminating an office person $7,000, and reducing overtime $8,000. You feel that this plan contains a higher probability of success than trying to increase unit sales.

Highly profitable firms use this same strategy to determine how they can maximize profits. In other words, on a corporate basis, what reasonable combination of overall unit volume, prices, and costs will maximize profits? Your firm for example might generate greater profits with higher prices and lower unit volume.

Summary

Your product should be priced to maximize profits. To understand the relationship between price and profits, you must determine the costs of your products/services by obtaining the direct labor, materials, and factory overhead necessary to produce each product/service in the line, and then adding a factor for general, selling, and administrative expenses. The difference between this total and the selling price is that particular item's pretax profit.

Now you must evaluate whether the pretax profit of each item meets the firm's profit goals, and in addition to this, determine what effect higher or lower prices would have on maximizing profits. If an item's pretax profit does not meet the firm's goals, you have five alternatives: (1) lower costs by taking something out of the item, becoming more labor efficient, seeking less expensive materials, or subcontracting the work; (2) raise prices to increase margins; (3) lower prices to increase unit volume and possibly raise margins; (4) make no changes, continue the present situation; (5) discontinue the item. You can use these same techniques to evaluate the effect on overall corporate profits of major changes in pricing strategy and/or cost cutting.

PROPERLY MERCHANDISING THE PRICE

You have determined what prices for which products/services will maximize dollar profits. Now, depending on industry tradition and competition, you must properly present or merchandise these prices. This section deals with off prices and price increases.

Off Prices

Rebates, premiums, coupons, terms, discounts, promotions, and advertising and freight allowances all represent means of varying a list price to arrive at an actual price. Within the framework of your industry and competitive position, you must decide whether to engage in these various types of off-price selling. If you do engage in them, the expense must be added to your net price, or reflected in the costs used to arrive at list prices.

For example, retailers traditionally buy ladies' blouses with 8% terms, and stores in California traditionally receive prepaid freight or landed prices. Therefore, a blouse company which wishes to remain competitive by accommodating customers and industry tradition must add 8% to its net price for terms, and for California customers must add an additional 2% to the price for freight. The firm must either add these to net prices or include them in costs when determining list prices. List price is what a firm charges, net price is what it receives.

For example, retailers insist on buying men's underwear for twice-a-year sales at 20% off list prices. Most manufacturers limit these off-price purchases to 20% of a customer's purchases for the previous twelve months. Therefore, to reflect the need for promotional prices, companies in this industry must increase net prices by 4% (20% of 20%), or increase list price costs by 4%.

Manufacturers and/or distributors of industrial nuts, bolts, rivets, chemicals, and cartons must offer quantity discounts to users to remain competitive. Five hundred pounds of chemicals are priced at less per pound than fifty. Companies in industries which traditionally offer quantity discounts must increase basic prices to reflect this, or include a factor for discounts in their costs.

Pet food and hair dryers are offered several times a year with a consumer coupon for a cash rebate from the manufacturer or a percentage discount from the retail price, which the manufacturer rebates to the store. Again, the manufacturer must reflect this as an expense in costs, or raise net prices to absorb it.

Often, firms which offer competitive items at the same list prices compete on a price basis by offering various rebates, coupons, terms, discounts, promotions, or advertising or freight allowances. Such firms can also effectively increase prices, revenues, and profits without raising list prices by reducing their rebates, coupons, terms, discounts, promotions, or advertising or freight allowances.

Often, small companies allow salespeople too much freedom in varying list prices, terms, discounts, promotions, or advertising or freight allowances. Most salespeople have more immediate economic interest in units and dollars of sales than in prices and profits. Their job is to make the sale, not to set prices. If given the freedom, salespeople will generally sell at lower prices, which may not maximize company profits. Management should establish list prices, terms, discounts, promotions, and advertising and freight allowances, and any variations should require the appropriate manager's approval.

Industry tradition and competitive position dictate that many firms offer their goods or services off-price. Since the customer demands this, don't fight it, just reflect the cost in your price. Rebates, premiums, coupons, terms, discounts, promotions, and advertising and freight allowances are merely ways of merchandising the final price.

Price Increases

Most customers dislike price increases, whether the item is industrial fasteners, shirts, testing equipment, or freight rates. Many customers view price increases as a reason to reexamine the product/service relative to competition, and to consider a change. Because of this, you must correctly merchandise price increases.

Announce price increases in advance, and allow customers a limited time to purchase at the old price. This dulls the negative impact of a price increase, shows customers that you care about their well-being, and if they purchase substantial quantities at the old price, it assures that they will continue as customers.

If possible, have field salespeople announce and explain price increases to their customers rather than you sending out an impersonal letter to each account. This personalizes the message. All these suggestions also enhance your human, caring small-company image.

Also, increasing prices for the entire line, by say 10% or $20.00, generally creates more attention and more customer animosity than increasing prices selectively. Selective model-by-model increases connote a certain sophistication and necessity, and are less noticed. Selective increases suggest that management has analyzed the situation, thought it out, and has found these changes necessary. Across-the-board increases suggest that you decided in a hallway conference that it was time to raise prices again.

TYPES OF PRICES

Consumers have developed attitudes and beliefs about certain retail price points. They associate even-dollar price points such as $4.00, $8.00, $10.00, $15.00, and $20.00 with quality products. They associate odd-numbered price points such as $3.99, $7.99, $9.99, $14.99, and $19.99 with bargains, and possibly inferior quality products. Many prestige stores, seeking a quality-product image, will not allow odd-penny pricing, while discounters use it continually. Depending on your customer and desired product/service image, decide between odd and even pricing.

Consumers associate multiple prices with value. For instance, a store may sell more socks or underwear at 3 for $9.00 than at $3.00 each. If your product/service lends itself to multiple sales, consider offering it in a 3- or 6-pack.

Oddball prices such as $1.11, $7.77, $9.99, $11.11, $22.22 attract consumer attention. If you sell items which stores promote regularly at less than list price, suggest some oddball price points during the sale period.

Skim pricing refers to higher-than-normal prices, which generally are used for new products/services with no direct competitors. The first panty hose, hand-held calculators, desk-top computers, industrial robots, tropical plant rentals, nonstop flights from Miami to London, and home kerosene heaters reflected skim pricing. Once competition started, these prices declined dramatically.

Penetration pricing refers to lower-than-normal prices and is used to eliminate or discourage competition. Once the threat of competition is removed, prices increase substantially. Braniff and American Airlines engaged in penetration pricing on routes they shared out of Texas. After Braniff's demise, American raised these prices. Penetration pricing of panty hose by large mills eliminated many competitors. Once that happened, prices rose. As discussed in the next section, penetration pricing can be illegal.

LEGAL ASPECTS OF PRICING

This chapter has discussed the many considerations necessary to maximize dollar profits through correct pricing. In order to accomplish this, you must also have a knowledge of the legal restrictions involved in pricing.

The Sherman Act of 1890 prohibits conspiracies in restraint of trade. The Clayton Act of 1914 prohibits practices which substantially lessen competition. Any concerted action by competitors, or any unfair action by a single company that has the result of limiting competition, is presumed to be an unreasonable restraint on commerce and is thus illegal.

All types of formal or informal agreements among competitors to set prices or to maintain uniform profit margins are illegal. Even informally exchanging price information with competitors at a trade association meeting or over cocktails has been considered a violation. If you find yourself in such a situation, change the conversation or leave.

The Robinson-Patman Act of 1936 prohibits discrimination in price, service, and facilities by a seller in the sale of like grade and quality to two or more buyers. Price discrimination consists of charging different prices to different customers for products/services of like kind and quality. Everything else being equal, the same types of customer should pay the same price for the same product/service.

Although it is illegal to discriminate in price among different purchasers of the same quality goods if such price discrimination injures a competitor, a firm can lower prices to meet competition if this is done without meaning to eliminate a competitor. Price includes terms, rebates, coupons, discounts, promotions, and advertising and freight allowances.

For example, it is illegal to sell at lower prices in one territory than another for the purpose of eliminating a competitor. It is also illegal to sell chain stores or large users at one price and specialty stores or small users at another, unless you can demonstrate a cost saving. If you offer a 3% advertising allowance and 5% terms with prepaid freight to Sears, you most likely will have to offer it to smaller accounts, and certainly to comparable accounts such as J.C. Penny. If you offer a 20%-off promotion on 20% of the previous year's unit purchases to Bloomingdale's, you probably must offer the same arrangement to a specialty store, and certainly must offer the same arrangement to Macys. If you give Standard Oil a 5% year-end rebate based on dollar volume, you probably must give the same rebate to smaller customers, and certainly to Mobil.

Larger firms sometimes use their size to coerce smaller firms into giving them preferential prices, terms, rebates, discounts, and allowances. Their action is generally considered illegal, as is yours if you comply. In such situations, you must temper business judgment with legal considerations, and certainly should consult an attorney.

SUMMARY

Your product/service should be priced to maximize profit dollars, taking into account both its value and its image to the user, plus competition. The pricing process involves determining what the market will bear by looking at your competitive advantage or place in the market, the type goods or services you offer, and the type of customer you serve. Next, you compute the cost and profit for each item in the line, and determine what specific effect higher or lower prices would have on present dollar profits. Finally, you evaluate whether each item's pretax profit meets the firm's profit goals, and if not, take appropriate action.

Pricing decisions also involve proper use of off prices, price increases, odd/even pricing, multiple prices, oddball pricing, skim pricing, and penetration pricing. Lastly, in maximizing dollar profits through pricing, you must recognize the appropriate legal restrictions.

10
Distribution

DETERMINING THE MOST EFFICIENT MEANS OF REACHING THE MARKET

To succeed in a marketplace dominated by larger businesses, the small businessperson must develop an efficient means of reaching the market. Without an appropriate distribution strategy, even a fine product/service which meets a need will fail. The sheer momentum of a larger business with inappropriate distribution allows it to continue. On the other hand, the proper distribution strategy for a smaller business establishes the foundation for it to compete successfully against such larger competitors.

Moreover, the flexibility of a smaller business allows it the opportunity to continually evaluate and quickly adjust its distribution strategy to meet ever changing market conditions. Often, large businesses are not sensitive to change, and cannot react quickly. The small businessperson should be aware of this competitive advantage.

Unfortunately, most small businesses are content to inherit their form of distribution from company tradition or industry pactice: "Our company has always sold smaller hardware stores within 500 miles of our factory using stocking distributors."

A third-generation family-owned knitwear manufacturer had established a successful business by selling to small retailers in rural towns through stocking distributors. In the 1960s and 1970s people left small towns and moved to larger cities, where knitwear was purchased at major department and chain stores. At the same time, major department and chain stores were opening branches at regional shopping centers in these rural areas. These large users bought directly from manufacturers and were serviced by company salespeople. The market share of small retailers in rural towns declined significantly, and all but a few stocking distributors went out of business.

The knitwear manufacturer continued following its traditional channels of distribution, with the result that its unit sales declined each year. In 1978 the management decided to hire company salespeople and sell major retailers in major cities, but by this time their momentum and market share had been seriously damaged.

Determining the most effective means of reaching a market requires creatively investigating alternatives to tradition. For each product/service or each product/service group, you need to analyze the variety of means and strategies for reaching your particular customer.

Basically this involves (1) identifying the customers for your product/service, (2) classifying your product/service by user perception, (3) for consumer products, choosing the correct retail outlet, (4) within the limits of your resources, choosing the type sales organization which best reaches the target customer, (5) choosing between highlight and scatter selling, and (6) realistically appraising your company's human and financial resources.

INTRODUCTION

Identifying the customer for your product or service appears deceptively simple, but some small businesses make a mistake at this basic juncture. The customer is not always who you think it is; some products/services are not purchased by the user, some products/services serve complex multiple customer groups, and some products/services become components for other products/services.

To select the proper form of distribution, you must understand how the customer perceives your product/service. Both consumer and business-to-business products and services can be classified as convenience goods, shopping goods, specialty goods, or unsought goods. These classifications reflect the buyer's preference for the goods, the buyer's willingness to seek them out.

For consumer products, choosing the correct retail outlet depends on your target customer, his or her shopping habits, his or her perceptions of your goods, the product/service image and pricing zone, and your firm's unit sales potential, objectives, and restrictions. Consumer shopping habits, expectations, needs, and satisfactions can be classified as personalized, ethical, economic, impulse, and apathetic.

The retail outlet, like the packaging, should reinforce rather than detract from the product image. A store's image is determined by its architecture, location, decor, layout, personnel, advertising, products, prices, and clientele. The retail outlet should carry other products whose positions in their pricing zones coincide to your position. Last, it is unrealistic to sell certain retail outlets if you cannot supply the quantities they need.

Retail outlets can be classified as supermarkets, drug stores, discount stores, catalogue showrooms, off-price factory outlets, discount department stores, chain stores, department stores, specialty stores, manufacturer-owned stores, franchises, and combinations. Each type of store appeals to a different type target customer, different shopping habits, and different consumer perceptions. Each type of store contains a different image and pricing zone.

Whether you sell consumer products to retail stores or commercial products/ services to other businesses, you must select an appropriate type of sales organization for reaching the customer. You may employ your own sales force, use sales representatives or jobbers who carry several lines, sell to a distributor or broker who sells in turn to the customer, or some combination. The choice depends on the type of goods and number of customers you sell, customer preferences and expectations, product and customer images, economics, and competition.

You must also decide whether to engage in highlight or scatter selling. A business can sell a limited number of large major accounts with a small compact sales organization or sell a wider variety of accounts, large and small, with a larger sales organization. Also, a business can sell in one or several regions of the country, nationally, or internationally.

In selecting the appropriate means of reaching the customer, a realistic appraisal of your company's available resources will influence choices between alternatives. You should take the time to evaluate your firm's management, financial, manufacturing, and sales capabilities.

IDENTIFYING THE CUSTOMER

To develop appropriate distribution, you must first identify the customer for each product/service or each product/service group. If your firm assembles nail-making machines, the customers are steel mills which produce nails. If your firm manufactures parabolic microwave antennas, the customers are telecommunication companies; utilities; railroads; and city, state, and federal government agencies. If your firm manfuactures blouses, the customers are the retail stores that sell blouses and the women who buy them. If your firm cleans hospitals, the customers are hospitals.

In defining the customer for your product/service, consider the geographic boundaries in which you wish to sell. Do you wish to sell nationally, regionally, or just in a particular state or city?

The more specifically you can identify the target customer, the easier it is to choose appropriate distribution. You can most accurately identify the customer for your product/service by first describing the broadest group of potential users and then narrowing the field to prime users.

Identifying the customer for your products or services appears deceptively simple, but some small businesses make a mistake at this basic juncture. The customer is not always who you think it is; some products/services are not purchased by the user, some products/services serve complex multiple customer groups, and some products/services become components for other products/services.

For example, most men's hosiery, underwear, shirts, and ties are purchased by women. Although men may be the users, both women and men are the customer. This is one reason why department stores sell far more men's furnishings than do men's specialty stores.

The first copying machines were marketed to the engineering departments of large firms for duplicating blueprints, schematics, building plans, materials lists, and designs. However, secretaries from other departments started using these machines for copying letters and documents. For years the copying machine manufacturers sold only the engineering departments, until these firms realized that the customers for their machines included all office personnel.

In the early 1970s, two companies developed the technology for portable whirlpool devices which were clamped on to bath tubs. Company X believed that the device would be purchased by older people with chronic ailments. Its marketing strategy, advertising, and distribution aimed at this group with a therapeutic and medical appeal. Advertising featured doctors' endorsements, and distribution was accomplished through geriatric outlets that sold wheelchairs, walkers, and canes. Company X finally disbanded, because older people (1) generally did not have the necessary funds for a purchase, (2) were afraid of the device, (3) could not easily operate or move it, and (4) did not want to be considered "crippled" or "sick."

Company Y believed that the device would be purchased by younger people for fun, relaxation, and alleviation of aches and pains caused by jogging, tennis, and skiing. Its advertising featured endorsements by athletes and entertainment personalities. Distribution was accomplished through sporting goods and department stores. Company Y has registered sales and profit gains for the past ten years.

Some products/services serve complex multiple customer groups, which makes identifying the specific customer difficult. Is the customer for office furniture: new businesses, firms that are moving, firms with old furniture, businesses with more than ten employees, or all offices? Is the customer for industrial robots: auto manufacturers, small-appliance manufacturers, metal fabricators, textile firms, or all factories? Is the customer for designer umbrellas: men or women, people under or over 40, consumers living in the North or South, households with under or over $25,000 of annual income, or the entire adult population?

Some products/services become components for other products/services, which further complicates identifying the customer. Semiconductor devices may be sold to firms manufacturing telephone switching equipment, which they in turn sell to telecommunication companies. Does the semiconductor firm sell design engineers at the switching equipment firms, or the telecommunications companies, or both? Industrial gears may be sold to firms manufacturing conveyor belts for steel mills. Does the gear firm sell design engineers at the conveyor belt firms, or the steel mills, or both?

The more specifically you can identify the target customer, the easier it will be to choose appropriate distribution. You can more accurately identify the customer for your products/service by first describing the broadest group of potential users, and then narrowing the field to prime users.

The broadest potential customer group for leasing ice-making machines with maintenance and ice delivery includes all restaurants, taverns, and food-processing plants. The narrower customer group includes restaurants, taverns, and food-processing plants which use over 100 pounds of ice a day, and the prime group includes only those which buy ice rather than those which own machines. The broad potential customer group for purchasing heat-reflecting window shades includes all private and commercial structures with untreated window glass. The narrower customer group involves older structures in Southern climates, and the prime group involves only those commercial structures with southern or western exposures.

In defining the customer for your product/service, consider the geographic boundaries in which you wish to sell. Do you wish to sell nationally, regionally, or just a particular state or city?

Your customer group, or target market, must be of sufficient size and buying power for you to operate at a profit. For example, Wyoming probably contains enough oil exploration activity to support a firm offering drilling supplies. Wyoming probably does not contain enough people to support a state magazine.

In identifying your customer group or target market, try to be as specific as possible. Remember, the customer is not always who you think it is.

CLASSIFYING PRODUCTS/SERVICES BY USER PERCEPTION

To select the proper form of distribution, you must understand the target customer's buying needs and habits, and how he or she perceives your product/service. Both consumer and business-to-business products and services can be classified as convenience goods, shopping goods, specialty goods, unsought goods, or new products. These classifications reflect the buyer's preference for the product or service and the buyer's willingness to seek it out.

Convenience goods are products/services which the customer needs but will not spend much time shopping for. Shopping goods are products/services which the customer wants to examine and compare before purchasing. Specialty goods are products/services which the customer will spend considerable time and effort searching out. Unsought goods are products/services which the customer does not presently want or feel he or she needs. New products represent a special type of unsought goods.

Convenience goods require broad non-exclusive distribution, while shopping goods require a more limited, more exclusive approach, and specialty goods the most selective distribution. Unsought goods sell best through your own sales force and poorest through retail outlets and distributors. New products require strong personal and management selling until user acceptance is established.

Convenience Goods

Convenience goods are products/services, many of them staples, which the customer needs but will not spend much time shopping for. Convenience goods require broad distribution. They include such consumer goods as photo processing, razor blades, most grocery products, gasoline, pet food, newspapers, nails, shampoo, and vitamins. They include such business-to-business commercial/industrial goods as office, maintenance, and shipping supplies, welding rods, grinding wheels, hand trucks, premiums, paper products, and small hardware items.

Consumers and purchasing agents will not seek out these goods; therefore they must be available through a wide variety of outlets. For consumer goods, this means selling competing and different kinds of retail outlets. For example, vitamins, razor blades, and shampoo might be sold to a wide variety of drug, grocery, chain, department, and discount stores in the same city. For business-to-business goods, this means selling through a wide variety of non-exclusive salespeople and distributors. For example, welding rods, grinding wheels, and office supplies might be sold through a wide variety of competing sales agents, jobbers, and stocking distributors in the same region.

In establishing your distribution for convenience goods, consider selling to or through as many alternative channels as practical. With this type of wide-open scatter selling, you have minimum control over the choice of sales organization, retailer, and distribution. The user will not seek you out or invest time in comparative shopping. When the customer wants to place an order, availability and reliable delivery rank higher than product benefits and salesmanship. Salespeople for convenience goods tend to be order takers.

Shopping Goods

Shopping goods are products/services which the customer wants to examine and compare before purchasing. The comparison may be based on price, product features, user benefits, or some combination. In any case, the user has time to and wants to "shop around" before buying. Shopping goods require more limited distribution than convenience goods. Shopping goods include both the homogeneous and heterogeneous items described in Chap. 9 on "Pricing."

Shopping goods include such consumer products/services as clothing, appliances, furniture, autos, maid services, smoke alarms, kerosene heaters, and pets. They include such business-to-business industrial/commercial goods as computers, testing instruments, machine tools, parabolic antennas, emergency lighting, ice-making machines, and wool yarn.

Since the consumer, purchasing agent, or retail store buyer is willing to seek out these goods, you may selectively limit and retain more control over choice of distribution, the sales force, and the retail outlets. For consumer goods, this means selling only certain types of outlets. For example, your line of clothing or furniture might only be sold through certain department stores. For business-to-business goods, this means selling through exclusive noncompetitive distributors, representatives, or your own sales force. For example, your line of ice machines, wool yarn, or emergency lighting would be sold by one organization or person in each territory.

In establishing your distribution for shopping goods, consider selling to or through a more limited number of retail outlets, distributors, representatives, and salespeople. In choosing your distribution, remember that shopping goods require salesmanship. The consumer, buyer, or purchasing agent needs help, advice, and information to make a purchase.

Specialty Goods

Specialty goods are products/services which the customer will spend considerable time and effort searching out, and therefore they require selective distribution. Often, this willingness to search out reflects strong brand, company, or store preference. Generally, specialty products and services have prestige images and status. If consumer goods, they have been advertised heavily through media, word of mouth, logos, embroideries, point-of-purchase displays, and packaging. Once purchased, consumer specialty items and some business-to-business specialty items have high visibility for the user, and generally contain easy identification for the user's associates. The user obtains status through purchasing the specialty item, and through association with others who have also purchased the item. Business-to-business specialty items are sometimes in short supply, difficult to manufacture, and difficult to obtain.

Specialty goods include such consumer products/services as Countess Mara ties, Godiva chocolates, Bombay gin, Michelin tires, the Sunday *New York Times,* Crabtree and Evelyn cosmetics, and store label merchandise from Bloomingdale's and Saks Fifth Avenue. They include such diverse business-to-business commercial/industrial products and services as law, accounting, consulting, investment and advertising firms with strong reputations for certain areas of expertise; specialized switching, holding, and recording telecommunication systems, cashmere yarn, company jets, high-strength metals, and high-performance electronic components.

Since the consumer, purchasing agent, or retail store buyer is willing to spend considerable time and effort seeking these goods out, you may be very selective and limited in your distribution, allowing you a great deal of control. For consumer goods, this means limiting your distribution to a few outlets in each area. For example, only a few select stores in each city carry Countess Mara ties or Godiva chocolates. Not every newsstand in Chicago carries the Sunday *New York Times*. For business-to-business goods, this means selling through a limited number of distributors, representatives, offices, or company salespeople. If your firm sold cashmere yarn, one salesperson could cover the United States. Prestigious advertising, legal, accounting, investment, and consulting firms only need offices in major cities, because clients will come to them.

As a business person, you have little control over whether the customer perceives your item as a convenience or shopping good. However, specialty goods are made, not born! Specialty goods status represents an excellent position for small businesses, because markets are limited, competition minimal, distribution costs reasonable, and prices flexible. Consider whether your product/service lends itself to specialty status.

In the early 1950s, a men's hosiery company knit a gold toe into each sock and limited distribution to one major department store in each town. The total number of accounts was limited to less than 500, and was sold by five salespeople working out of one office in New York City. The company made a basic, quality product, and soon became the largest, most profitable firm in the men's branded hosiery industry. This firm created a specialty product.

In establishing your distribution for specialty goods, consider selling to or through a very limited number of retail outlets, distributors, representatives, and salespeople. Limiting distribution helps to maintain your exclusive specialty image. In choosing your distribution, remember that the people or stores who represent you must carry an image which reinforces your product/service.

Unsought Goods

Unsought goods are products/services which the customer does not presently want or does not presently feel he or she needs. At this point in time, the benefits of such goods do not appear obvious to the potential user. He or she is unwilling to shop for this classification of goods. Unsought goods sell best through your own sales force and poorest through distributors and retail outlets.

Unsought goods include such consumer items as life insurance, encyclopedias, home security systems, magazine subscriptions, pay TV, charitable donations, and photographic family portraits. They include such business-to-business items as business-interruption insurance; trade directory listings; water coolers; works of art; legal, tax, or accounting reference manuals; and association memberships.

Since the consumer, purchasing agent, or retail store buyer will not seek out such products/services, the provider must seek out the users. Therefore, you sell unsought goods through telemarketing and personal visits. For example, life insurance, pay TV, business-interruption insurance, directory listings, association memberships, commercial reference manuals, and encyclopedias are all sold over the phone, followed up by a personal visit.

Since these goods are unsought by users, the provider has total control over choice of distribution. Also for this reason, unsought consumer products sell poorly in retail stores, and unsought business-to-business products sell poorly through distributors. You will obtain the best results by establishing your own sales force and investing considerable time in hiring, training, and supervising its members. The salesperson must arouse a need in the prospect for the unsought goods. This requires good salespeople and good management.

New Products

New products represent a special type of unsought goods. As you create a demand for new products using the techniques discussed in Chap. 8, they emerge into convenience, shopping, or specialty goods.

New products require strong personal selling until a user perception pattern develops and user acceptance is established. With new consumer goods, you initially limit distribution by using retail outlets which specialize in personal selling. For example, hand-held calculators were first introduced through electronics specialty stores such as Radio Shack and Shutterbug. Today, ten years later, you can purchase hand-held calculators at department, hardware, office supply, chain, discount, and drug stores. When a small business introduces a new consumer product, it generally requires strong management selling to place it in appropriate retail outlets.

When a small firm introduces a new business-to-business product, it again requires strong management selling. The sales manager or president should accompany salespeople, representatives, or distributors in visiting prospects. This gives the new product/service more importance, and obtains more attention from the purchasing agent, design engineer, or plant manager. When a hospital cleaning firm introduced a new service for cleaning sterile operating rooms, the sales manager or president accompanied their salespeople during presentations to major prospects.

Annual Review

Business is a dynamic process; products mature, markets and customer perceptions change. For this reason, whether your firm sells convenience, shopping, specialty, or unsought goods, you should reexamine their distribution annually to determine the appropriateness. A sudden change in laws governing corporate taxation might transform tax manuals from unsought goods to shopping goods. A decrease in the cost of home video games might transform video game cassettes from shopping to convenience goods.

Summary

Both consumer and business-to-business products and services can be classified as convenience goods, shopping goods, specialty goods, unsought goods, or new products. These classifications reflect the buyer's preference for the product or service and the buyer's willingness to seek them out. While convenience goods require broad distribution, shopping goods lend themselves to a more limited approach, and specialty goods require the most selective distribution. Unsought goods and new products/services require a great deal of personal selling.

CHOOSING THE CORRECT RETAIL OUTLET

For consumer products, choosing the correct retail outlet depends on your target customer, his or her shopping habits, his or her perceptions of your goods, the product/service image and pricing zone, and your firm's unit sales potential, objectives, and restrictions. Retail outlets can be classified as supermarkets, drug stores, discount stores, off-price factory outlets, catalogue showrooms, discount department stores, chain stores, department stores, specialty stores, manufacturer-owned stores, franchises, and combinations.

Introduction

Shopping Habits.   To correctly choose the most appropriate retail outlet for your goods, you must understand the target customer's shopping expectations, satisfactions, and needs, because one type of store will satisfy these expectations and needs better than another. Shoppers and shopping expectations, needs, and satisfactions can be classified as personalized, ethical, economic, impulse, and apathetic.

Personalized shoppers expect and enjoy personal recognition from store personnel. Ethical shoppers enjoy patronizing and supporting small local retailers rather than large or multistore chains. Economic shoppers enjoy getting the most for their money and therefore show the most concern for price and value.

Impulse shoppers shop for the sake of shopping, with little preconceived idea of purchasing a particular item. Apathetic shoppers do not enjoy the shopping experience and perceive it as strictly functional.

Perceptions. To select the proper retail outlet for consumer goods, you must also understand how the target customer perceives your product/service, because one type of store will prove more compatible with those perceptions than another. How the consumer perceives your goods reflects the buyer's preference and willingness to seek them out. The greater the desire or preference for an item, the fewer the requirements for availability. As discussed previously, consumer products/services can be classified as convenience goods, shopping goods, specialty goods, unsought goods, and new products.

Since the target customer will not seek out convenience goods, they must be available through a wide variety of retail outlets. The target customers for convenience goods generally include personalized, ethical, economic, impulse, and apathetic shoppers.

Since the target customer will seek out shopping goods, you may selectively limit the number and type of retail outlets. The target customers for shopping goods include primarily personalized, ethical, and economic shoppers.

Since the target customer is willing to spend considerable time seeking out specialty goods, you may further selectively limit the number and type of retail outlets in each area. The target customers for specialty goods include primarily personalized and ethical shoppers.

Unsought goods sell poorly in all types of retail outlets. They sell best through telemarketing and personal sales.

New consumer products sell best through retail outlets which excel in personal selling, such as specialty and department stores, rather than through retail outlets providing self-service, such as supermarkets, chains, and discount stores. The target customers for new products include primarily personalized, impulse, and ethical shoppers.

Image and Pricing Zone. To select the proper retail outlet for consumer goods, you must also consider your product/service's image and pricing zone. The retail outlet, like the packaging, should reinforce rather than detract from the product image. Also, the retail outlet should carry other products whose positions in their pricing zones coincide with your product's position. A store's image is determined by its architecture, location, decor, layout, personnel, advertising, products, prices, and clientele. Although all these factors are inter-related in projecting a store's image, the most important factor is its clientele. Consumers wish to shop at stores patronized by others like themselves.

Sales Potential. To select the proper retail outlet for consumer goods, you also must consider your firm's unit sales potential, objectives, and restrictions. It is unrealistic, for example, to consider selling national mass merchants if you cannot supply the quantities they need. In such a situation, you might seek other appropriate retail outlets which require smaller quantities such as regional and city-wide discount, chain, or supermarket stores.

Type of Stores. Retail outlets can be classified as supermarkets, drug stores, discount stores, factory outlets, catalogue showrooms, discount department stores, chain stores, department stores, specialty stores, manufacturer-owned stores, franchises, and combinations. Each type of store appeals to different type target customers, different shopping habits, and different consumer perceptions. Each type of store contains a different image, pricing zone, and delivery requirements.

If your firm offers a convenience item with a nonprestige image to economic, apathetic, or impulse shoppers, and the item is priced at the lower end of its zone; and if your firm can reliably deliver large quantities; then you should consider selling to supermarkets or drug stores. If your firm offers shopping goods with a lower quality image to economic shoppers, and the items are priced at the lower end of their zone; and if your firm can reliably deliver huge quantities; then you should consider selling to discount stores. If your firm offers branded shopping goods with a good quality image to economic shoppers, and the items are priced in the middle to upper end of their zone; and if your firm can reliably deliver huge quantities; then you should consider selling factory outlets, catalogue showrooms, and discount department stores. If your firm offers shopping goods with a medium quality image to economic shoppers, and the item is priced at the middle of its zone; and if your firm can reliably deliver large quantities; then you should consider selling to chain stores. If your firm offers branded or designer shopping or specialty goods or a new product with a quality, status, or prestige image to economic, personalized, or impulse shoppers, and the item is priced in the moderate to upper end of its zone; and if your firm can deliver moderately large quantities; then you should consider selling department stores. If your firm offers branded or designer shopping goods, specialty goods, or a new product with a quality, status, or prestige image to personalized, ethical, or impulse shoppers, and the item is priced at the upper end of its zone; and if you can economically ship small orders; you should consider selling specialty, manufacturer-owned, and franchised stores.

Although this section deals with the sale of consumer goods through retail stores, consumers can also be sold through direct mail, telemarketing, and door-to-door salespeople. Direct mail includes catalogues, statement stuffers, peridoical advertising and brochures.

The Target Customer

Once you have correctly defined the target customer for your consumer product/service (as discussed earlier in the chapter), you must determine where that customer wishes to shop for your type of goods. Often the choices are many.

The target customers for high-protein dog food are owners of large dogs or show dogs. Do these customers prefer to shop for their pet food at kennels, pet shops, grocery stores, or discount stores? The target customers for designer jeans are women under 30. Do these customers prefer to shop in specialty, department, chain, or discount stores? The target customers for oversized stretch denim Long Haul jeans (discussed in Chap. 8 on "New Products") are truck drivers and blue-collar workers. Do these prefer to shop at truck stops, chain stores, or discount stores?

If the target customer for your portable bathtub-mounted whirlpool device is older people with chronic ailments, you would consider selling through stores which also offer wheelchairs, walkers, and canes. However, if the target customer is younger people purchasing the device for fun, relaxation, and alleviation of aches and pains caused by jogging, tennis, and skiing, you would consider selling through sporting goods, department, or chain stores.

The Target Customer's Shopping Habits

Different types of target customers receive different types of satisfaction from shopping. The shopping experience encompasses a wide range of expectations, and satisfies a wide range of needs. To correctly choose the most appropriate retail outlet for your goods, you must understand the target customer's shopping expectations, satisfactions, and needs, because one type of store will satisfy these expectations and needs better than another. Shoppers and shopping expectations, needs, and satisfactions can be classified as personalized, ethical, economic, impulse, and apathetic.

Most individual consumers exhibit combinations of these shopping habits, and few could be accurately described as purely one or the other. Consumers may also exhibit different shopping habits toward different types of goods. Also keep in mind that your product/service may appeal to several target customer groups, each having different shopping habits. In choosing the most appropriate retail outlet, you must weigh the relative importance of each element in the combination.

Personalized Shoppers. Personalized shoppers expect and enjoy a great deal of personal recognition, service, and attention from store personnel. They enjoy talking with the owner or manager and being on a first-name basis with salespeople. They feel comfortable shopping in and have great loyalty to stores where they are known. Store owners value them as repeat customers. However, they demand a great deal of attention and service such as custom tailoring, delivery, and return privileges. A personalized shopper will buy clothes at a shop where he or she can discuss styles with the salespeople, or where he or she trusts the owner's taste.

Countess Mara ties, designer gowns, and Oxxford Clothing, for example, are sold through such outlets, because their target customers are personalized shoppers. Many "leaders" and "early adopters" described in Chap. 9 on "Pricing" are personalized shoppers. If your target customers include a high percentage of personalized shoppers, choose specialty or department stores as retail outlets.

Ethical Shoppers. Ethical shoppers enjoy patronizing and supporting small local retailers rather than large or multistore chains. They enjoy shopping in their particular neighborhood or their town. They identify with the smaller store, and derive a sense of belonging and satisfaction from helping the smaller store compete against larger national or regional chains. Store owners value them as loyal repeat customers. An ethical shopper will buy vitamins at the corner drug store or canned goods at the corner grocery store rather than walking a few blocks to a regional chain. For example, health foods are sold through local and neighborhood stores, because their target customers are ethical shoppers. If your target customers include a high percentage of ethical shoppers, choose local or neighborhood stores as retail outlets.

Economic Shoppers. Economic shoppers enjoy getting the most for their money and therefore, show the most concern for price and value. They will shop around to find the best value, the best relationship between price and quality. For goods of similar quality or for goods where quality cannot be easily compared, the economic shopper will search out the least expensive offering. He or she feels most comfortable shopping in supermarkets, chain, discount, and factory outlet stores, and least comfortable shopping in department, specialty, and neighborhood stores. Shopping in large stores gives them a sense of value. They show little loyalty to any particular retailer. Many "early and late majority" types of customers described in Chap. 9 are economic shoppers.

An economic shopper will buy tennis shoes and balls at Sportmart, Herman's, or Athlete's Foot rather than at a pro shop. An economic shopper will buy books at Crown's, B. Dalton, Waldenbooks, or Kroch's & Brentano's rather than at the neighborhood book store.

For example, work clothes, athletic socks, children's pajamas, auto accessories, plastic dishes, small tools, and children's toys are sold primarily through chain and discount stores because their target customers are economic shoppers. If your target customers include a high percentage of economic shoppers, choose supermarkets, catalogue showrooms, chains, factory outlets, and/or discount stores as retail outlets.

Impulse Shoppers. Impulse shoppers enjoy the excitement and adventure of an unplanned trip to the store. They shop for the sake of shopping, with little preconceived idea of purchasing a particular item. They enjoy the experience and environment of a retail store. They feel comfortable shopping in any type of retail outlet, and don't exhibit loyalty to any particular store.

People who go to the grocery store without a list are impulse shoppers. The man who unexpectedly buys a suit because he saw a nice one in a store window at lunch is an impulse shopper. If your target customers include impulse shoppers, location of your goods within the store is very important. Your goods require highly visible displays in good traffic areas.

Impulse shoppers patronize all types of stores. Therefore, if your target customers are impulse shoppers, choice of appropriate retail outlets will depend on other factors such as your goods' image and pricing zone. Examples of items frequently purchased by impulse shoppers include stuffed animals, specialty food items, sunglasses, and national magazines.

Apathetic Shoppers. Apathetic shoppers do not enjoy the shopping experience and perceive it as stricly functional. They are the opposite of impulse shoppers, because shopping makes them feel uncomfortable. They will shop at the closest, easiest, and most convenient retail outlet which carries the desired merchandise. Apathetic shoppers do not frequent shopping centers and downtown stores. They feel equally uncomfortable in all types of retail outlets, and have no store loyalty.

An apathetic shopper would buy a wristwatch at the corner drug store even if there was a broader selection at a store several blocks away. Examples of products frequently purchased by apathetic shoppers include necessities (staples) such as soap, milk, and light bulbs. If your target customers include a high percentage of apathetic shoppers, distribute your goods through as wide a variety of neighborhood and local retail outlets as possible.

Summary. As you can see, for the consumer, shopping is more than just buying goods. Shopping is a ritual, a social experience, an adventure, an expression of freedom, power, confidence, affluence, values, and self. The store selected usually reflects the shopper's self-image and life style. You must choose retail outlets which best suit your target customer's shopping habits, whether these be personalized, ethical, economic, impulse, or apathetic.

How the Target Customer Perceives Your Products/Services

To select the proper retail outlet for consumer goods, you must understand how the target customer perceives your product/service, because one type of store will prove more compatible with those perceptions than another. How the consumer perceives your goods reflects the buyer's preference and willingness to seek them out. The greater the desire or preference for an item, the fewer the requirements for availability. As discussed previously, consumer products/services can be classified as convenience goods, shopping goods, specialty goods, unsought goods, and new products.

Convenience Goods. Convenience goods are products/services the customer wants but will not spend much time shopping for. They include such items as razor blades, most grocery products, photo finishing, gasoline, newspapers, charcoal, ice, nails, and shampoo. Since the customer will not seek out these goods, they must be available through a wide variety of competing retail outlets. The target customers for convenience goods generally include personalized, ethical, economic, impulse, and apathetic shoppers. If the target customer perceives your product/service as convenience goods, you should consider selling a wide variety of competing and different types of retail outlets. For example, razor blades or shampoo might be sold to a wide variety of drug, supermarket, grocery, chain, department, and discount stores in the same city.

Shopping Goods. Shopping goods are products/services the customer wants to examine and compare before purchasing. The comparison may be based on price, product features, user benefits, or some combination. The customer has the time and desire to "shop around" before buying. Shopping goods include most clothing, furniture, maid services, and appliances. The target customers for shopping goods include primarily personalized, ethical, and economic shoppers. Since the customer will seek out these goods, you may selectively limit the number and type of retail outlets. For example, your line of clothing or furniture might be sold only to certain department and specialty stores in each city.

Specialty Goods. Specialty goods are products or services which the customer will spend considerable time and effort searching out. Often this willingness to search out reflects strong brand or store preference. Specialty goods include such items as Countess Mara ties, Godiva chocolates, Bombay gin, Crabtree and Evelyn beauty products, Michelin Tires, the Sunday *New York Times,* and Club Med vacations. The target customers for specialty goods include primarily personalized and ethical shoppers. Since consumers are willing to spend considerable time seeking out these goods, you may selectively limit the number and type of retail outlets in each area. For these reasons, Countess Mara ties are only sold through select specialty and department stores which offer a great deal of service. For these reasons, Godiva chocolates and Crabtree and Evelyn beauty products are only sold through company-owned or franchised retail stores, and a few select department stores.

Unsought Goods. Unsought goods are products/services the customer does not presently want or feel that he or she needs. The benefits of such goods do not appear obvious to potential users, and they are unwilling to shop for this classification of goods. Unsought goods include life insurance, encyclopedias, home security systems, pay TV, and magazine subscriptions. Since these goods are unsought by users, they sell poorly in any type of retail outlet, and must be sold instead through telemarketing and personal sales.

New Products. New products represent a special type of unsought goods. As you create a demand for them, they emerge into convenience, shopping, or specialty goods. The target customers for new products include primarily personalized, impulse, and ethical shoppers. New products require strong personal selling until a user perception pattern develops. Therefore, you distribute them through retail outlets that excel in personal selling, such as specialty or department stores, rather than through retail outlets providing self-service, such as supermarkets, chains, and discount stores. For example, video games were first introduced through electronic specialty stores. However, two years after their introduction, consumers also could purchase them in chain and discount stores.

Summary. To select the proper retail outlet for consumer goods, you must understand how the target customer perceives your product/service, because one type of store will prove more compatible with those perceptions than another. The greater the desire or preference for an item, the fewer the requirements for availability. Consumers perceive products/services as convenience goods, shopping goods, specialty goods, unsought goods, and new products.

The Product/Service and Retail Outlet's Image and Pricing Zone

To select the proper retail outlet for consumer goods, you must consider your product/service's image and pricing zone. The retail outlet, like the packaging, should reinforce rather than detract from the product image. Also, the retail outlet should carry other products whose positions in their pricing zones coincide to your position.

A store's image is determined by its architecture, location, decor, layout, personnel, advertising, products, prices, and clientele. Stores with distinctive outside designs imply that distinctive products may be found inside. Stores in prestigious locations such as Fifth Avenue in New York, Michigan Avenue in Chicago, and Wilshire Boulevard in Los Angeles connote a prestige image; while stores without carpets, with narrow aisles, and with selling fixtures close together give the impression of good values. Stores with an abundance of well-dressed helpful sales clerks connote quality, while self-service stores with one clerk dressed in blue jeans connote low overhead and reasonable prices. Advertising that utilizes a great deal of white space creates a prestige image, while cluttered advertising connotes bargains. A retail outlet that carries fine products obtains an image as a fine store, whereas a retail outlet that sells low-price merchandise obtains an image as a cheap store. A retail outlet that sells branded merchandise 10% below competition obtains a value-oriented image.

Most important to a store's image are the people who shop there, because consumers like to shop at stores patronized by others like themselves. This reinforces the consumer's self-image. A store's architecture, location, decor, layout, personnel, advertising, prices, and products tell the consumer a great deal about its clientele. As you can see, all these factors are interrelated in projecting a store's image.

The image of the retail stores you choose influences the consumer's image of your product, and therefore should reinforce it. If your product's image is value-for-the-price, then choose stores with a value image, such as chains, mass merchants, and supermarkets. If your product's image is status, then choose stores with a status image, such as better department and specialty stores. For example, canvas suitcases can be sold through Sears, Penney's, Target, and Zayre's, whereas leather suitcases should be sold through luggage shops and department stores.

The retail outlets you choose should reinforce your product's pricing zone. The outlets should carry other products whose positions in their pricing zones coincides with your position. If an item is priced at the upper or lower end of its zone, it should be sold through outlets which carry other, noncompetitive products similarly priced. You would not sell $40 men's shirts through stores selling $100 suits. A vendor offering upper-end goods will encounter difficulty raising prices to a store which primarily carries lower-end merchandise.

In choosing retail outlets for your firm's products/services, consider the match between images and pricing zones. Pick those stores whose images and pricing zones most closely coincide with those for your product.

Unit Sales Potential, Objectives, and Restrictions

To select the proper retail outlet for consumer goods, you also must consider your firm's unit sales potential, objectives, and restrictions. It is unrealistic to consider selling national mass merchants if you cannot supply the quantities they need. If your firm is capable of shipping 2,000,000 pairs of ladies' hosiery annually, but if selling K Mart would require shipments of 3,000,000 pairs annually, then you cannot realistically consider selling this retail outlet.

You might instead consider selling a smaller regional discount chain such as Bradlee's in New England, whose annual ladies' hosiery requirements might be 500,000 pairs. However, you may not wish to be dependent upon one customer for 25% of your firm's sales. In such a situation, you might seek other appropriate retail outlets with even smaller requirements, such as city-wide discount, chain, or supermarket stores.

Type of Retail Outlets

Retail outlets can be classified as supermarkets, drug stores, discount stores, off-price factory outlets, catalogue showrooms, discount department stores, chain stores, department stores, specialty stores, manufacturer-owned stores, franchises, and combinations. Each type of store appeals to different types of target customers, different shopping habits, and different consumer perceptions. Each type of store contains a different image, pricing zone, and quantity requirements.

Supermarkets.   The average supermarket carries more than 50,000 branded, store label, and generic items, many of them nonfood products. Because most households must visit the supermarket at least once a week, convenience goods sell well. A majority of supermarket customers are economic shoppers, with some apathetic and impulse shoppers mixed in. Supermarkets have a strong price appeal and a relatively low-quality, impersonal image. Items are priced at the lower end of their zone. Customers serve themselves, delivery service is seldom offered, and the choice of colors, sizes, and labels is limited. However, supermarket items are almost always in stock. Supermarkets have tremendous customer traffic and sell huge quantities of goods. If your firm offers a convenience item with a nonprestige image to economic, apathetic, or impulse shoppers, and the item is priced at the lower end of its zone; and if your firm can reliably deliver huge quantities; then you should consider selling to supermarkets.

Drug Stores.   In recent years drug stores have greatly expanded their product lines. Because most households must visit a drug store at least once a week, convenience goods sell well there. A majority of drug store customers are economic shoppers, with some apathetic and impulse shoppers mixed in. Drug stores have a strong price appeal, and a relatively low-quality, impersonal image. Items are priced at the lower end of their zone. Customers serve themselves, delivery service is seldom offered, and the choice of colors, sizes, and labels is limited. Drug stores have high customer traffic and sell large quantities of goods. If your firm offers a convenience item with a nonprestige image to economic, apathetic, or impulse shoppers, and the item is priced at the lower end of its zone; and if your firm can reliably deliver large quantities; then you should consider selling to drug stores.

Discount Stores. Discount stores carry many different types of products, most of which could be classified as unbranded shopping goods. Some discount stores like K Mart offer everything from appliances to clothing to furniture. Other discount stores specialize in one category of merchandise such as toys, shoes, appliances, sporting goods, food, or health and beauty products. The vast majority of discount store customers are blue-collar and lower-echelon white-collar shoppers. Discount stores have a strong price appeal, and a low-quality, impersonal image with items priced at the lower end of their zone. Customers serve themselves, no delivery service is offered, and the choice of colors, sizes, styles, models, and labels is limited. However, items are always in stock. Discount stores sell huge quantities of goods and have tremendous customer traffic. If your firm offers shopping goods with a lower quality image to economic shoppers, and the items are priced at the lower end of their zone; and if your firm can reliably deliver huge quantities; then you should consider selling to discount stores.

Factory Outlets, Catalogue Showrooms, Discount Department Stores. Factory outlets, catalogue showrooms, and discount department stores all sell branded, quality shopping goods below suggested retail prices used by other types of outlets. Authentic factory outlets are owned by the company whose products they primarily sell. For instance, Bass Shoe and French Shriner each own a chain of factory outlet stores, which primarily carry their overstocked, discontinued, or irregular shoes. However, these outlets also carry some regular merchandise bought from other vendors, including shoes and hosiery.

If your firm has a problem selling irregulars, seconds, discontinued, or overstocked styles and models, consider opening your own factory outlet store. If you have inexpensive space available, such a store can prove highly profitable.

Many factory outlet stores, such as Marshall's, have no corporate connections to the merchandise they carry. Such stores began by purchasing irregulars, overstocked, and discontinued goods from a wide variety of vendors. However, as these stores grew, they added regular first-quality merchandise, but sold it below the suggested list price. Most non-manufacturer-owned factory outlet stores specialize in apparel, but others offer such goods as camping equipment, sporting goods, furniture, home furnishings, housewares, paint, and wallpaper.

Catalogue showrooms, such as Service Merchandise Company, sell through direct mail catalogues, brochures, and media advertising, in addition to their own showrooms where the catalogue items are displayed. Customers may order by phone, by mail, or by visiting the showroom. At the showroom, consumers select the desired item and order it from a clerk. After a few minutes, the item is delivered to the customer from an adjacent warehouse. Catalogue showrooms specialize in jewelry, watches, housewares, small appliances, giftware, silverware, cameras, radios, and luggage. All merchandise is branded, and sold below suggested retail prices.

Discount department stores, such as Mervyn's, primarily offer quality branded merchandise at below suggested list prices. They offer all types of shopping goods.

Factory outlets, catalogue showrooms, and discount department stores have a strong off-price appeal, but a quality, value, impersonal image, with items priced in the middle to upper end of their pricing zone. These stores cater to economic shoppers, customers serve themselves, and no delivery service is offered. The selection of colors, sizes, makes, and models is vast at discount department stores and catalogue showrooms, but limited at factory outlet stores. Discount department stores and catalogue showrooms attempt to remain in stock at all times. All three types of outlet sell huge quantities of goods and have tremendous customer traffic. If your firm offers branded shopping goods with a good quality image to economic shoppers, and the items are priced in the middle to upper end of their zone; and if your firm can reliably deliver huge quantities; then you should consider selling factory outlets, catalogue showrooms, and discount department stores.

Chain Stores. Chain stores such as Sears Roebuck, J. C. Penney, and Montgomery Ward carry many different categories of shopping products and services. Chain stores do not specialize in one category such as shoes, clothing, furniture, or appliances. The majority of products are sold under the store labels rather than brands. Chain store customers are primarily economic shoppers who enjoy "one-stop" shopping and have faith in the store labels. The chain store label reduces the consumer's risk of being wrong. Chain stores have a "middle-of-the-road" quality image and moderate price appeal, with most items priced in the center of their respective zones.

If service is desired, customers can obtain it from store personnel, and home delivery of certain merchandise such as appliances is available. However, most goods are displayed for self-service, and any delivery is added to the price. Choice of colors, styles, models, and labels is limited, and stores are not always in stock. Chain stores sell large quantities of goods and have high customer traffic. If your firm offers shopping goods with a medium quality image to economic shoppers, and the item is priced at the middle of its zone; and if your firm can reliably deliver large quantities; then you should consider selling to chain stores.

Chain stores also sell services such as insurance, security brokerage, home and auto repair, and health care. These services are often subcontracted locally, and can represent an interesting means for a small service organization to market themselves.

Department Stores. Department stores carry many different types of shopping and specialty goods rather than concentrating on one category. The majority of products are sold under national brands and designer labels, although store labels are important in certain departments. Department store customers are economic, personalized, and impulse shoppers who enjoy "one-stop" shopping and have faith in the store's choice of merchandise. Department stores have a quality, status, prestige image and offer items priced in the middle to upper end of their zones. Store personnel serve customers, answer questions, and assist in the purchase. Because of this, department stores can sell new products. Home delivery service is offered, occasionally at no charge. Choice of colors, models, styles, sizes, and labels is extensive, but stores are frequently out of stock. Department stores sell moderately large quantities of goods and have good customer traffic. If your firm offers branded, designer, shopping, or specialty goods, or a new product with a quality, status, or prestige image to economic, personalized, or impulse shoppers, and the item is priced in the moderate to upper end of its zone; and if your firm can deliver moderately large quantities; then you should consider selling department stores.

Specialty Stores. As the name implies, specialty stores specialize in one particular type of product such as gourmet food, women's or men's apparel, computers, sporting goods, or furniture. Personalized, impulse, and ethical shoppers purchase shopping/specialty goods and new products under national brands or designer labels at specialty stores. Customers have faith in the store's choice of merchandise. Specialty stores have a quality, status, prestige image, and offer items priced in the upper end of their zones. Store personnel know the customers, serve them, answer questions, and generally try to make shopping a pleasant experience. Choice of colors, models, styles, and sizes may be limited, and stores are often out of stock. Specialty stores sell small quantities of goods and have limited customer traffic. If your firm offers branded or designer shopping goods, specialty goods, or a new product with a quality, status, or prestige image to personalized, ethical, or impulse shoppers, and the item is priced at the upper end of its zone; and if you can economically ship small orders; you should consider selling specialty stores.

Manufacturer-Owned Stores and Franchises. Some manufacturers desire or require a great deal of control over the sale of their products. They may therefore manage their own retail outlets or franchise retail stores in certain areas.

For instance, Florsheim Shoes, Bally of Switzerland, and Crabtree and Evelyn own or franchise their own stores. These manufacturer-owned retail outlets have the same characteristics as specialty stores, and carry goods besides those manufactured by the owner. If you are considering selling specialty stores, then consider selling appropriate manufacturer-owned or franchised retail outlets.

Combinations and Changes. Some retail outlets represent various combinations of supermarkets, drug stores, discount stores, factory outlets, catalogue showrooms, discount department stores, chain stores, department stores, specialty stores, and manufacturer-owned or franchised stores. These classifications are not always mutually exclusive. Moreover, since business is a dynamic process, retailers are continually varying their strategy to take advantage of changing markets.

For example, many Jewel supermarkets now have Osco drug stores under the same roof. Similarly, many Stop and Shop supermarkets now have Bradlee's discount stores under the same roof. Kohl supermarkets share space with Kohl discount stores. Carson, Pirie, Scott, a Midwest department store, and Filene's, a New England department store, run a factory outlet type operation in their basements. Many Macy's department stores have specialty shop operations in their basements. Bernie Shulman's in suburban Cleveland, Drug Emporium in Columbus, Drug Place in Cincinnati, and Drug Mart in Dayton are examples of a new retailing phenomenon, discount drug stores, which sell everything from health and beauty products to bread, soft drinks, and housewares at rock-bottom prices.

J. C. Penney no longer offers auto service centers or major appliances, and in some branches is trading up with branded merchandise, wood parquet floors, and carpeting. In years to come, Penney's has announced its intention to de-emphasize paint, hardware, and lawn and garden supplies.

With sales of hi-fi equipment declining, stereo stores are disappearing or turning themselves into electronic supermarkets offering hi-fi, video, computers, and telephones. Similarly, most butcher shops have succumbed to supermarkets.

Summary. Retail outlets can be classified as supermarkets, drug stores, discount stores, catalogue showrooms, factory outlets, discount department stores, chain stores, department stores, specialty stores, manufacturer-owned stores, franchises, and combinations. Each type of store appeals to different types of target customers, different shopping habits, and different consumer perceptions. Each type of store contains a different image, pricing zone, and quantity requirements. Supermarkets and drug stores primarily sell nonprestige, lower-priced convenience items. Discount stores primarily sell lesser-quality shopping goods priced at the lower end of their zone. Factory outlets, catalogue showrooms, and discount department stores primarily sell branded shopping goods with a good quality image at attractive prices. Chain stores primarily sell medium-quality, medium-priced, unbranded shopping goods at middle-of-the-road prices. Department, specialty, manufacturer-owned, and franchised stores primarily sell branded shopping and specialty goods with a quality, status, or prestige image at better prices to personalized, ethical, and impulse shoppers.

In choosing the correct retail outlet, remember that most consumers will not travel more than fifteen minutes from their home to shop. Also keep in mind that department and specialty stores do not like items and brands which they sell to be also offered by supermarkets, drug, discount, factory outlet, catalogue showrooms, discount department, or chain stores. Such distribution causes pricing problems and hurts the image of the department store or specialty store.

TYPE OF SALES ORGANIZATION

Whether you sell consumer products to retail stores or commercial products/ services to other businesses, you must select the appropriate type of sales organization for reaching the customer. You may employ your own full-time sales force, use sales representatives or jobbers who carry several lines, sell to or through a distributor or broker who sells in turn to the customer, or some combination. The choice depends on the type of goods and number of customers you sell, customer preferences and expectations, product and customer images, economics, and competition. The decision concerning the proper form of sales organization becomes more complicated for companies with several related product lines.

Introduction

As discussed previously, both consumer and business-to-business products and services can be classified as convenience goods, shopping goods, specialty goods, unsought goods, or new products. Since convenience goods' distribution must be broad-based and since availability is more important than salesmanship, they can best be sold through stocking distributors, jobbers, and brokers. On the other hand, shopping goods' distribution is more limited and salesmanship is required; and so, depending on an item's sophistication, it may be sold through your own full-time sales force or part-time sales representatives. Specialty goods are sold to a very limited number of customers who can be efficiently served by a small full-time sales force. Unsought goods and new products require a great deal of salesmanship and can best be sold through your own full-time sales force with the help of management.

Industrial purchasing agents and retail store buyers have certain expectations or preferences concerning the type of sales force they deal with. Often these expectations reflect industry tradition, and the importance of your product/service to the purchaser.

The image of your type of distribution or type of sales organization must reinforce your product image and customer self-image. If your product or service or customers have a status, quality, prestige, or specialty image, you require channels of distribution and a sales organization with a status, quality, prestige, or specialty image. If your product/service or customers have a value-for-the-price image, you require channels of distribution and a sales organization with a value-for-the-price image.

For a smaller firm, economics also plays an important role in how you reach the customer. Your own full-time salespeople are usually more expensive than part-time representatives. In choosing among alternative types of sales organizations, you must determine whether a manageable territory has enough dollar volume to support a full-time salesperson. Territories which require a great deal of travel but do not contain a great deal of potential business may lend themselves to a part-time salesperson, or to an organization whose salespeople carry several noncompeting lines.

For many smaller firms, hybrid structures prove effective. This means using a full-time company salesperson in a dense territory where many customers cluster, and representatives, jobbers, brokers, or distributors who carry several lines in sparse territories where customers are few and far between.

The decision concerning the proper form of sales organization becomes more complicated for companies with several related product lines. If the product lines have compatible images and product classifications, and are bought by the same customers, purchasing agents or buyers, then they can be sold effectively by the same type sales organization. If not, you require a more detailed analysis.

In deciding between the use of full-time salespeople, part-time representatives, distributors, brokers, jobbers, or some combination, consider how your most successful competitors handle this choice. However, analyze your competitors' results before following their examples.

Type of Goods/Number of Customers

As discussed previously, both consumer and business-to-business products/services can be classified as convenience goods, shopping goods, specialty goods, unsought goods, or new products. These classifications reflect the buyer's preference for the goods, the buyer's willingness to seek them out.

Convenience goods are products/services which the customer wants but will not spend much time shopping for, and so distribution must be broad-based.

Most small businesses cannot afford a broad-based full-time sales force. Convenience goods do not require a great deal of salesmanship, but they do require fast, reliable delivery, which can best be accomplished by maintaining local inventories. Therefore, convenience goods lend themselves to distribution through stocking distributors, jobbers, or brokers who sell and carry inventory for many noncompeting lines. Many stocking distributors, jobbers, and brokers are themselves small businesses with their own sales force reaching a broad customer base, but within a small geographic area.

Shopping goods are products/services which the customer wants to examine and compare before purchasing. The buyer or purchasing agent has time to and wants to "shop around." Shopping goods do not require distribution as broad-based as convenience goods, and fast delivery is less critical. However, shopping goods do require salesmanship, because the buyer needs help, advice, and information to make a purchase. Generally speaking, more sophisticated shopping goods, which require a great deal of training and missionary work to sell, lend themselves to a full-time company sales force, but other shopping goods can be sold by part-time sales representatives who carry other noncompeting lines.

Specialty goods are products/services which the customer will spend considerable time and effort seeking out. Normally, specialty goods are sold to a limited number of customers who can be efficiently served by a small full-time salesforce.

Unsought goods and new products/services are items which the customer does not presently want or feel he or she needs. Therefore, they require a great deal of salesmanship and can best be sold through your own full-time sales force with the help of management.

In choosing the distribution for your goods, consider the customer's willingness to seek them out. Convenience goods generally require distribution by a network of brokers, jobbers, or distributors; specialty, unsought goods and new products can best be sold by a small full-time sales force; and shopping goods can be sold by either a full-time sales force or part-time representatives.

Customer Preference and Expectations

Industrial purchasing agents and retail store buyers have certain expectations or preferences concerning the type of sales force with which they wish to deal. You must take their expectations and preferences into account when choosing appropriate means of reaching the customer.

Often these expectations reflect industry tradition, and/or the importance of the product/service to the purchaser. An item of which the buyer or purchasing agent buys a great deal, or which is very expensive, or is critical to the customer's operation, or requires a great deal of vendor service may require a full-time salesperson; on the other hand an inexpensive, low-volume, uncritical, nonservice item may not.

For example, a discount store furniture buyer may expect to be called on by part-time sales reps, while the blouse buyer may prefer full-time company salespeople. A men's wear specialty store buyer may expect to be called on by part-time sales representatives, while a department store dress buyer may prefer to be called on by a full-time company salesperson.

The purchasing agent for maintenance supplies at a chemical company may expect to be called on by a distributor, while the purchasing agent for automatic controls may prefer to see a sales engineer. The purchasing agent for food provisions at a hospital may prefer to work with a food broker, while the purchasing agent for cleaning and laundry services may expect to be called on by a full-time company salesperson.

Compatible Image

The image of your type of distribution or type of sales organization must reinforce your product image and your customer's self-image. If your product/service or customers have a status, quality, prestige, or specialty image, you require channels of distribution and a sales organization with a status, quality, prestige, or specialty image. If your product/service or customers have a value-for-the-price image, you require channels of distribution and a sales organization with a value-for-the-price image.

For example, typewriters can be sold through distributors, but word processors require a sales engineer. Flat stock steel can be sold through brokers, but titanium alloys require a technical representative. Unbranded underwear can be sold through jobbers, but designer neckties require their own sales force.

You can sell the Army Post Exchanges through a sales representative organization, but the buyer at Bloomingdale's wants to work with a full-time company salesperson. You can sell drilling supplies to independent oil exploration firms through distributors, but the purchasing agent at Standard Oil wants to work with a full-time company salesperson.

Economics

For a smaller firm, economics play an important role in how you reach the customer. Your own full-time salespeople, even if they are on 100%-commission compensation, are usually more expensive than part-time sales representatives, jobbers, distributors, or brokers. A full-time sales organization requires fringe benefits which add at least 16% to their basic compensation, while a part-time sales organization generally requires no fringe benefits. Also, usually a part-time organization pays its own travel, entertainment, and office expenses, while an employer pays for at least some portion of a full-time organization's expenses. Although you may pay part-time salespeople a higher basic compensation to partially offset their fringe benefits and expenses, this does not equal the cost of supporting full-time people.

Because stocking distributors, jobbers, and brokers not only sell, but usually assume some credit and inventory responsibility, you must pay them more, through the margin you allow them, than the compensation paid to part-time field sales representatives. You must decide whether these additional services are worth the cost. In the case of jobbers, distributors, and brokers, your cost is generally not reflected in sales compensation, but in the lower price you charge them.

In choosing between alternative types of sales organizations, you must determine whether a manageable territory has enough dollar volume to support a full-time salesperson. Territories which require a great deal of travel but do not contain a great deal of potential business may lend themselves to a part-time salesperson or organization carrying several noncompeting lines.

Generally, you have, or at least feel you have, more control over full-time people because their only source of income derives from selling your product or service. However, with proper recruiting, training, compensation, motivation, communication, planning, and appraisal, you can build a successful sales force around full- or part-time people, jobbers, brokers, or distributors. Most important of all for a small business sales organization is the proper human resource.

Combinations

For many smaller firms, hybrid sales structures prove effective. This means using a full-time company salesperson in a dense territory where many customers cluster, and representatives, jobbers, brokers, or distributors who carry several lines in sparse territories where customers are few and far apart.

For example, a semiconductor manufacturer might employ full-time salespeople in Boston, Dallas, Phoenix, and Los Angeles but part-time sales representatives elsewhere. A panty hose manufacturer might employ full-time salespeople in New York, Chicago, and Los Angeles; part-time sales representatives in Boston, Philadelphia, Atlanta, Miami, Dallas, Cleveland, Detroit, and San Francisco; and distributors or jobbers for the rest of the country.

Multiple Product Lines

The decision concerning the proper form of distribution or type of sales organizations becomes more complicated for companies with several related product lines. If a sweater company offers both men's and ladies' styles, or both branded and unbranded garments, or a separate line of full-fashion knit jerseys, can management utilize the same type of sales force for all lines? If a firm which assembles nail-making machines also offers a line of rivet-producing equipment, or cutting fluids, would the same form of distribution or type of sales organization provide acceptable results for both lines?

If the product lines have compatible images and product classifications, and are bought by the same customers, purchasing agents, or buyers, then they could be sold effectively by the same salesperson. If the product lines do not have compatible images and/or product classifications, and/or are not sold to the same customers, purchasing agents, or buyers, then you require a more detailed analysis.

Again, for smaller businesses the human resource reigns supreme. A good salesperson probably can sell related product lines; a weak salesperson has difficulty with one. The same salesperson carrying related product lines might generate higher commission income, or justify higher salaries allowing you to attract more or better full-time people. The same person carrying related product lines might enable the company to have more salespeople with smaller, more efficient territories.

Competition

In any sales management decision, an important consideration is competition. Does your most successful comparable competitor employ full-time salespeople, part-time representatives, distributors, brokers, jobbers, or some combination? How does it deal with related product lines? How does your least successful competitor deal with these issues? Analyze your competition's results before following their examples.

Summary

Whether you sell consumer products to retail stores or commercial products/ services to other businesses, you must select the appropriate type of sales organization to reach the customer. You may employ your own full-time sales force, use sales representatives or jobbers who carry several lines, sell through or to a distributor or broker who sells in turn to the customer, or some combination. The choice depends upon the type of goods and number of customers you sell, customer preferences and expectations, product and customer images, economics, and competition. From a practical standpoint, what is right is what works best. Often the small businessperson must try different approaches, measure the results, and have an open mind.

HIGHLIGHT VS. SCATTER SELLING

Determining the most profitable means of reaching a market requires choosing between highlight and scatter selling. Few small businesses evaluate whether their resources, markets, and competitive advantage favor the shotgun or rifle approach for the number and size of customers to be solicited and serviced. Most small businesspeople just accept the current approach as the proper one.

For example, a business can choose to sell only large major accounts with a small compact sales organization, or sell a variety of accounts, large and small, with a large sales organization. Also, a business can elect to sell in one or several regions of the country, nationally, or internationally. These choices exist regardless of whether your firm offers convenience, shopping, specialty, or unsought goods. You can attempt to sell all the appropriate accounts in all regions of the country or you can limit distribution.

Limiting your distribution to a few major users only requires a small compact sales organization, thus reducing selling expenses and the need for sales control. Credit risks are generally less, but your firm may become overly dependent on several large customers. Also, with large users you must be able to handle large orders.

To sell and service many accounts, large and small, requires a larger sales organization, greater sales expense, and more sales management. Credit risks are generally higher, and your firm must have the staff and facilities to process many small orders.

Limiting your distribution to one or several areas of the country also reduces the size and cost of your sales force, but again increases your dependency on a smaller regional customer base. Many California companies only sell to West Coast customers because they have a freight and delivery advantage. Most small businesses have strong and weak territories. You should at least consider eliminating the weak ones and concentrating your resources on the strong.

A combination of highlight and scatter selling also deserves consideration as a marketing strategy. In certain territories, it might be advantageous to sell only major accounts; in other territories, it might be advantageous to sell all potential accounts. This would depend on the size of the territory, cost of traveling the territory, the size and number of potential customers, and the salesperson.

As sales manager you should decide which alternative highlight or scatter selling or some combination seems most appropriate to the strengths and weaknesses of your business. To accomplish this, the following questions require answers. Is the business capable of supplying appropriate quantities and services to a few large accounts, or is it better suited for processing and shipping many small orders? What are the economics of a large sales force versus a small one? Does the company have the resources to supervise, control, and support a large sales organization? Who is the competition with major accounts; who is the competition in the broader market? Does the company have a different competitive advantage with large accounts than with small ones? What percentage of the market do large accounts represent? What percentage of the market do small accounts represent? Are they growing? How loyal are larger accounts as opposed to smaller ones? Can the company afford the risk of losing large customers?

EVALUATING RESOURCES

In deciding the most effective means of reaching a market, and in most sales management/marketing decisions, a realistic appraisal of your company's available resources is important. Realistically evaluating resources is important for any business, but critical for a smaller one because resources are often limited.

For example, if a firm doesn't have an experienced sales manager, it would be difficult to hire, train, and control a large sales organization. Similarly, with a net worth of $100,000 and annual positive cash flow of $20,000, it would be unrealistic to enter a market which requires large advertising expenditures or major new equipment purchases. Also, if your annual manufacturing capacity is 200,000 dozen, you have no business approaching large customers who require shipment of 5,000 dozen a week. Instead, you would need to direct your sales organization toward smaller accounts.

I suggest the following exercise to assist you in evaluating resources. Leave the office for a half day, but take with you four pieces of lined paper and a pen. Place one of the following headings on each page: Management, Capital, Manufacturing, Sales.

On the Management page list all your firm's key managers, their titles, duties, strengths and weaknesses. On the Capital page place a summary of the firm's most recent balance sheet, 12-month cash flow projection, and credit lines. On the Manufacturing page list the firm's production capacity limits by function, key skilled and supervisory people, and age of critical equipment. On the Sales page list each territory, its salesperson, and key customers with strengths and weaknesses of each. Also list each product or product category with its competitive strengths and weakensses. Include the itemized sales expense page from your most recent profit-and-loss statement.

You will find this exercise rewarding and revealing. In capsule form, these lists are your firm's resources. By accumulating and reviewing these lists in one sitting, you will discover new relationships, opportunities, limitations, and some inconsistencies in your organization, all of which will assist you in making decisions concerning distribution.

SUMMARY

To succeed in a marketplace dominated by larger businesses, the small businessperson must develop an efficient means of reaching the market. Determining the most effective means of reaching a market requires creatively investigating alternatives to tradition. For each product/service or each product/service group, you need to analyze the variety of means and strategies for reaching your particular customer.

Basically this involves (1) identifying the customers for your product/service, (2) classifying your product/service by user perception, (3) for consumer products, choosing the correct retail outlet, (4) within the limits of your resources, choosing the type sales organization which best reaches the target customer, (5) choosing between highlight and scatter selling, and (6) realistically appraising your company's human and financial resources.

11
Advertising, Packaging, Promotion, and Publicity

A firm communicates product information to users and potential users through salespeople, advertising, packaging, promotion, and publicity. The choice between channels and among alternative forms and media within each channel depends on the type of information you wish to communicate and the audience you wish to reach. Each alternative performs varying functions and provides different kinds of information. The use of several channels, forms, or media reinforces the message and increases the likelihood of a purchase.

Previous chapters have dealt at length with communicating through salespeople, and so this chapter will only deal with the other channels of communicating product information. They are advertising, packaging, promotion, and publicity.

Pre-selling, creating a demand for your product or service through advertising, promotion, and publicity, is helpful for most businesses, essential for some. If a prospective customer or the ultimate user has an awareness of your product or service and knows its selling points or advantages, the salesperson's job and the retailer's job is that much easier.

In addition, advertising and publicity reach users and prospective users less expensively than a salesperson's visit. However, advertising and publicity are one-sided forms of communication. A salesperson can answer a user's questions and clarify benefits, whereas an advertisement does not allow feedback. Moreover, much advertising and publicity fall on deaf ears, readers or listeners who are not part of your target market. Only a small portion of advertising actually reaches your target audience.

It is especially important for a small business to differentiate the physical and/or psychological nature of its product/service from competition. Advertising represents an extremely effective means for developing differentiation between products/services.

Many small-business sales managers feel their firms do not have the financial and human resources necessary to properly support advertising, promotion, and publicity. Costs seem out of reach, and the technical aspects of creating an ad appear incomprehensible. This chapter attempts to show how the small businessperson can effectively use advertising, packaging, promotion, and publicity to increase sales. We will discuss how to maximize your advertising budget, how to choose among various types of advertising, how to communicate through packaging, sales promotion, and publicity, how to create an effective message, and finally how to organize and plan your advertising program. The portion of this material covered in Chap. 8, "The Development and Introduction of New Products," will be included but not fully treated here. For more detail on these subjects, refer to Chap. 8.

INTRODUCTION

As a small businessperson, you maximize the advertising budget by soliciting your suppliers, retail store customers, and distributors for advertising allowsances. Most small businesses buy from and sell through larger companies with substantial advertising allowances.

Types of advertising can be divided into: printed media such as newspapers, consumer magazines, trade publications, direct mail catalogues, product brochures, reprints, statement stuffers, and handbills; broadcast media such as AM and FM radio; cable, VHF, and UHF television; point-of-purchase displays and fixtures; position media such as billboards and signs; and miscellaneous such as display advertising in Yellow Pages and directories. The choices between media and among alternatives within each media depend on the type of information you wish to communicate and the audience you wish to reach. The use of several media or several alternatives within each media reinforces the message and increases the likelihood of a purchase.

Packaging communicates product information by attracting attention, arousing interest, and expressing the product's characteristics. A package should reinforce, not detract from, the product image.

Sales promotion communicates product/service information by reinforcing salespeople, advertising, packaging, and publicity. Sales promotion includes contests, premiums, gifts, coupons, rebates, customer entertainment, and trade shows.

Publicity communicates product/service information to customers and prospects through articles in various publications. A product/service that receives publicity in a periodical acquires exposure, status, and credibility, building confidence in its purchase.

You create an effective advertising message by gaining the reader's or listener's attention, inviting interest, arousing needs and desires, and then finally suggesting goals and actions which satisfy those needs. In the message, you use appropriate symbols to represent needs, desires, goals, and products. You demand minimal attitude changes and utilize proven learning techniques. You must also consider the legal restrictions placed on advertising.

Finally, you specifically organize and plan the advertising program by budgeting financial resources, evaluating human resources, setting goals and objectives, defining the target audience, selecting the appropriate form and media, choosing the appropriate message, content, and image, determining the frequency and timing of the message, and lastly, measuring results through feedback. Hopefully, your program will inform and persuade users to purchase your product or service.

BUDGET

The advertising budget consists of what your company can afford from internal resources along with what you can obtain from suppliers and customers. Most small businesses buy from and sell through larger companies with substantial advertising allowances. Often, the small company neglects to take advantage of the easily available dollars from these sources. The clever small-business sales manager should fully explore these opportunities.

What percentage of sales should your business allocate to advertising? Sales volume and profit margins in some small businesses limit advertising expenditures from internal sources to $1,000 annually. Other firms may have more latitude and devote up to 8% of sales to advertising. Generally speaking, industrial/commercial products and services require up to 4% of sales for advertising, while consumer products require between 4% and 8%. Obviously, unbranded merchandise requires less than branded. Markets where products, technology, and fashions change often will require more advertising than markets where change is less frequent. If your competitive advantage, type of product/service, and type of customer allow some flexibility in pricing, your firm can allocate a greater percentage of sales and a greater percentage of internally generated funds to advertising.

For example, companies selling beverages, ethical drugs, soaps, and detergents generally spend 7% to 8% of their sales dollar on advertising and promotion. On the other hand, companies selling farm equipment, chemicals, paper products, and office furniture generally spend less than 2% of their sales dollar on advertising and promotion. In 1982 Proctor and Gamble spent $577,000,000 just on television advertising.

Regardless of your advertising budget's size or the amount generated from internal sources, solicit your suppliers for an advertising allowance. Advertising should increase your sales, and therefore your purchases from the supplier, justifying the allowance. A company which annually sold $6,000,000 of furniture polish contributed only $60,000, or 1% of sales, to its $500,000, or 8%, advertising budget; the rest came from chemical suppliers. A company which annually sold $2,500,000 of industrial testing instruments raised its entire $100,000 advertising budget from suppliers.

Therefore, if your firm makes perfume, approach your fragrance and packaging suppliers for an advertising allowance. If you rent tropical plants, approach the seed and fertilizer concerns which you patronize. If you make power supplies for lasers, approach the battery companies. If you rent ice machines, approach the ice machine manufacturer. If you mold flexible bottles, approach the chemical firm which supplies the plastic.

If you sell a consumer product or service through major retailers, you should contact key retail customers and prospects concerning cooperative advertising. In such an arrangement, you and the store share the ad's cost, since both of you benefit from the product's/service's sale. The ad, whether in a newspaper or magazine, or on radio or television, announces that your product/service can be purchased at that particular store. Generally, the store will design and place the ad, eliminating your preparatory costs, and allowing you the additional benefit of their lower advertising rate. Since major retailers continually buy large volumes of space and time, their rates are lower than those available to you. Sometimes, the store pays half the ad's media cost, sometimes less. Normally, you receive a good-size order for the item being advertised, which automatically pays for some of your share.

If the perfume firm sold to Macy's, the store should be asked to pay for half the cost of a *New York Times* holiday advertisement; possibly the fragrance supplier would pay the other half. If you sell a telephone-answering device through Radio Shack, you might ask the buyer to share the cost of a regional consumer magazine ad.

Similarly, if you sell an industrial/commercial product/service through distributors, approach them to share in the advertising cost of reaching the user. Again, you both benefit from the sale. If you manufacture office furniture and sell through distributors with showrooms and a sales force, you might ask a distributor to pay for half the cost of advertising in a regional trade publication. If you sell grinding wheels to machine shops through stocking distributors, you might ask a distributor to pay for half the cost of a display ad in a local trade directory. You might ask your abrasive supplier to pay the other half.

As you can see from these examples, a small internally generated advertising budget can be greatly augmented from supplier advertising allowances, and retailer or distributor cooperative advertising. Most supplier advertising allowances and cooperative retailer programs are not used by smaller firms, because they don't believe in advertising, are unwilling to do the necessary paperwork, feel the amounts are too small, or don't want to invest their share. However, the wise small-business sales manager should contact suppliers, distributors, and/or retailers and explore this source of advertising funds.

TYPES OF ADVERTISING

Advertising can be divided into: printed media such as newspapers, consumer magazines, trade publications, direct mail catalogues, product brochures, reprints, statement stuffers, and handbills; broadcast media such as radio and television; point-of-purchase displays and fixtures; position media such as billboards and signs; and miscellaneous such as display advertising in Yellow Pages and directories. The choice between media and among the alternatives within each media depends upon the type of information you wish to communicate and the audience you wish to reach. Each alternative performs varying functions and provides different kinds of information. Use of several media or several alternatives within each media will reinforce the message and increase the likelihood of success.

Newspapers

Newspapers are most cost-efficient for advertising consumer products/services with wide appeal and local distribution. Consumers use newspapers as a source of immediate comparative product and price information on which they base buying decisions. You will increase the ad's cost efficiency by choosing the newspaper and section and day which best reaches your target audience. The major disadvantages of newspaper advertising are short life and poor print quality.

Because newspapers deal with daily activities and have limited geographic distribution, readers use them to identify with their community. Readers have faith and confidence in the integrity and believability of their newspapers' contents.

Newspapers are most cost-efficient for advertising consumer products/services with wide appeal and local distribution because newspapers allow you to concentrate advertising in a local market, while at the same time reaching a wide variety of readers. Newspapers are least cost-efficient for advertising most industrial/commercial products or services because the readership contains too small a percentage of potential users.

In some cities, you can advertise in neighborhood, foreign language, and ethnic newspapers, which allows you to narrow the audience. You can also narrow the audience by advertising in a particular newspaper section such as Sports, Business, Food, Help Wanted, Fashion, Theaters, Autos, Home and Garden, or Obituaries.

In addition, some newspapers have expanded sections with expanded readership on certain days, such as Business on Monday, Food on Thursday, Sports on Saturday, and Help Wanted on Sunday. You can take advantage of the expanded general readership of most dailies by advertising on Sundays. Depending on the readership and circulation, newspapers charge different rates for advertising on different days and in various sections. You should select the day and section which best reaches your target audience.

Consumers use newspapers as a source of immediate comparative product and price information on which they base buying decisions. Because of this, a more descriptive advertising approach, which emphasizes price and benefits, produces the best results. Because readers have faith and confidence in the integrity and believability of the newspaper, it also provides a good medium for advertising new products.

The major disadvantage of newspaper advertising is short life; generally, the reader discards a paper after one reading. Also, because of the relatively poor print and reproductive quality on ads, visual content must be kept simple, limiting the type of message.

If you wish to advertise the price of a consumer product/service which can be purchased immediately in a specific local store or stores, and can be described in words better than in pictures, especially a new product or service, then newspapers can produce the best affordable results for your small business. The wider the item's appeal, and the more stores offering it within the local market, the more cost-efficient the ad. You will increase the ad's cost efficiency, or results per dollar, by choosing the newspaper and section and day which best reaches your target audience.

For example, if you were introducing a new kerosene home space heater in Chicago at a special low price, and if you sold ten local stores with good inventory, you should try some cooperative newspaper advertising in late November. Since men purchase space heaters, you might place ads in the sports section. Because foreign-speaking people often live in older housing without central heating, you might try some foreign language papers. The ad could contain a simple line drawing of the device with bold type emphasizing the cost saving and the personal comfort benefits. Then in smaller type the ad would list names, addresses, and phone numbers of stores carrying the heaters.

A local funeral parlor or cemetery could inexpensively advertise its services on the obituary page. The ad would require a simple statement of purpose and no pictures. This is an example of very specialized newspaper advertising.

Magazines

Generally, magazines are much more specialized in content and much more national in distribution than newspapers. Magazines allow you to reach a consumer and/or business audience having specific shared interests. Different magazines appeal to different audiences. Readers identify with their special interest or trade group through magazines. Magazines have better print quality, are more personal, and more difficult to throw away than newspapers. Decision makers use magazines as a source of general comparative product information which eventually, but not immediately, influences buying decisions. This section deals with both consumer magazines and trade publications.

Magazines deal more with feature articles than news, and are usually read at leisure in the privacy of a home or office, where the reader can more rationally select products/services which seem to meet his or her personal needs, or the needs of his or her firm. Because magazines are read at leisure in the privacy of a home or office, they may be kept for months. Readers generally do not use magazines as a source of comparative price or specific product information upon which to base immediate buying decisions. Magazine advertising influences future purchases rather than immediate ones. Because of the excellent print and reproductive quality in magazine ads, visual content can be fully utilized. This allows you more versatility than newspaper advertising in choosing the content and the message.

Magazines are most cost-efficient for consumer and industrial/commercial products and services with specialized appeal and national distribution. Magazines allow you to inexpensively reach a specific market. Some national magazines allow firms to further narrow the audience or market and reduce costs by advertising in regional editions.

Similarly, in most major cities, magazines exist which specialize in articles and listings about local events, politics, the arts, and restaurants. These magazines have local audiences with common interests in the arts, restaurants, and politics.

Consumer Publications. If you sell a consumer product/service nationally to a special interest group, such as skiers, or runners, or auto enthusiasts, and if it lends itself to visual presentation, then magazines can produce affordable results for your small business. Analyze which magazines reach your specific customer group.

A small optics company in Colorado made quality nonprescription plastic sunglasses for skiers. They ran a small ad each month in several ski magazines with a picture of an attractive couple wearing their sunglasses on the slopes. The ad listed major retail outlets by city which carried the glasses, and contained a return coupon and toll-free number for information on cities not listed. The ads produced many consumer responses, which allowed the company to further expand its number of retail outlets, and increase sales at existing outlets.

A dog trainer in conjunction with an agricultural feed firm developed a line of high-protein dog food. When offered through grocery stores and advertised in local newspapers, the product failed, because it was too good and too expensive for that market. However, when it was advertised in *Dog World* magazine and sold through kennels, pet shops, and clubs as a premium product for show animals, sales increased dramatically. The advertisement contained a picture of a proud owner displaying her award-winning dog at a show. The advertisement also contained a return coupon and toll-free number for more information.

Trade Publications. If you sell an industrial/commercial product/service nationally, or if you sell a consumer product/service to retail stores, then trade publications allow your small business to inexpensively reach your specific market. Although trade publications include both daily trade papers and weekly, monthly, and quarterly trade magazines, they all are specialized in content, national in distribution, and read by a special-interest audience, so I shall discuss them together in this section. *Standard Rate and Data* lists over 4,000 trade publications (magazines and papers) including *Airport Service Management, American Laundry Digest, Apartment Construction News, Automotive Engineering, Broadcast Daily, Chemical Age, Chemical Equipment, Coal Industry News, Computer Data, Convenience Store Merchandiser, Cost Engineering, Design News, Forest Products Journal, Gas Digest, Golf Digest, Hardware Merchandising, Hospital Financial Management, Frozen Food Age, Laboratory Management, Light Metal Age, Meat Plant Magazine, Mens Wear, Musical Products News, Nuclear Instruments, Paper Trade Journal, Pollution Engineering, Pulp and Paper, Rubber World, Sporting Goods Business, Telephone Engineering and Management, Textile Industries, Womens Wear Daily,* and *Yard and Garden Product News.*

If you sell an industrial/commercial product/service nationally, determine what trade publications reach the decision makers you sell. Ask your major customers and prospects; consult responses to your market research survey. You probably read the same publications. Because these publications generally have limited circulation, their rates are reasonable; because these publications have special-interest readership, your results are excellent. A small semiconductor firm decided to use one electronics publication for reaching design engineers and another for reaching purchasing agents.

If you offer a consumer product/service nationally through retail stores, you must first convince the retailer to buy your item before both of you can convince the consumer to buy it. We have discussed how you reach the consumer through advertising, but it is equally important and much less expensive to reach the retailer. As with the industrial market, determine what trade publications reach the retail decision makers. A small ladies' blouse company decided to advertise in one women's wear publication for reaching buyers and another for reaching merchandise managers.

As in consumer advertising, trade magazines have better reproductive quality than trade papers, although trade papers offer magazine-quality inserts. As in consumer advertising, trade magazines have a longer life than trade papers.

Trade papers and magazines have specialized sections, editions, and days for different types of goods and services. In the apparel trade papers, Monday is knit goods day and Thursday financial services. Readership for sweater ads would be better on Mondays, and readership for banking and factoring ads would be better on Thursdays.

The electronics trade magazines contain certain specialized sections for components, equipment, and quality control. A semiconductor manufacturer might receive better readership by advertising in the component section, while a test instrument firm might receive better readership by advertising in the equipment or quality control sections. In addition, most trade publications have special issues with increased circulation and rates for major trade shows.

Buyers, purchasing agents, and decision makers use trade publications as a source of general comparative product information which eventually, but not immediately, influences buying decisions. Because of this, ads which feature user benefits produce the best results. In trade magazines you can use pictures to obtain the reader's attention and tell the story, but in trade newspapers simple art work produces the best results.

A small engineering firm specializing in pollution control advertised monthly in various trade publications reaching the steel, utility, paper, and chemical industries. It showed pictures of pollution problems and briefly listed the firm's technical capabilities. A toll-free number and return coupon generated many responses.

A small designer tie firm advertised twice monthly in the men's apparel trade paper, listing its products, price ranges, and markups next to a simple drawing of an attractive design. The ads invited interested buyers to call a toll-free number or visit the New York showroom. The ads inexpensively generated many qualified leads.

As this section shows, magazines are most cost-efficient for consumer and industrial/commercial products and services with specialized appeal and national distribution. Magazines allow you to inexpensively reach a specific market with good print quality. Explore which magazines and trade publications reach your customers.

Direct Mail and Handbills

A small firm can inexpensively advertise and sell its products/services through catalogues, brochures, reprints, statement stuffers, and handbills. As discussed in Chap. 8 on "The Development and Introduction of New Products," both industrial and consumer products/services can be advertised and sold through direct mail.

Many retail stores send out numerous consumer catalogues each year, and also mail statement stuffers with their charge card billings. Credit card companies also send stuffers with each billing. Consumer and business-to-business mail order firms sell and advertise almost exclusively through catalogues. In addition, many consumer and industrial businesses regularly mail product literature, reprints, letters, in-house sales catalogues, and brochures to their customers and prospects. These are all effective forms of direct mail advertising.

Store Catalogues.   For consumer products sold through retail outlets, store catalogues offer the small business an inexpensive means of pre-selling the ultimate user. Most major retailers print numerous specialty catalogues of items which can be purchased by mail, by phone, or in the store. In December, for example, the store catalogue might feature toys, in February linens, and in May outdoor items. Through such catalogues, your message will reach thousands of affluent consumers. Although only a small percentage of those receiving the catalogue respond by immediately making a purchase, the rest become aware of the item and at a later date may purchase it at any retail outlet. Stores mail catalogues to their charge card customers in addition to people on lists purchased from direct mail services. Customers can also obtain catalogues in the stores.

Retailers confine their catalogues to their store's trading markets. However, with multistore, multiregion retailers, trading markets may expand beyond city and state lines. Also, some buying organizations such as True Value Hardware and Frederick Atkins offer catalogues to member stores. Therefore, some store catalogues are local, some regional, and some national.

Generally, stores sell space in their catalogues, but then place large orders with the advertisers for the goods involved. Immediate sales from the catalogues should pay for your space costs, and so the additional market exposure, the advertising value, costs nothing.

Generally, vendors submit samples or pictures and the store advertising personnel prepare the copy and presentation. Because of excellent print and reproductive quality, visual content can be fully utilized. Consumers read catalogues at leisure in the privacy of their homes and may keep them for months.

Consumers use catalogues as a source of immediate product and price information on which they base buying decisions at the issuing store. Most retail catalogues emphasize product appeal and value. Consumers also use catalogues as a source of general comparative product information on which they base future buying decisions at other stores.

Numerous small businesses in the apparel, furniture, toy, and small appliance fields use their entire limited advertising funds for retail catalogue advertising. A firm which manufactured lawn sprinklers built a multimillion-dollar business using only this form of advertising.

Contact the advertising departments of your retail customers and prospects concerning space in their catalogues. Generally the reward is well worth the cost.

Specialty Catalogues.   Whether your firm sells a consumer or an industrial product/service, nonretail store specialty catalogues offer an inexpensive means of pre-selling. Specialty catalogues offer a wide variety of products and services including cigars, Christmas ornaments, chocolates, outdoor apparel, camping equipment, household gadgets, tools, motorcycle accessories; maintenance, material handling, safety, and communication equipment; maintenance, office, laboratory, printing, and computer supplies; small computers, electronic typewriters, chemicals, and containers. Through such catalogues, your message can reach thousands of affluent consumers and appropriate corporate purchasing agents. These catalogues are mailed nationally to previous customers in addition to people and firms on lists purchased from direct mail agencies, trade associations, and trade publications. The lists attempt to classify consumers by income and special interests, such as camping or home ownership. The lists attempt to classify firms by industry and size. For consumers, where you live very much affects your buying habits. Target marketing allows mail order firms to pinpoint prime prospects by their zip codes.

Although only a small percentage of those receiving the catalogues respond by immediately purchasing your product/service, the rest become aware of the item. At a later date, some of these people will recognize your product/service at conventional retail outlets or when presented by a field salesperson, and may possibly purchase it.

Some specialty catalogues charge vendors for space, others do not. In the former case, immediate sales from the catalogue should pay for your space costs; and in either case, the additional market exposure, the advertising value, costs nothing.

Generally, vendors submit samples or pictures and the catalogue advertising personnel prepare the copy and visual presentation. Because of the excellent print and reproductive quality, visual content can be fully utilized.

Consumers and purchasing agents read these catalogues at leisure in the privacy of their home or office and may keep them until the next issue is received. Consumers use these catalogues both as a source of immediate product and price information on which they base immediate buying decisions, and as a source of general comparative information on which they base future buying decisions. Most consumer specialty catalogues emphasize product appeal and value.

Businesses use business catalogues as a source of general comparative product information which eventually, but not immediately, influences buying decisions. Most business-to-business specialty catalogues emphasize user benefits and price.

A well-known but small hiking boot manufacturer advertises only in specialty catalogues, even though other retail outlets also sell the shoes. Several small chemical, computer supply, and container firms established brand identification by advertising through specialty catalogues.

Contact specialty catalogue publishers who sell to your target customers. Specialty catalogues can produce immediate sales and considerable advertising value.

Sales Catalogues. Many firms print catalogues which describe their line and list current prices. Such catalogues range from bound versions with color photography to multilithed typewritten pages stapled together. Firms mail these in house catalogues to their customers and prospects, plus salesmen use them in their presentations. In the case of consumer products, the catalogues go to retail store buyers.

These catalogues keep your firm's name in front of customers and prospects between the salesperson's visits, and also act as reference pieces for ordering. The catalogue contains detailed price information, detailed product information, and instructions for ordering. Customers keep these catalogues until a new one is issued, which varies from once to four times annually. Because these catalogues serve as reference documents, they should be well organized and contain easy-to-use indexes.

Brochures and Reprints. Besides mailing their catalogues to customers and prospects, firms also mail flyers, press releases, reprints of ads and articles, special-interest bulletins, and brochures on specific models or styles. Sending reprints of ads and articles concerning your products/services assures that customers and prospects see them, even though they might have missed the original published version. Generally, brochures contain attractive photography, product descriptions, and a list of benefits, along with a return coupon and telephone number for more information. The copying-maching industry uses such brochures extensively.

By selecting the correct mailing list, a firm can pinpoint who receives these forms of printed advertising, and can assume that it will be seen by the appropriate person. The sources for this mailing list would be company records on customers, salespeople's suggestions on prospects, names from trade shows, plus appropriate lists purchased from trade associations, trade publications, reference books, and direct mail companies. You must address in-house sales catalogues, brochures, flyers, reprints, press releases, and bulletins to the specific party you wish to read them. Don't mail them to a customer or prospect without including the buyer or purchasing agent's name.

Besides mailing product information to store buyers, consumer product firms can also advertise by mailing product literature directly to potential users. Such mailings often contain coupons for rebates at a local store or announcements of special prices. In the case of some products/services such as home fire alarms, pay TV, or insurance, the mailing might include a return coupon for more information.

As mentioned in Chap. 8 on "The Development and Introduction of New Products," you may wish to draw special attention to your mailing by using Western Union Mailgrams or the U.S. Postal Service's E-Com (electronic computer originated mail). Whatever the form, mailings represent an inexpensive way for smaller businesses to keep their names in front of customers and prospects between a salesperson's visits.

Statement Stuffers.   For consumer products/services, credit card and retail store statement stuffers allow a small business to advertise at minimum cost. Diners Club, American Express, Mobil, Visa, Mastercharge, etc., search out products which might be appropriate for one of their monthly stuffers. Your message can reach millions of affluent people, and will be paid for by the orders received from credit card holders. The same stuffer is seldom sent to all card holders, but rather to select groups who have previously purchased a similar item, live in a certain region of the country, or charge over a certain amount annually. Although only a small percentage of those receiving the stuffer respond by buying the product from the credit card company, the other 98% become aware of the item and may purchase it later through a conventional retail outlet.

Most national credit card concerns subcontract the management of their entire direct mail programs, including statement stuffers, to specialists. Since the pictures and the text do the selling, these firms design stuffers with a great deal of visual appeal and detailed product information, emphasizing price, value, and benefits. Like newspaper advertising, though, statement stuffers have a short life. Many are not even read.

Retail stores also sell and advertise through statement enclosures, and for the small business, these too offer an inexpensive means of advertising. The benefits and mechanics are similar to those of a national credit card stuffer, except you generally reach a smaller regional audience. Although only a small percentage of those receiving the stuffer respond with an immediate purchase, the remainder become aware of the item and may buy it later at another retail outlet.

Retail store statement stuffers may be designed by either the vendor or the retailer's advertising department. Since the product is also available for inspection and purchase at the store, a less detailed description is required. Generally, the vendor pays the cost of printing the stuffer, and the retailer pays the cost of mailing it with its monthly charge-card billing. Repeat items such as detergents, hosiery, underwear, cosmetics, and house paint especially lend themselves to retail store statement enclosures because, based on previous purchases, the consumer knows just what he or she wants. All statement stuffers should contain an easy-to-use order form and a toll-free number to call for ordering.

If you sell a consumer product through retail stores, contact the advertising department of customers and prospects concerning statement stuffers. If you sell a consumer product which at all lends itself to statement stuffers, contact the major credit card companies. You might also contact a direct mail consultant to assist in this area.

Handbills.   Handbills are yet another inexpensive form of printed advertising. They can be slipped in mailboxes to advertise a house painter, placed under windshield wipers to advertise a repair service, or handed out to passersby in front of a store to advertise a sale. Generally, handbills are simple, don't contain pictures, and have a short life. Handbills allow you to reach a wide variety of consumers in a particular area or neighborhood. If your business's target customers live in a particular area or pass by a particular street corner each day, handbills can prove an inexpensive means of reaching them.

Radio

Within the broadcast media, radio represents the most effective consumer product/service advertising for a small business because specific types of consumer audiences can be reached inexpensively. Broadcast media do not lend themselves to advertising commercial/industrial products in a cost-effective manner because the listenership contains too small a percentage of potential users. All broadcast advertising must overcome the recall problem. The listener has no practical way of saving the message for later reference. In addition, radio advertisements must get their message across in 15 to 30 seconds to a listener who is most likely engaged in some other primary distracting activity.

Radio programming and, therefore, radio audiences vary a great deal, making it easy for an advertiser to reach certain types of listeners and markets. Popular music stations reach young people, while classical music stations reach affluent adults, and talk shows reach housewives and expressway commuters. You can further narrow the radio audience by advertising on foreign language programs, on sporting events, on Sunday night opera, or on Monday night jazz. Also, audience size and rates vary depending on the day of the week and the time of day.

The radio audience is more clearly defined than that of a newspaper, but has less in common and fewer shared interests than that of a magazine. Because radio is live, it is quite human, and listeners develop strong loyalties to personalities and stations. Like that of a newspaper, radio's audience is limited geographically, and listeners must be able to purchase or use the advertised product/service locally. A few FM stations are now broadcasting in distant cities via satellite, allowing interested advertisers to reach more distant markets.

Most radio advertisements must get their message across in 15 to 30 seconds to a listener who is most likely engaged in some other primary distracting activity. The message must be sent without pictures, and there is no way of recalling the message for later reference. These factors limit the effectiveness of radio advertising, and make it more appropriate for some consumer products/services than others. Because of these limitations, consumers seldom use radio as a source of immediate comparative product information on which they base buying decisions.

If you sell a consumer product/service to a well-defined market, and the product/service lends itself to a 30-second verbal presentation, then radio advertising can produce good sales results at affordable costs. For example, better music FM radio stations are an effective means of advertising theater, symphony, opera, fine restaurants, foreign cars, banks, art galleries, jewelry, and fur coats. As another example, popular music AM radio stations are an effective means of advertising soft drinks, domestic cars, fast-food shops, records, blue jeans, rock concerts, and cosmetics.

A dog kennel in Detroit owes its success to advertising four times a week on the local jazz station. An auctioneer in Los Angeles filled her showroom every week by advertising on the local FM better music station. A successful regional Wisconsin beer advertises only on local radio stations.

Television

Television allows you to advertise locally or nationally and reach a wide variety of listeners. Because television appeals to both visual and auditory senses, and because it appears live, products/services can be vividly presented in actual use. Although television is an extremely forceful advertising medium, it shares radio's recall problem. The viewer presently has no practical, inexpensive way of saving the message for future reference.

Even though television reaches a large and diverse consumer audience with tremendous realism, the present cost of advertising places it outside the reach of most small businesses. In 1983 the average 30-second network television ad cost $91,000, and a 30-second ad during the Super Bowl cost $400,000. However, the growth of UHF stations, cable television, home video taping equipment, and personal computers will soon expand television's capabilities and allow small businesses opportunities to advertise at affordable costs.

Local UHF stations already reach a smaller, more specialized audience than VHF for a fraction of the advertising cost. At present they are especially cost-efficient for reaching a foreign language or sporting event audience. In some cities, stations presently specialize in financial and commodity market reporting. Such stations lend themselves to inexpensive advertising by small financial service firms, such as discount brokers. As UHF broadcasting expands, and each station becomes more specialized in content, small businesses will be able to reach specific target audiences inexpensively.

By 1990 various forms of cable and other limited-distribution commercial television will also allow advertisers to inexpensively reach specific markets. The variety of programming available on cable television will allow advertisers to reach specific types of consumers with greater precision than FM radio. Programming will include channels exclusively offering adult education, art films, sporting events, news, religious services, theater, soap operas, travelogues, shopping, and talk and quiz shows. Because television appears live, and because programming will be so specialized, viewers will develop strong loyalties to specific stations which appeal to their interests, and to the personalities appearing on those stations.

Moreover, cable television programming, home computers, and video tape equipment soon will allow consumers to shop for certain items from their homes. Viewers will use their computers to ask the cable station for comparative presentations of specific products/services which the video tape equipment will store. After the presentations, viewers may order their choice, use the telephone or a store visit to obtain more information, or put the data back in tape storage for future reference.

The emotional impact and effectiveness of television advertising surpasses all other medias. Television allows the advertiser to use color, action, symbols, image, reason, price, value, realism, fantasy, wish fulfillment, and status to their fullest extent. Although television is not a cost-efficient means for the small business to presently advertise, it will be soon.

Point-of-Purchase Displays and Fixtures

For products sold through retail outlets, point-of-purchase displays obtain the user's attention and outline the item's features. Selling fixtures present the product in an attractive, organized fashion making it more appealing to the consumer. The customer is in the store; now you want him or her to buy your product.

Point-of-purchase displays can show the item in use, list its benefits, or just announce a sale price. Pictures and copy must be large so they can be read from a distance, and too much information can confuse the reader. Consumers use point-of-purchase displays as a source of immediate comparative product and price information on which they base buying decisions. For this reason, displays are especially important for new products. The firm that makes "Rusty Jones" car undercoatings offers its dealers a cutout of "Rusty Jones" which sits on top of new autos in the dealer's showroom. The cutout contains copy emphasizing that this service is guaranteed for the life of the cars.

For a manufacturer of consumer products, offering selling fixtures to retail outlets represents a useful advertising aid. Fixtures present the product in an attractive, organized fashion making it more appealing to the customer. Appropriate fixtures also aid the retailer by using space efficiently. As a manufacturer or distributor, a small business can buy large quantities of custom fixtures for its product and resell them at cost, with a saving to the retailer. Good fixtures help your salespeople and your customers to sell more products. Some manufacturers of toys, Christmas ornaments, hardware, plumbing supplies, and men's and ladies' furnishings put their entire advertising budget into fixtures and point-of-purchase displays.

Billboards and Signs

Billboards and signs can prove an effective form of low-cost advertising if your business sells to a well-defined market whose members frequent certain locations. A small charter aircraft concern generated new business by renting signs in airports and using billboards on the airport approach roads. A local hotel and restaurant in Minot, N.D., produced good results from renting billboard space on the highway coming into this small town.

However, most billboards and signs are not cost-efficient for small businesses because the readership contains too small a percentage of potential customers. Billboard costs can be reduced by sharing the space with other noncompetitive firms.

Yellow Pages and Directories

Many small businesses exist from sales generated by their display ads in the Yellow Pages. The ice-machine rental company ran large display ads under "Ice Machines" and "Ice Delivery." The ads produced two sales a week. The heat-reflecting window shade company received good responses from Yellow Page ads placed under "Shades" and "Air Conditioners."

In addition to the printed Yellow Pages, you can now list your firm with services that provide this information over the phone. Customers call for the names and telephone numbers of firms offering certain products/services.

Some industries rely on directories for critical information. For example, *Standard Rate and Data* provides current advertising information on newspapers and magazines. A small trade magazine might generate business by placing a display ad in the appropriate section. Explore whether your business could benefit from advertising in the Yellow Pages or in trade directories. Generally, costs are reasonable.

PACKAGING

A firm also communicates product information to users and potential users through packaging. A package must attract attention, arouse interest, create confidence in the purchase decision, and express the product's characteristics. A package should reinforce, not detract from, the product image. For example, a quality product should not have a cheap-looking package. A price- and value-oriented product should not have a luxurious-looking package. The Tanqueray gin bottle exudes status, while the Gordon's gin bottle connotes value.

In businesses which sell through self-service retailers, the consumer often buys the package, not the product. In many cases, the package must sell the product; it must create an emotional response which says "try me."

Many of these packaging objectives can be accomplished through the correct choice of shape, graphics, pictures, colors, and lettering, which are discussed later in this chapter. For example, bold colors such as red and black express strength and durability, while soft colors such as pastels express femininity and quality. Packaging of generic products is generally simple and plain with bold black letters on a white background reinforcing the value image.

Packaging need not be expensive to be attractive. A well-designed package often costs only a fraction more than a poorly designed one, and sells many more units. Once a year, test your packaging on a group of 30 potential customers. Their responses will indicate whether it communicates the desired information and produces the desired reaction. Before changing a package, be sure to perform a thorough test-marketing procedure as described in Chap. 8.

SALES PROMOTION

Sales promotion reinforces and is reinforced by salespeople, advertising, packaging, and publicity in communicating product/service information to potential users. Sales promotion includes such items as contests, premiums, gifts, coupons, rebates, customer entertainment, and trade shows.

A men's hosiery company included a dollar bill in the foot of one sock out of each twelve pairs; a point-of-purchase display advertised the fact. A men's underwear company sent consumers a free brief in exchange for ten of its labels; cooperative newspaper advertising announced this offer. A handkerchief firm offered a seventh "hanky" free if you bought six, and advertised it on their package. A "do-it-yourself" tool company had a contest to name a new product; the contest and the new product were advertised on the radio. A small regional chemical company invited all its customers to a golf outing once a year. A tax shelter financial service sends customers paperweights in the form of oil drilling rigs. A car rental firm offers gifts to regular customers, and a hotel offers a free rental car to regular customers. These examples illustrate the wide variety of sales promotion ideas; the cost depends on the project. Most small businesses use some form of sales promotion.

Trade shows, discussed at length in Chap. 8 on "The Development and Introduction of New Products," can be an effective sales promotion device for small firms. Most trade shows present industrial/commercial products and services such as machine tools and data processing to business users, or consumer products such as shoes or outerwear to retailers. There are also some trade shows which present specialized consumer products directly to the consumer, such as ski equipment and apparel, sail and power boats, automobiles, photographic, and camping equipment.

Trade shows combine promotion and advertising with personal selling by allowing you to show the actual product, and engage in two-way communication with a specific group of users. Exhibiting at a trade show gives your product/service more credibility, which builds user confidence. Generally, attendees use trade shows as a source of comparative price and product information upon which they base future purchasing decisions. A trade show exhibit must be reinforced by advertising your presence in appropriate trade publications, sending direct mail announcements to attendees, and having product literature available for interested parties.

Since the cost can be considerable—space alone averaged $46 a square foot in 1981—be sure you pick the trade show which is attended by the most appropriate audience, by the appropriate decision makers. You can reduce the cost by sharing your booth with another compatible firm. In addition to the large well-known and rather expensive shows, there are thousands of less expensive regional and very specialized sub-industry trade shows. Often, these less costly smaller shows produce better results because of limited competition. The 1982 annual *Directory of Trade and Industrial Shows* published by *Successful Meetings* lists over 10,000 trade shows. Pick the trade show attended by the people responsible for buying your product/service.

The key to a successful trade show lies in effectively contacting a maximum number of qualified prospects and customers. The exhibit itself should quickly tell your story through an unusual display, or if appropriate, a demonstration showing use, benefits, and competitive advantage. Offer cards for interested people to fill in their names and addresses. The appropriate field salesperson or retailer should then receive these cards, and follow up with a sales call.

Selling at a trade show necessitates preparation and special training, since presentations are numerous and short. You must teach trade show salespeople how to give an effective two-minute presentation, and how to properly qualify prospects with appropriate questions. Ten qualified prospects might walk by while a salesperson talks with a browser or an unidentified competitor. You must also teach salespeople how to quickly and systematically obtain information from prospects. Often a check list or form which forces salespeople to write down the information proves helpful.

Before a show starts, you should remind salespeople that prospects/customers become turned off by salespeople who smoke, drink coffee, or eat at the booth. Customers also become turned off by salespeople who pace nervously, talk endlessly with fellow workers, or stand with arms folded across their chests. In addition, a trade show salesperson should dress conservatively, wear an appropriate badge, not use the booth phone for personal business, not prejudge a visitor based on looks, and show enthusiasm by standing rather than sitting.

Some small computer and software firms spend half their advertising budgets successfully attending twenty trade shows a year. A small firm producing chemicals for institutional rug cleaning attends over seventy shows annually. Many small firms without a field sales force rely entirely on trade shows for selling.

Investigate the possibility of trade shows, contests, premiums, gifts, rebates, coupons, customer entertainment, and other forms of sales promotion to see if the cost/benefit relationship favors their usage. Be sure to reflect the expense in costing your product/service.

PUBLICITY

Publicity created by press releases represents the least expensive means of communicating product/service information to customers and potential users, thus making publicity extremely appropriate for small businesses with limited financial resources. A product/service which receives publicity in a periodical acquires exposure, status, and credibility, building confidence in its purchase. News is more readily accepted as being credible than an advertisement. However, with publicity, you do not have final control over what is published.

To create an effective publicity program, each month you should write a newsworthy story about one of your products/services, have photographs made, and submit the package to select publications. If the product/service has an industrial end use, submit the material to appropriate trade publications. For consumer products, you must pre-sell both the retailer and the retailer's customers; therefore, for consumer products or services, submit the material to both retail trade and consumer publications. Select publications read by your potential customer or ultimate user.

Magazines and newspapers always have space to fill. Interesting product/ service press releases represent an inexpensive means for an editor to obtain good material. Eye-catching photographs with captions produce good results.

Be sure the press release contains information on how and where to purchase the product or service. Resources permitting, you might begin by consulting a professional public relations firm. You will quickly learn the techniques and be able to perform this function admirably yourself.

You can obtain free exposure for consumer products/services in newspapers and certain consumer magazines by using the following techniques. First, decide which section of the publication should receive your press release. If the product is an oven cleaner or squirrel trap, you would submit material to the home and garden editor. If the product is apparel, you would submit material to the fashion editor. If the service guarantees tire repairs for two years, you would submit material to the auto editor.

Next, buy copies of reference books which list publications and their specific editors. For newspapers the reference book is *Editor and Publisher International Year Book,* The Encyclopedia of The Newspaper Industry, 575 Lexington Avenue, New York, New York. For newspapers and magazines the reference book is *The IMS Ayer Directory of Publications,* 426 Pennsylvania Avenue, Fort Washington, Pennsylvania. Then select cities of interest, publications of interest, and submit the press release package to each appropriate editor by name. The results of such a program will amaze you.

You would follow a similar procedure for publicizing an industrial/commercial product or service in trade journals, and a consumer item in retail trade publications. Listings of trade publications can be found through *Standard Rate and Data* and the *Standard Periodical Directory.*

Make reprints of worthwhile published articles which appear as a result of your press release. Combine these reprints with sales bulletins and direct mail pieces, and send them to salespeople, customers, and prospects. Recipients consider reprints important, and will take the time to read them.

Publicity through press releases is especially well suited for small firms because of the nominal cost and excellent results. A small business with limited resources appears much larger and very successful when its name and products/services appear often in print.

SUMMARY

A firm communicates product information to users and potential users through salespeople, advertising, packaging, promotion, and publicity. The choices depend on the types of information you wish to communicate, and the audience you wish to reach.

The advertising budget consists of what your company can afford from internal resources and what you can obtain from suppliers and customers. Advertising can be divided into: printed media such as newspapers, magazines, and direct mail; broadcast media such as radio and television; point-of-purchase displays and fixtures; position media such as billboards and signs; and miscellaneous, such as Yellow Pages and directories.

Newspapers

Newspapers are most cost-efficient for advertising consumer products/services with wide appeal and local distribution. Consumers use newspapers as a source of immediate comparative product and price information on which they base buying decisions. The major disadvantage of newspaper advertising is short life and relatively poor print or reproductive quality in ads.

Magazines

Generally, magazines are much more specialized in content, more national in distribution, more personal, and more difficult to throw away than newspapers. Magazines are most cost-efficient for consumer and industrial/commercial products/services with specialized appeal and national distribution. If you sell an industrial/commercial product/service nationally, or if you sell a consumer product/service to retail stores, then trade publications allow your small business to inexpensively reach your specific market. Because of the excellent print and reproductive quality in magazine ads, visual content can be fully utilized. Consumers, buyers, and purchasing agents use magazines as a source of general comparative product information which eventually, but not immediately, influences buying decisions.

Direct Mail and Handbills

A small firm can inexpensively advertise and sell its products through such direct mail devices as catalogues, brochures, reprints, and statement stuffers. Both industrial and consumer products/services can be advertised and sold through direct mail. Many retail stores send out numerous consumer catalogues each year, and mail statement stuffers with charge cards billings. Credit card companies also send stuffers with each billing. Consumer and business-to-business specialty mail order firms sell and advertise exclusively through catalogues. In addition, many consumer and industrial businesses regularly mail product literature, advertising and publicity reprints, in-house sales catalogues, and brochures to their customers and prospects.

Handbills allow you to reach a wide variety of consumers in a particular area or neighborhood. They can be slipped in mailboxes, placed under windshield wipers, or handed out to passersby.

Radio

Among the broadcast media, radio represents the most effective advertising for a small business offering a consumer product/service, because specific types of consumer audiences can be reached inexpensively. However, both radio and television advertising must overcome the recall problem. The listener or viewer has no practical way of saving the message for later reference. Because of this limitation, consumers generally do not use radio or television as a source of immediate comparative product information on which they base buying decisions. Broadcast media do not lend themselves to cost-effectively advertising commercial/industrial products, because the listenership contains too small a percentage of potential users.

Television

Television allows you to advertise locally or nationally and reach a wide variety of listeners. Because television appeals to both visual and auditory senses, and because it appears "live," products/services can be vividly presented in actual use. Although television reaches a large diverse consumer audience with tremendous realism, the present cost places it outside the reach of most small businesses.

However, by 1990 various forms of cable, UHF, and other limited-distribution commercial television will allow small-business advertisers to inexpensively reach specific markets. The variety of programming available on cable television and UHF will allow advertisers to reach specific types of consumers with greater precision than FM radio. In addition, cable television programming, home computers, and video tape equipment will allow consumers to shop for certain items from their homes.

Point-of-Purchase Displays and Selling Fixtures

For products sold through retail outlets, point-of-purchase displays obtain the user's attention and outline the item's features. Point-of-purchase displays can show the item in use, list its benefits, or just announce a sale price. The customer is in the store, now you want him or her to buy your product.

For a manufacturer of consumer products, offering selling fixtures to retail outlets represents another useful advertising aid. Fixtures present the product in an attractive, organized fashion making it more appealing to the customer, and saving space for the retailer.

Billboards and Signs

Billboards and signs can prove an effective form of low-cost advertising if your business sells to a well-defined market whose members frequent certain locations. However, most billboards and signs are not cost-efficient for small businesses because the readership contains too small a percentage of potential customers.

Yellow Pages and Directories

Display ads in the Yellow Pages and industry directories have inexpensively generated new customers for many small businesses. You should investigate this type of low-cost, effective advertising.

The choice among these various forms of advertising and among specific media within each form depends upon the type of information you wish to communicate, and upon the audience you wish to reach. For example, you reach consumers through newspapers, radio, television, statement stuffers, and catalogues. You reach industrial purchasing agents through trade publications, catalogues, brochures, and reprints of ads.

Packaging

Packaging should reinforce the product image created by advertising. A package must attract attention, arouse interest, and express the product's characteristics through the correct choice of shape, graphics, pictures, colors, and lettering.

Sales Promotion and Publicity

Sales promotion includes such items as contests, premiums, gifts, coupons, rebates, customer entertainment, and trade shows. Sales promotion reinforces salespeople, advertising, packaging, and publicity in communicating product/service information to customers and potential users.

Publicity created by press releases represents the least expensive means of communicating porduct/service information, which makes it extremely appropriate for a small business. A product/service which receives publicity in a periodical acquires exposure, status, and credibility, building confidence in its purchase.

Using several forms of product communication, for example advertising and publicity, or several forms of advertising such as printed and broadcast media, reinforces your message and increases the likelihood of success. Similarly, use of several individual media such as two trade publications reinforces the message and increases the likelihood of success.

CONTENT

We have discussed how to maximize your advertising/promotion budget, how to evaluate and choose among the various advertising media, and how to capitalize on packaging, promotion, and publicity. In this section, we will discuss creating the content of messages communicated through advertising, packaging, promotion, and publicity.

Introduction

Communication in general and advertising, packaging, promotion and publicity in particular consist of the transmission of information, ideas, and emotions through symbols, words, pictures, and figures. Advertising, packaging, promotion, and publicity are forms of persuasive communication designed to sell a product/service.

To accomplish this persuasion, advertising, packaging, promotion, and publicity must first gain the receiver's attention. No matter how good the product or service, an ad which does not gain the reader's, listener's, or viewer's attention proves useless. The vast majority of all advertising goes unnoticed. Illustrations or photographs obtain attention in visual ads and packaging.

Once attention is gained, the advertisement, packaging, promotion, and publicity must invite interest, or favorable attention. You accomplish this through effective copy. An advertisement must make an initial statement which draws the respondent's interest to the detailed message.

Next, the advertising message must arouse needs and desires in the receiver and suggest a way of providing satisfaction. The more needs or goals satisfied by a product/service, the more attractive it becomes to the potential purchaser.

Consumer needs can be classified as physical, safety, social, esteem, and individual development. The most effective advertising results from showing consumers how they can achieve a more favorable self-image.

Business buyers' needs reflect their desires to improve company performance, advance themselves in the organization, make their jobs easier, avoid mistakes and problems, and satisfy their egos. Business buyers have a strong need to feel important and be respected.

Lastly, advertising, packaging, promotion, and publicity must suggest goals which fulfill the needs they arouse, and suggest the action necessary to achieve these goals. If a choice exists, purchasers will choose the easiest, cheapest, or most desirable action to achieve their goals.

People think, communicate, and perceive in terms of symbols, and therefore the products/services they buy also have symbolic meanings. The products/services purchased symbolize the needs, desires, and goals which they satisfy. Advertising, packaging, promotion, and publicity must communicate in appropriate symbols.

Advertising, packaging, promotion, and publicity are most effective when they demand minimal attitude changes; they are least effective when they demand attitude changes which threaten the receiver. Therefore, you should use copy and pictures which best fit the receiver's attitudes and which demand minimal change.

Advertising, packaging, promotion, and publicity are forms not only of communication but also of learning. To choose the most effective content for a message, you must understand what techniques produce the best learning results. Although unpleasant messages may sometimes be learned as easily as pleasant ones, both are learned better than messages which produce little or no emotional response. Continuous repetition of the message over long periods produces the most learning and best results. Points presented at the beginning and end of the message are remembered better than those in the middle. Also, to optimize learning, advertisers must adapt their language to the particular audience to be reached.

The content of advertising, packaging, promotion, and publicity must take into account legal restrictions. The Federal Trade Commission Act of 1914 prohibits unfair or deceptive practices in advertising. For example, advertising cannot be used to "bait and switch," and cannot employ false testimonials or ambiguous statements.

Attention

Advertising, packaging, promotion, and publicity initially must gain the receiver's attention. No matter how good the product or service, an ad which does not gain the readers', listeners', or viewers' attention proves useless. The vast majority of all advertising goes unnoticed.

In designing a visual ad or a package, you can use illustrations or photographs to obtain the reader's or viewer's attention. An ad for the men's long underwear with feet showed Santa Clause and Superman wearing the garment. An ad for the small less expensive forklift truck showed it lifting $12,000,000 worth of gold bars. An ad for an employment service shows an empty desk with the phone off the hook.

The need to gain attention is the reason why press releases and resulting publicity produce better results when accompanied by photographs, and why choice of color is so important to packaging. A press release for the parabolic antenna company contained a picture showing an entire field filled with antennas.

On radio and television, advertisers employ unusual sounds to obtain the listener's attention. A regional brewer, for instance, introduces its radio ads for beer with the sound of running water; a local casualty insurance agency with the sound of sirens; a maid service with the sound of a doorbell.

Interest

Once attention is gained, the advertising, packaging, promotion, and publicity must invite interest, or favorable attention. You accomplish this through effective copy. An advertisement must make an initial statement which draws the respondent's interest to the detailed message.

In designing a visual ad or a package, you can use typography such as bold, block, script, or Roman type faces to emphasize the initial statement. You can also ask an interesting question pertaining to the product/service.

An initial statement which shows errors in how to do something can effectively create interest. For example, an ad for a copying machine might read, "The bid deadline was missed because the copying machine did not work." An ad for overnight freight service might read, "The order was canceled because the shipment arrived late." An ad for car undercoatings might read, "A rusty car has less resale value." In advertising which shows errors, moderate fear-appeals prove more effective than strong fear-appeals.

The captions under publicity pictures, the headlines in press releases, the initial statement in a radio or TV ad, all must create enough interest to draw the respondent to your detailed message. No matter how worthwhile your product or service, an ad which does not gain the reader's, listener's, or viewer's interest proves a waste of money.

Desire

The advertising message must arouse needs and desires in the receiver and suggest a way of providing satisfaction. The more needs or goals satisfied by a product/service, the more attractive it becomes to purchasers. You arouse consumer needs by creating copy which makes the consumer want a product or service (wish fulfillment). You develop business needs by creating copy which shows a purchasing agent or store buyer how your product or service can solve a problem, improve results, or help the person achieve certain career and professional goals. Although business needs are more pragmatic than consumer needs, all buying behavior is a complex mixture of reason and emotion.

Consumer Needs. Consumer needs can be classified as: physical, such as hunger, thirst, and warmth; safety, such as security and health; social, such as love, affection, and belonging; esteem, such as prestige and respect; and individual development, such as self-fulfillment and independence. The most effective advertising results from showing consumers how they can achieve a more favorable self-image, because consumers evaluate a product/service's worth by how it contributes to their own self-image. The target customer will reject products whose images are not compatible with his or her own self-image. In perceiving an image, consumers do not distinguish between the physical and psychological characteristics of a product/service.

For example, you successfully create a desire for home smoke detectors and dead-bolt locks by appealing to the need for safety and security. You successfully create a desire for cosmetics by appealing to the need for affection. You successfully create a desire for *The New York Times* by appealing to the need for prestige. You successfully create a desire for business franchises by appealing to the need for independence.

Most advertisements actually appeal to a group of needs. For example, the franchise ad might appeal to both independence and financial security; the cosmetic ad to both affection and self-image.

Business Buyer Needs. A purchasing agent, plant manager, design engineer, retail store buyer, or merchandise manager does not achieve the same personal satisfaction or need-fulfillment from a business purchase as a consumer does from an individual purchase. Moreover, the initial decision on a business purchase often is made by more than one person, which further complicates need fulfillments. Business buyers' needs reflect their desires to improve company performance, advance themselves in the organization, make the job easier, avoid problems and mistakes, and satisfy their egos.

Business buyers, first of all, want their companies to succeed. They participate by buying goods and services which lower costs, improve efficiency, improve sales, and, most important, increase corporate profits.

Business buyers themselves want to move up the corporate ladder toward management. They fulfill this need by drawing attention to themselves through making successful changes in what is purchased and how.

Business buyers also want to make their jobs easier. They fulfill this need by obtaining as much service as possible from vendors, and by avoiding problems and mistakes through dealing with reliable resources.

Finally, many business buyers have strong egos, and most have a need to feel important and be respected. Any business-to-business ad which does not "massage" the buyer's ego loses a certain amount of effectiveness.

Successful business-to-business advertising, then, results from showing buyers and purchasing agents how your product/service can satisfy their needs. For example, you successfully create a desire for a new nail-making machine by showing that it produces better nails faster and less expensively. You successfully create a desire for designer gloves by advertising the exceptionally good markup. You advertise commercial heat-reflecting window shades by showing that they can keep the boss's office cooler. You advertise an underwear line by emphasizing that your salespeople count stock once a month, and the mill ships within 24 hours of order receipt. In all these ads you appeal to the buyer's ego by alluding to him or her as a professional. As these examples illustrate, most business-to-business advertisements appeal to a group of needs rather than just one.

Consumers and business buyers both desire to reduce the risks of being hurt or being wrong. For example, purchasing agents do not wish to buy products which do not deliver the promised benefits. Similarly, consumers do not wish to buy products which make them appear foolish to their peers.

Action

Once the ad has the reader's, listener's, or viewer's attention and interest, and has aroused a need or desire, it must suggest goals and action which can satisfy these needs. An advertisement must motivate the reader or listener to make a purchase, or investigate the product/service further (the goal), and then suggest action to achieve these goals, such as "Call this toll free number," "visit (a certain store)," "Return this coupon," "Call your local sales representative," or "Consult the Yellow Pages." If a choice exists, purchasers will choose the easiest, cheapest, or most desirable action to achieve their goals. Therefore, the simpler the action, the more likely it will be taken. An ad which motivates the recipient to purchase a product/service, but does not suggest ways of attaining it, has failed.

For example, once your ad has created a desire for a home smoke alarm by appealing to the reader's need for safety, the ad must suggest action for satisfying this desire by including a telephone number, return mail coupon, or store name through which the product may be purchased. For another example, once your ad has created an interest in a small forklift truck by appealing to the purchasing agent's or plant manager's desire to lower cost, improve efficiency, and move up in the organization, now the ad must suggest action for satisfying this interest by including a telephone number, return mail coupon, or the local sales representative's name and address.

Symbols

People often think, communicate, and perceive in terms of symbols, and therefore the products/services they buy also have symbolic meanings. The products/services purchased symbolize the needs, desires, and goals which they satisfy. We don't sell products/services, we satisfy needs; and to the user, products/services have symbolic meanings which satisfy those needs. The purchaser's choice becomes easier when one object is symbolically more harmonious with his or her goals, needs, desires, feelings, and self-image than another. As an advertiser, you must understand these symbols and motivations from the user's standpoint.

Symbols also represent the product's/service's image, and buyers perceive products/services in terms of their images. A competitor can copy your product/service features, but any attempt by a competitor to copy your image merely strengthens your position. For this reason, creating the correct image through advertising, promotion, packaging, and publicity assures an important competitive advantage. You must understand how to communicate the product's/service's image through the symbolic meanings of lines, figures, and colors.

A book on sales management and marketing satisfies a need for self-fulfillment and becomes a symbol of knowledge. Advertisements for such a book must use words and illustrations which enhance this image. Heat-reflecting window shades satisfy a consumer need to be physiologically comfortable, and they become a symbol of coolness. Advertising for this product might include illustrations of the sun's hot rays outside a window, and lines or colors suggesting coolness inside the building. The small forklift truck satisfies a need to be efficient and save money and symbolizes strength. Advertising for this product might include heavy, dark lines and sharp angles which symbolize strength.

As these examples show, the symbolic meanings of lines, figures, and colors become very important in advertising and packaging. Smooth, softly shaded, thin lines project feminine qualities, while heavy, dark lines and sharp angles symbolize strength and masculinity. Jagged lines express informality, while straight lines convey formality. A diagonal line expresses motion, change, excitement, and progress; a vertical line expresses growth, striving, balance, spiritual uplifting, dignity, and honesty; and a horizontal line expresses calm, rest, and stability. Ovals and circles convey feminine qualities, squares convey unity and harmony, and triangles liveliness. White symbolizes cleanliness and purity; black symbolizes strength, mystery, and mourning; red symbolizes danger, excitement, and power; blue symbolizes coolness, cleanliness, and purity;

yellow symbolizes youth, cheerfulness, and optimism; and green symbolizes safety and nature.

As an advertiser, you must understand what needs your products/services satisfy and what symbolic meaning they have for the user. As an advertiser, you also must understand how to accurately communicate the product's image in symbols.

Attitudes

Advertising, packaging, promotion, and publicity are most effective when they demand minimal attitude changes; they are least effective when they demand attitude changes which threaten the receiver. Consumers generally will expose themselves only to ideas which reinforce their beliefs, and will accept only messages which seem appropriate to their attitudes, messages which are inconsistent with a person's attitudes will be rejected or distorted to fit those attitudes.

The lettuce-leaf cigarette demanded considerable and threatening attitude changes on the part of smokers. The use of robots initially demanded considerable and threatening attitude changes on the part of major industries. The advertising of home smoke alarms reinforced attitudes and beliefs about safety. The advertising of small forklift trucks reinforced attitudes and beliefs about cost savings and efficiency.

Regardless of the product/service, use copy and pictures in advertising which best fit the receiver's attitudes and which demand minimal change. For example, advertise the fact that robots can perform jobs which humans find unpleasant, or that lettuce-leaf cigarettes can be smoked in a crowd without offending others. You as the advertiser must find ways to present benefits so that the potential user will view them in a favorable light.

Learning Techniques

Advertising, promotion, packaging, and publicity are all forms of communication which involve learning. In order to use them most effectively for communication, you must understand what techniques produce the best learning results. Learning techniques include a message's emotional content, repetition, order of material, and language.

Although unpleasant messages may sometimes be learned as easily as pleasant ones, both are learned better than messages which produce little or no emotional response. An annoying advertisement produces more learning than a dull one, but a message promising the audience a rewarding experience works the best. A dull ad does not obtain the reader's or listener's attention. Generally, a pleasant message obtains more interest than an unpleasant one.

For advertising to be effective, it must be repeated. Continuous repetition of the message over long periods produces the most learning and best results. Therefore, a small business can achieve better results for the dollars invested by repeating ads less frequently but over longer time periods.

Also, a small business can achieve better results for the dollars invested by not varying ads with the same message. Repetition of identical material is generally as effective as repeating the same message but with variations in the story. Moreover, any variations increase your advertising expense.

The order of material in an ad, package, or press release is very important. Points presented at the beginning and end of the message are remembered better than those in the middle. If you list five benefits, the first and last should be the two most important.

For effective learning and communication, the advertiser must adapt his or her language to the particular audience to be reached. An art gallery advertising on a classical music station might refer to an artist as reflecting "the ambience of the times." On the other hand, a bottler advertising on a popular music station would not be communicating effectively by saying the soft drink "adds to the ambience of a party." Trade publication ads should use the trade terminology understood by the readers, whether it be "electrical resistance" or "tear strength." Readers and listeners learn more from ads which "speak their language."

Legal Issues

You must temper the content of advertising, promotion, packaging, and publicity with legal considerations. Advertising which deceives, uses "bait and switch" techniques, or employs false testimonials is considered illegal.

The Federal Trade Commission Act of 1914 prohibits unfair or deceptive practices in advertising, and assigns the Federal Trade Commission the responsibility for enforcing this. For example, you cannot compare your lowest prices to a competitor's highest prices and then claim that your product/service is less expensive. A firm which rents automobiles cannot advertise its fleet rate as compared to a competitor's single-day, single-vehicle rate and claim that it is less expensive.

Advertising cannot be used to "bait and switch." An automobile rental agency cannot advertise the reduced rate on its sub-compact and then charge customers a higher rate on larger cars because the agency has only one sub-compact.

Advertising cannot employ false testimonials or ambiguous statements. All claims must have a reasonable basis, and all claims of superiority must be proven. You cannot claim that your nail-making machine is faster than competition unless you can prove it. You cannot have your brother-in-law, who is a doctor, state in an ad that your nail-making machine never requires maintenance.

The Federal Trade Commission states that unfair and deceptive advertising statements need have only the "capacity or tendency to deceive." A party bringing action does not have to prove fraud was intended, only that a "fair probability" of deception existed. However, "permissible puffery," "an expression of mere opinion by the seller not made as a representation of fact," is allowed. As you can see, it is best to consult a knowledgeable attorney on such matters.

Summary

You create an effective advertising message by gaining the reader's, viewer's, or listener's attention, inviting interest, arousing needs and desires, and then finally suggesting goals and actions which satisfy those needs. In the message, you use appropriate symbols to represent needs, desires, goals, and products. You demand minimal attitude changes and utilize proven learning techniques. You must also consider the legal restrictions placed on advertising.

Effective advertising does not have to be expensive. I recently saw a three-inch one-column black-and-white ad for an adult baseball camp which met all the above requirements. The ad showed a baseball with the following copy written on it. In large type it stated, "Have your baseball fantasies fulfilled." In smaller type it offered an opportunity to play baseball for a week with a vintage major league team. It told the dates, location, price, and how to call for more information.

ORGANIZING AND PLANNING YOUR ADVERTISING PROGRAM

Organizing and planning your advertising program involves using available human and financial resources to inform and persuade users to purchase your product or service. This requires you to evaluate available human resources; set goals and objectives; define the target audience; budget expenses; select the appropriate advertising form and media; choose the appropriate message, content, and images; determine the frequency and timing of the message; and measure the advertising results through feedback.

Human resources include your company personnel plus qualified people at advertising agencies, at the media, free-lance commercial artists and copy writers, suppliers, and retail customer personnel. From this group, you decide who will have responsibility for various aspects of the program.

A successful advertising program must have specific goals and objectives which are related to the goals and objectives of your overall marketing plan. What specifically do you wish the advertising program to accomplish?

You define your target audience by deciding who are the customers or potential users of your product/service, and who are the decision makers? To be effective, your advertising must reach the appropriate customer, user, and/or decision maker.

You budget expenses by estimating the funds available from internally generated sources along with monies available from suppliers, customers, and distributors. You then prepare monthly worksheets detailing how these funds will be spent.

The choices among the various forms of advertising and various media depend on the type of information you wish to communicate and the target audience you wish to reach. Use of several media reinforces the message and increases the likelihood of success.

Next you decide on the message, content, symbols, and images necessary to persuade or inform the target audience. In doing this, you must demand minimal attitude changes and use techniques which produce the best learning results.

Then you determine the frequency and timing of the message. For advertising to be effective, it must be repeated.

Last you seek feedback concerning the advertising's effectiveness. Did it achieve your desired goals?

Human Resources

An advertising program is no better than the people who manage and create it. You must evaluate the available human resources and decide who will have responsibility for various aspects of the program. In a small firm, this generally means going outside the company for help. Human resources include your company personnel plus qualified people at advertising agencies, at the media, free-lance commercial artists and copy writers, suppliers, and retail customer personnel.

Advertising agencies employ experienced specialists who can contribute greatly to your program's success. Seek an agency which has experience in your product/service area, and has dealt with small businesses. Interview the person who will be responsible for your account, and contact other firms who have used the agency. Take advantage of the agency's expertise, but remember that you have ultimate responsibility for the program's success.

Advertising agencies receive up to a 15% commission from the media they use. In addition, agencies charge clients fees for certain services. Some agencies are not interested in small-business accounts because potential revenues are too small.

If you cannot use an advertising agency, you can obtain assistance from media personnel, commercial artists, and free-lance copy writers. Personnel at newspapers, magazines, radio and television stations can help you prepare copy and choose appropriate editions, sections, or times. They can also supply detailed information on their publication's or station's audience. Reference books such as *Standard Rate and Data* can supply less specific but comparative information on reader and listenership.

Free-lance commercial artists with experience in preparing ads can provide expertise in the visual presentations. Free-lance copy writers can provide expertise in the written or spoken presentations. Often, advertising agencies which do not handle small accounts can recommend you to free-lance artists and copy writers. Be sure to interview them and check their references.

Small businesses which rely on larger suppliers for an advertising allowance can often use the supplier's advertising department or advertising agency to manage its program. Small businesses which share the cost of cooperative ads with their larger retail store customers generally must use the store's advertising department or agency. In coop advertising, the store prepares and places the ad. In both these situations you lose some or all control over the advertising, but gain expert human resources at no cost.

Before you begin the advertising program, evaluate available human resources and assign responsibility for each task. You may rely on your own company personnel, an advertising agency, media people, free-lance commercial artists and copy writers, and supplier and retail customer personnel.

Goals and Objectives

A successful advertising program must have specific goals and objectives which are related to the goals and objectives of your overall marketing plan. What do you wish the advertising to accomplish? What type of information do you want to communicate? What learning and action do you want to initiate? During what time period do you want which results?

It is not enough to say that the goals and objectives of your advertising program are to sell more goods. As the following examples illustrate, you must be more specific.

For a new product/service with little competition, the advertising objectives would be primarily to educate users about the product's primary benefits. For example, the first season's ads for the initial kerosene home space heaters emphasized warmth, economy, and safety. The introductory ads for first-generation small-business computers emphasized ease of operations, versatility, uses, and reasonable cost.

As products/services mature, advertising objectives change, with more emphasis on combating competition. The second winter, kerosene heater ads emphasized price and features which differentiated one competitor from another. The third winter, kerosene heater ads emphasized brand names, reliability, and price. A year after the initial introductory ads, small-business computer advertising emphasized competitive advantages such as speed, memory capacity, and cost. Eventually the ads emphasized brand name, software, systems capabilities, service, and cost.

Before commencing an advertising program, decide on its goals and objectives. What specifically do you wish this advertising to accomplish?

Defining the Target Audience

Who are the customers or potential users of your product/service, and who are the decision makers? To be effective, your advertising must reach the appropriate customer, user, and/or decision makers. These people are your target audience.

The potential customer for a tax shelter is a person in the 40% or higher tax bracket. The potential customer for a nail-making machine is a steel mill, and the decision makers are purchasing agents, engineers, and plant managers. The potential users of ties are men, but the purchasers are men and women. The potential consumers for home smoke alarms are people who live in older houses and apartments. The potential customers for emergency lighting are commercial buildings and public places; the decision makers are building owners and managers, theater owners and managers, and municipal purchasing agents.

Before you can decide on how best to reach and influence your customer, you must decide who is the customer. As discussed in Chaps. 9 and 10, you also need this same knowledge to determine proper pricing and distribution.

Budgeting

Your advertising budget includes internally generated funds, along with monies available from suppliers and retail customers or distributors. You must decide how to allocate these funds among the various forms of advertising and media to achieve your desired goals and objectives. Once you decide on the allocation, you prepare a detailed budget as described in Chap. 7.

Such a budget involves monthly worksheets listing the various types of advertising and their anticipated expense. You then justify these monthly figures with a more detailed plan. In what specific newspaper or magazine do you plan to run how many column inches? What product/service will the ad feature? How much will each ad cost? What specific supplier or retailer will share in the cost?

Selecting the Appropriate Advertising Form and Media

The choices among the various forms of advertising and various media depend on the type of information you wish to communicate and the target audience you wish to reach. The type of information depends on the advertising program's goals and objectives. Use of several media reinforces the message and increases the likelihood of success.

If you wish to advertise the price of a consumer product/service which appeals to a broad audience, and if it can be purchased immediately in specific local stores and described better in words than pictures, then newspapers can produce good results for a small business. You will increase the ad's cost efficiency, or results per dollar, by choosing the newspaper and section and day which will best reach your target audience.

If you sell a consumer product/service nationally to a common interest group, such as skiers, runners, or dog owners, and if the item lends itself to visual presentation, then magazine advertising can produce affordable results for your small business. If you sell an industrial/commercial product/service-nationally, or if you sell a consumer product/service to retail stores, then trade publication advertising can allow your small business to inexpensively reach your specific market (target audience).

If you sell a consumer product/service to a well-defined market, and the product/service lends itself to a 30-second verbal presentation, then radio advertising can produce good sales results at affordable prices. Cable and UHF television offer similar advertising benefits, but allow the realism of a visual presentation.

Consumer, retail store, and business-to-business catalogues along with credit card and retail store statement stuffers also allow you to inexpensively reach certain target audiences. Most catalogues and statement stuffers use appealing visual presentations to emphasize product appeal and value.

On the other hand, handbills allow you to reach a wide variety of consumers in a particular area or neighborhood. Generally, handbills are simple, don't contain pictures, and have a short life.

Point-of-purchase displays, fixtures, and packaging obtain the user's attention and outline the item's features and image once a potential user is in a store. Consumers use them as a source of immediate comparative product information on which they base buying decisions.

Billboards and signs can prove an effective form of low-cost advertising if your business sells to a well-defined market whose members frequent certain locations. Display ads in the Yellow Pages and other directories also reach potential users. Sales promotion, trade shows, and publicity through press releases reinforce other forms of advertising and prove especially valuable for new products/services.

In selecting the appropriate advertising form and media, you may choose among newspapers, consumer magazines, trade publications, radio, television, catalogues, statement stuffers, handbills, point-of-purchase displays, fixtures, billboards, and display ads in Yellow Pages and directories. The choice depends on the type of information you wish to communicate and the target audience you wish to reach. Of course, all this must be tempered by the money available in your budget.

Choosing the Appropriate Message, Content, and Image

Once you have selected the appropriate advertising form and media, you are ready to create the message. Communication in general and advertising, packaging, promotion, and publicity in particular are the transmission of information, ideas, and emotions through symbols, words, pictures, and figures. To accomplish this communication, advertising, packaging, promotion, and publicity must first gain the receiver's attention through illustrations, photographs, and/or unusual sounds; then invite interest, or favorable attention, through an initial statement, copy, and typography; next use appropriate copy to arouse needs and desires in the receiver; and finally, suggest ways or goals which can satisfy or fulfill the needs it has aroused, and suggest the action necessary to achieve these goals.

To the purchaser, the product/service symbolizes the needs, desires, and goals which it satisfies. Therefore, your advertisement must communicate these symbols. To do this, you must have an appreciation of the symbolic meanings of lines, colors, and figures.

Advertising, promotion, and publicity are most effective when they demand minimal attitude changes; they are least effective when they demand changes which threaten the receiver. Regardless of the product/service, use copy and pictures in advertising which best fit the receiver's attitudes and demand minimal change.

To choose appropriate content, you must understand what techniques produce the best learning results. An annoying commercial produces more learning than a dull one, but a message promising the audience a rewarding experience works best. Points presented at the beginning and the end of a message are remembered better than those in the middle. The advertiser must also adapt his or her language to the particular audience to be reached.

Determining the Frequency and Timing of the Message

For advertising to be effective, it must be repeated. You achieve the best results for the money spent by repeating ads with identical material. You achieve the best results for the money spent by repeating ads less frequently, but over longer periods of time. Saturation campaigns are not cost-efficient for small businesses. With this in mind, you can decide how often, and over what time period, you wish to repeat specific ads.

Measuring the Advertising Results through Feedback

Last, you seek feedback concerning the advertising's effectiveness. Did it achieve your desired goals? What form of advertising or media proved most effective?

For a small business with a limited advertising budget, measuring advertising results proves difficult. Did advertising cause last year's sales increase, or did the sales force work harder? Did cooperative advertising increase sales at a particular store, or was it the weather?

The more specific the target audience, and the more specific the action asked for, the easier it is to measure your advertising results. If you engaged in cooperative advertising with one store in Chicago, and its sales of your product increased substantially more than other Chicago stores which carried the same items, the difference probably resulted from advertising. If you engaged in FM broadcast advertising of one item in one city for one year, and sales of that item in that area increased substantially more than in other areas, the difference probably resulted from advertising.

You can measure advertising results by asking for feedback from readers and listeners. Ads can ask the audience to call a number or return a coupon for more information. Ads can ask the audience to mention the newspaper, magazine, or station when purchasing the item and receive a rebate. Clerks in retail stores can ask shoppers how they heard of an item, and then tabulate the responses.

You should give your salespeople reprints of ads to show buyers and purchasing agents. The salespeople can ask whether the ad was seen, and how it was received. Also, the salespeople can reinforce the advertising by leaving reprints with customers and prospects.

When advertising in trade publications, you can hire a college student to call buyers, purchasing agents, merchandise managers, or design engineers to inquire whether they read the ad, and what they remember from it. This is a form of market research which will tell you whether or not the intended message was received.

If the intended message was not received by the target audience, or if sales did not increase, or if the advertising did not meet some other objective, then you should consider changing the media, content, or frequency. Your advertising budget represents a finite number of dollars, and as a small business, you must use limited resources effectively.

Conclusion

Although small businesses often do not use advertising, because they do not understand it, many small businesses owe their existence to the proper use of advertising. A manufacturer of portable whirlpools which attach to bathtubs only enters geographic markets reached by better music FM radio stations and UHF television stations. This firm knows that its target audience can be reached by these media, and that advertising on them will produce predictable results. For similar reasons, a manufacturer of specialty home repair tools will only enter geographic markets where the weekly *TV Guide* readership exceeds a certain number.

A discount brokerage house can accurately predict the number of new accounts it will open from advertising in various financial publications. Similarly, a specialty chemical firm can accurately predict the number of qualified leads it can generate from advertising in various trade publications. Analyze whether your firm can use advertising more effectively by utilizing the techniques suggested in this chapter.

References

Sales Management

Patty, Robert C. *Managing Salespeople*. Reston, Virginia: Reston Publishing Company, 1979.

Beer, Michael. *The Many Arts of Sales Management*. Radnor, Pa.: Chilton Publishing Company, 1980.

Wortman, Leon A. *Sales Managers Problem Solver*. New York: Ronald Press, 1983.

Haas, K. B., and Ernest, J. W. *Creative Salesmanship: Understanding Essentials*. Beverly Hills, Calif.: The Glencoe Press, 1969.

De Voe, Merril. *How To Tailor Your Sales Organization to Your Market*. Englewood Cliffs, N.J.: Prentice-Hall, 1964.

Steinkamp, W. H. *How To Sell and Market Industrial Products*. Philadelphia, Penn.: Chilton Book Co., 1970.

Smyth, Richard C., and Murphy, Matthew J. *Compensating and Motivating Salesmen*. New York: American Management Association, Inc., 1969.

Krause, Wm. H. *How To Hire and Motivate Manufacturers Representatives*. New York: Amacom, 1976.

Steinbrink, John. *Compensation of Salesmen Survey*. Chicago, Ill.: Dartnell, 1983.

Marketing

Cohen, William A., and Reddick, Marshall E. *Successful Marketing for Small Businesses*. New York: AMA Com, 1981.

Smith, Cynthia S. *How To Get Big Results from a Small Advertising Budget*. New York: Hawthorn Books Inc., 1973.

Carmon, James M., and Kenneth P. Uhl. *Phillips and Duncan's Marketing Principles and Methods*. Homewood, Ill.: Richard D. Irwin, 1973.

McCarthy, E. Jerome. *Basic Marketing: A Managerial Approach*. Homewood, Ill.: Richard D. Irwin, 1975.

Britt, Stuart H. *Marketing Managers Handbook*. Chicago: Dartnell.

Entrepreneurship

Batty, Gordon B. *Entrepreneurship for the Eighties*. Reston, Virginia: Reston Publishing Company, 1981.

Allen, Louis L. *Starting and Succeeding in Your Own Small Business*. New York: Grosset and Dunlap, 1968.

Mancuso, Joseph R. *The Small Business Survival Guide, Sources of Help for Entrepreneurs*. Englewood Cliffs, N.J.: Prentice Hall Inc., 1980.

MacFarlane, William N. *Principles of Small Business Management*. New York: McGraw-Hill, 1977.

Index

324 INDEX

Qualifying prospects, 32, 167–171
Questionnaire, market research, 194–197
Quota, evaluation, 171

Radio, advertising, 290, 291
Raising prices, 236
Random sample, market research, 198
Rating system, salesperson appraisal, 172, 173
Rebates, 240, 294–296
Recall problem, radio and T.V., 290–292
Receiver, communication, 115
Recognition, motivation, 94, 95, 145, 166, 257
Reducing territory, 97
Reducing travel and entertainment expenses, 64
Reference checking, 15
Referrals, prospecting, 33
Related markets, product development. 187, 188
Rent, 160
Repetition, advertising, 308
Representative group, market research, 197–199
Reprints, advertising, 288, 289
Restraint of trade, 243
Resumes, hiring, 11
Retail catalogues, 210, 211, 286, 287
Retail outlets, 263–267
Return on investment, new products, 189–191
Return privileges, test marketing, 200
Reusable package, 184
Reviving ideas, new products, 188
Rewarding positive action, compensation, 49
Rewarding superior performance, compensation, 50
Robinson-Patman Act, 243
Role playing, sales meeting, 143
Route analysis, customers, 86, 87, 167–171
Route sheets, salesperson, 3, 124–127, 167–171

Salaries, expense, 160
Salary, compensation, 53–56
Sales aids, 4, 32
Sales call
 critique, 39
 objectives, 38, 40
 self-analysis, 39

Sales catalogues, 288
Sales club, motivation, 94
Sales contests, 104–112
 budget, 109, 110
 objectives, 108, 109
 poorly conceived, 105
 prizes, 110
 promotion, 111, 112
 rules, 112
 time frame, 110
 types, 106–108
  direct competition, 106
  individual goal, 107, 108
  teams, 106, 107
Sales force expenses, 159–161
Sales force organization, 72–78
 by customer, 74–75
 by function, 76
 by geography, 75, 76
 by product line, 72–74
 combinations, 77
 human resource, 77, 78
 no restrictions, 76, 77
Sales forecasts, 3, 148–158
 changes outside company, 154, 155
 changes within company, 153, 154
 company forecast, 151–158
 evaluation, 157
 final forecast, 155, 156
 forecast form, 149, 150
 format, 149, 150
 management review, 156, 157
 objectives, 157
 past/present sales trends, 151–153
 preliminary forecast, 149–155
 process, 151–156
 worst and best case, 155
Sales and Marketing Management Magazine, 53, 61, 71, 80, 139
Sales meetings, 41, 100, 137–146
 costs, 139
 formal group meetings, 141–144
  administrative matters, 141
  problem areas, 141, 142
 formal individual meetings, 144
  informal social gatherings, 144
  official social gatherings, 145
 format and agenda, 140, 141
 frequency, 139, 140
 location, 139